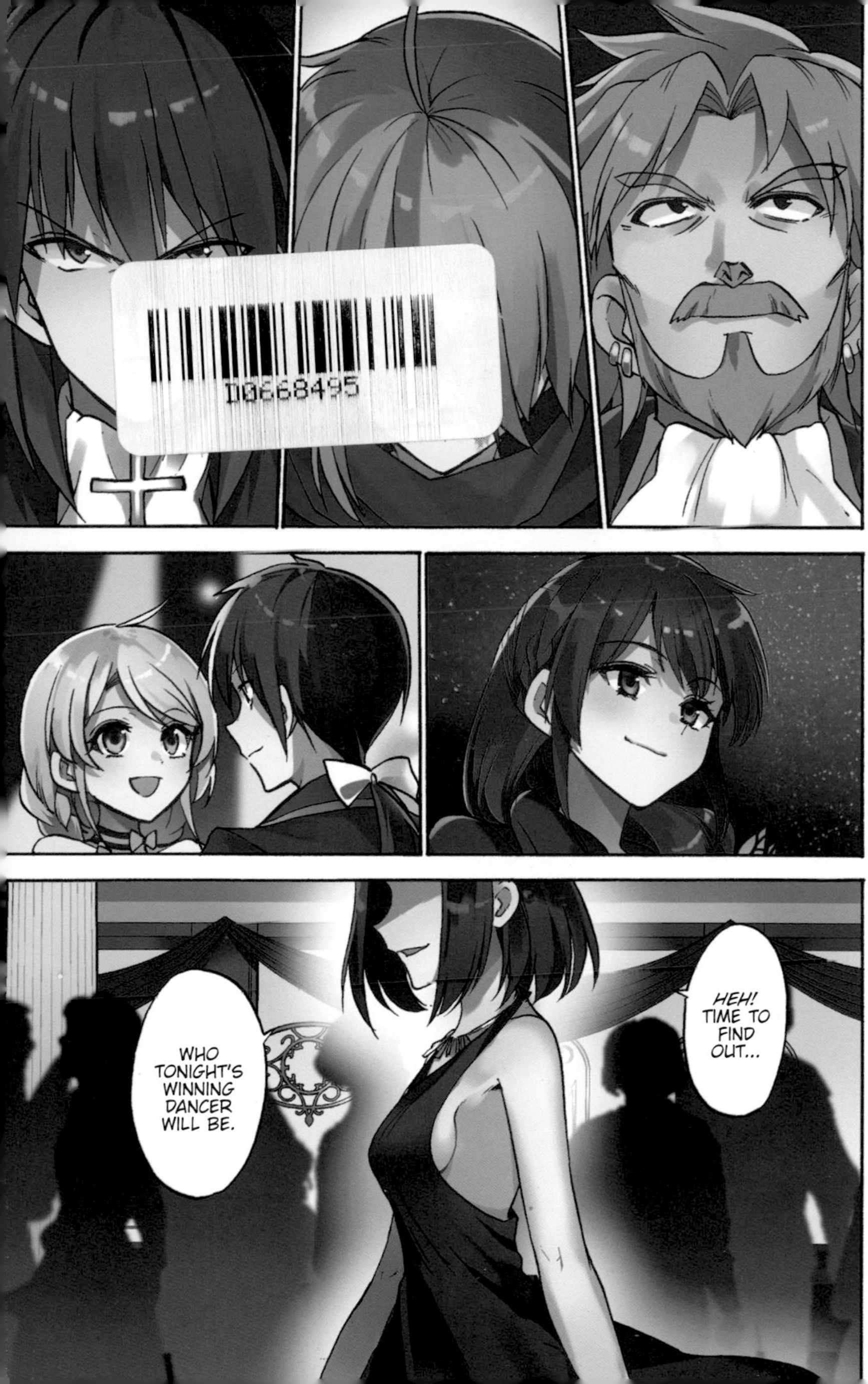
HEH! TIME TO FIND OUT...
WHO TONIGHT'S WINNING DANCER WILL BE.

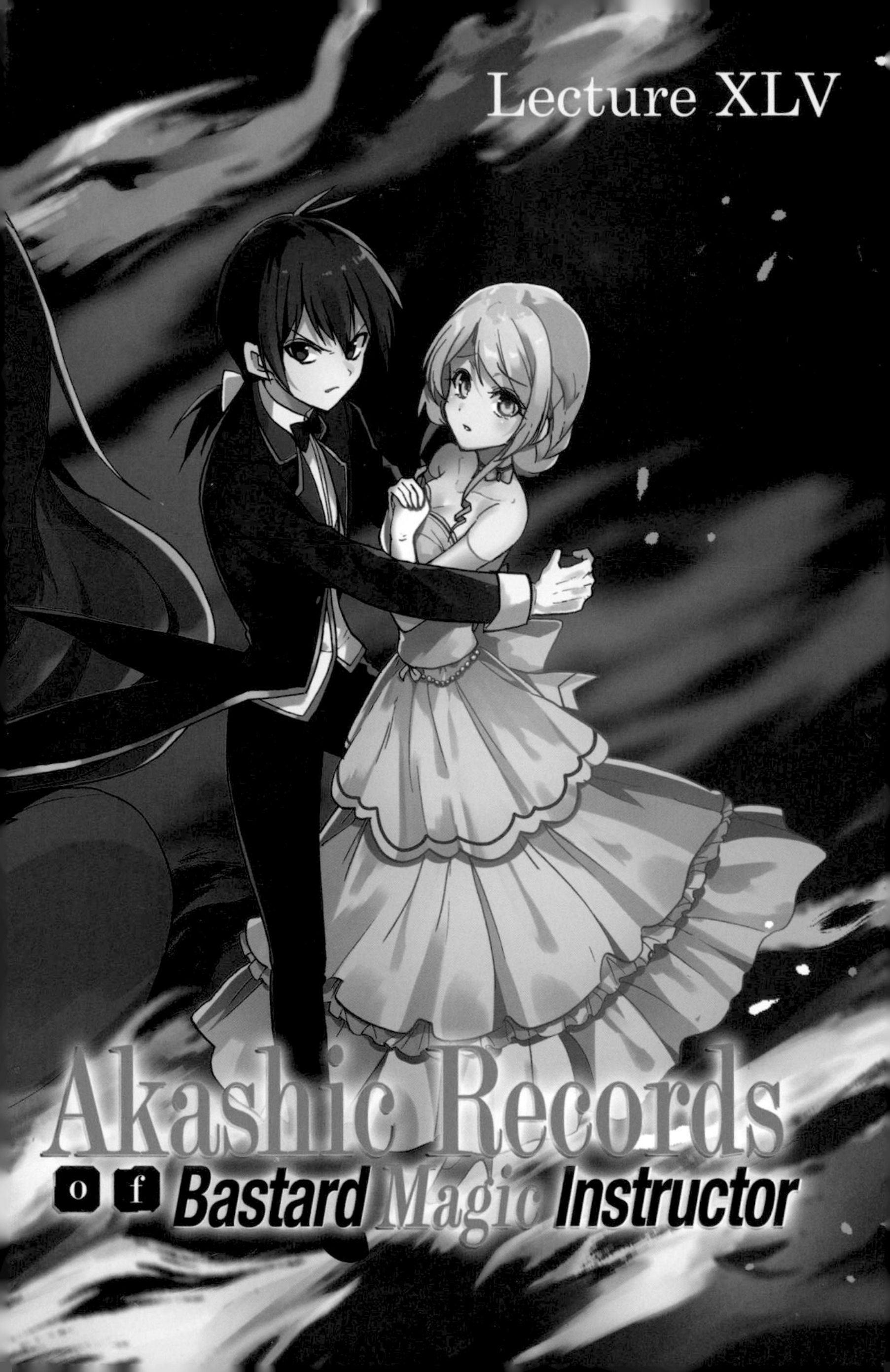
Lecture XLV
Akashic Records
of Bastard Magic Instructor

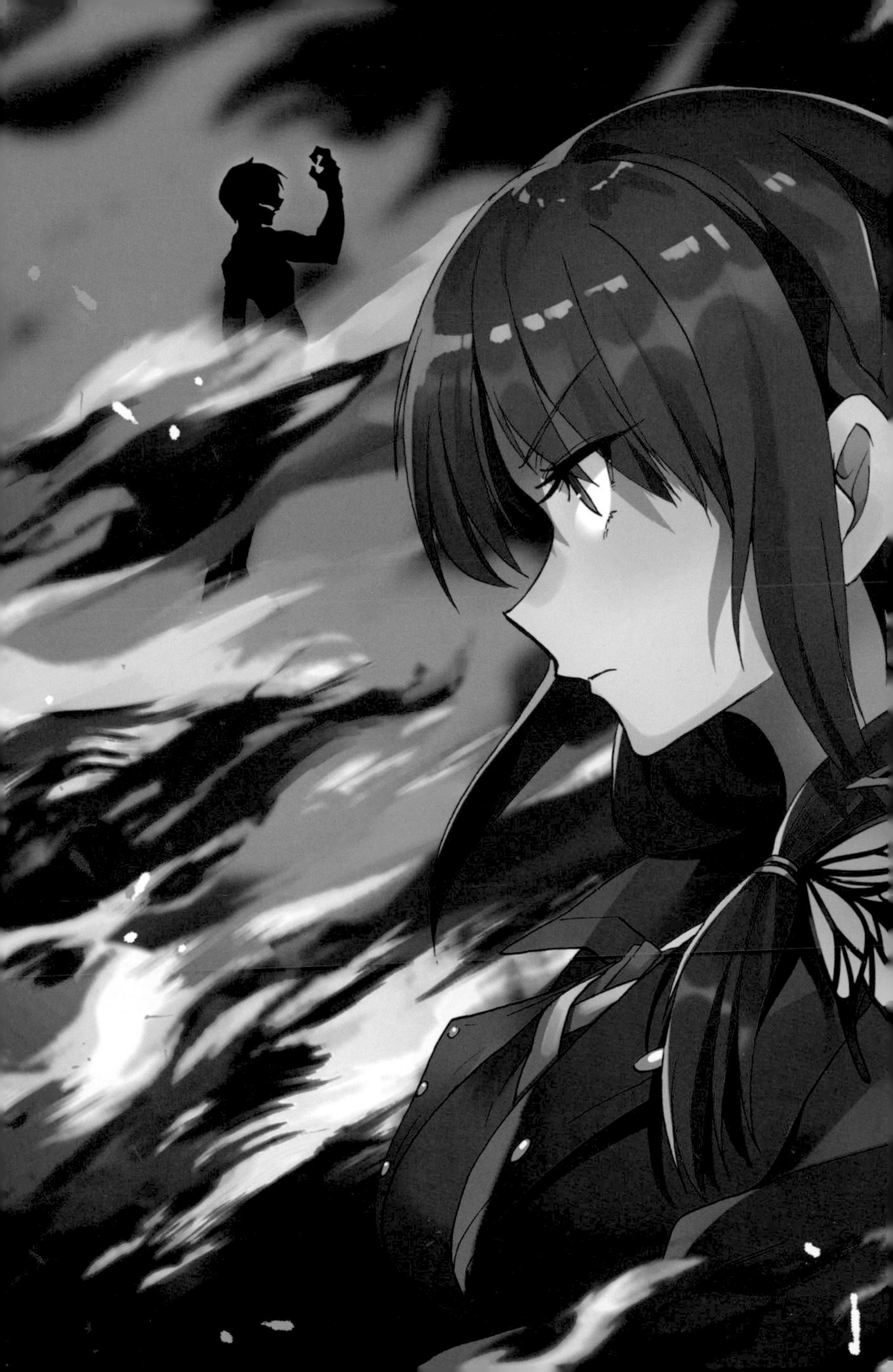

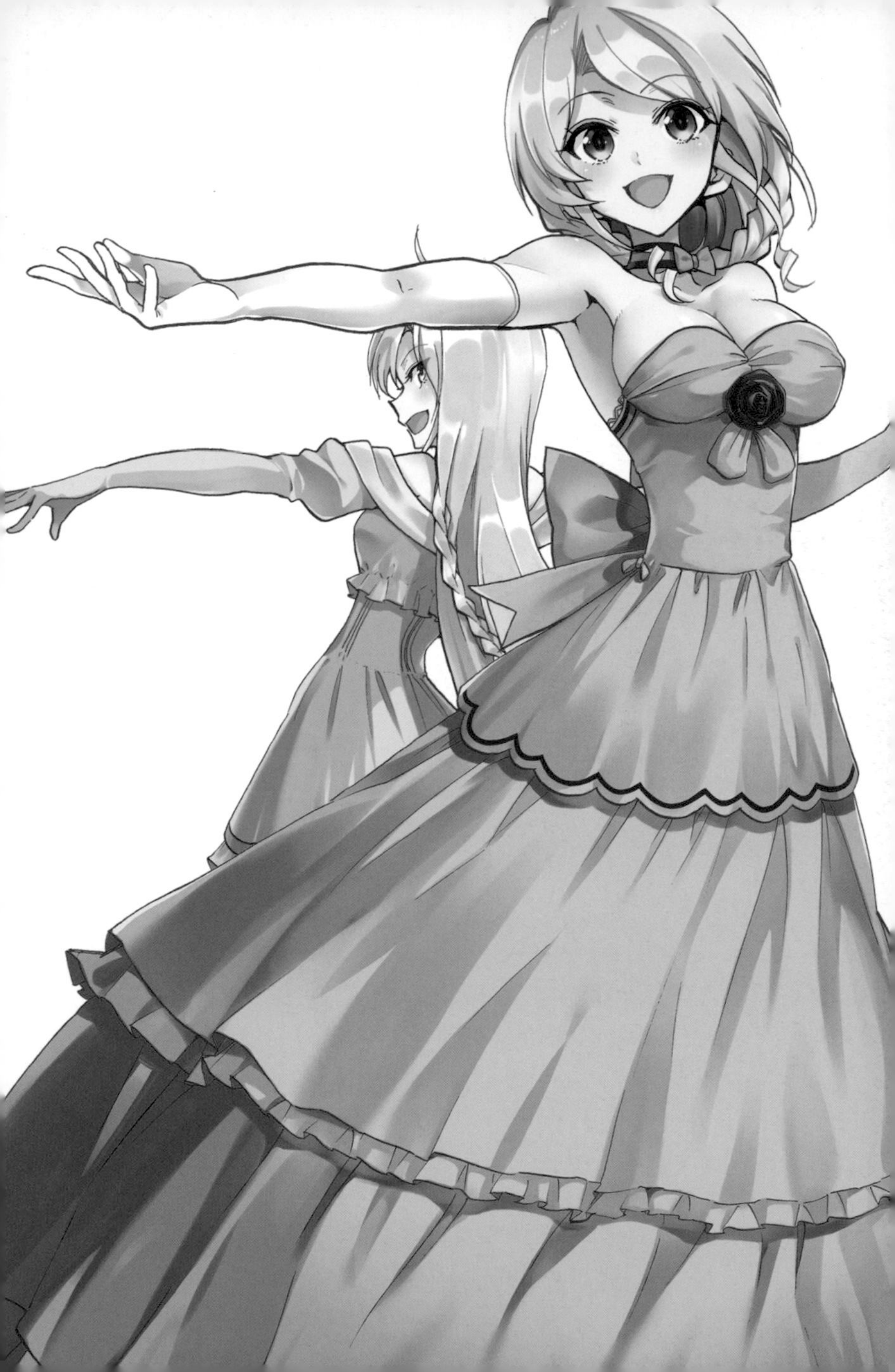

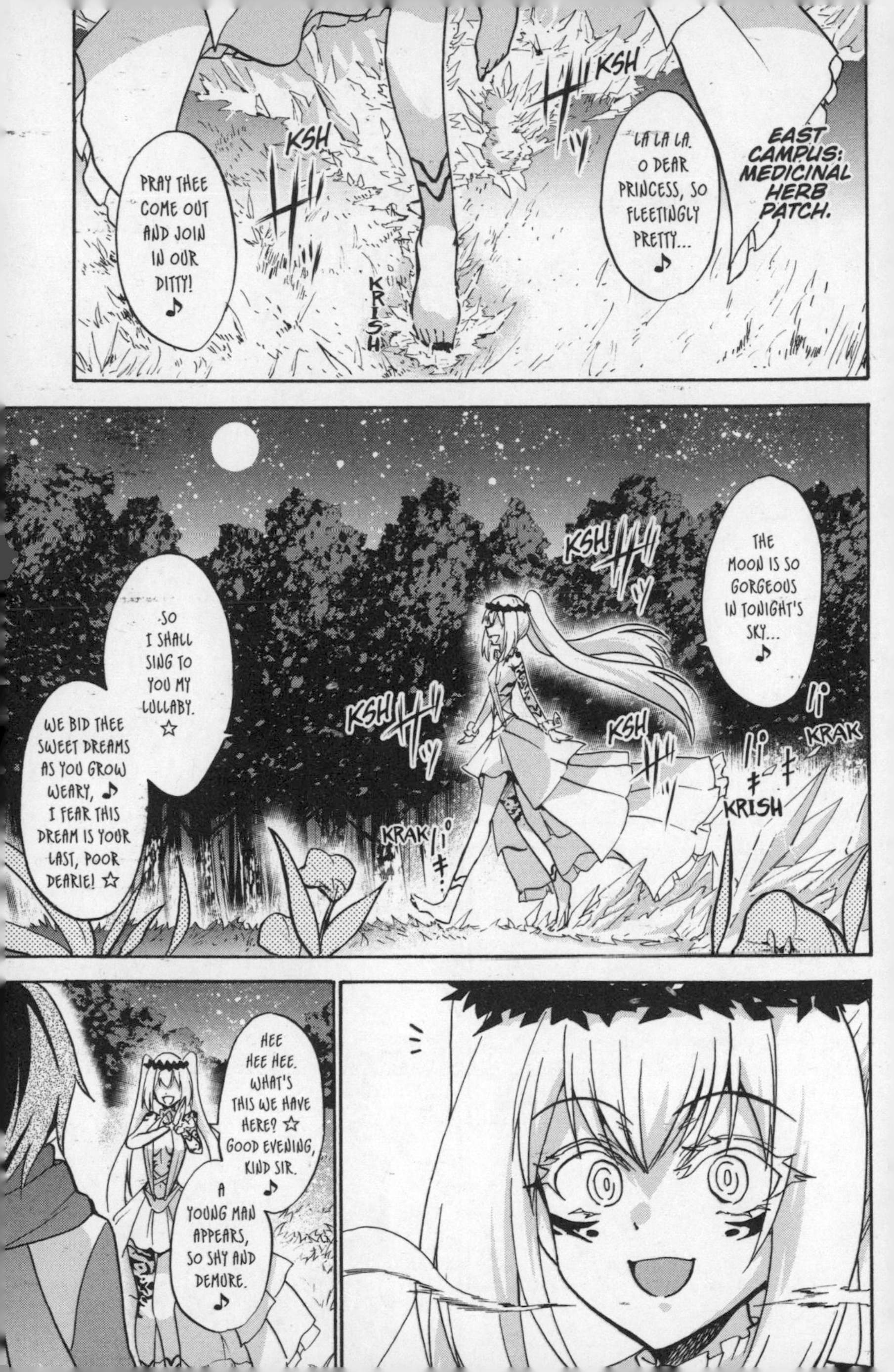
EAST CAMPUS: MEDICINAL HERB PATCH.
KSH
LA LA LA. O DEAR PRINCESS, SO FLEETINGLY PRETTY... ♪
KSH
PRAY THEE COME OUT AND JOIN IN OUR DITTY! ♪
KRISH
THE MOON IS SO GORGEOUS IN TONIGHT'S SKY... ♪
KSH
KRAK
KRISH
KSH
KSH
SO I SHALL SING TO YOU MY LULLABY. ☆
WE BID THEE SWEET DREAMS AS YOU GROW WEARY, ♪ I FEAR THIS DREAM IS YOUR LAST, POOR DEARIE! ☆
KRAK
HEE HEE HEE. WHAT'S THIS WE HAVE HERE? ☆ GOOD EVENING, KIND SIR. ♪
A YOUNG MAN APPEARS, SO SHY AND DEMURE. ♪

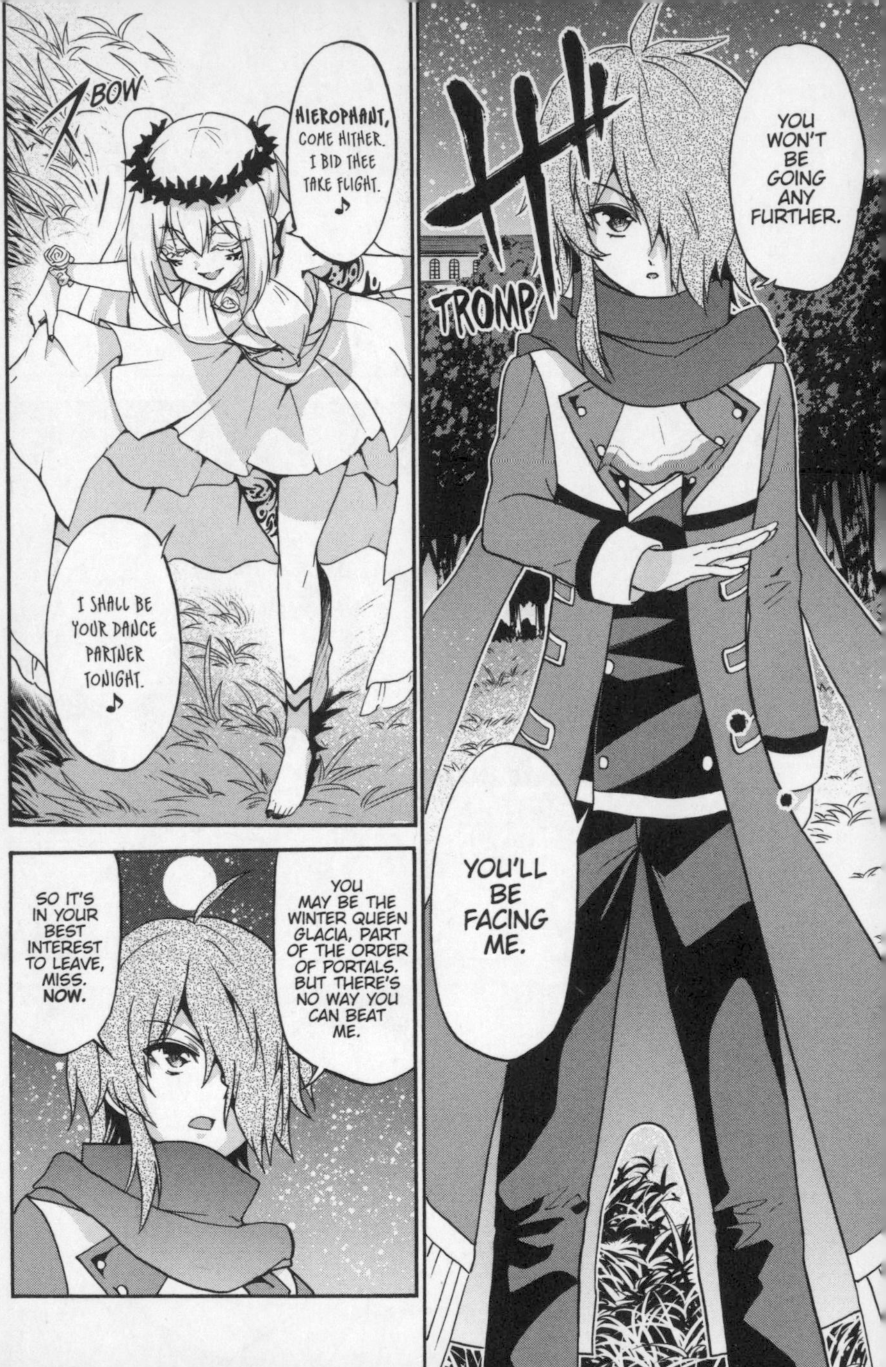
YOU WON'T BE GOING ANY FURTHER.
TROMP
YOU'LL BE FACING ME.
BOW
HIEROPHANT, COME HITHER. I BID THEE TAKE FLIGHT. ♪
I SHALL BE YOUR DANCE PARTNER TONIGHT. ♪
YOU MAY BE THE WINTER QUEEN GLACIA, PART OF THE ORDER OF PORTALS. BUT THERE'S NO WAY YOU CAN BEAT ME.
SO IT'S IN YOUR BEST INTEREST TO LEAVE, MISS. NOW.

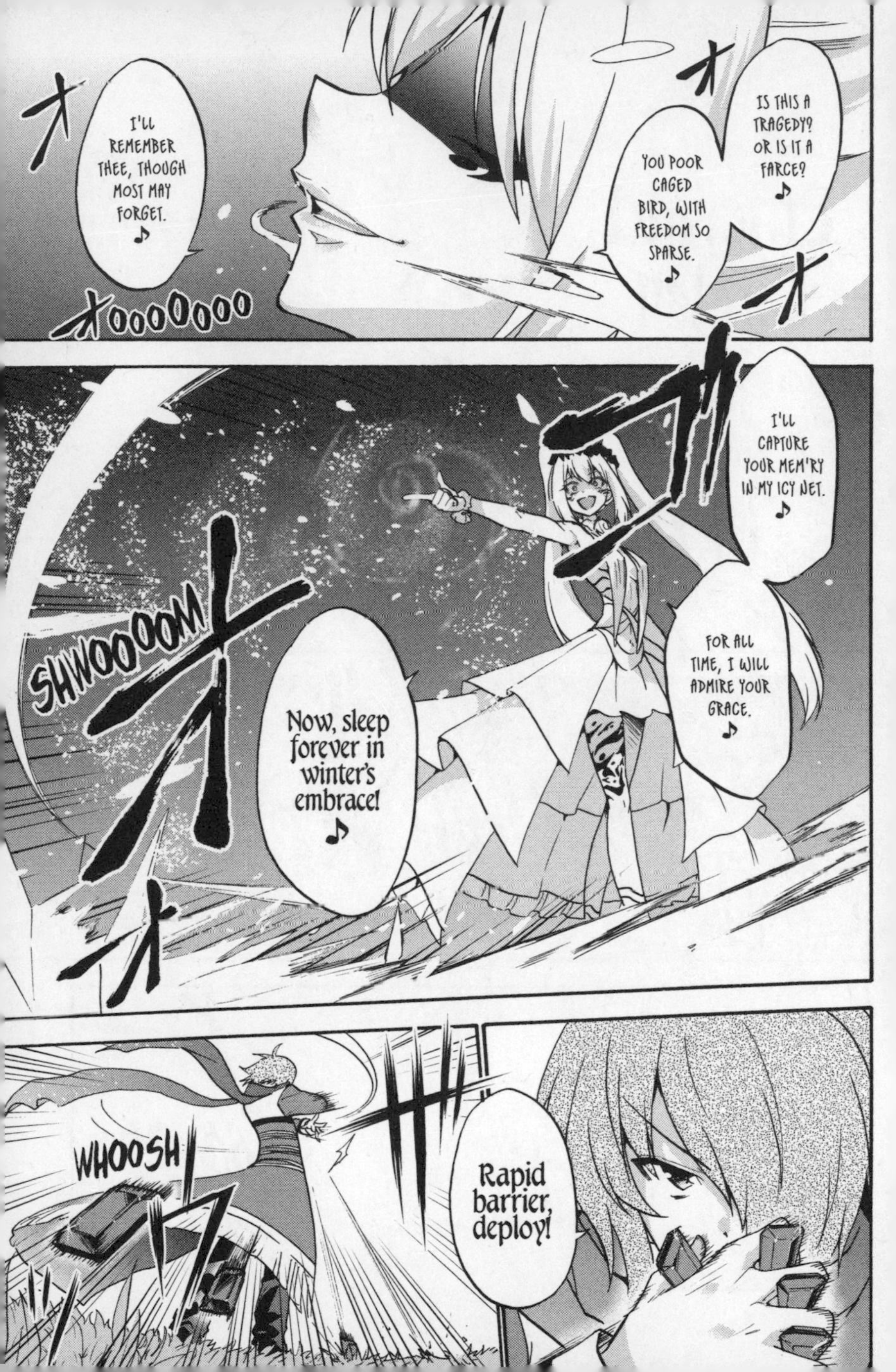
IS THIS A TRAGEDY? OR IS IT A FARCE? ♪
YOU POOR CAGED BIRD, WITH FREEDOM SO SPARSE. ♪
I'LL REMEMBER THEE, THOUGH MOST MAY FORGET. ♪
オOOOOOOO
I'LL CAPTURE YOUR MEM'RY IN MY ICY NET. ♪
FOR ALL TIME, I WILL ADMIRE YOUR GRACE. ♪
Now, sleep forever in winter's embrace! ♪
SHWOOOOM
Rapid barrier, deploy!
WHOOSH

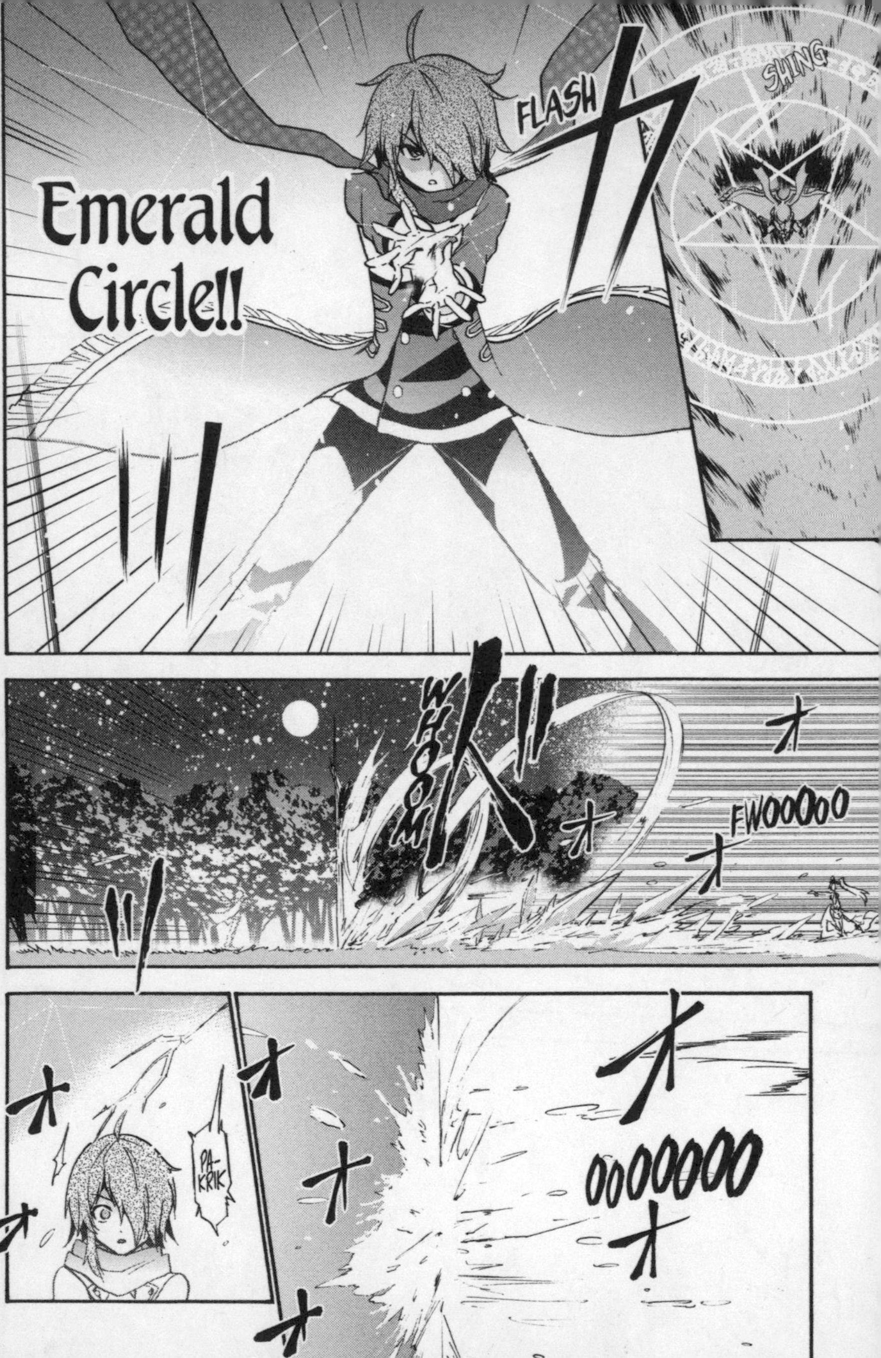
SHING
FLASH
Emerald Circle!!
FWOOOOO
WHOOM
OOOOOOO
PA-KRIK

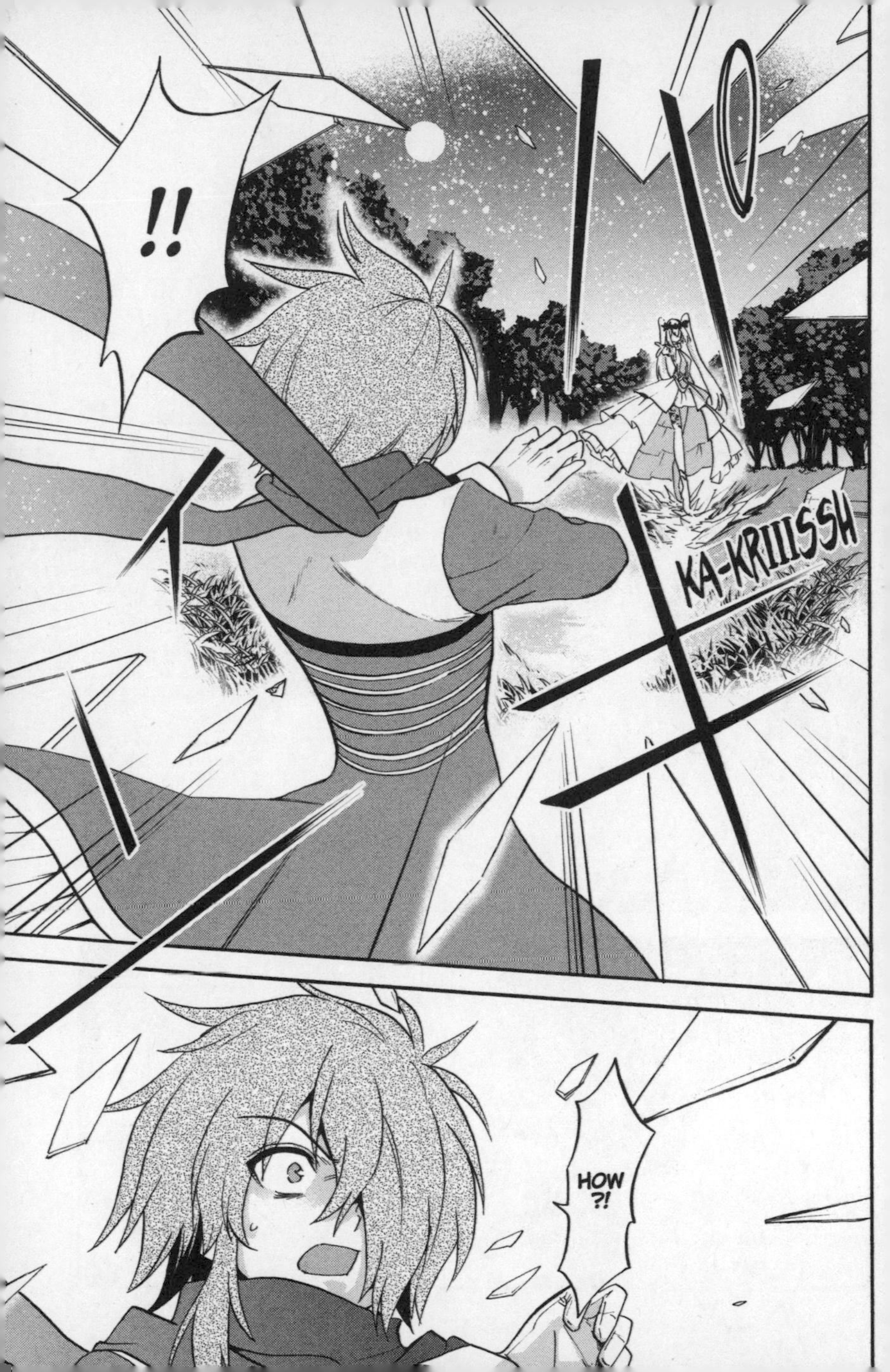
!!
KA-KRIIISSH
HOW?!

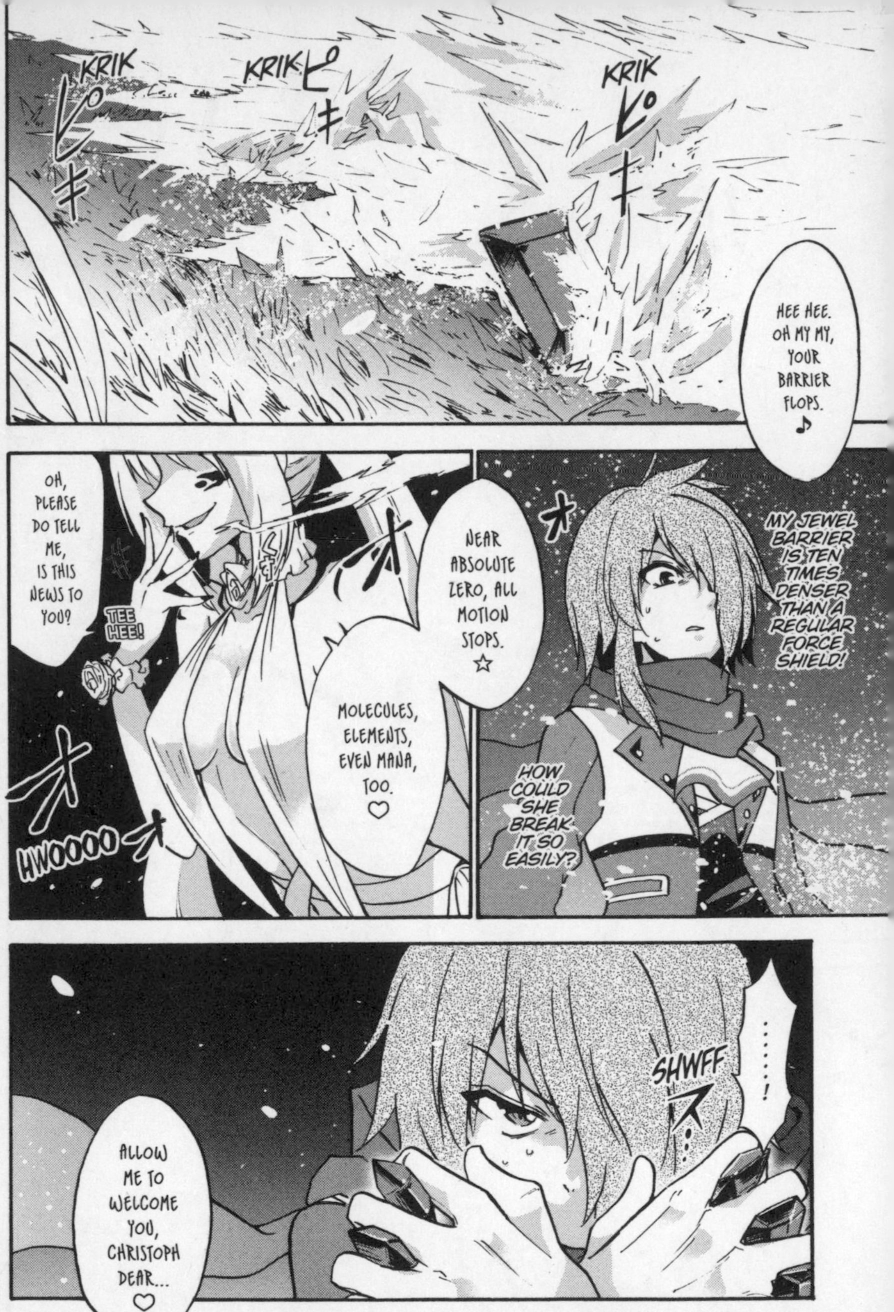
KRIK
KRIK
KRIK
HEE HEE. OH MY MY, YOUR BARRIER FLOPS. ♪
MY JEWEL BARRIER IS TEN TIMES DENSER THAN A REGULAR FORCE SHIELD!
HOW COULD SHE BREAK IT SO EASILY?
NEAR ABSOLUTE ZERO, ALL MOTION STOPS. ☆
MOLECULES, ELEMENTS, EVEN MANA, TOO. ♡
OH, PLEASE DO TELL ME, IS THIS NEWS TO YOU?
TEE HEE!
HWOOOO
......!
SHWFF
ALLOW ME TO WELCOME YOU, CHRISTOPH DEAR... ♡

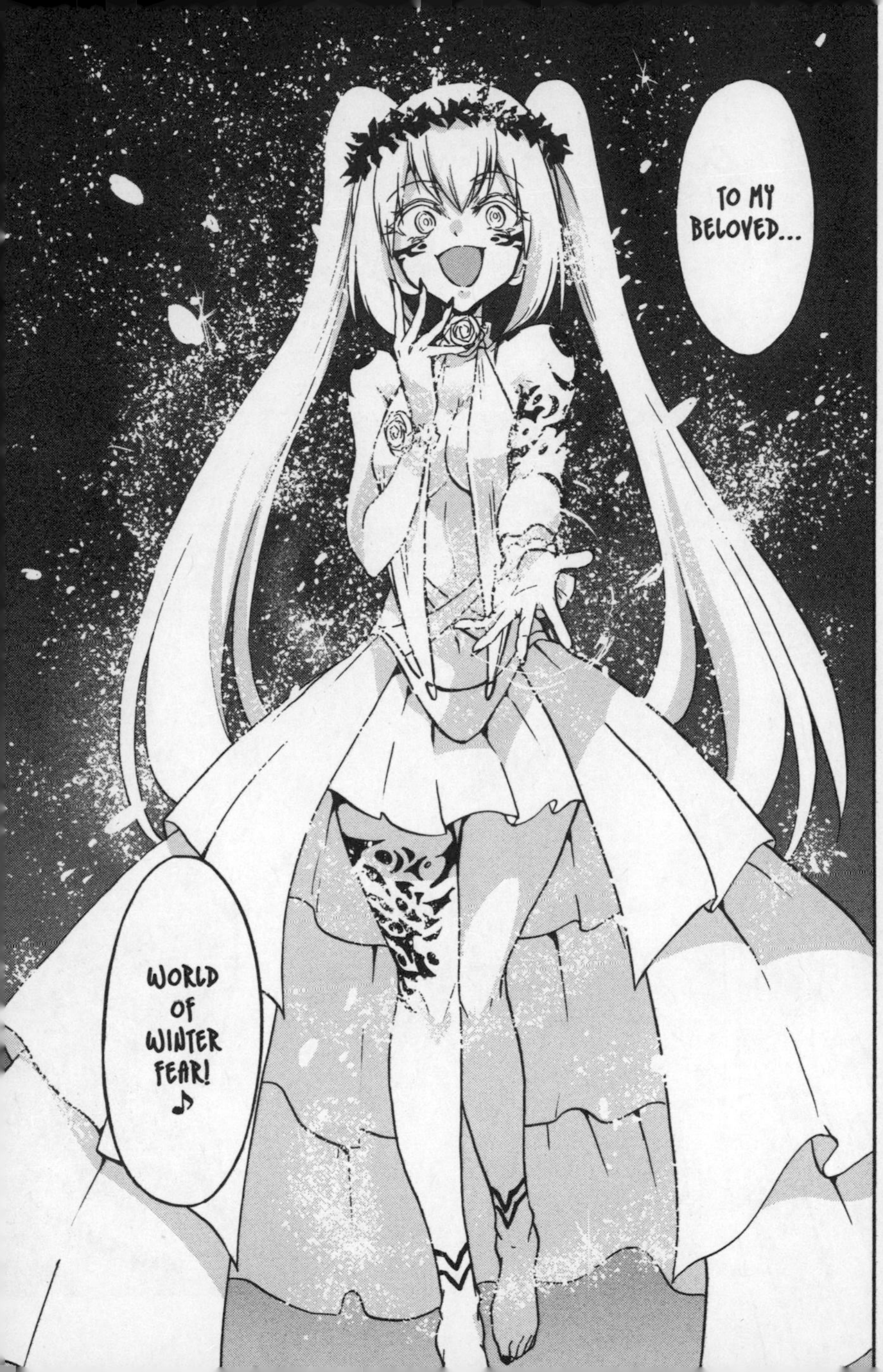
TO MY BELOVED...
WORLD OF WINTER FEAR! ♪

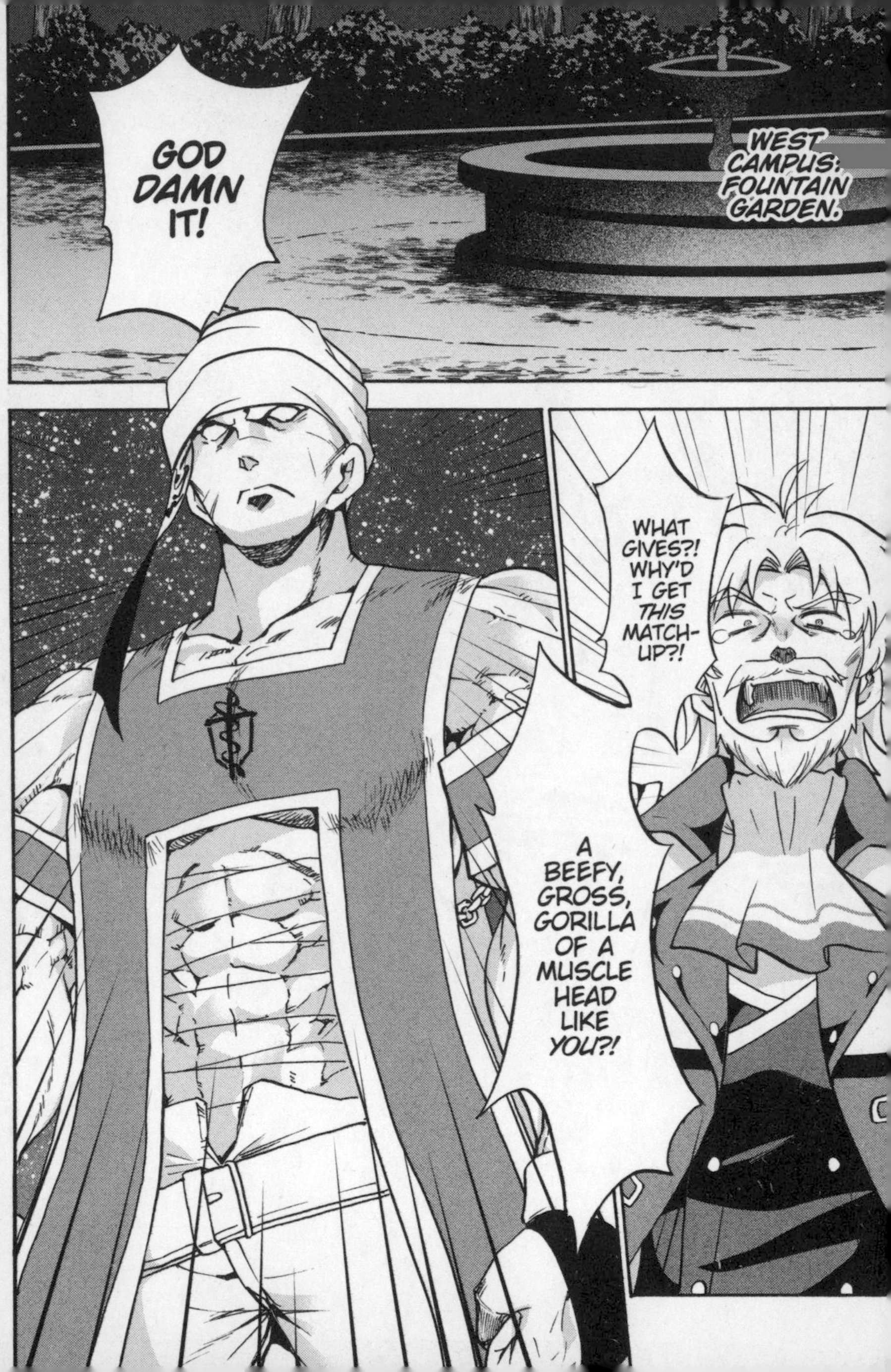
WEST CAMPUS: FOUNTAIN GARDEN.
GOD DAMN IT!
WHAT GIVES?! WHY'D I GET *THIS* MATCH-UP?!
A BEEFY, GROSS, GORILLA OF A MUSCLE HEAD LIKE *YOU*?!

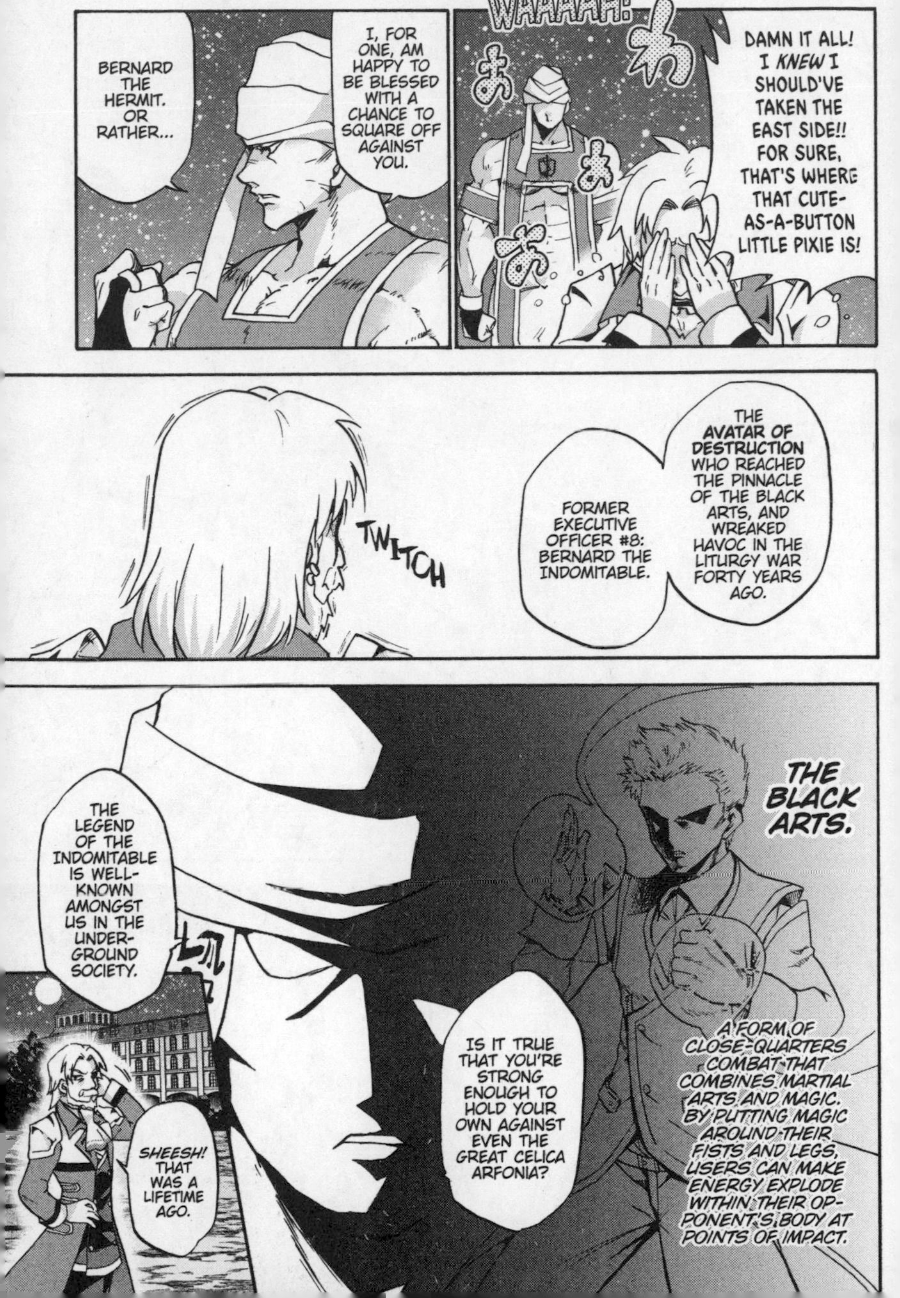
WAAAAH!
わあああ
DAMN IT ALL! I *KNEW* I SHOULD'VE TAKEN THE EAST SIDE!! FOR SURE, THAT'S WHERE THAT CUTE-AS-A-BUTTON LITTLE PIXIE IS!
I, FOR ONE, AM HAPPY TO BE BLESSED WITH A CHANCE TO SQUARE OFF AGAINST YOU.
BERNARD THE HERMIT. OR RATHER...
THE **AVATAR OF DESTRUCTION** WHO REACHED THE PINNACLE OF THE BLACK ARTS, AND WREAKED HAVOC IN THE LITURGY WAR FORTY YEARS AGO.
FORMER EXECUTIVE OFFICER #8: BERNARD THE INDOMITABLE.
TWITCH
THE BLACK ARTS.
THE LEGEND OF THE INDOMITABLE IS WELL-KNOWN AMONGST US IN THE UNDERGROUND SOCIETY.
A FORM OF CLOSE-QUARTERS COMBAT THAT COMBINES MARTIAL ARTS AND MAGIC. BY PUTTING MAGIC AROUND THEIR FISTS AND LEGS, USERS CAN MAKE ENERGY EXPLODE WITHIN THEIR OPPONENT'S BODY AT POINTS OF IMPACT.
IS IT TRUE THAT YOU'RE STRONG ENOUGH TO HOLD YOUR OWN AGAINST EVEN THE GREAT CELICA ARFONIA?
SHEESH! THAT WAS A LIFETIME AGO.

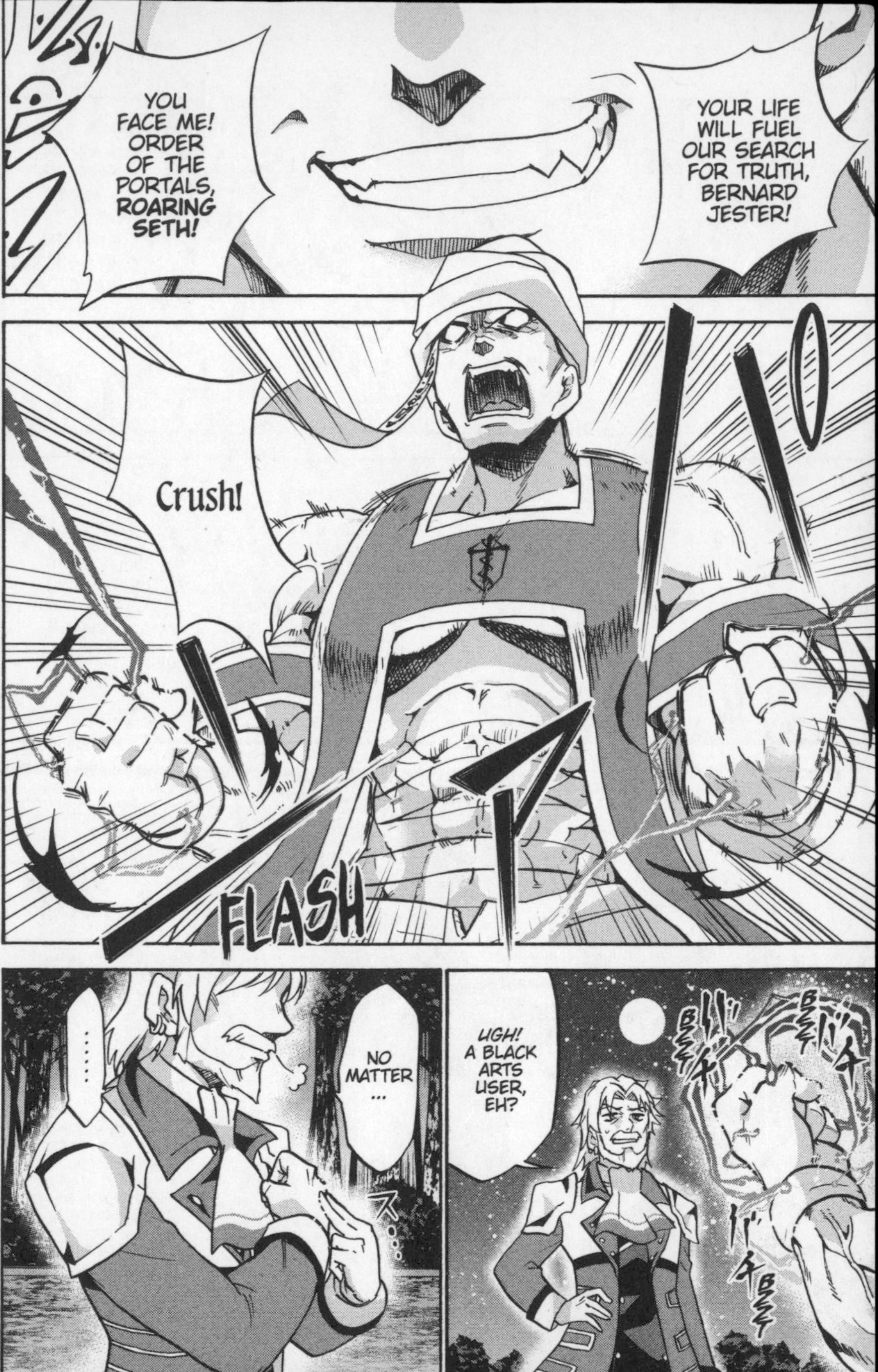
YOUR LIFE WILL FUEL OUR SEARCH FOR TRUTH, BERNARD JESTER!
YOU FACE ME! ORDER OF THE PORTALS, ROARING SETH!
Crush!
FLASH
UGH! A BLACK ARTS USER, EH?
NO MATTER ...
......

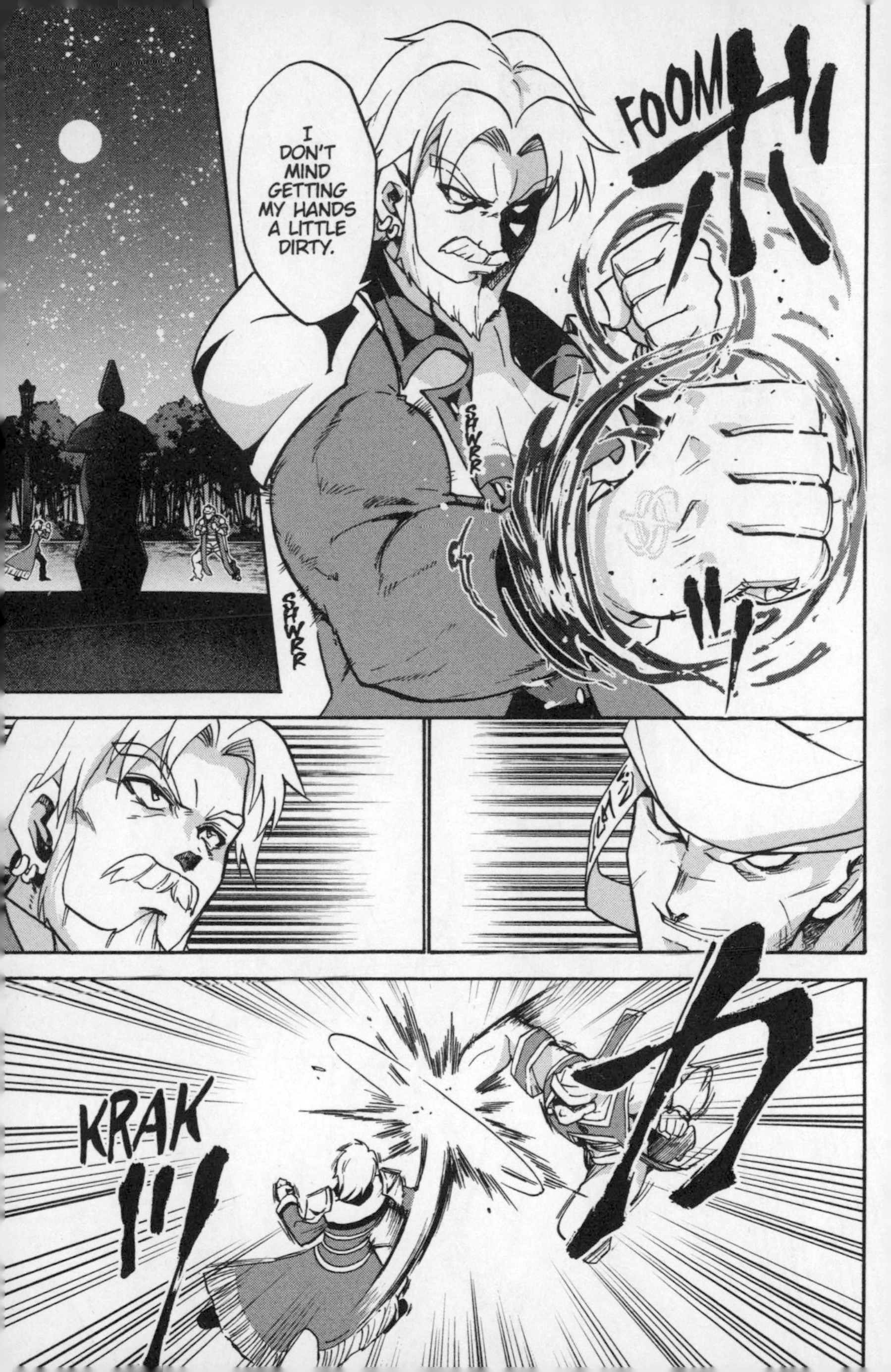

FOOM
I DON'T MIND GETTING MY HANDS A LITTLE DIRTY.
SHWRR
SHWRR
KRAK

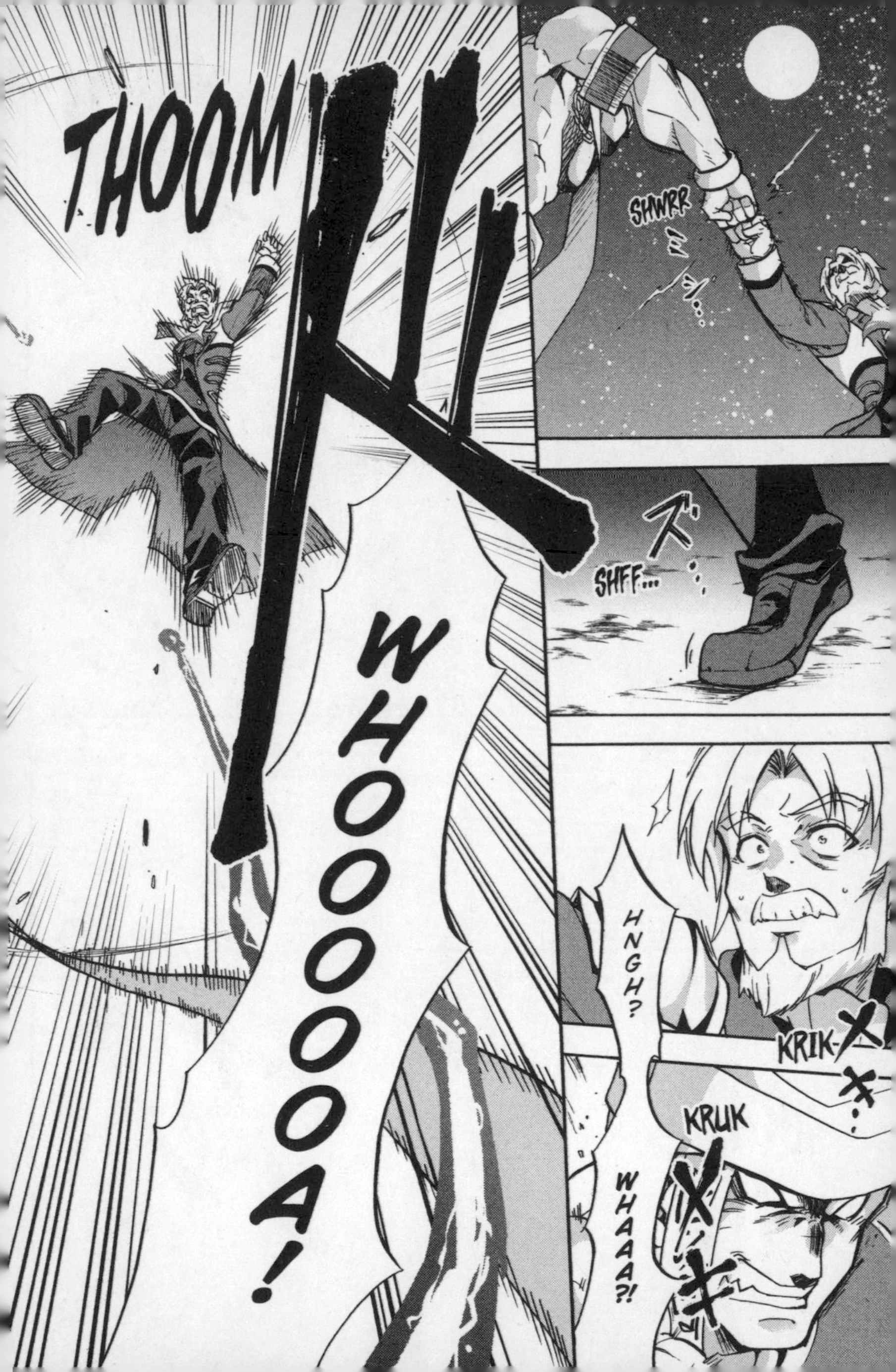
SHWRR
ミッ...
ズ...
SHFF...
HNGH?
KRIK-
KRUK
WHAAAA?!
THOOM
WHOOOOOA!

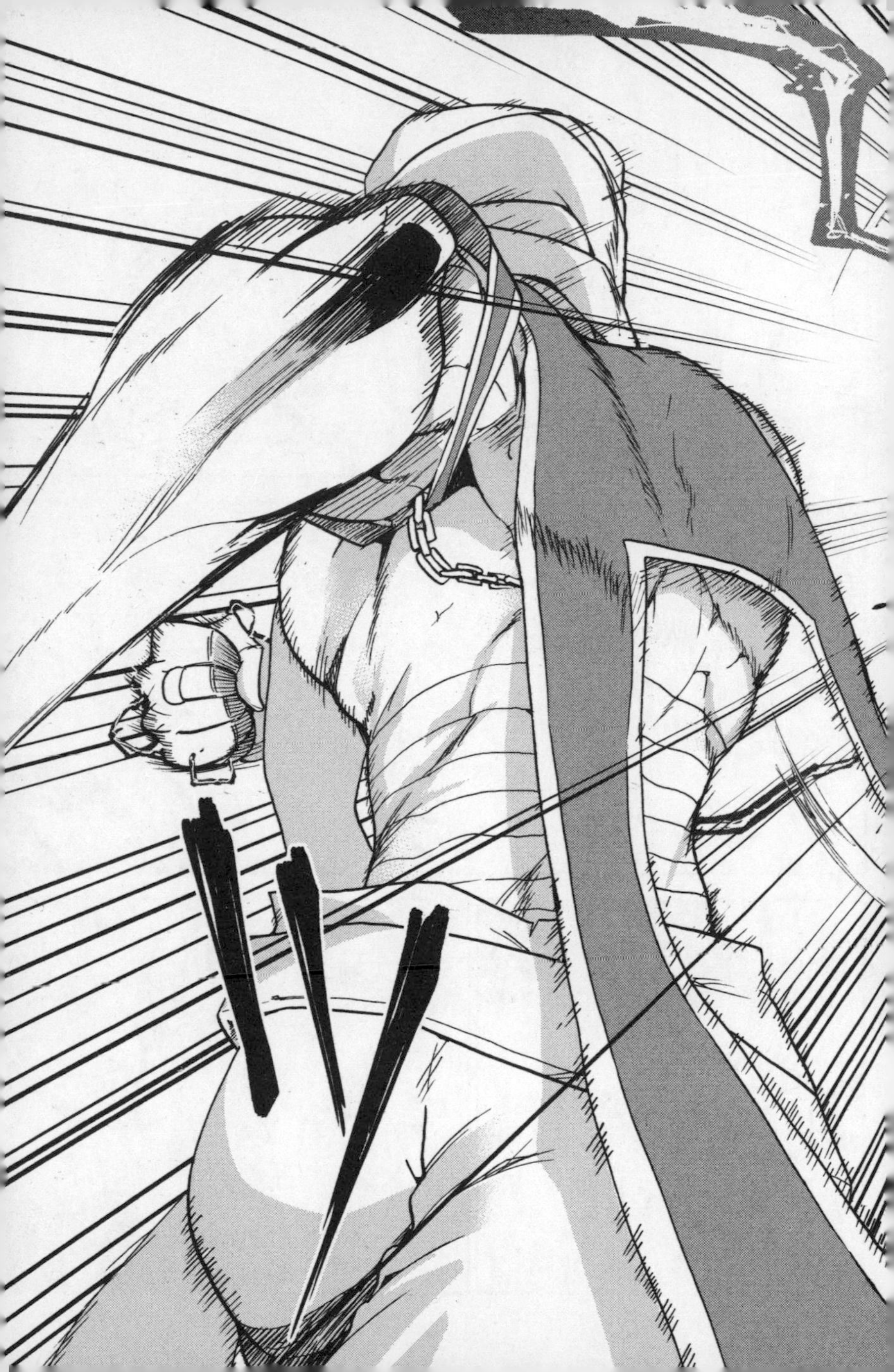

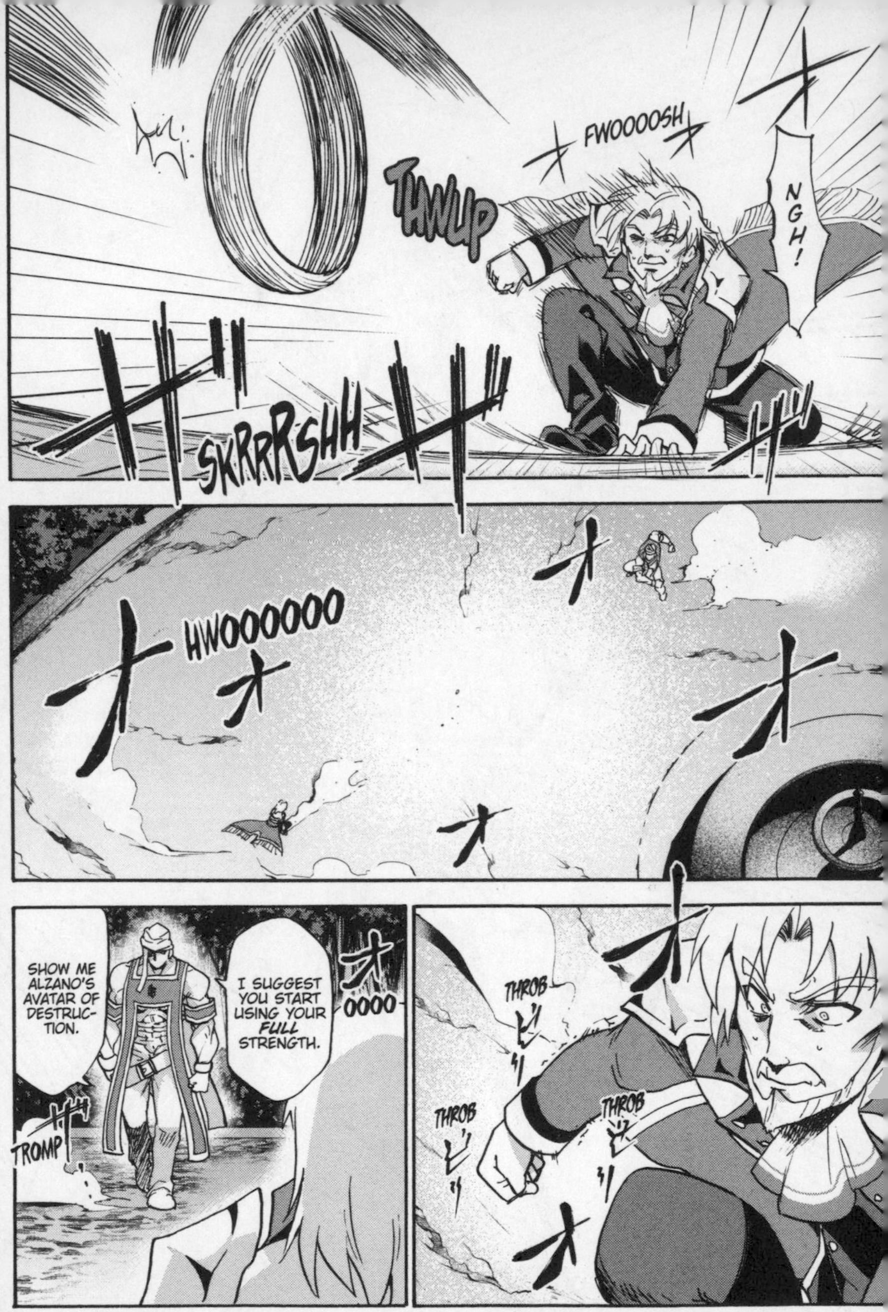
NGH!
FWOOOOSH
THWUP
SKRRRSHH
HWOOOOOO
THROB
THROB
THROB
OOOO
I SUGGEST YOU START USING YOUR *FULL* STRENGTH.
SHOW ME ALZANO'S AVATAR OF DESTRUC-TION.
TROMP

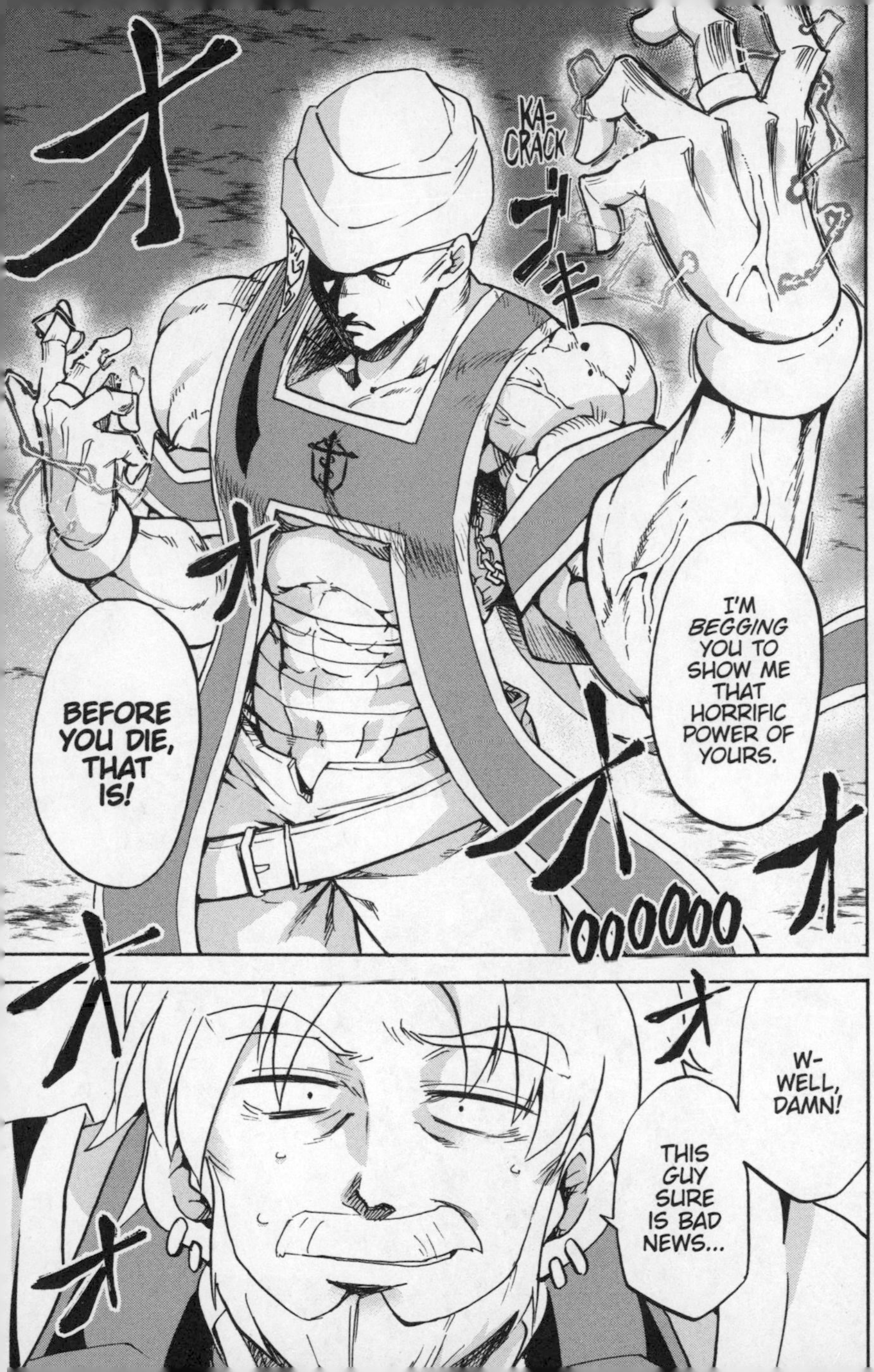
KA-CRACK
I'M BEGGING YOU TO SHOW ME THAT HORRIFIC POWER OF YOURS.
BEFORE YOU DIE, THAT IS!
OOOOOO
W-WELL, DAMN!
THIS GUY SURE IS BAD NEWS...

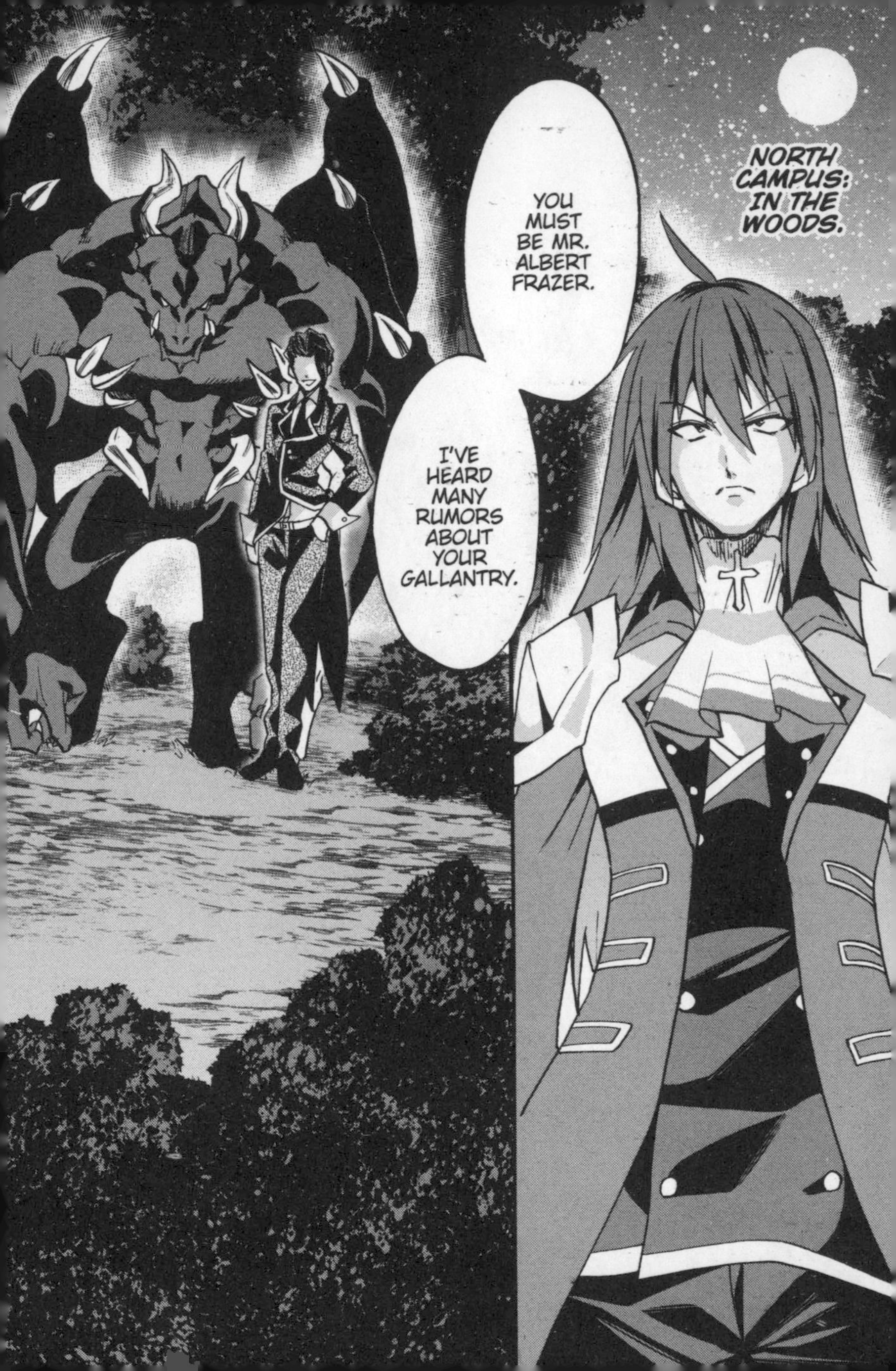
NORTH CAMPUS: IN THE WOODS.
YOU MUST BE MR. ALBERT FRAZER.
I'VE HEARD MANY RUMORS ABOUT YOUR GALLANTRY.

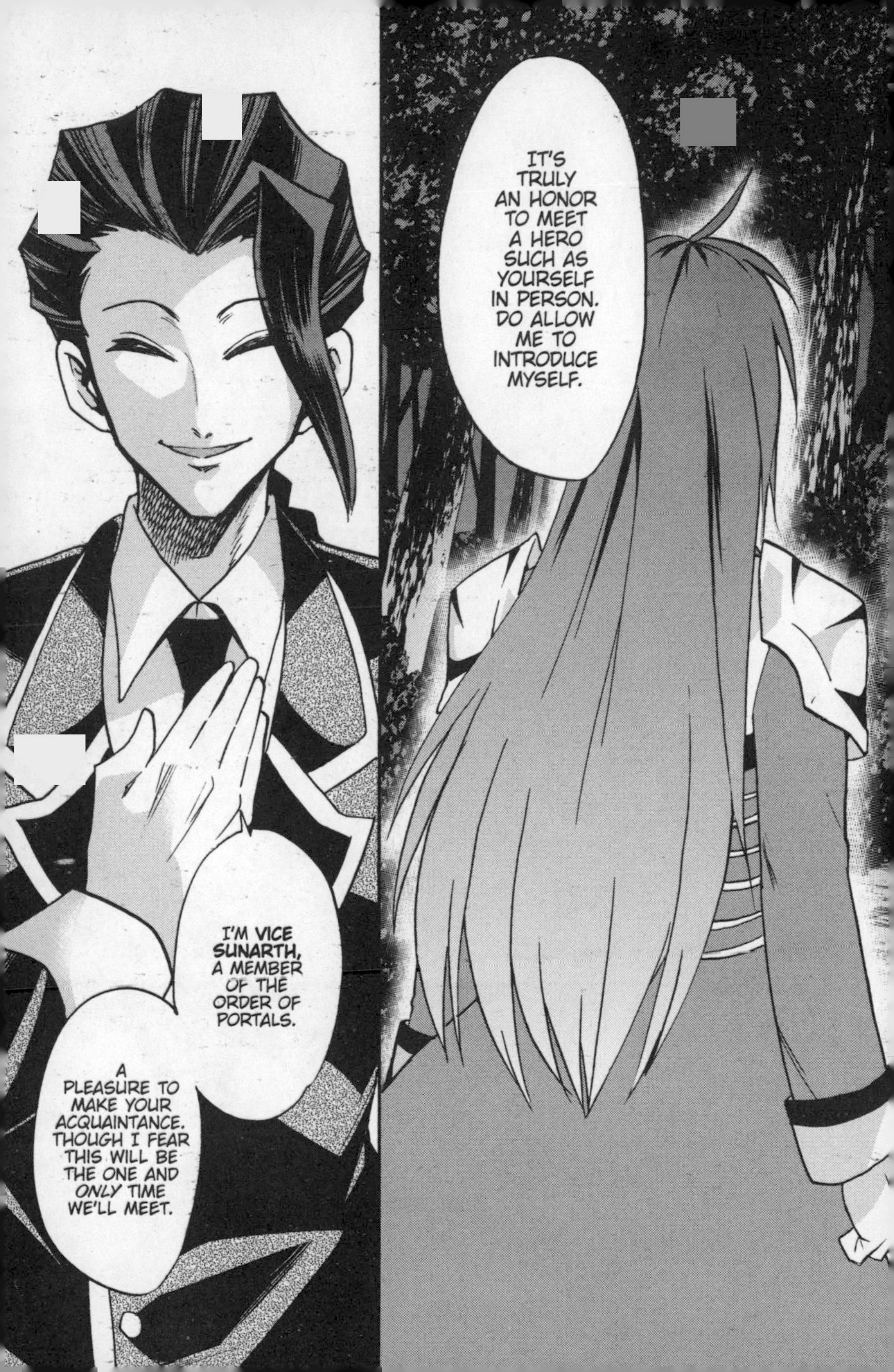
IT'S TRULY AN HONOR TO MEET A HERO SUCH AS YOURSELF IN PERSON. DO ALLOW ME TO INTRODUCE MYSELF.
I'M VICE SUNARTH, A MEMBER OF THE ORDER OF PORTALS.
A PLEASURE TO MAKE YOUR ACQUAINTANCE. THOUGH I FEAR THIS WILL BE THE ONE AND ONLY TIME WE'LL MEET.

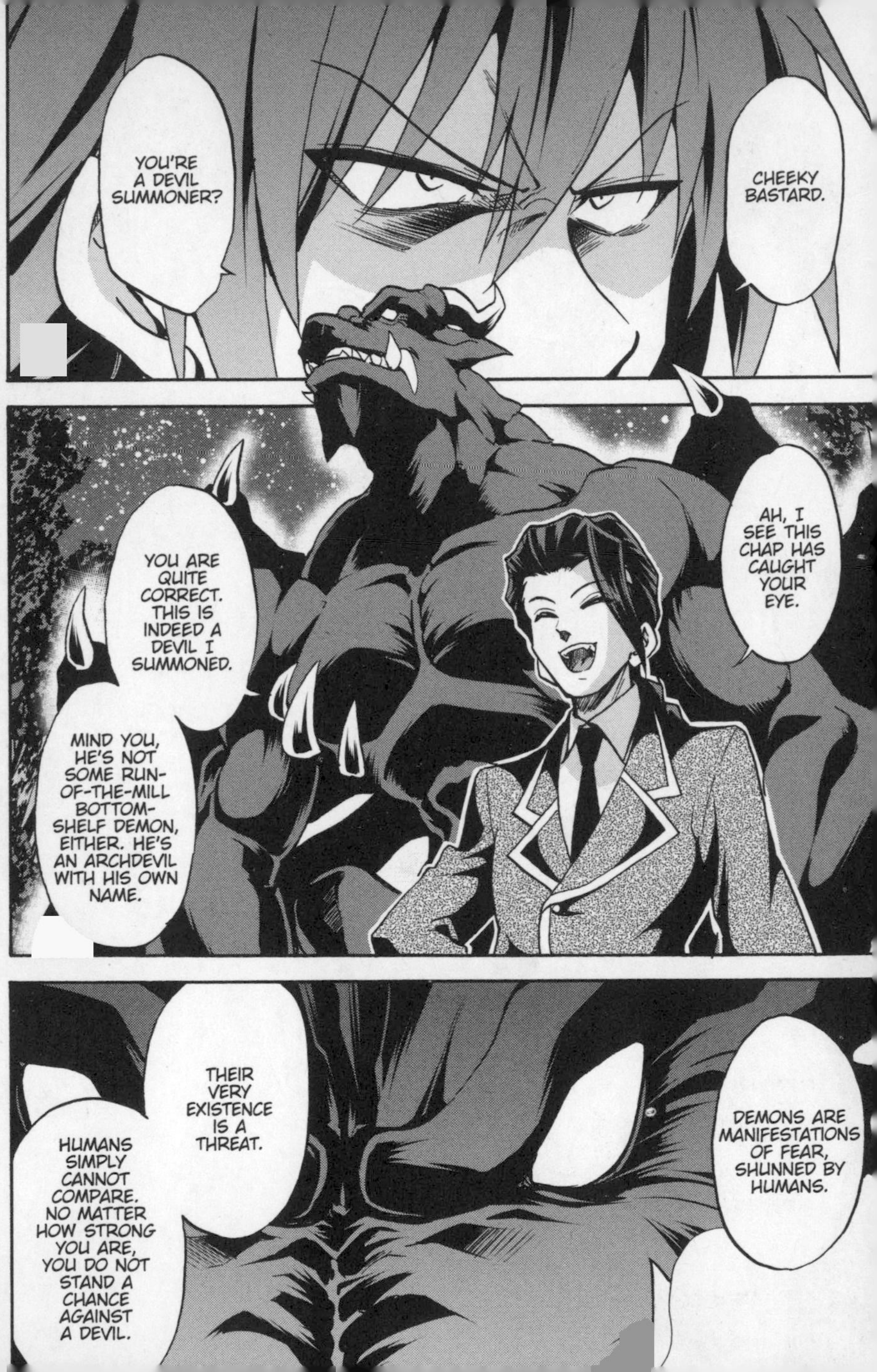
CHEEKY BASTARD.
YOU'RE A DEVIL SUMMONER?
AH, I SEE THIS CHAP HAS CAUGHT YOUR EYE.
YOU ARE QUITE CORRECT. THIS IS INDEED A DEVIL I SUMMONED.
MIND YOU, HE'S NOT SOME RUN-OF-THE-MILL BOTTOM-SHELF DEMON, EITHER. HE'S AN ARCHDEVIL WITH HIS OWN NAME.
DEMONS ARE MANIFESTATIONS OF FEAR, SHUNNED BY HUMANS.
THEIR VERY EXISTENCE IS A THREAT.
HUMANS SIMPLY CANNOT COMPARE. NO MATTER HOW STRONG YOU ARE, YOU DO NOT STAND A CHANCE AGAINST A DEVIL.

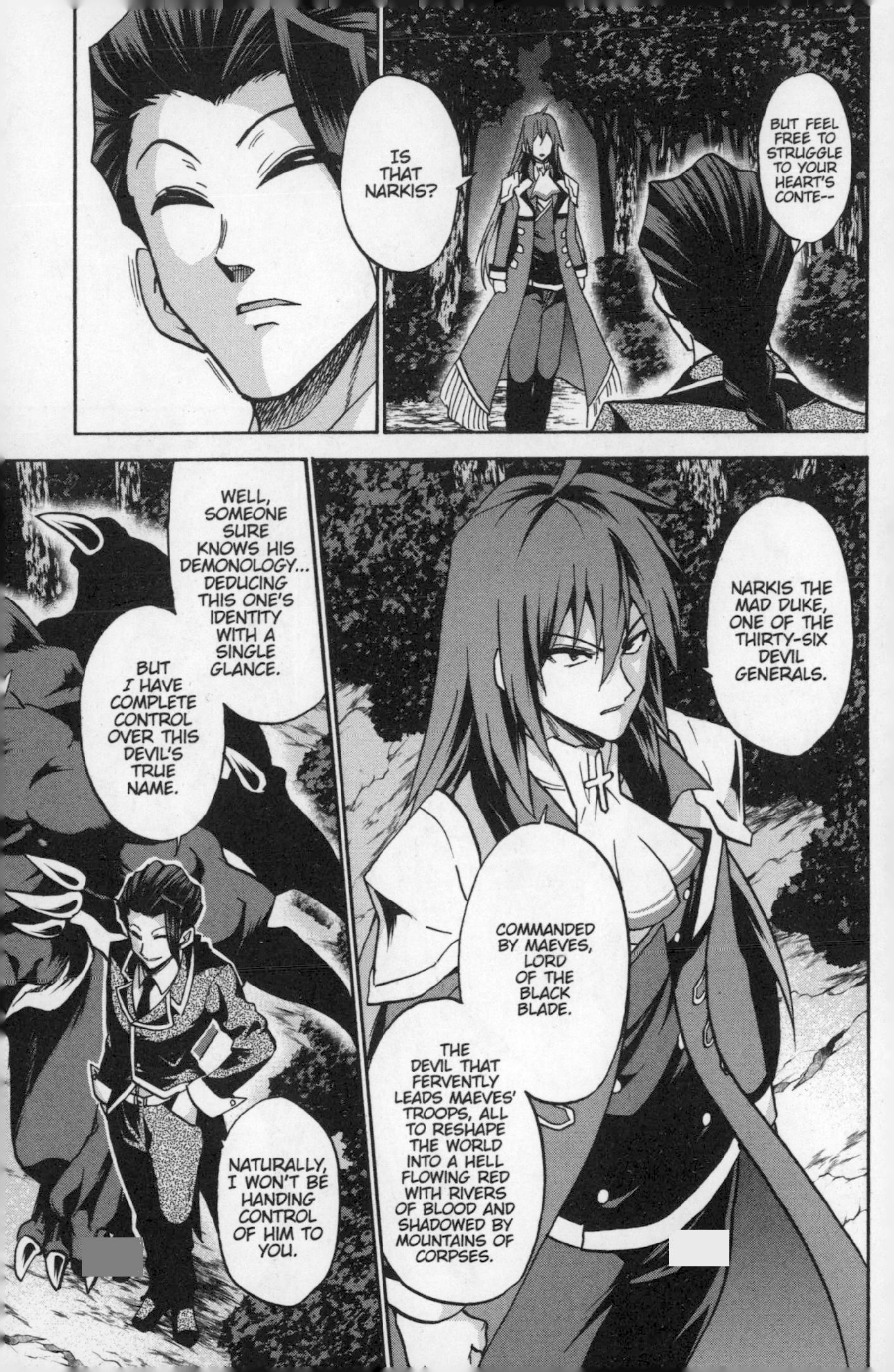
BUT FEEL FREE TO STRUGGLE TO YOUR HEART'S CONTE--
IS THAT NARKIS?
NARKIS THE MAD DUKE, ONE OF THE THIRTY-SIX DEVIL GENERALS.
COMMANDED BY MAEVES, LORD OF THE BLACK BLADE.
THE DEVIL THAT FERVENTLY LEADS MAEVES' TROOPS, ALL TO RESHAPE THE WORLD INTO A HELL FLOWING RED WITH RIVERS OF BLOOD AND SHADOWED BY MOUNTAINS OF CORPSES.
WELL, SOMEONE SURE KNOWS HIS DEMONOLOGY... DEDUCING THIS ONE'S IDENTITY WITH A SINGLE GLANCE.
BUT I HAVE COMPLETE CONTROL OVER THIS DEVIL'S TRUE NAME.
NATURALLY, I WON'T BE HANDING CONTROL OF HIM TO YOU.

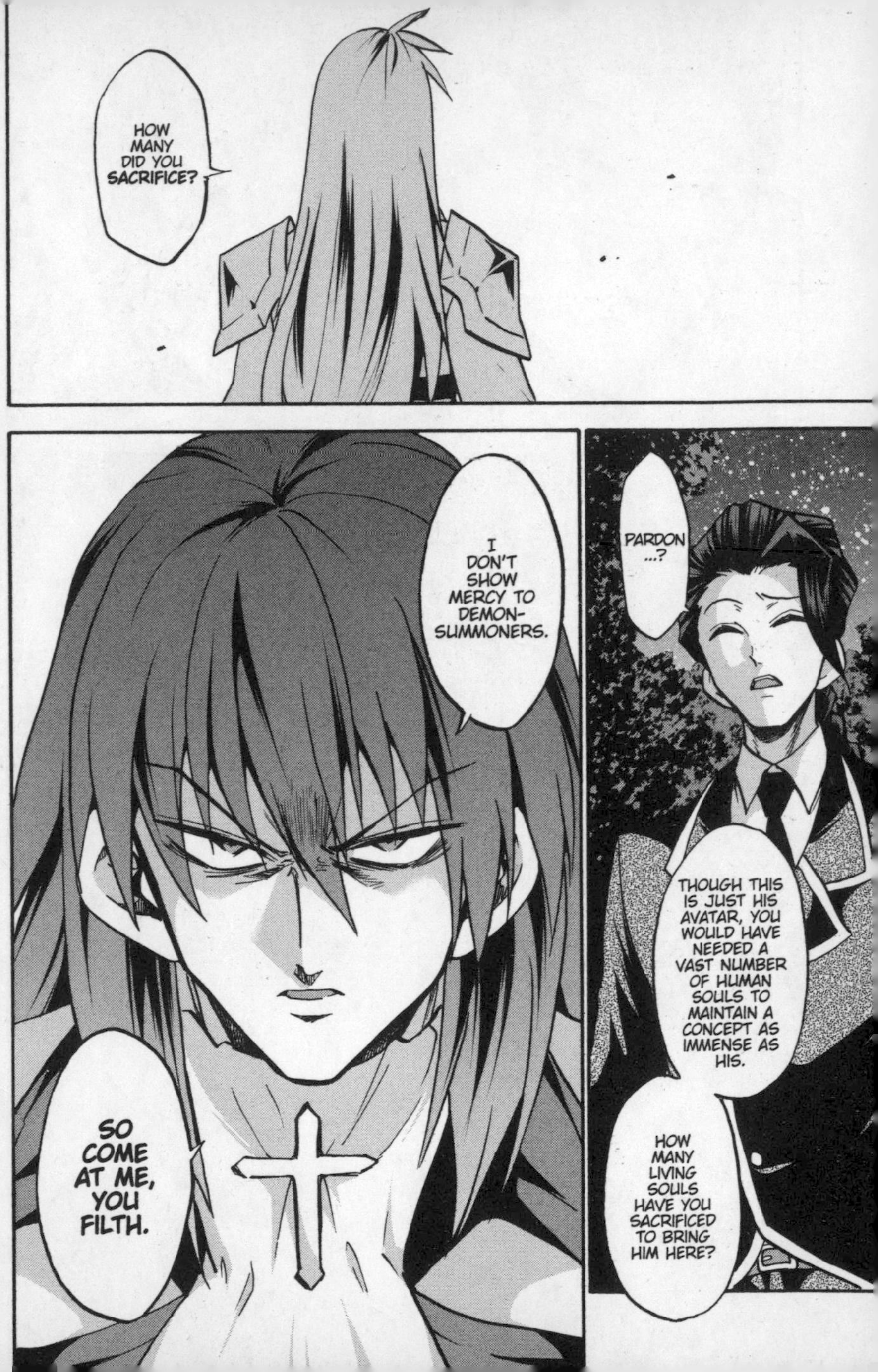
HOW MANY DID YOU SACRIFICE?
PARDON ...?
THOUGH THIS IS JUST HIS AVATAR, YOU WOULD HAVE NEEDED A VAST NUMBER OF HUMAN SOULS TO MAINTAIN A CONCEPT AS IMMENSE AS HIS.
HOW MANY LIVING SOULS HAVE YOU SACRIFICED TO BRING HIM HERE?
I DON'T SHOW MERCY TO DEMON-SUMMONERS.
SO COME AT ME, YOU FILTH.

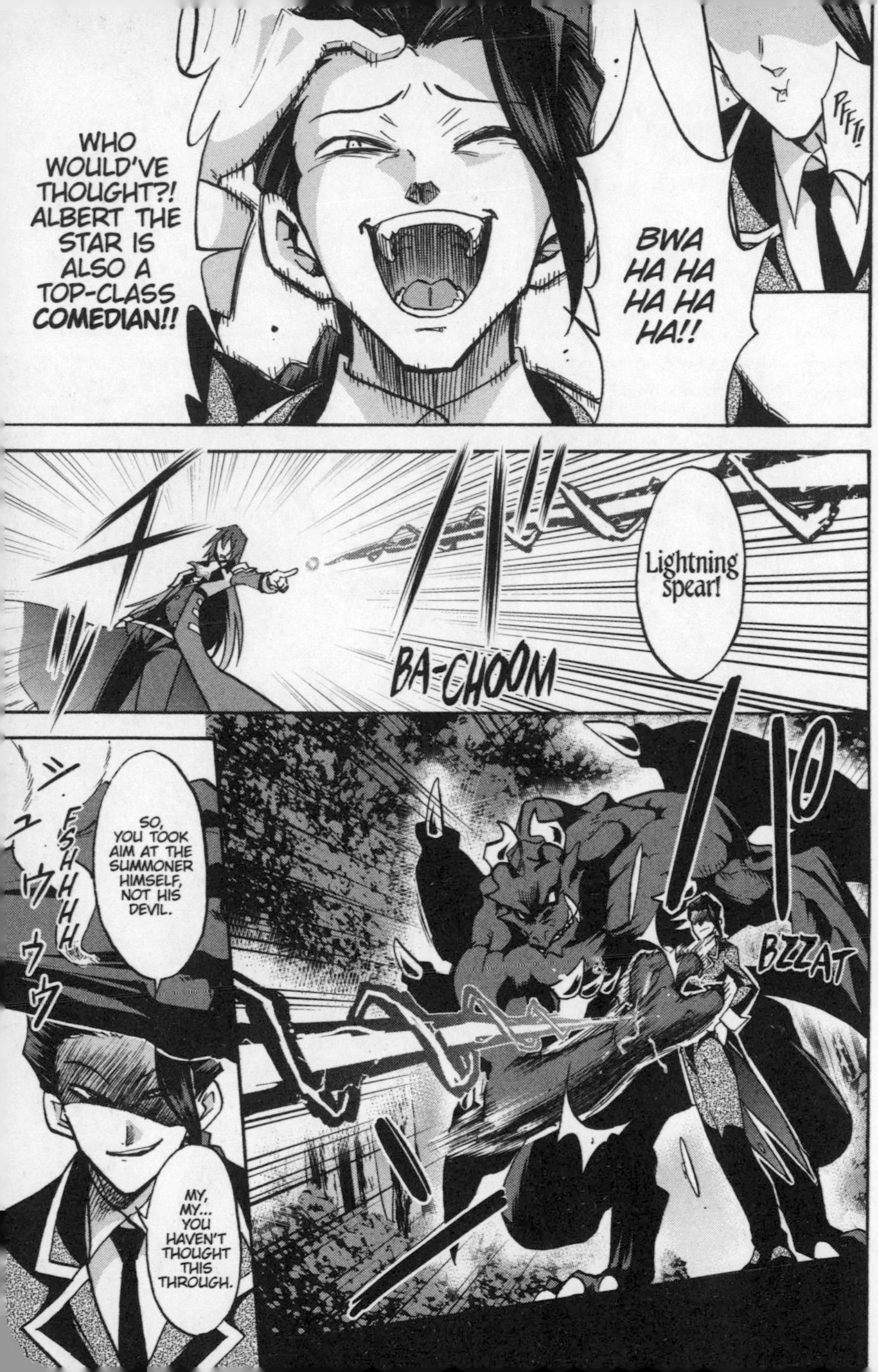
PFFT!!
BWA HA HA HA HA HA!!
WHO WOULD'VE THOUGHT?! ALBERT THE STAR IS ALSO A TOP-CLASS COMEDIAN!!
Lightning spear!
BA-CHOOM
BZZAT
FSHHHH
SO, YOU TOOK AIM AT THE SUMMONER HIMSELF, NOT HIS DEVIL.
MY, MY... YOU HAVEN'T THOUGHT THIS THROUGH.

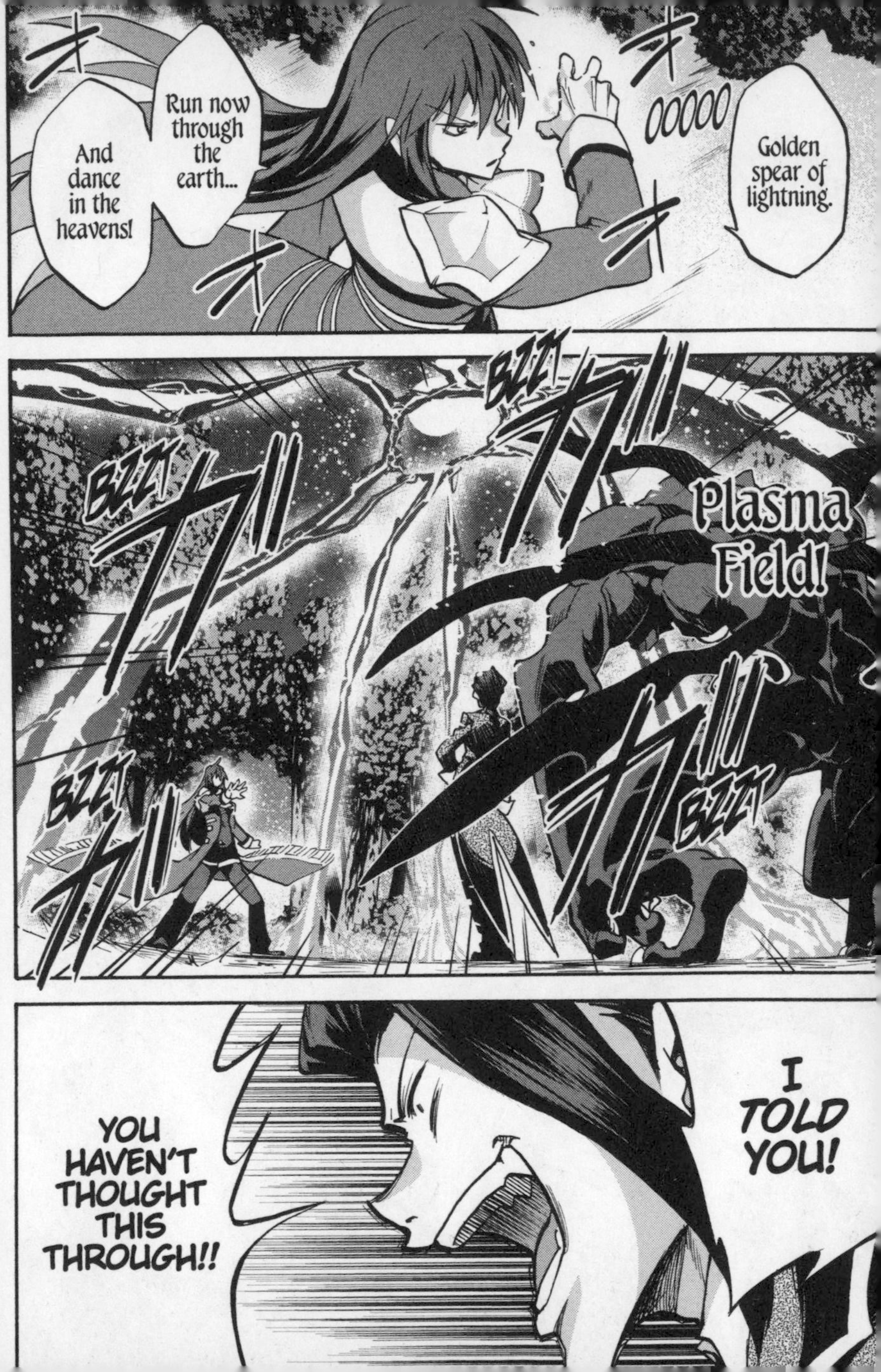
Golden spear of lightning.
OOOOO
Run now through the earth...
And dance in the heavens!
Plasma Field!
I TOLD YOU!
YOU HAVEN'T THOUGHT THIS THROUGH!!

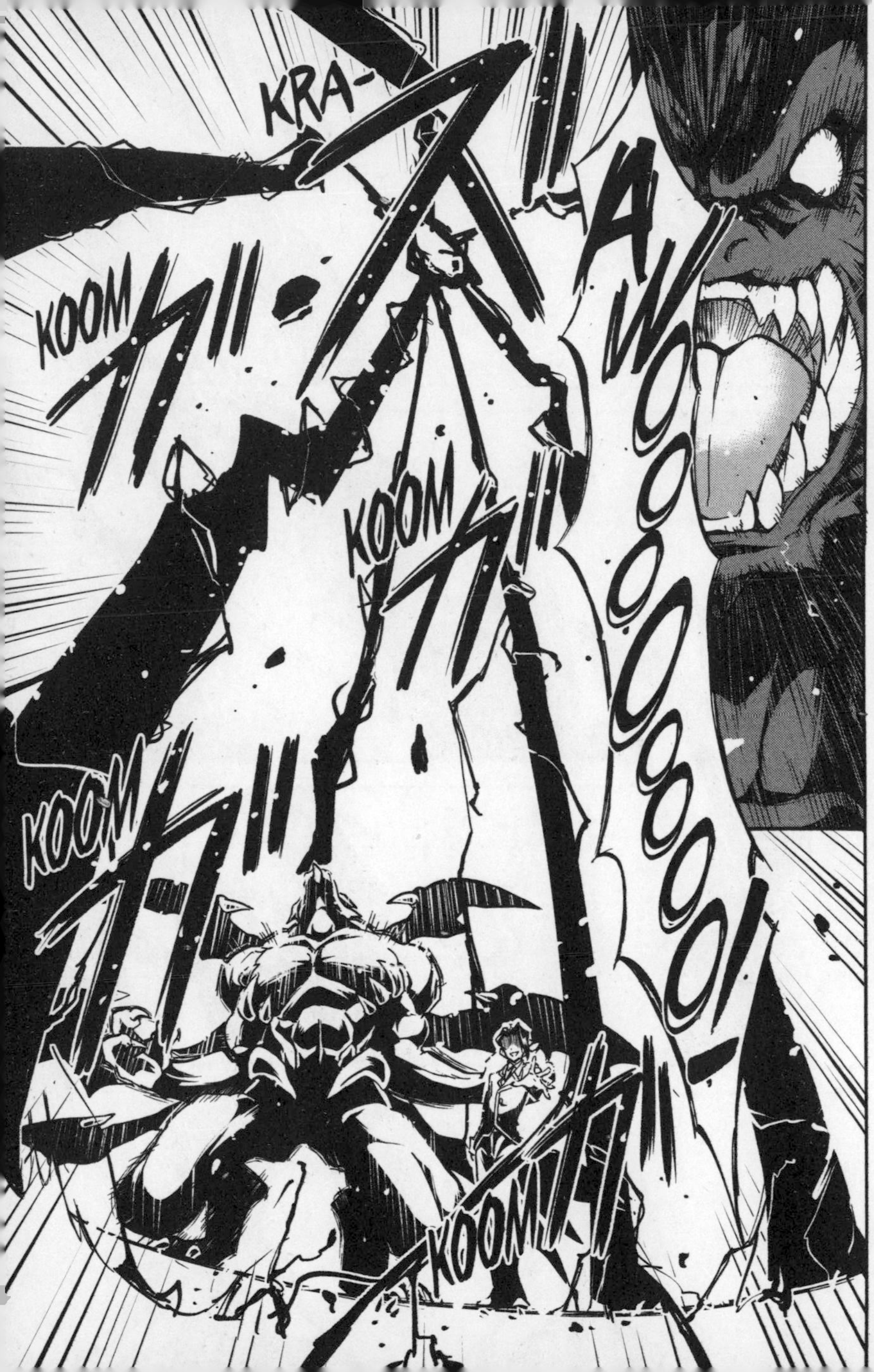
AWOOOOOOOOOOO-!
KRA-
KOOM
KOOM
KOOM
KOOM

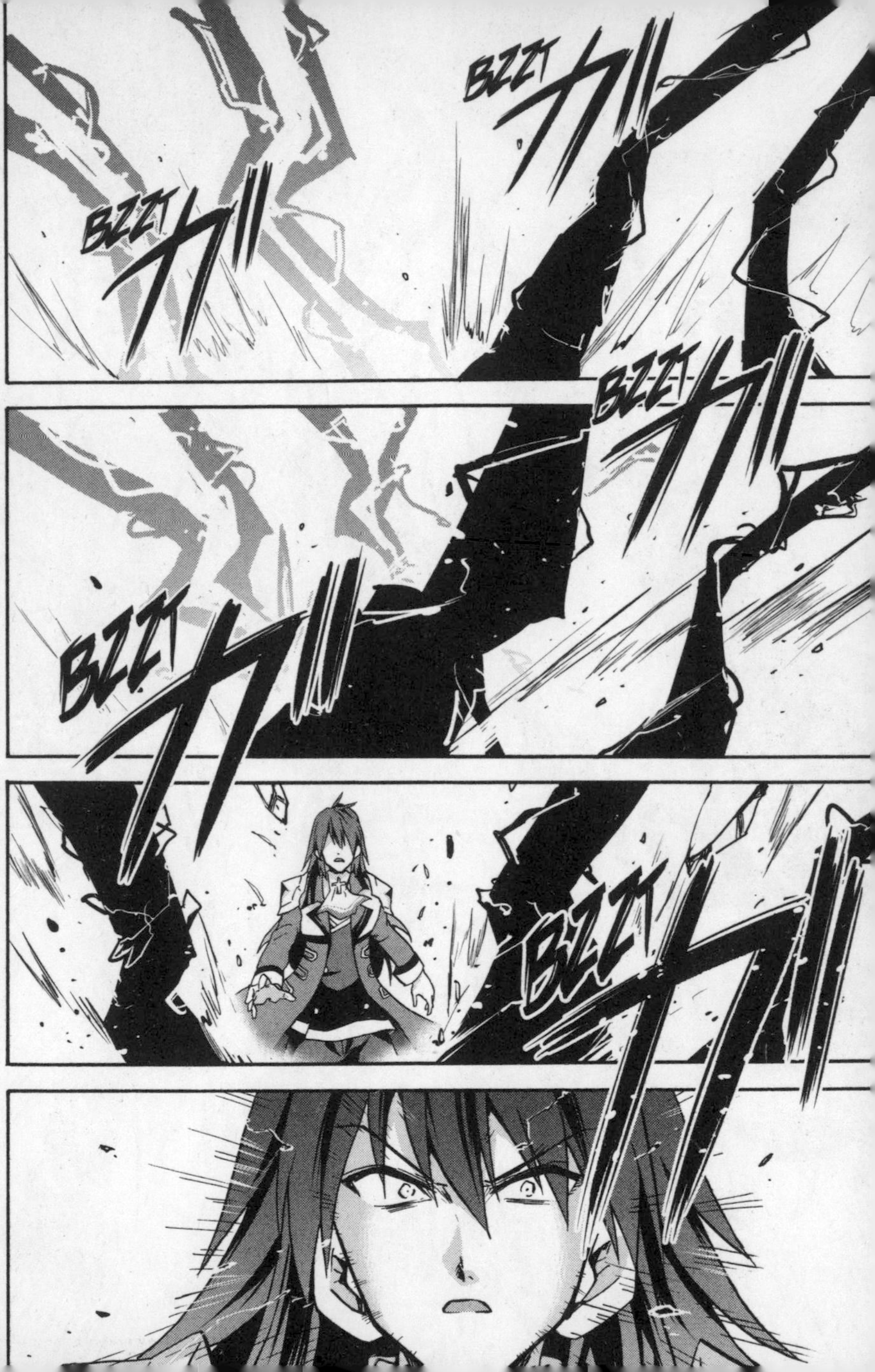
BZZT
BZZT
BZZT
BZZT
BZZT

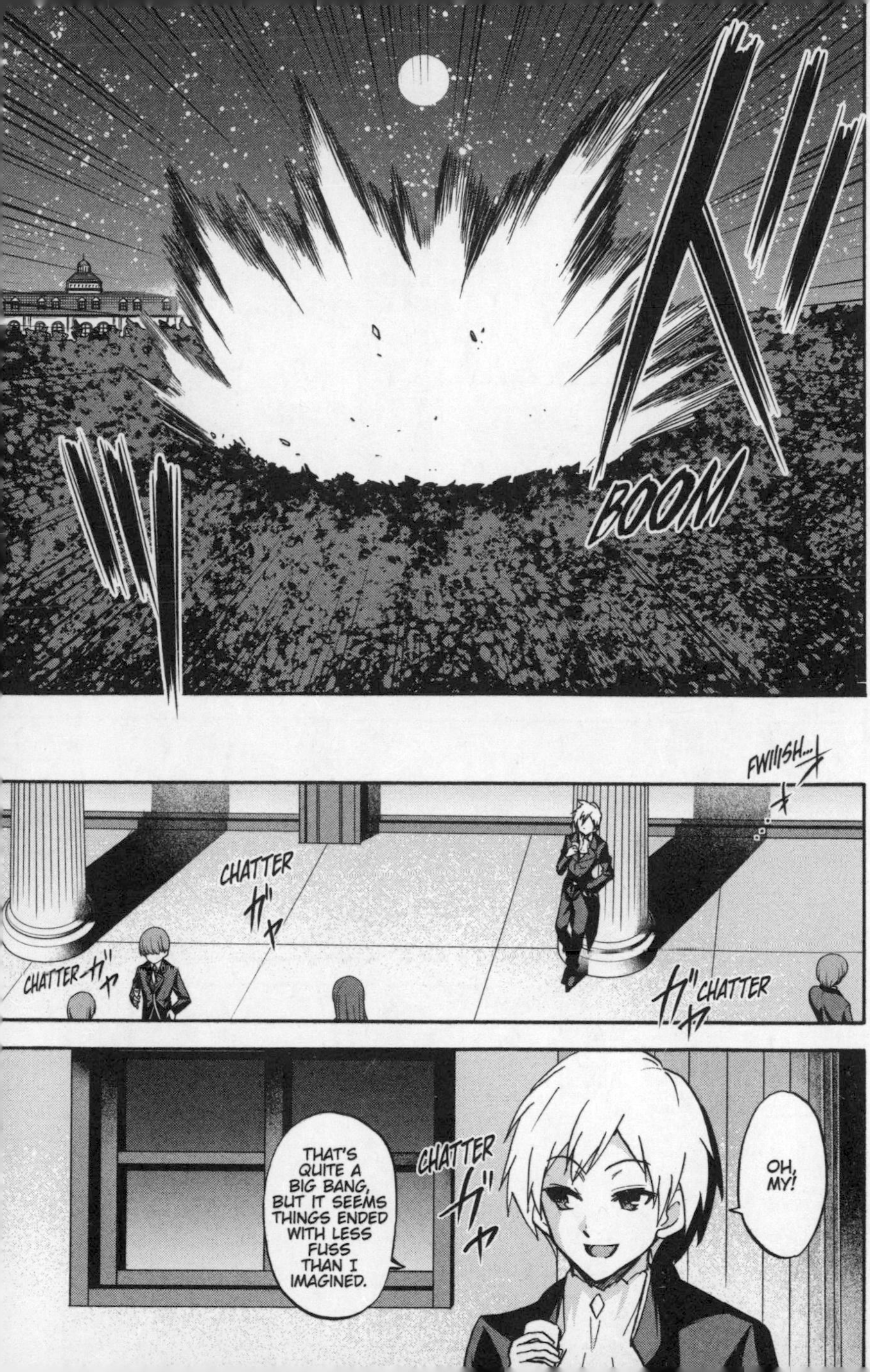
BOOM
FWIIISH...
CHATTER
CHATTER
CHATTER
OH, MY!
CHATTER
THAT'S QUITE A BIG BANG, BUT IT SEEMS THINGS ENDED WITH LESS FUSS THAN I IMAGINED.

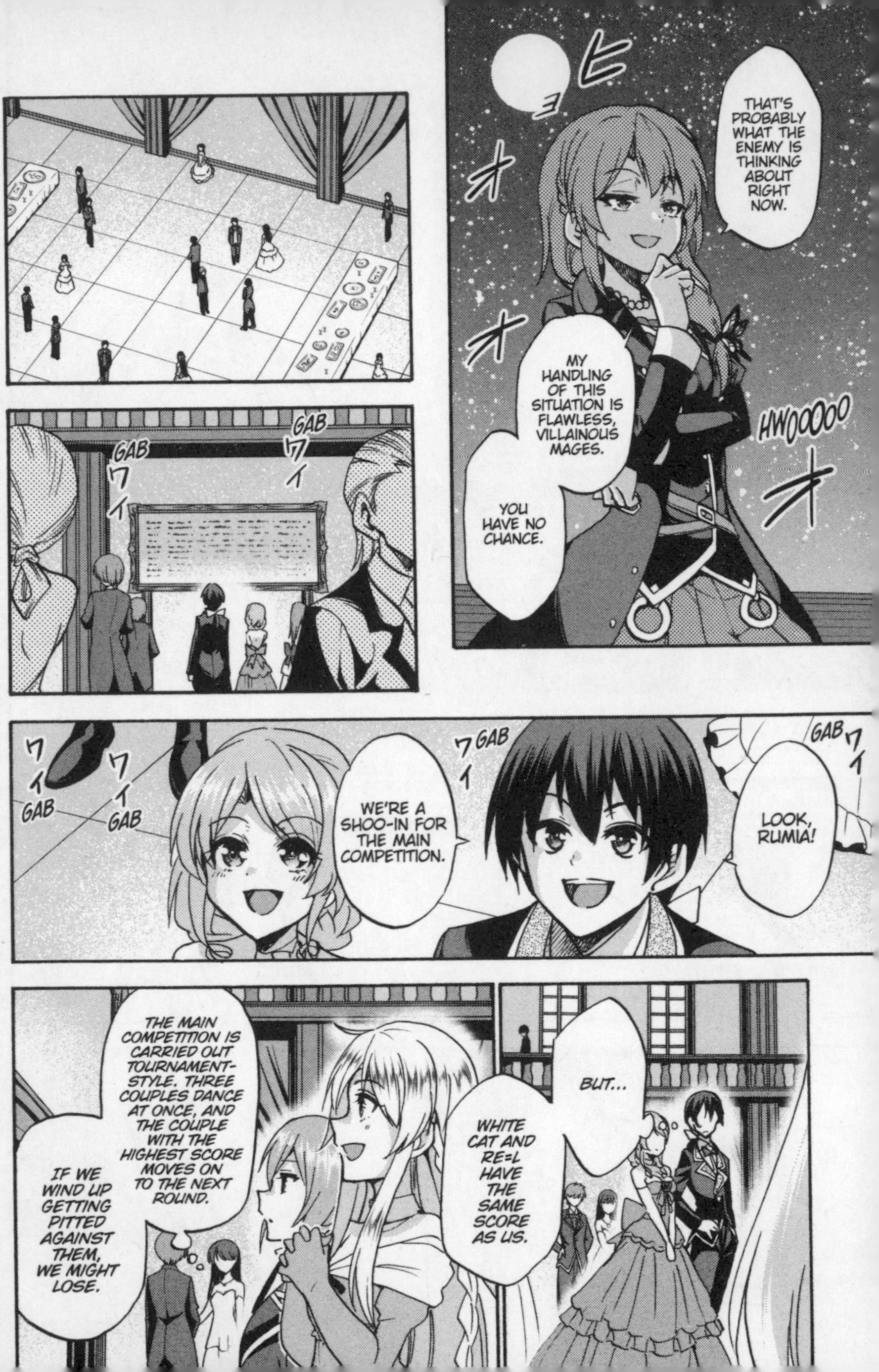
THAT'S PROBABLY WHAT THE ENEMY IS THINKING ABOUT RIGHT NOW.
MY HANDLING OF THIS SITUATION IS FLAWLESS, VILLAINOUS MAGES.
HWOOOOO
YOU HAVE NO CHANCE.
GAB
GAB
GAB
LOOK, RUMIA!
GAB
WE'RE A SHOO-IN FOR THE MAIN COMPETITION.
GAB
GAB
BUT...
WHITE CAT AND RE=L HAVE THE SAME SCORE AS US.
THE MAIN COMPETITION IS CARRIED OUT TOURNAMENT-STYLE. THREE COUPLES DANCE AT ONCE, AND THE COUPLE WITH THE HIGHEST SCORE MOVES ON TO THE NEXT ROUND.
IF WE WIND UP GETTING PITTED AGAINST THEM, WE MIGHT LOSE.

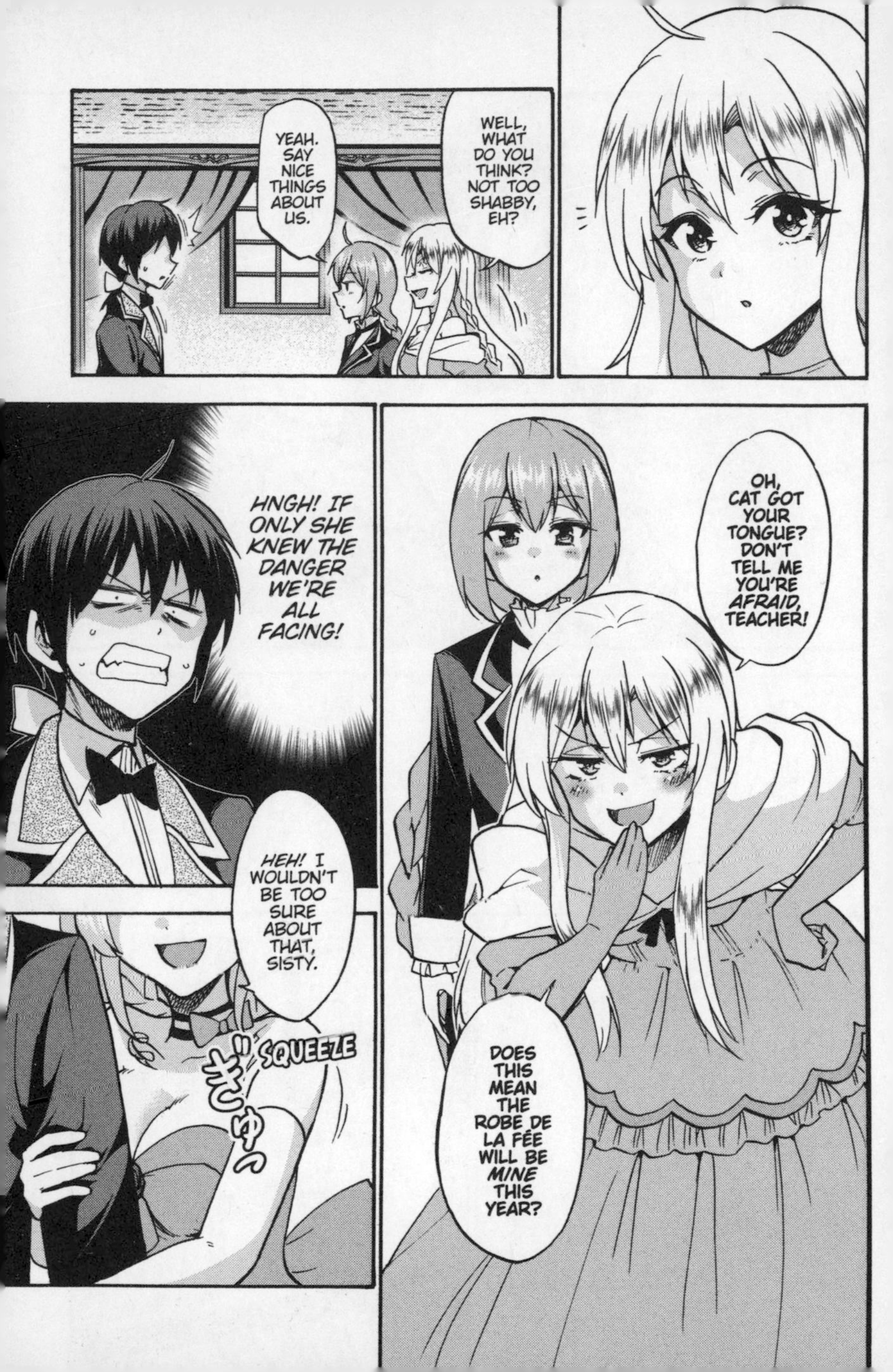
WELL, WHAT DO YOU THINK? NOT TOO SHABBY, EH?
YEAH. SAY NICE THINGS ABOUT US.
OH, CAT GOT YOUR TONGUE? DON'T TELL ME YOU'RE AFRAID, TEACHER!
DOES THIS MEAN THE ROBE DE LA FÉE WILL BE MINE THIS YEAR?
HNGH! IF ONLY SHE KNEW THE DANGER WE'RE ALL FACING!
HEH! I WOULDN'T BE TOO SURE ABOUT THAT, SISTY.
SQUEEZE

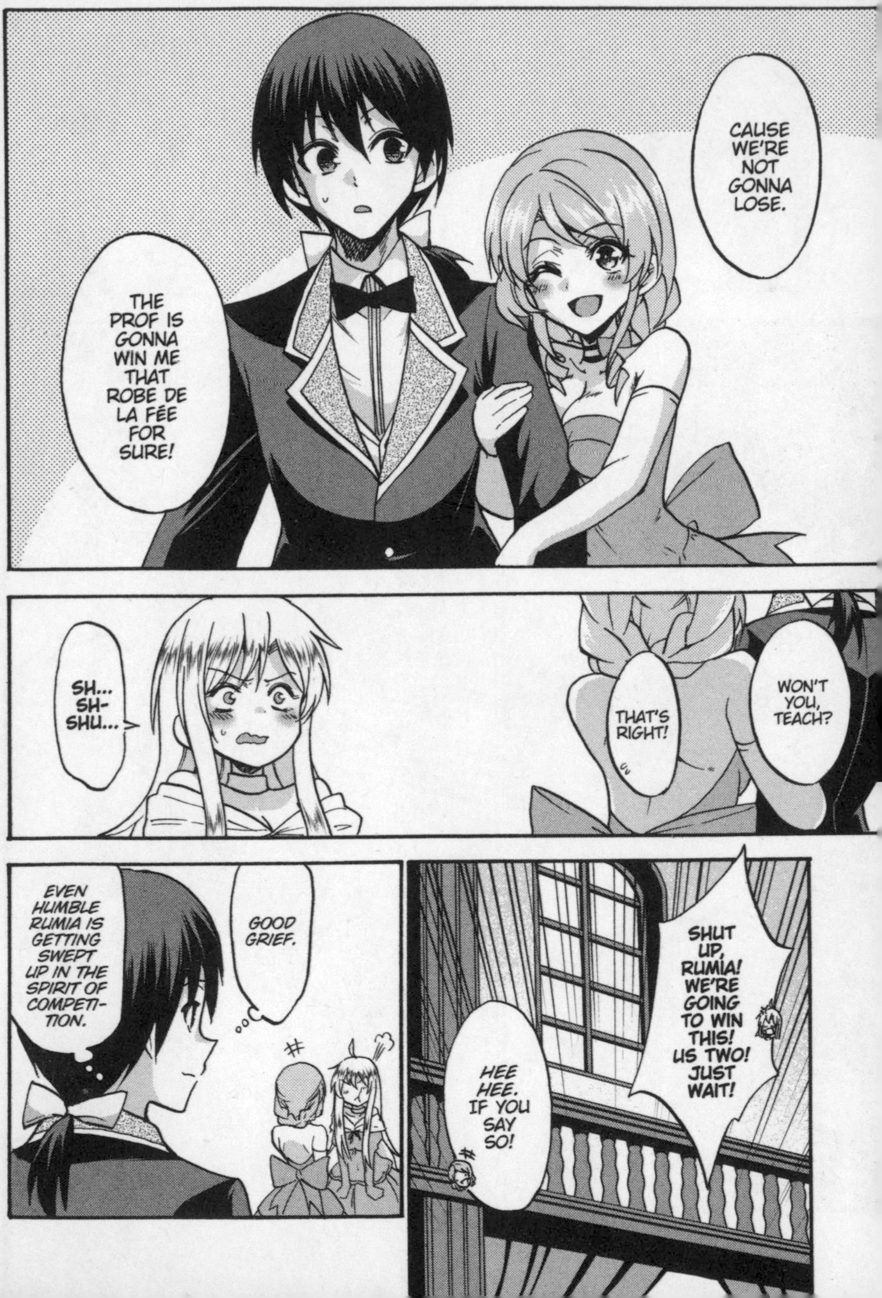
CAUSE WE'RE NOT GONNA LOSE.
THE PROF IS GONNA WIN ME THAT ROBE DE LA FÉE FOR SURE!
WON'T YOU, TEACH?
THAT'S RIGHT!
SH... SH-SHU...
SHUT UP, RUMIA! WE'RE GOING TO WIN THIS! US TWO! JUST WAIT!
HEE HEE. IF YOU SAY SO!
GOOD GRIEF.
EVEN HUMBLE RUMIA IS GETTING SWEPT UP IN THE SPIRIT OF COMPETITION.

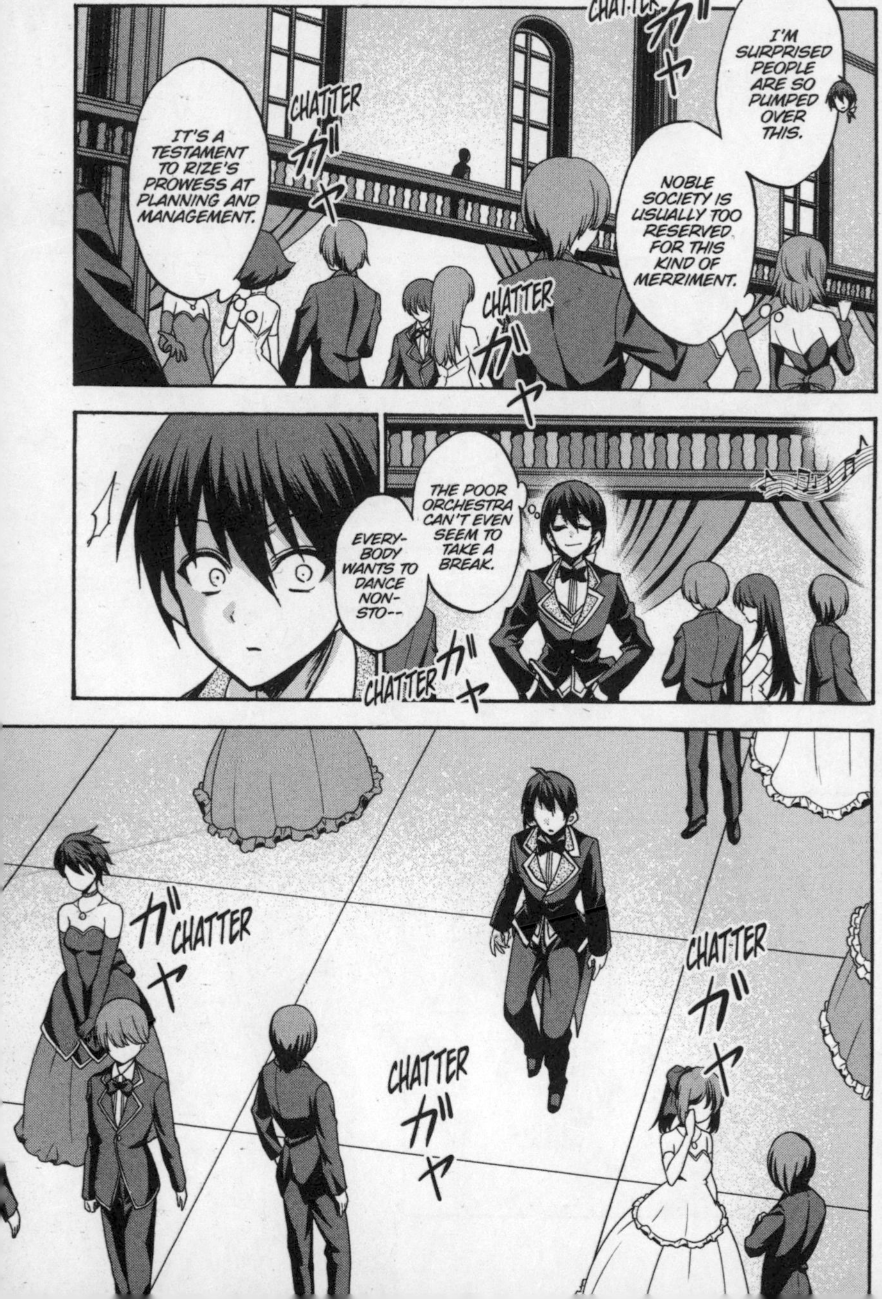
CHATTER ガヤ
I'M SURPRISED PEOPLE ARE SO PUMPED OVER THIS.
NOBLE SOCIETY IS USUALLY TOO RESERVED FOR THIS KIND OF MERRIMENT.
CHATTER ガヤ
CHATTER ガヤ
IT'S A TESTAMENT TO RIZE'S PROWESS AT PLANNING AND MANAGEMENT.
THE POOR ORCHESTRA CAN'T EVEN SEEM TO TAKE A BREAK.
EVERY-BODY WANTS TO DANCE NON-STO--
CHATTER ガヤ
CHATTER ガヤ
CHATTER ガヤ
CHATTER ガヤ

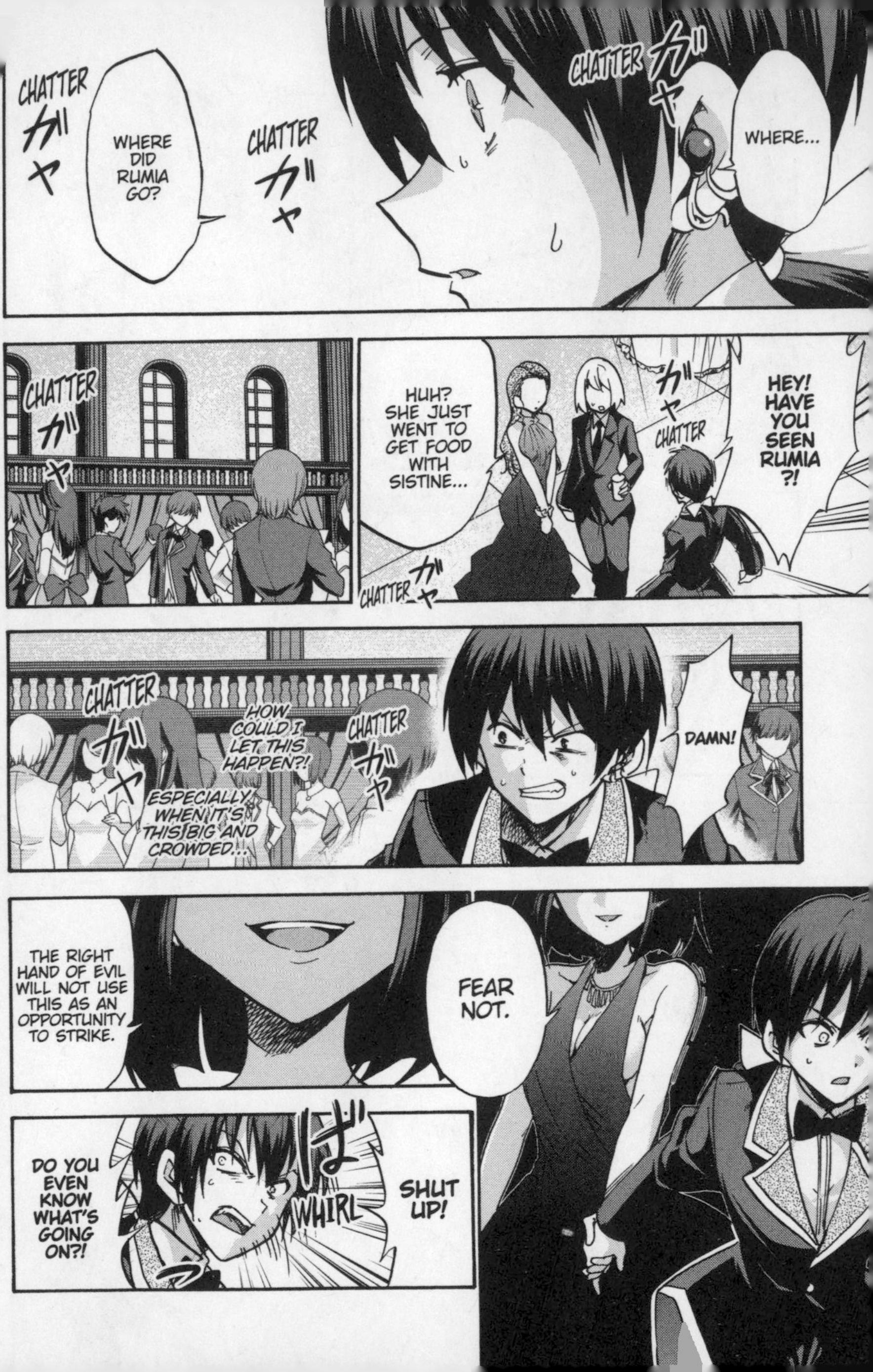

WHERE...
CHATTER ガヤ
CHATTER ガヤ
WHERE DID RUMIA GO?
CHATTER ガヤ
HEY! HAVE YOU SEEN RUMIA?!
CHATTER ガヤ
HUH? SHE JUST WENT TO GET FOOD WITH SISTINE...
CHATTER ガヤ
CHATTER ガヤ
DAMN!
CHATTER ガヤ
HOW COULD I LET THIS HAPPEN?!
CHATTER ガヤ
ESPECIALLY WHEN IT'S THIS BIG AND CROWDED...
FEAR NOT.
THE RIGHT HAND OF EVIL WILL NOT USE THIS AS AN OPPORTUNITY TO STRIKE.
SHUT UP!
ばっ WHIRL
DO YOU EVEN KNOW WHAT'S GOING ON?!

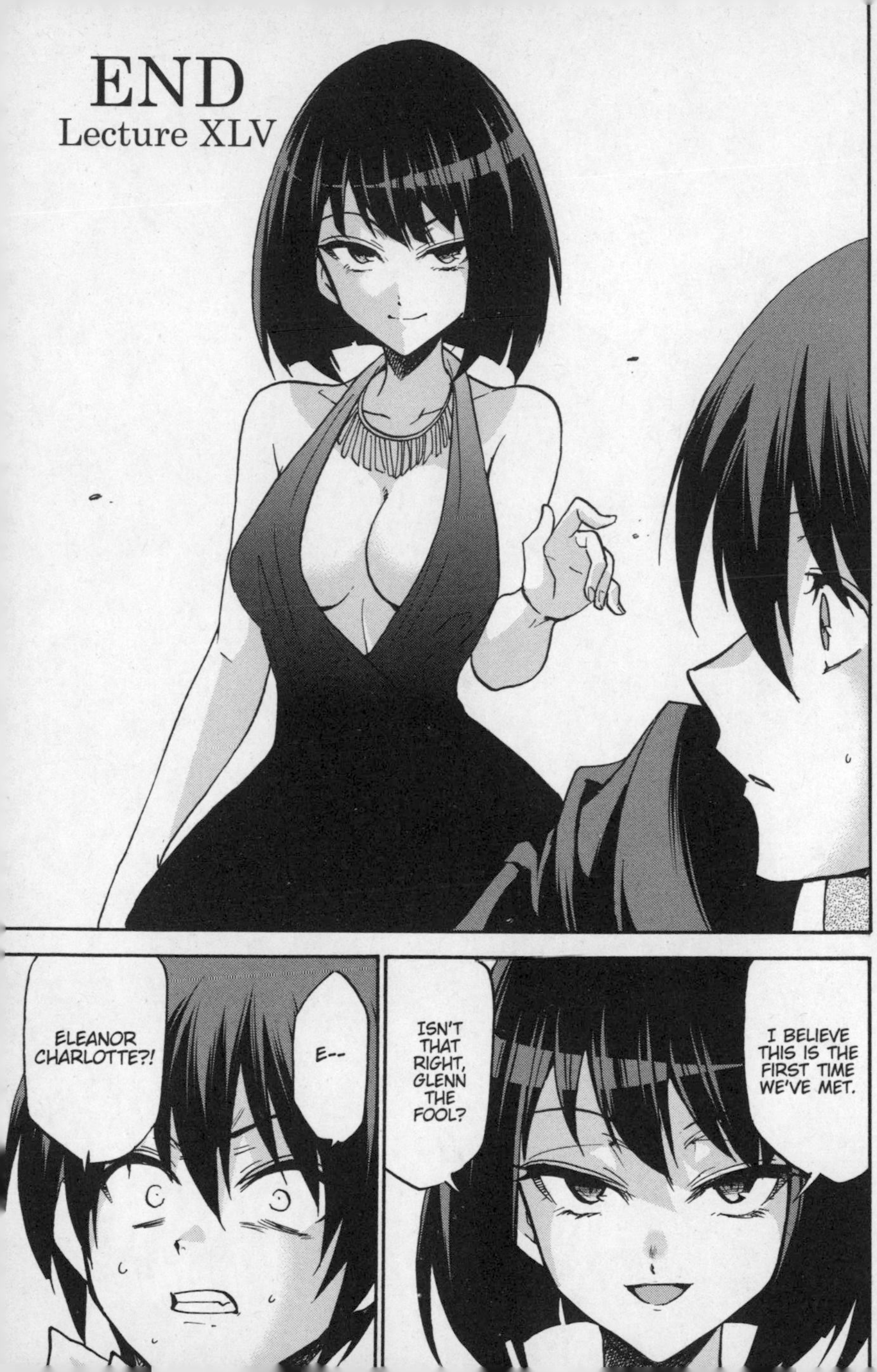
END
Lecture XLV
I BELIEVE THIS IS THE FIRST TIME WE'VE MET.
ISN'T THAT RIGHT, GLENN THE FOOL?
E--
ELEANOR CHARLOTTE?!

Akashic Records

of *Bastard* Magic *Instructor*

Lecture XLVI

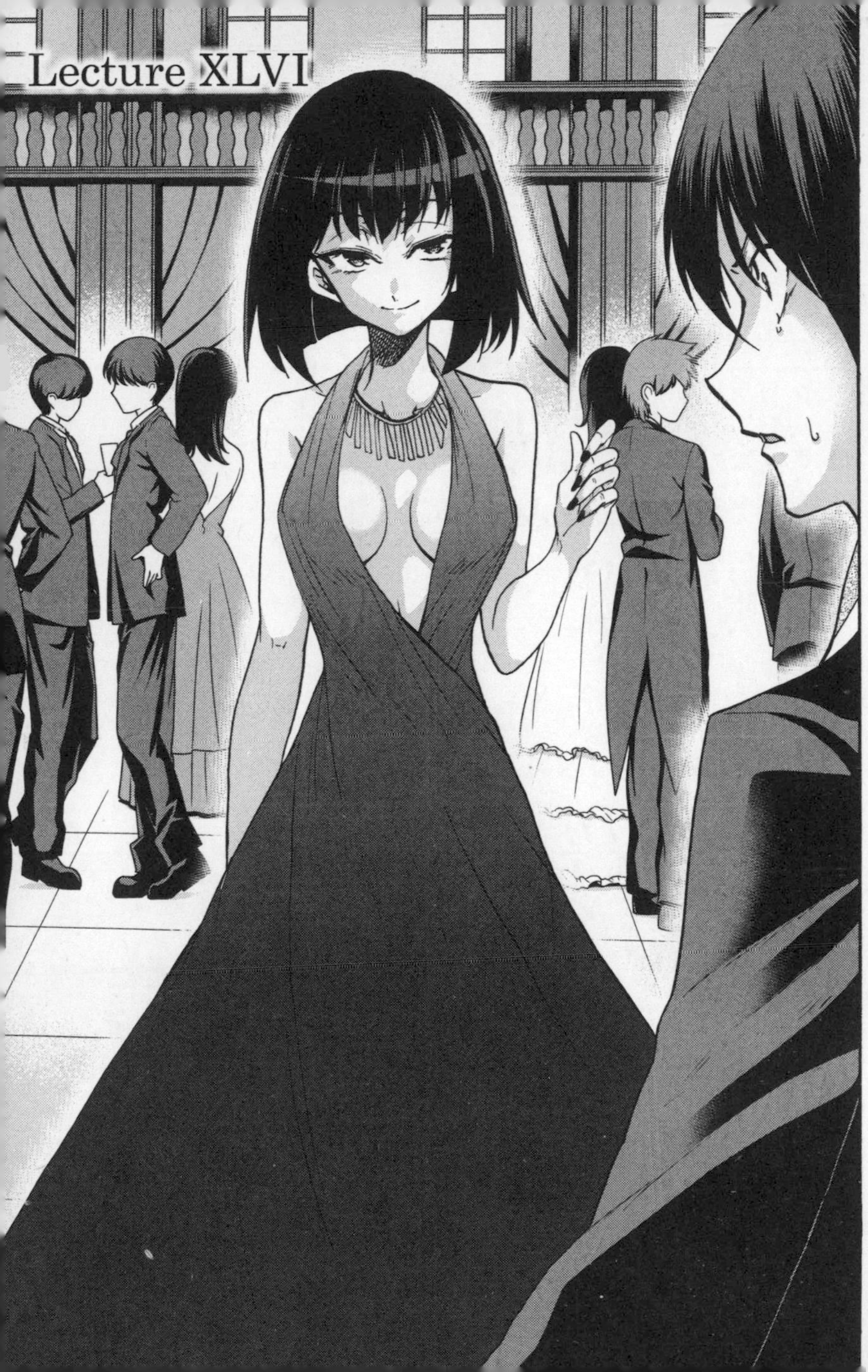

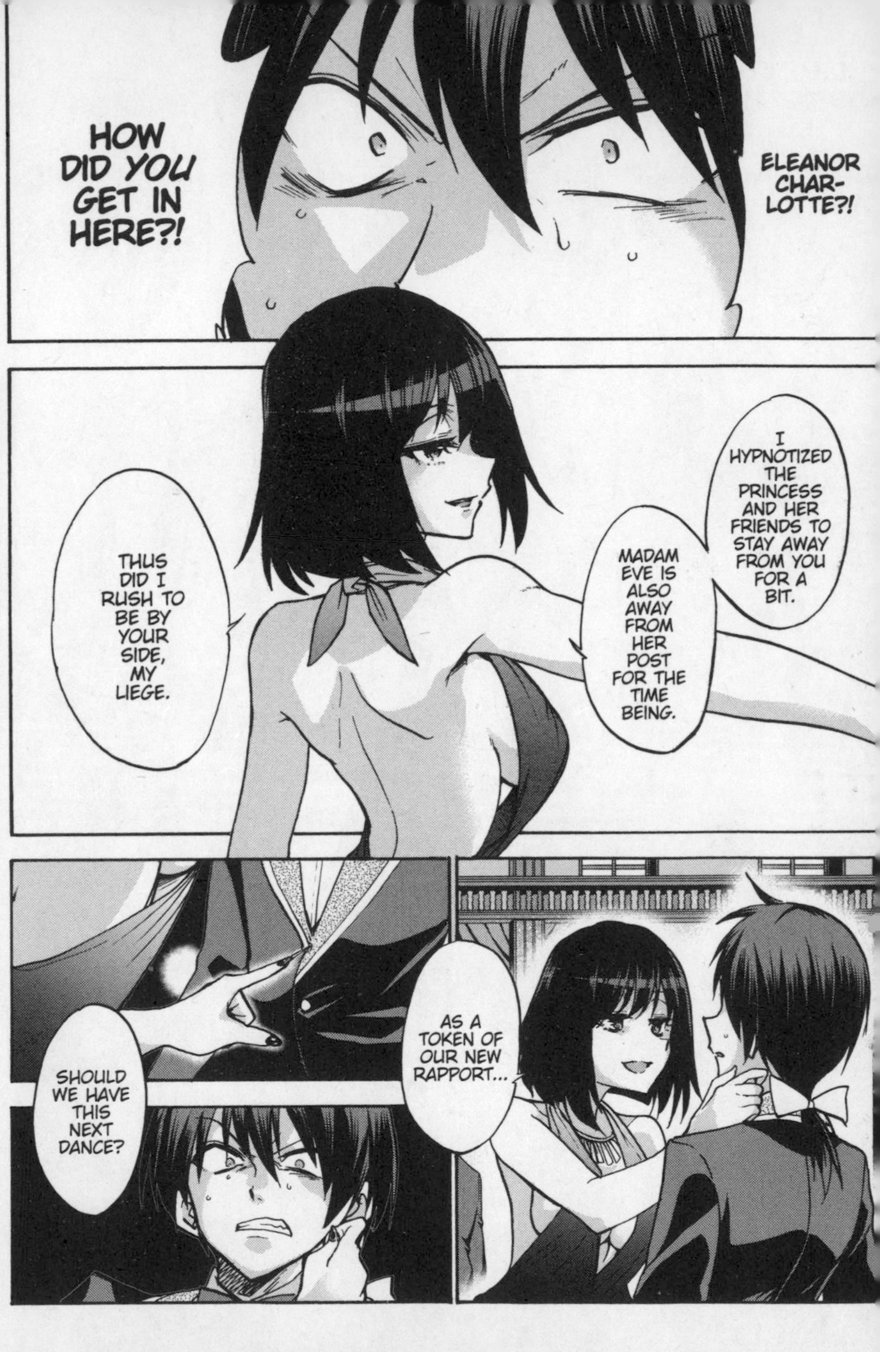
ELEANOR CHARLOTTE?!
HOW DID YOU GET IN HERE?!
I HYPNOTIZED THE PRINCESS AND HER FRIENDS TO STAY AWAY FROM YOU FOR A BIT.
MADAM EVE IS ALSO AWAY FROM HER POST FOR THE TIME BEING.
THUS DID I RUSH TO BE BY YOUR SIDE, MY LIEGE.
AS A TOKEN OF OUR NEW RAPPORT...
SHOULD WE HAVE THIS NEXT DANCE?

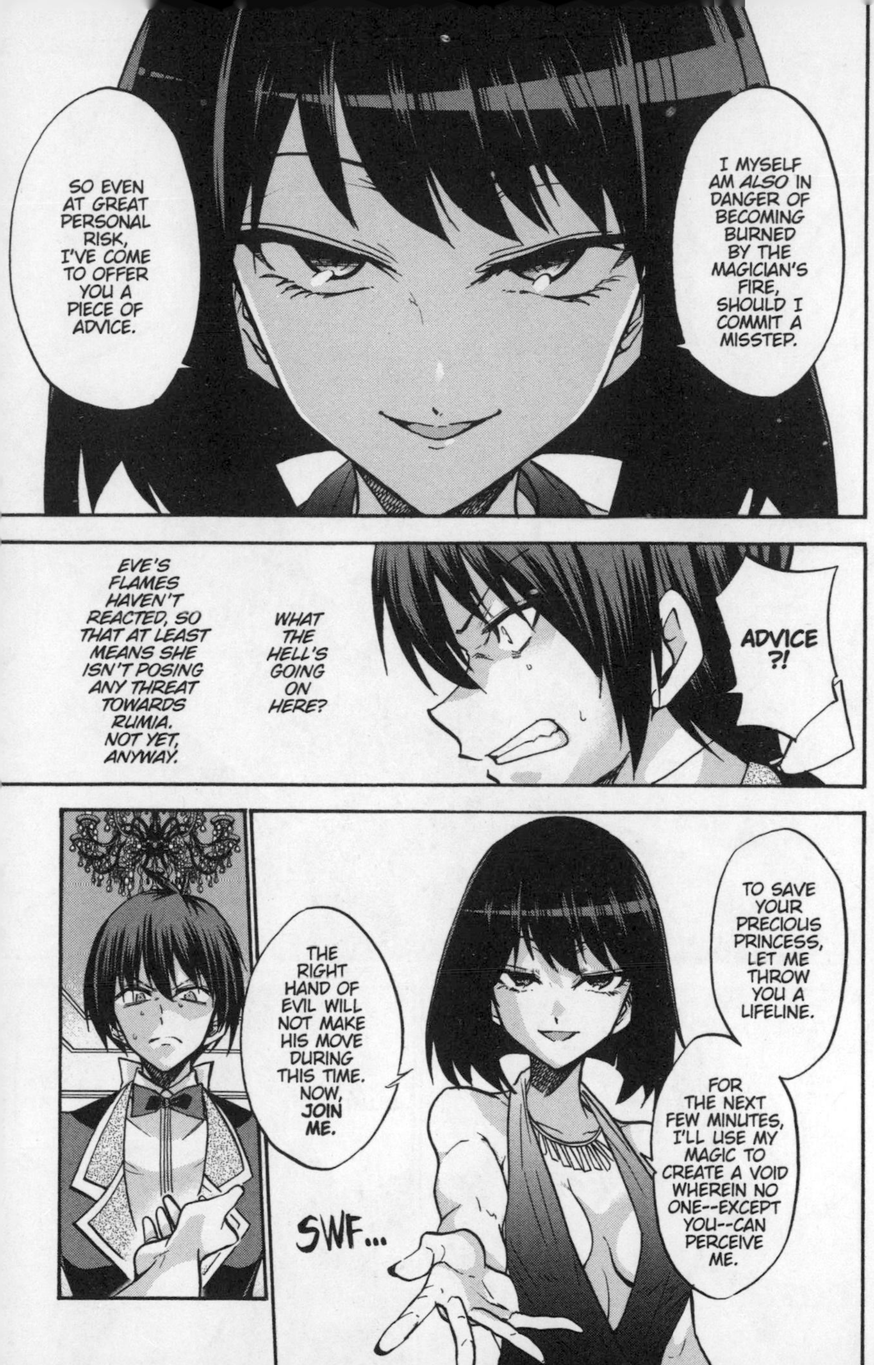

I MYSELF AM *ALSO* IN DANGER OF BECOMING BURNED BY THE MAGICIAN'S FIRE, SHOULD I COMMIT A MISSTEP.
SO EVEN AT GREAT PERSONAL RISK, I'VE COME TO OFFER YOU A PIECE OF ADVICE.
ADVICE?!
WHAT THE HELL'S GOING ON HERE?
EVE'S FLAMES HAVEN'T REACTED, SO THAT AT LEAST MEANS SHE ISN'T POSING ANY THREAT TOWARDS RUMIA. NOT YET, ANYWAY.
TO SAVE YOUR PRECIOUS PRINCESS, LET ME THROW YOU A LIFELINE.
FOR THE NEXT FEW MINUTES, I'LL USE MY MAGIC TO CREATE A VOID WHEREIN NO ONE--EXCEPT YOU--CAN PERCEIVE ME.
THE RIGHT HAND OF EVIL WILL NOT MAKE HIS MOVE DURING THIS TIME. NOW, **JOIN ME.**
SWF...

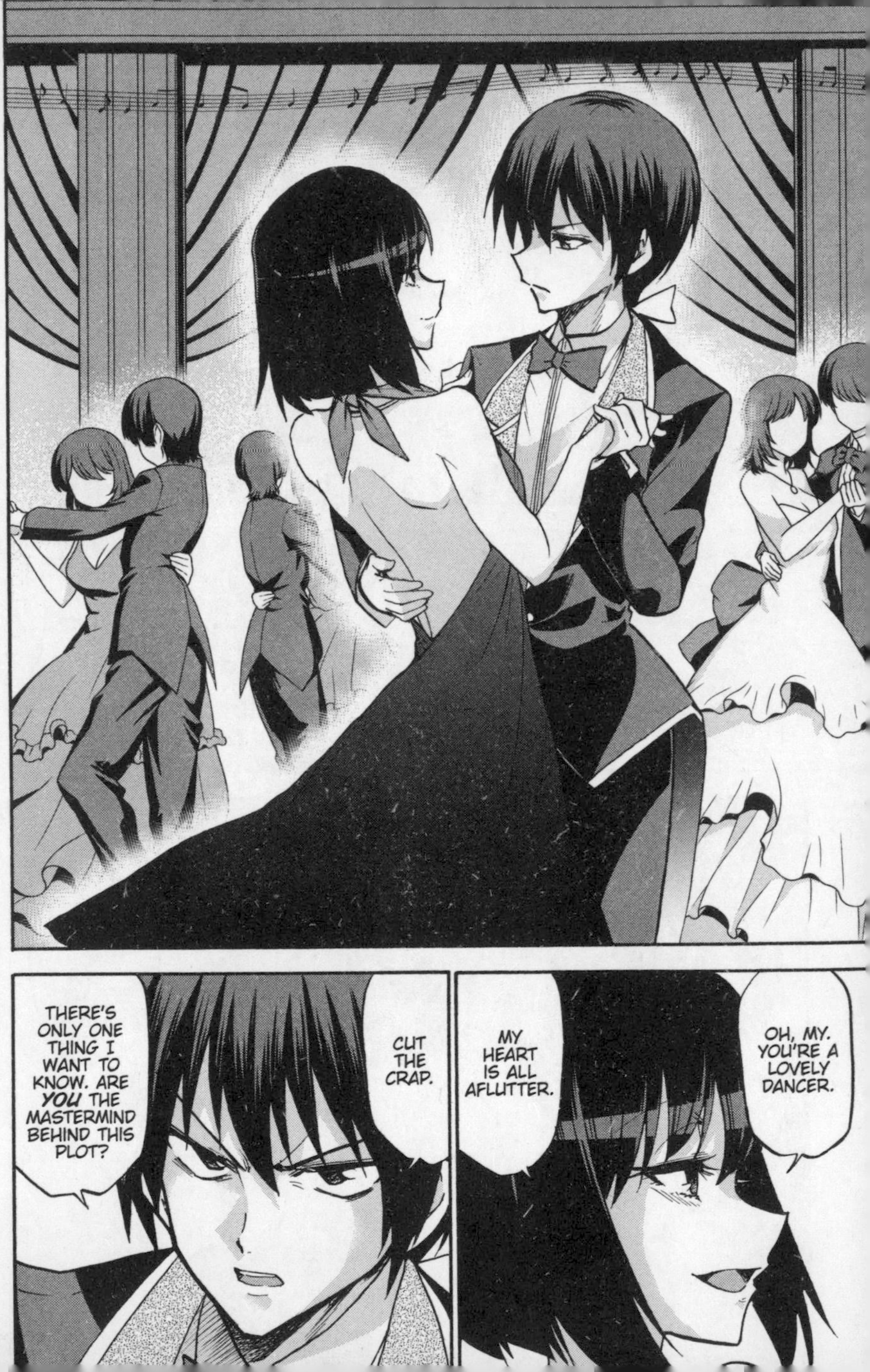
OH, MY. YOU'RE A LOVELY DANCER.
MY HEART IS ALL AFLUTTER.
CUT THE CRAP.
THERE'S ONLY ONE THING I WANT TO KNOW. ARE *YOU* THE MASTERMIND BEHIND THIS PLOT?

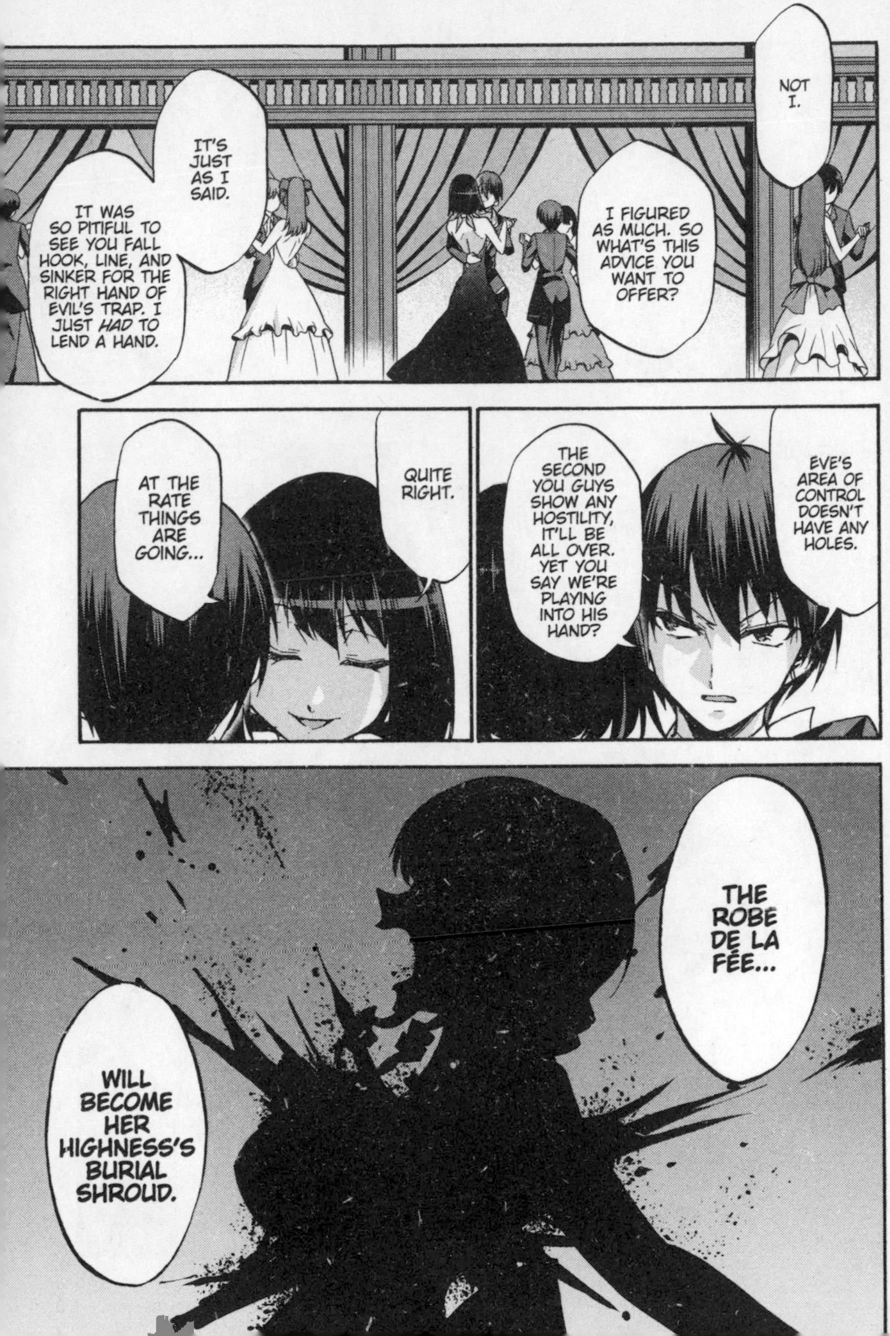
NOT I.
I FIGURED AS MUCH. SO WHAT'S THIS ADVICE YOU WANT TO OFFER?
IT'S JUST AS I SAID.
IT WAS SO PITIFUL TO SEE YOU FALL HOOK, LINE, AND SINKER FOR THE RIGHT HAND OF EVIL'S TRAP. I JUST *HAD* TO LEND A HAND.
EVE'S AREA OF CONTROL DOESN'T HAVE ANY HOLES.
THE SECOND YOU GUYS SHOW ANY HOSTILITY, IT'LL BE ALL OVER. YET YOU SAY WE'RE PLAYING INTO HIS HAND?
QUITE RIGHT.
AT THE RATE THINGS ARE GOING...
THE ROBE DE LA FÉE...
WILL BECOME HER HIGHNESS'S BURIAL SHROUD.

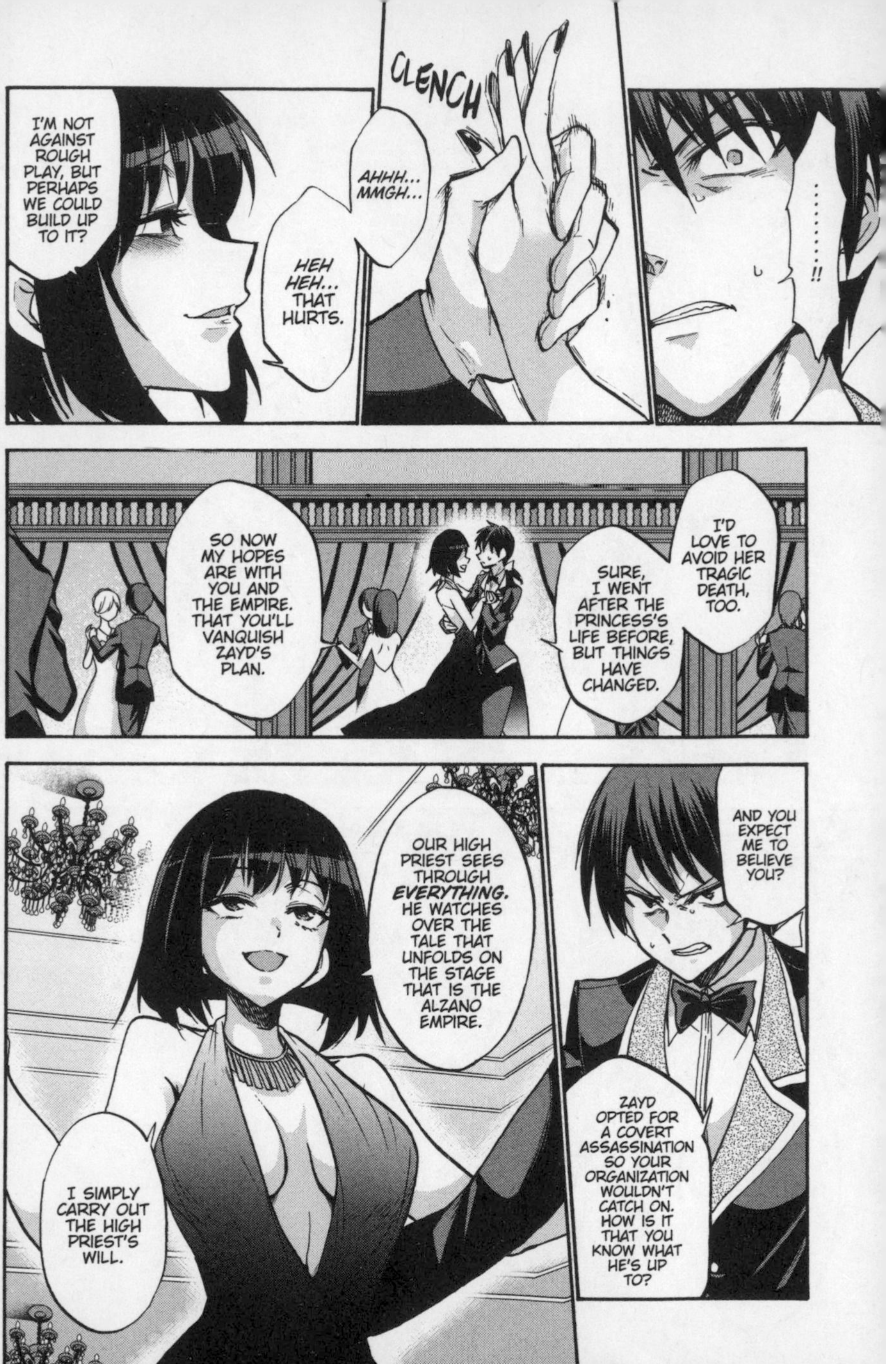
......!!
CLENCH
AHHH... MMGH...
HEH HEH... THAT HURTS.
I'M NOT AGAINST ROUGH PLAY, BUT PERHAPS WE COULD BUILD UP TO IT?
I'D LOVE TO AVOID HER TRAGIC DEATH, TOO.
SURE, I WENT AFTER THE PRINCESS'S LIFE BEFORE, BUT THINGS HAVE CHANGED.
SO NOW MY HOPES ARE WITH YOU AND THE EMPIRE. THAT YOU'LL VANQUISH ZAYD'S PLAN.
AND YOU EXPECT ME TO BELIEVE YOU?
ZAYD OPTED FOR A COVERT ASSASSINATION SO YOUR ORGANIZATION WOULDN'T CATCH ON. HOW IS IT THAT YOU KNOW WHAT HE'S UP TO?
OUR HIGH PRIEST SEES THROUGH EVERYTHING. HE WATCHES OVER THE TALE THAT UNFOLDS ON THE STAGE THAT IS THE ALZANO EMPIRE.
I SIMPLY CARRY OUT THE HIGH PRIEST'S WILL.

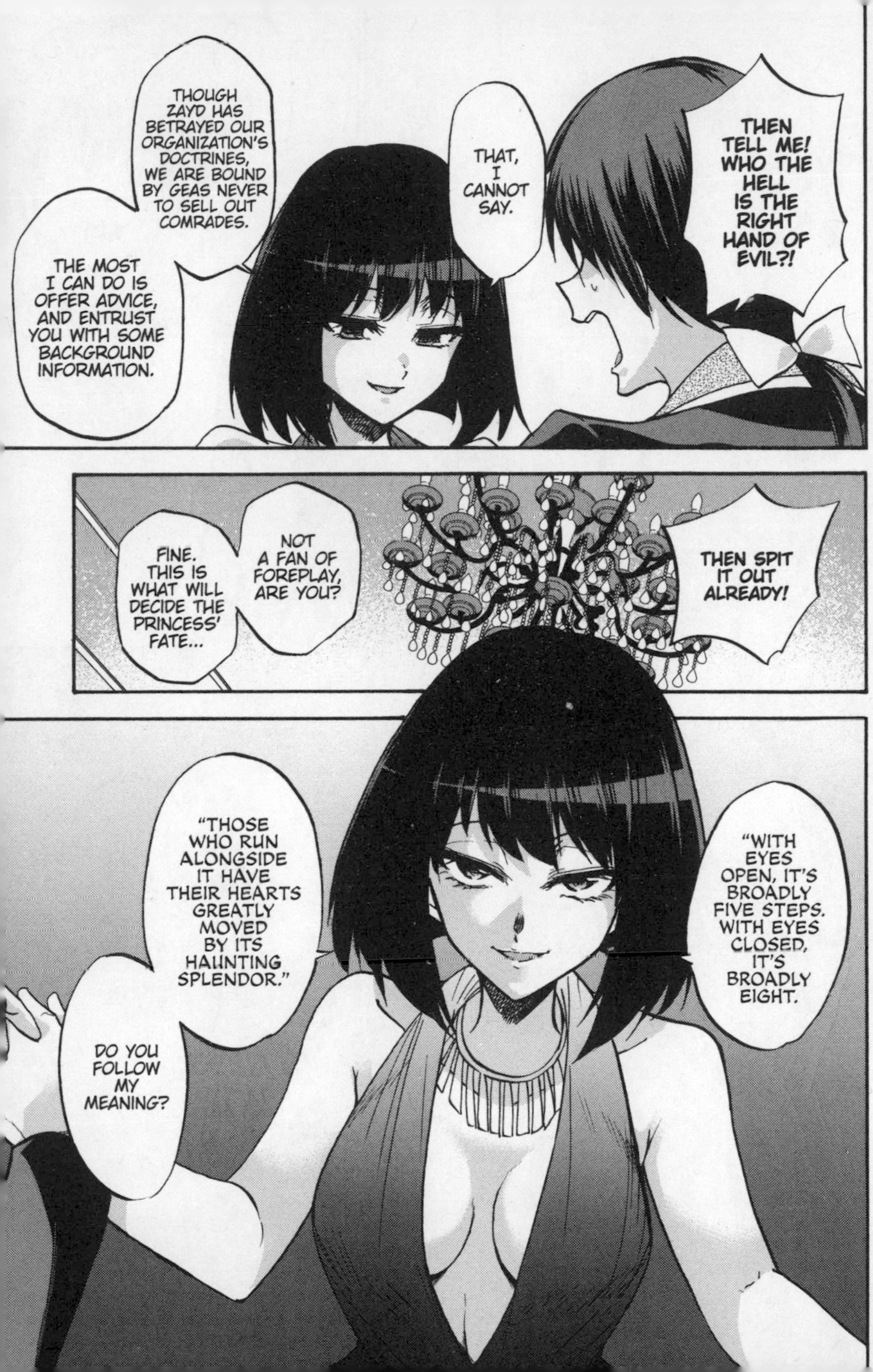
THEN TELL ME! WHO THE HELL IS THE RIGHT HAND OF EVIL?!
THAT, I CANNOT SAY.
THOUGH ZAYD HAS BETRAYED OUR ORGANIZATION'S DOCTRINES, WE ARE BOUND BY GEAS NEVER TO SELL OUT COMRADES.
THE MOST I CAN DO IS OFFER ADVICE, AND ENTRUST YOU WITH SOME BACKGROUND INFORMATION.
THEN SPIT IT OUT ALREADY!
NOT A FAN OF FOREPLAY, ARE YOU?
FINE. THIS IS WHAT WILL DECIDE THE PRINCESS' FATE...
"WITH EYES OPEN, IT'S BROADLY FIVE STEPS. WITH EYES CLOSED, IT'S BROADLY EIGHT.
"THOSE WHO RUN ALONGSIDE IT HAVE THEIR HEARTS GREATLY MOVED BY ITS HAUNTING SPLENDOR."
DO YOU FOLLOW MY MEANING?

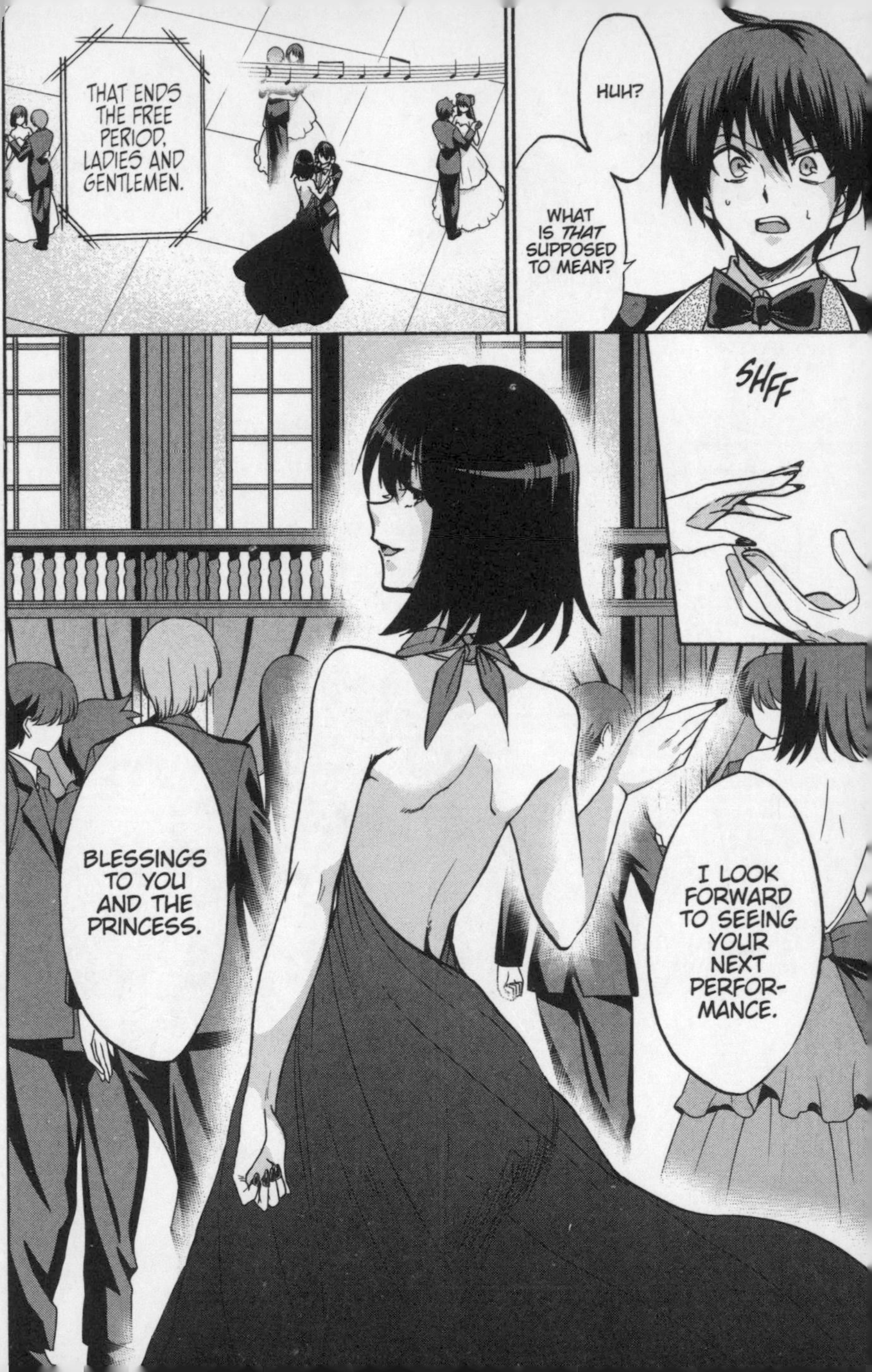
HUH?
WHAT IS *THAT* SUPPOSED TO MEAN?
THAT ENDS THE FREE PERIOD, LADIES AND GENTLEMEN.
SHFF
I LOOK FORWARD TO SEEING YOUR NEXT PERFOR-MANCE.
BLESSINGS TO YOU AND THE PRINCESS.

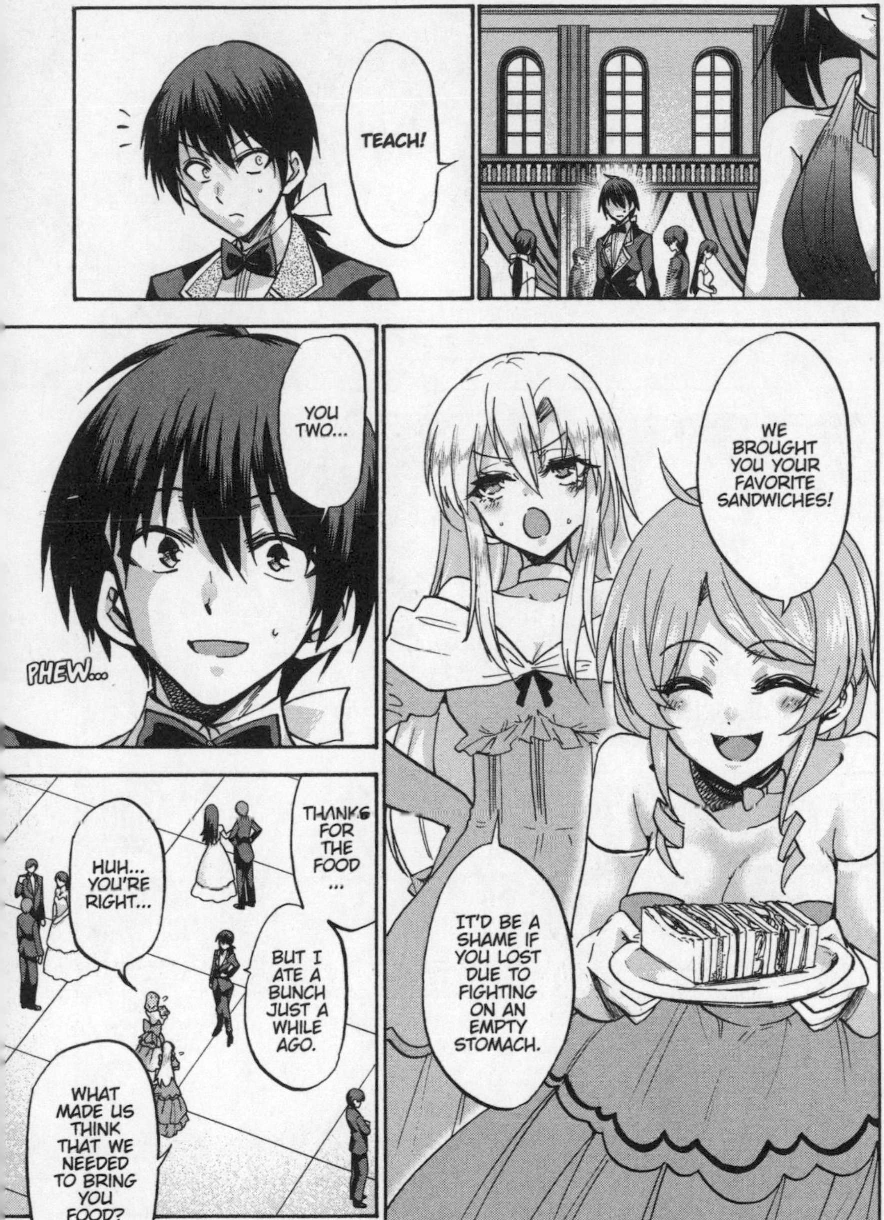
TEACH!
WE BROUGHT YOU YOUR FAVORITE SANDWICHES!
IT'D BE A SHAME IF YOU LOST DUE TO FIGHTING ON AN EMPTY STOMACH.
YOU TWO...
PHEW...
THANKS FOR THE FOOD...
BUT I ATE A BUNCH JUST A WHILE AGO.
HUH... YOU'RE RIGHT...
WHAT MADE US THINK THAT WE NEEDED TO BRING YOU FOOD?

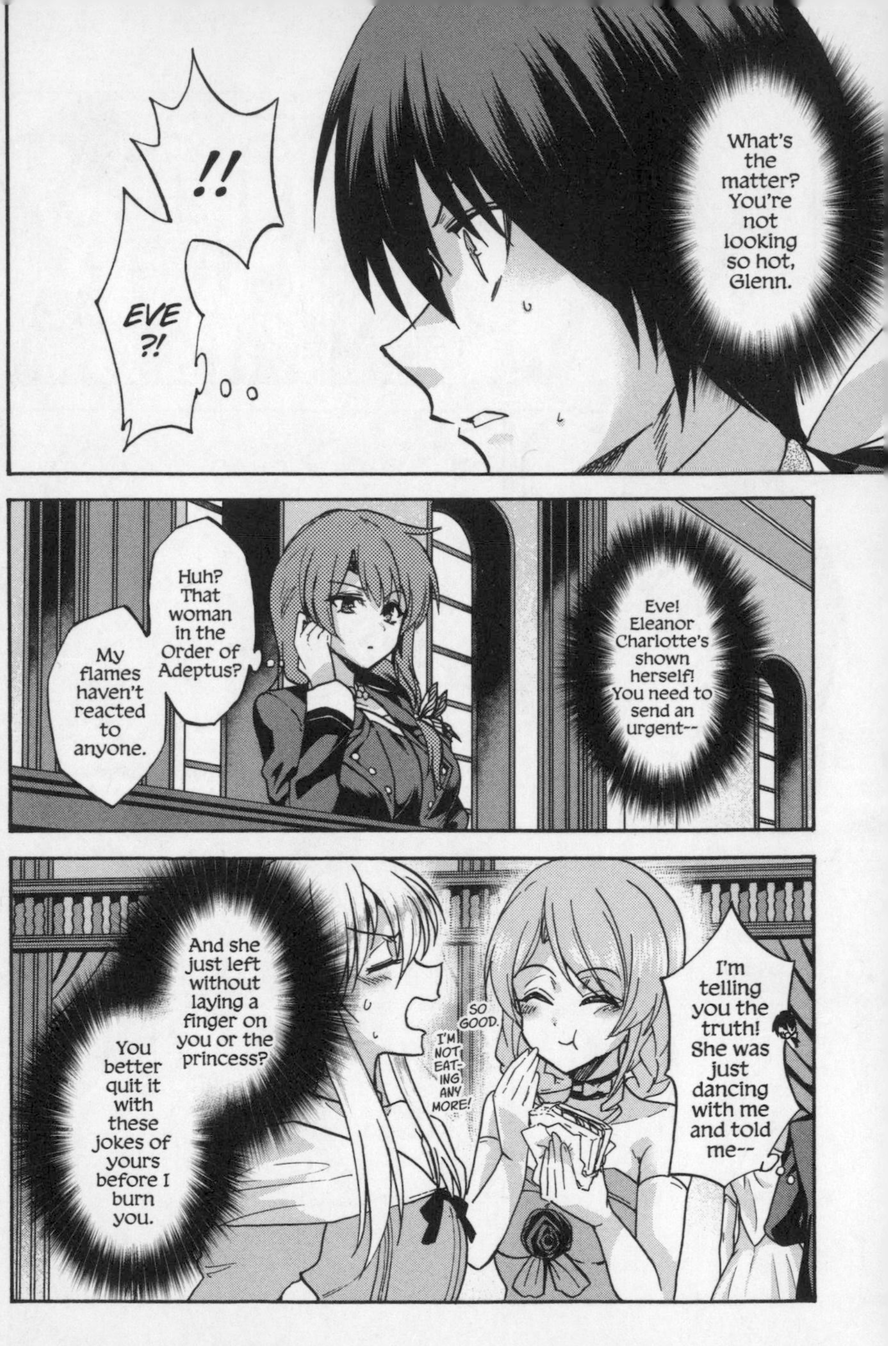
What's the matter? You're not looking so hot, Glenn.
!!
EVE?!
Eve! Eleanor Charlotte's shown herself! You need to send an urgent--
Huh? That woman in the Order of Adeptus?
My flames haven't reacted to anyone.
I'm telling you the truth! She was just dancing with me and told me--
SO GOOD.
I'M NOT EATING ANY MORE!
And she just left without laying a finger on you or the princess?
You better quit it with these jokes of yours before I burn you.

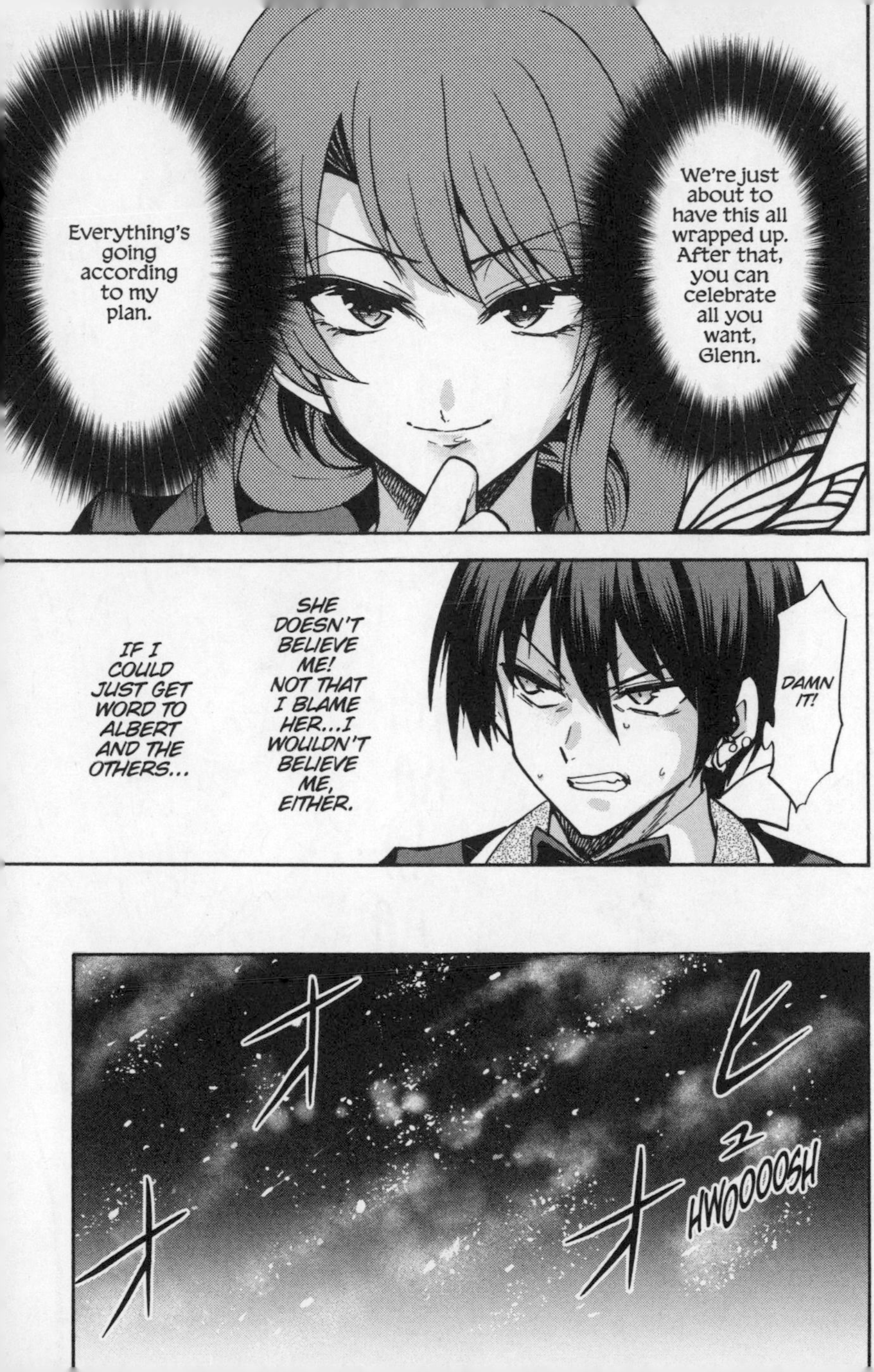
We're just about to have this all wrapped up. After that, you can celebrate all you want, Glenn.
Everything's going according to my plan.
DAMN IT!
SHE DOESN'T BELIEVE ME! NOT THAT I BLAME HER...I WOULDN'T BELIEVE ME, EITHER.
IF I COULD JUST GET WORD TO ALBERT AND THE OTHERS...
HWOOOOSH

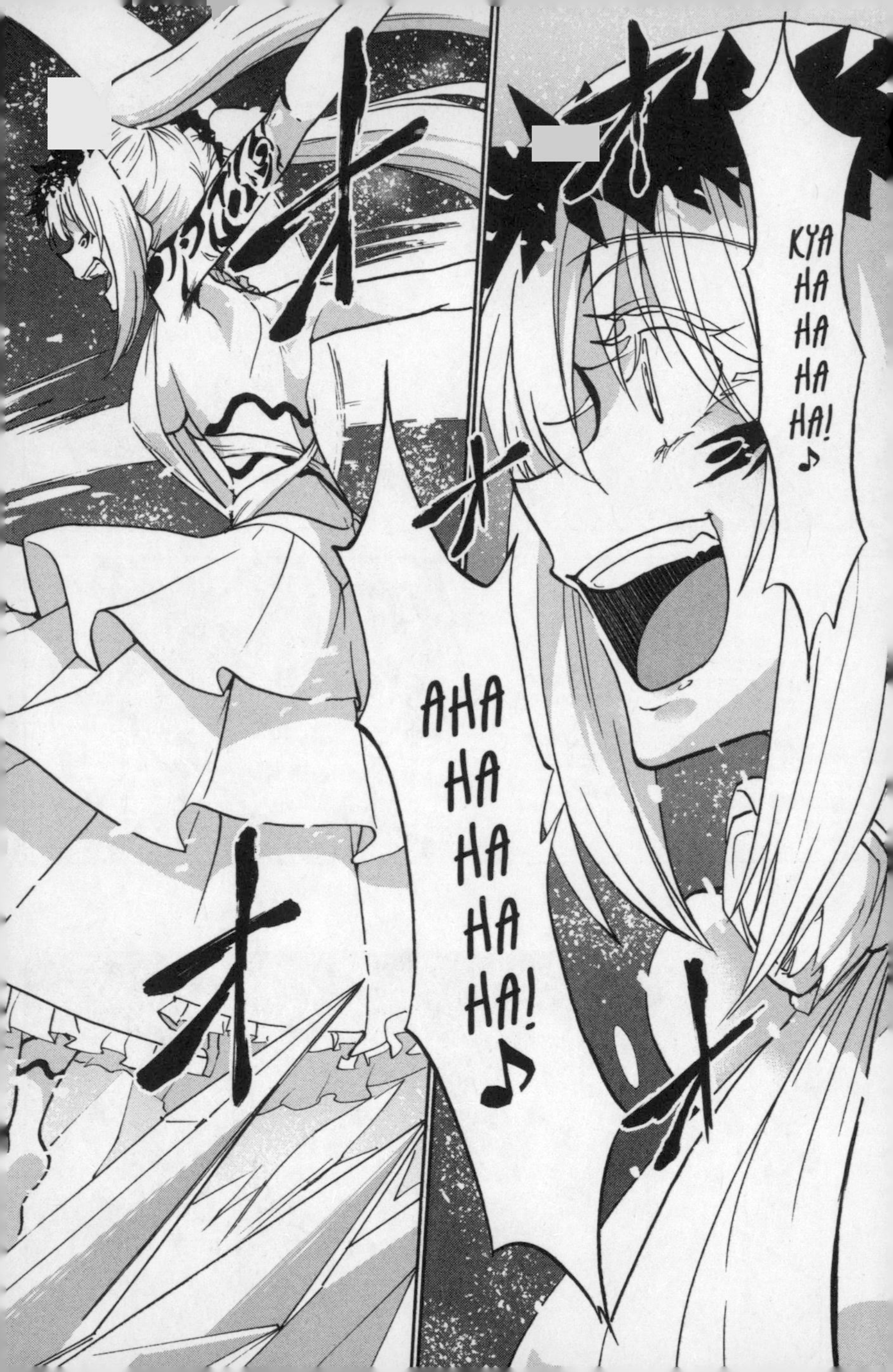
KYA HA HA HA HA! ♪
AHA HA HA HA HA HA! ♪

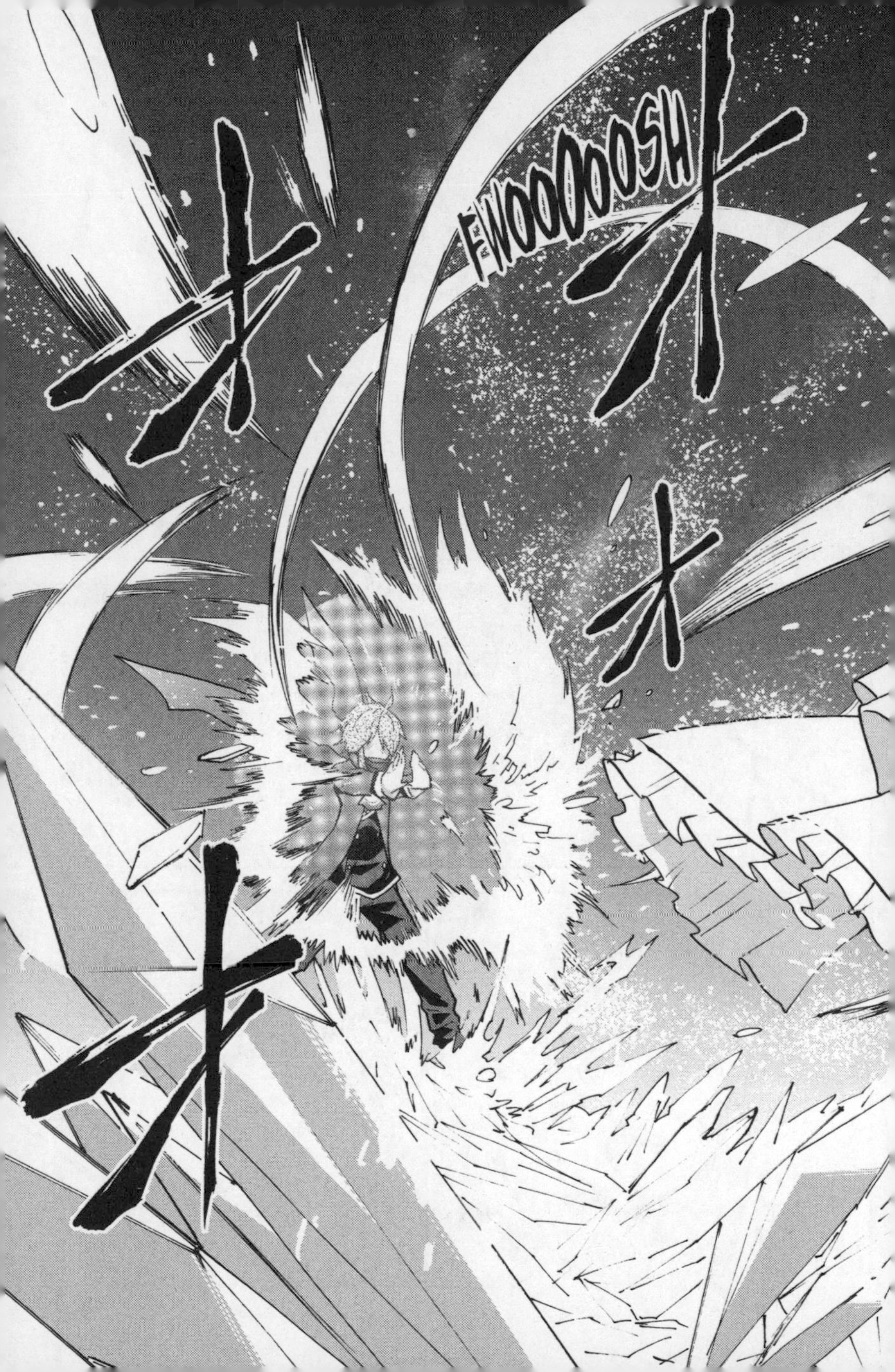
FWOOOOOSH

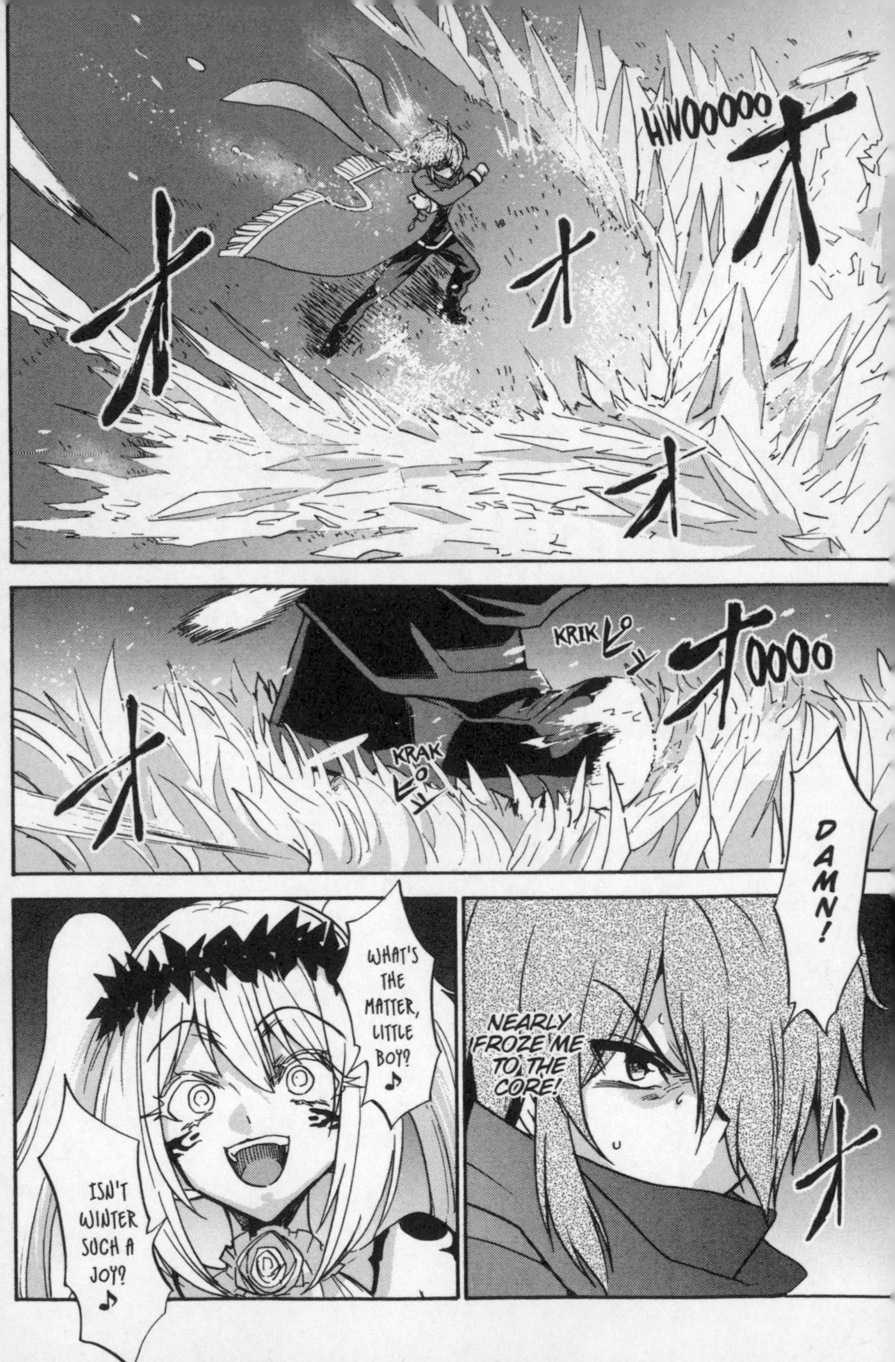
HWOOOOO
KRIK
OOOO
KRAK
DAMN!
NEARLY FROZE ME TO THE CORE!
WHAT'S THE MATTER, LITTLE BOY? ♪
ISN'T WINTER SUCH A JOY? ♪

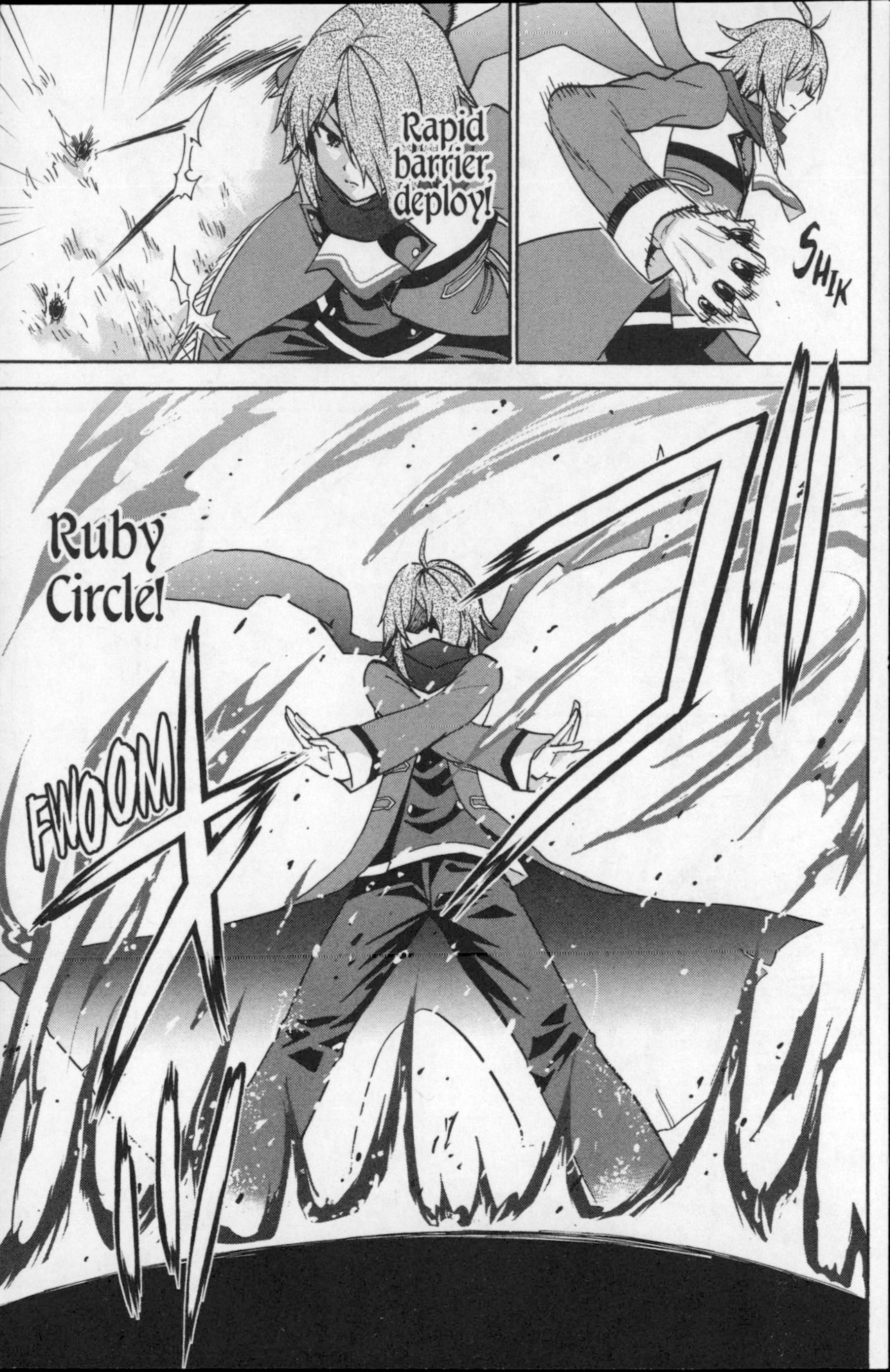
SHIK
Rapid barrier, deploy!
Ruby Circle!
FWOOM

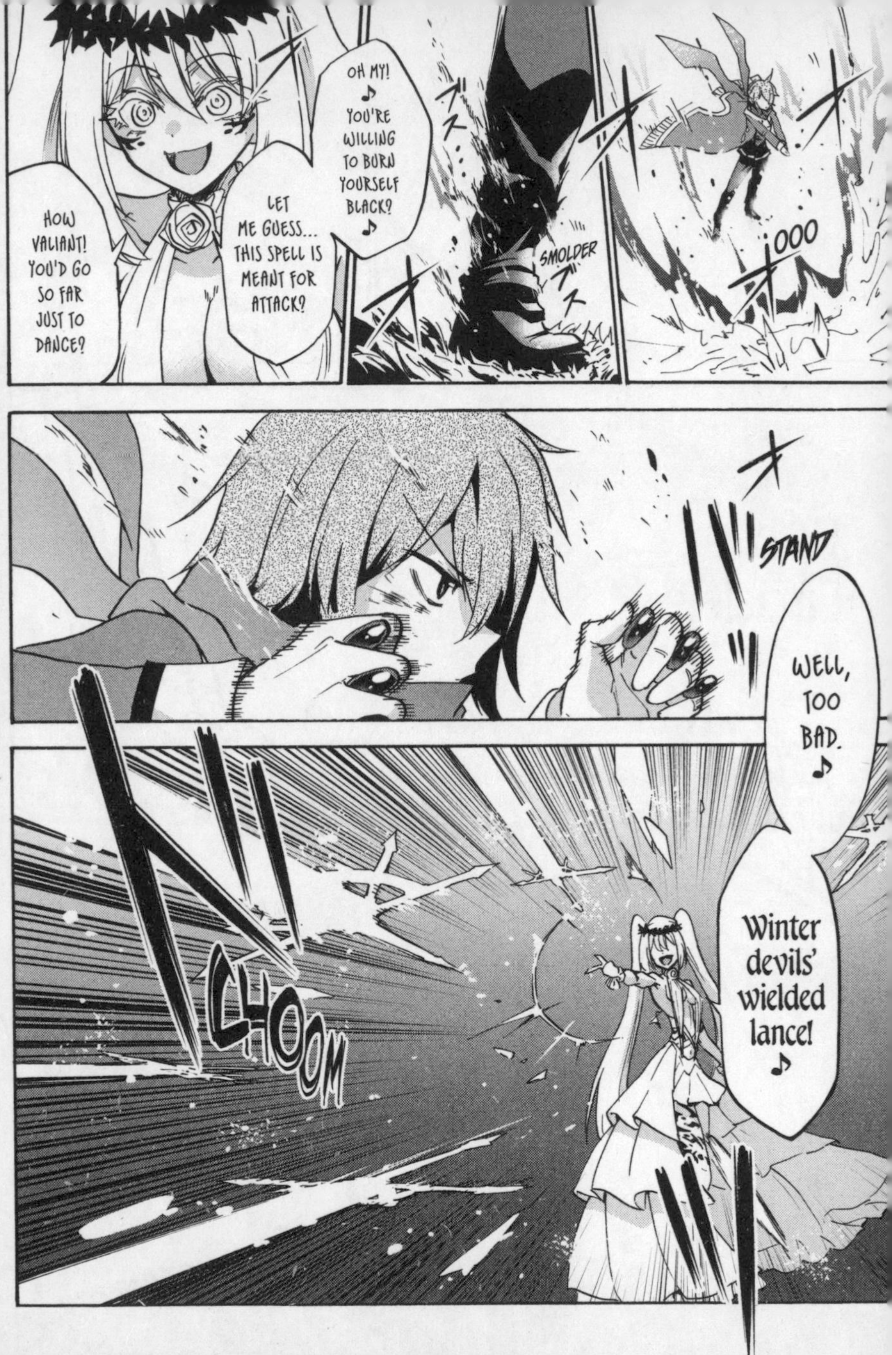
OOO
SMOLDER
OH MY! ♪ YOU'RE WILLING TO BURN YOURSELF BLACK? ♪
LET ME GUESS... THIS SPELL IS MEANT FOR ATTACK?
HOW VALIANT! YOU'D GO SO FAR JUST TO DANCE?
STAND
WELL, TOO BAD. ♪
Winter devils' wielded lance! ♪
CHOOM

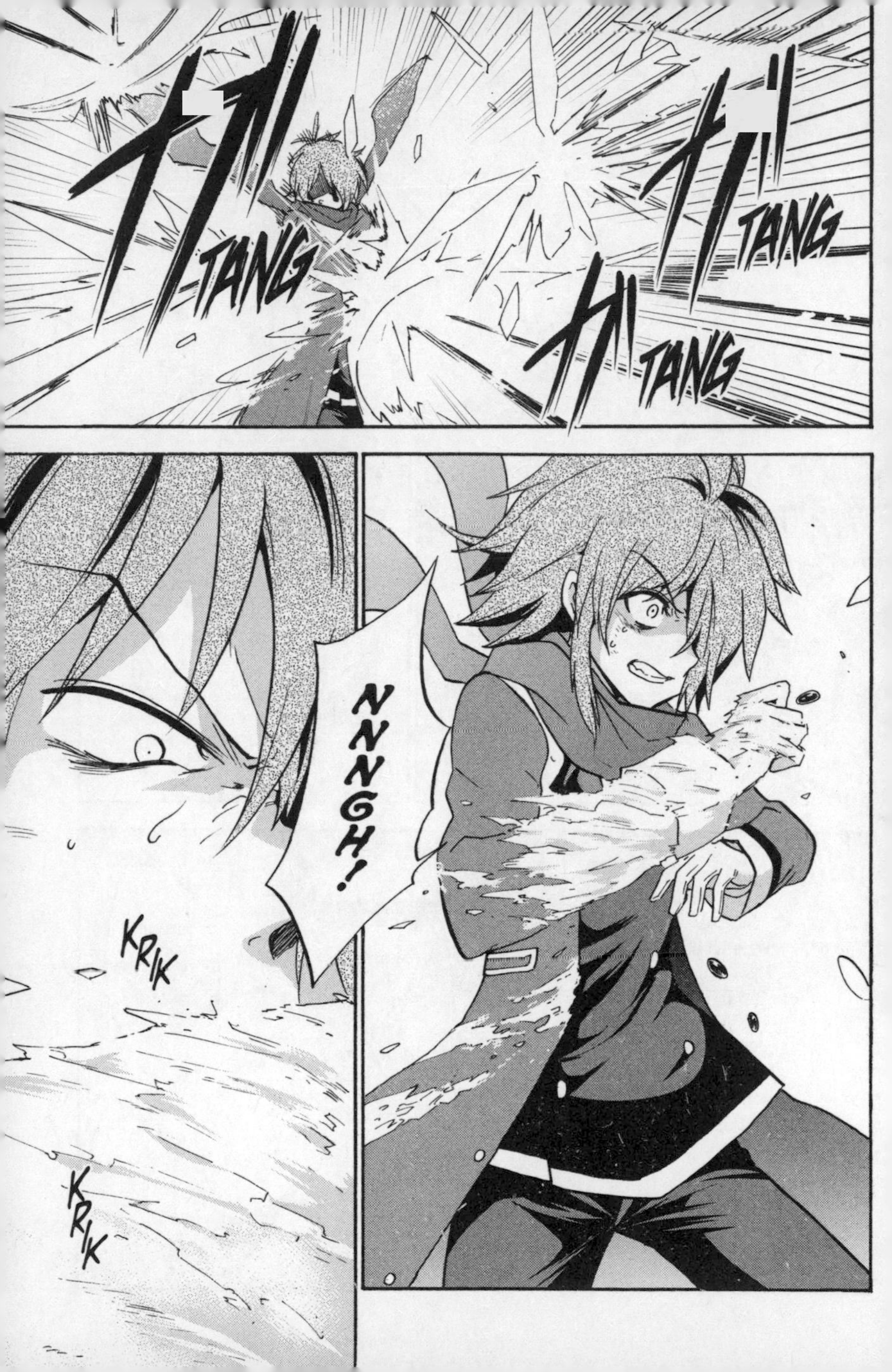
TANG
TANG
TANG
NNNGH!
KRIK
KRIK

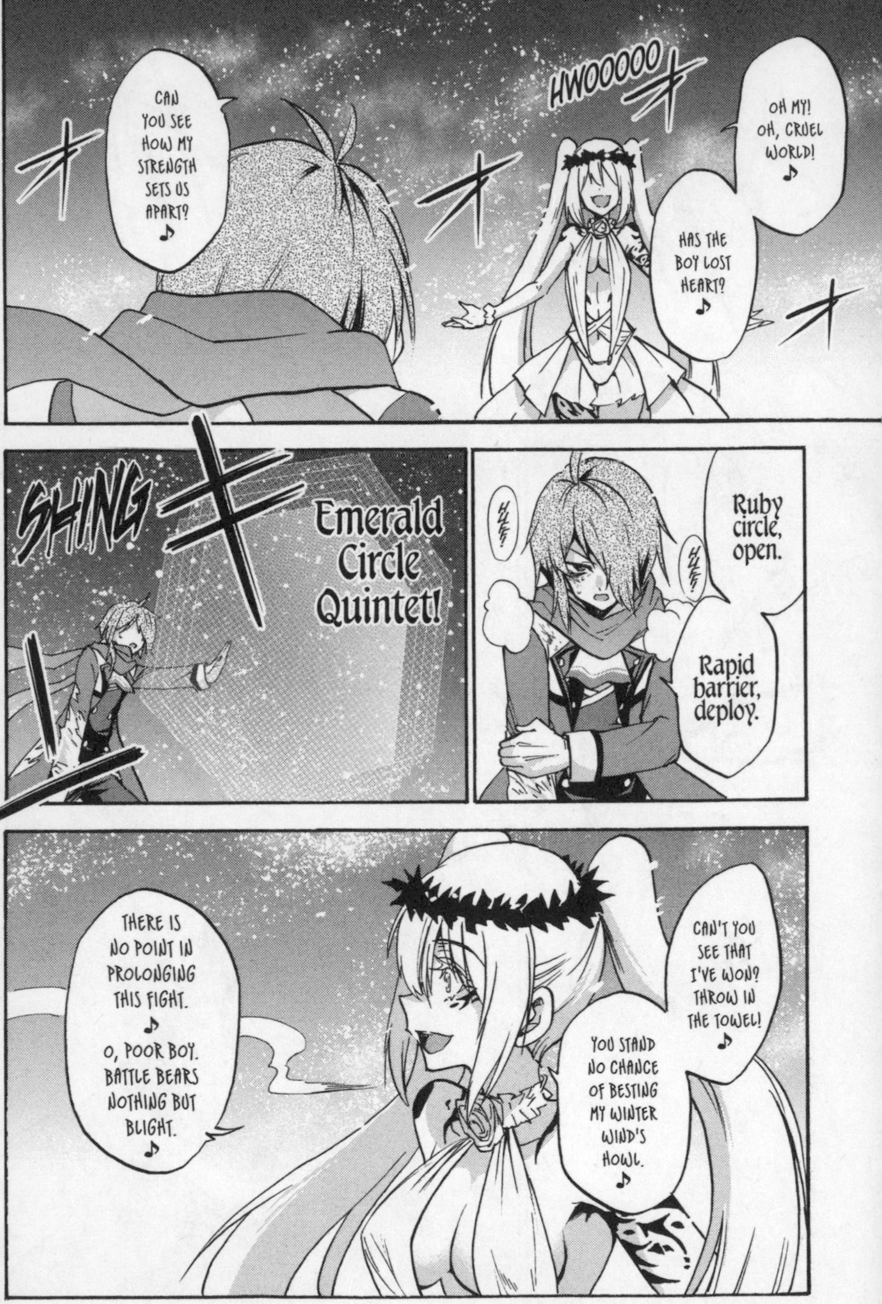
HWOOOOO
OH MY! OH, CRUEL WORLD! ♪
HAS THE BOY LOST HEART? ♪
CAN YOU SEE HOW MY STRENGTH SETS US APART? ♪
HUFF
HUFF
Ruby circle, open.
Rapid barrier, deploy.
SHING
Emerald Circle Quintet!
CAN'T YOU SEE THAT I'VE WON? THROW IN THE TOWEL! ♪
YOU STAND NO CHANCE OF BESTING MY WINTER WIND'S HOWL. ♪
THERE IS NO POINT IN PROLONGING THIS FIGHT. ♪ O, POOR BOY. BATTLE BEARS NOTHING BUT BLIGHT. ♪

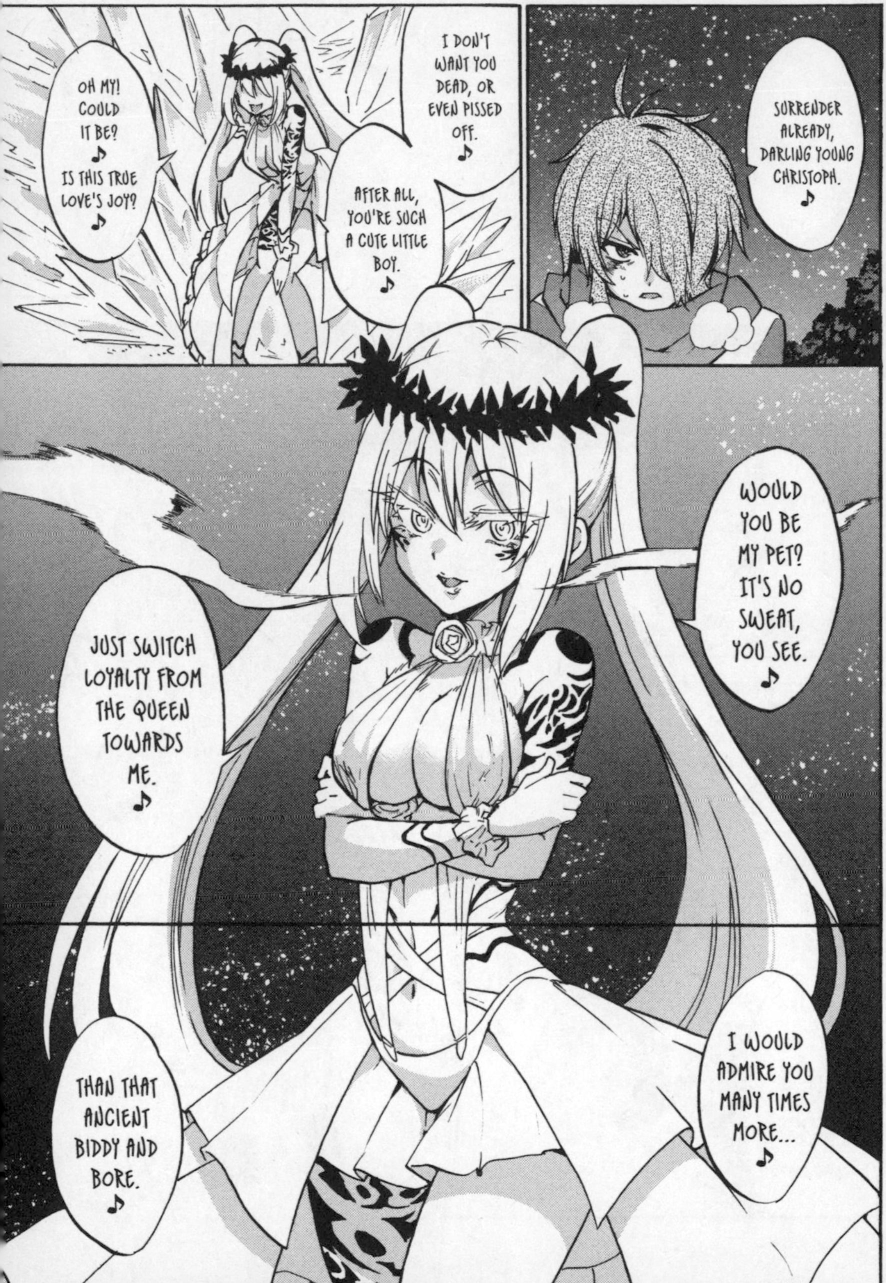
SURRENDER ALREADY, DARLING YOUNG CHRISTOPH. ♪
I DON'T WANT YOU DEAD, OR EVEN PISSED OFF. ♪
OH MY! COULD IT BE? ♪ IS THIS TRUE LOVE'S JOY? ♪
AFTER ALL, YOU'RE SUCH A CUTE LITTLE BOY. ♪
WOULD YOU BE MY PET? IT'S NO SWEAT, YOU SEE. ♪
JUST SWITCH LOYALTY FROM THE QUEEN TOWARDS ME. ♪
I WOULD ADMIRE YOU MANY TIMES MORE... ♪
THAN THAT ANCIENT BIDDY AND BORE. ♪

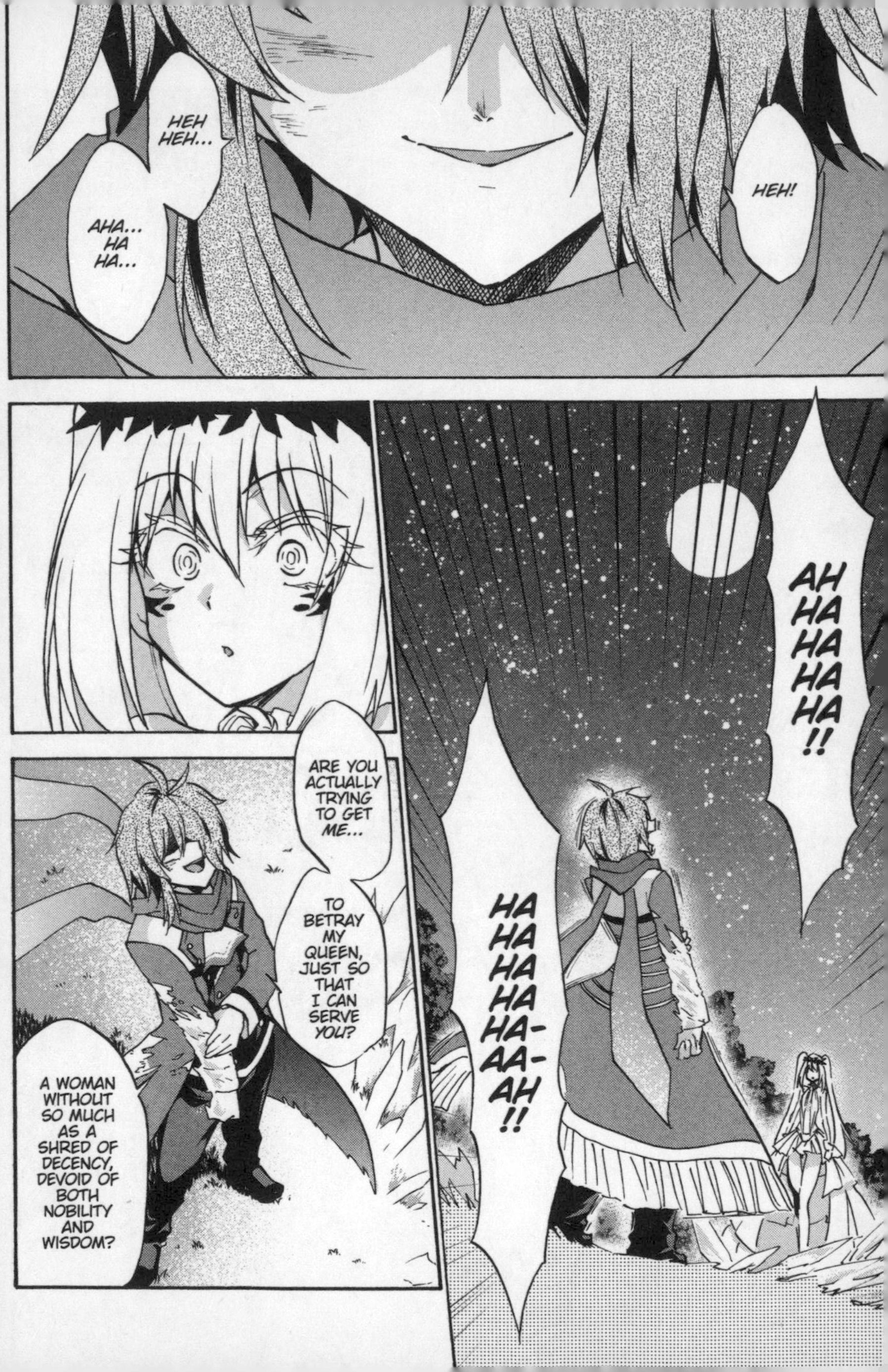
HEH!
HEH HEH...
AHA... HA HA...
AH HA HA HA HA!!
HA HA HA HA HA-AA-AH!!
ARE YOU ACTUALLY TRYING TO GET ME...
TO BETRAY MY QUEEN, JUST SO THAT I CAN SERVE YOU?
A WOMAN WITHOUT SO MUCH AS A SHRED OF DECENCY, DEVOID OF BOTH NOBILITY AND WISDOM?

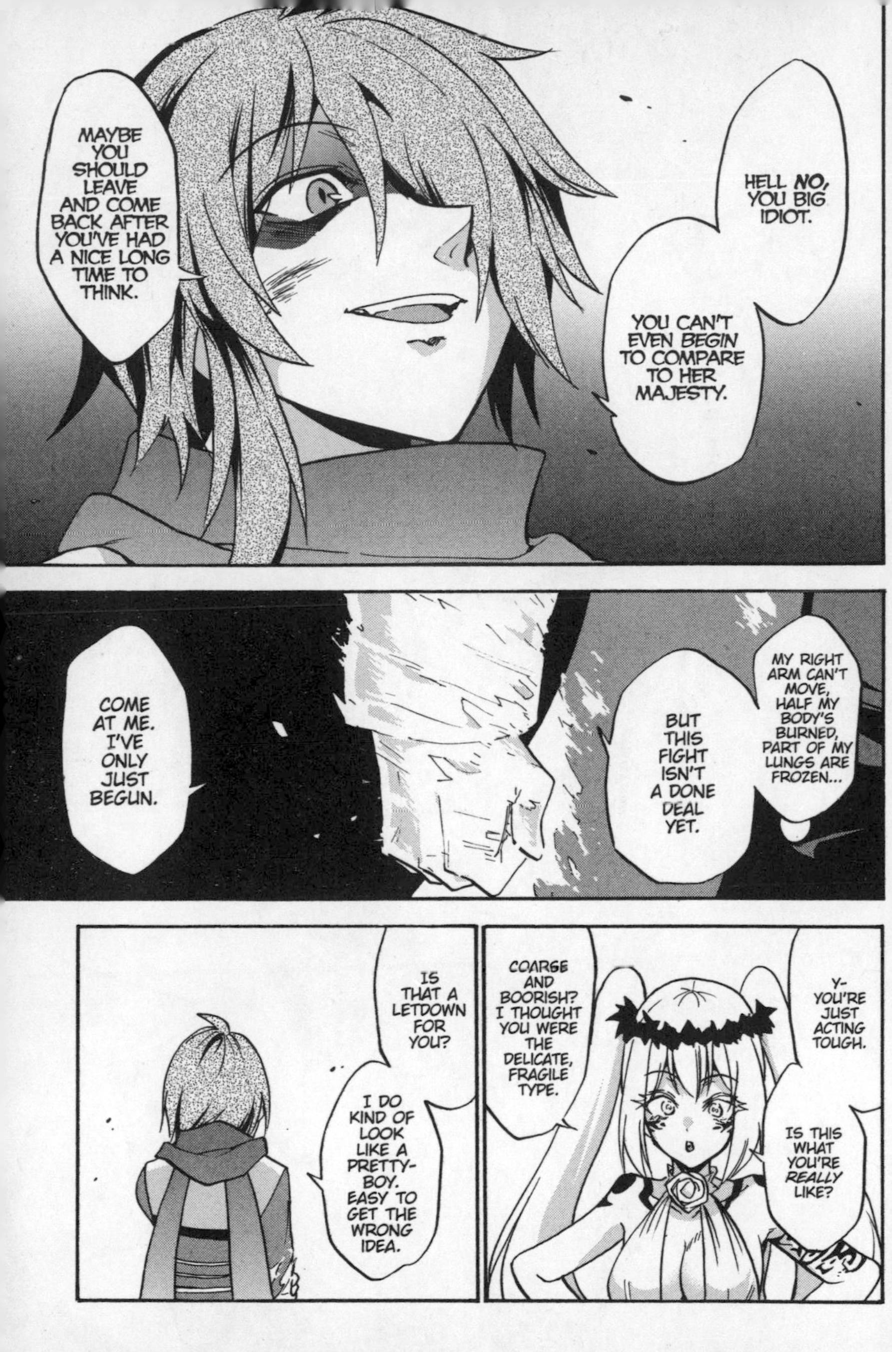
HELL *NO*, YOU BIG IDIOT.
YOU CAN'T EVEN BEGIN TO COMPARE TO HER MAJESTY.
MAYBE YOU SHOULD LEAVE AND COME BACK AFTER YOU'VE HAD A NICE LONG TIME TO THINK.
MY RIGHT ARM CAN'T MOVE, HALF MY BODY'S BURNED, PART OF MY LUNGS ARE FROZEN...
BUT THIS FIGHT ISN'T A DONE DEAL YET.
COME AT ME. I'VE ONLY JUST BEGUN.
Y- YOU'RE JUST ACTING TOUGH.
IS THIS WHAT YOU'RE *REALLY* LIKE?
COARSE AND BOORISH? I THOUGHT YOU WERE THE DELICATE, FRAGILE TYPE.
IS THAT A LETDOWN FOR YOU?
I DO KIND OF LOOK LIKE A PRETTY-BOY. EASY TO GET THE WRONG IDEA.

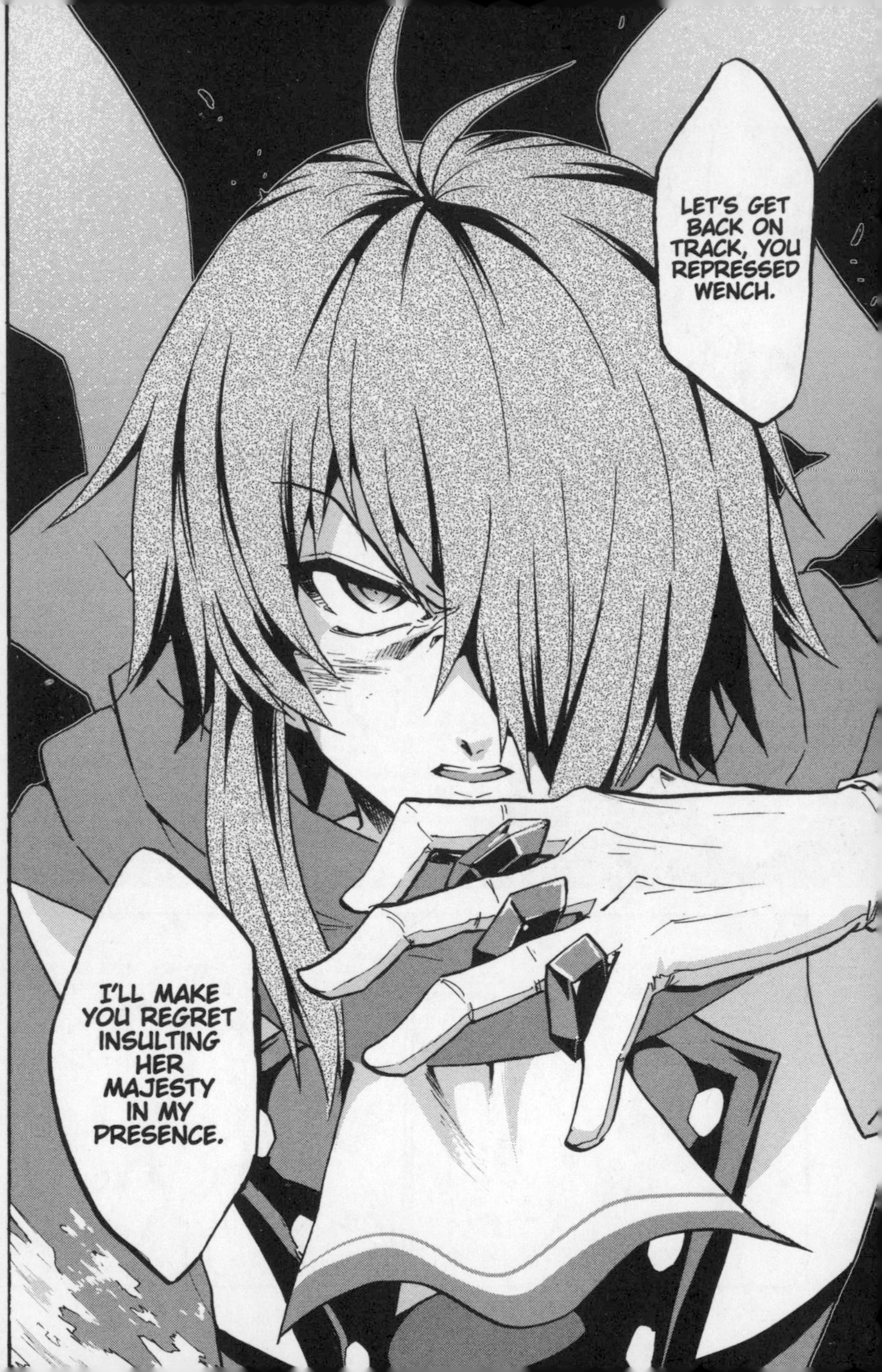
LET'S GET BACK ON TRACK, YOU REPRESSED WENCH.
I'LL MAKE YOU REGRET INSULTING HER MAJESTY IN MY PRESENCE.

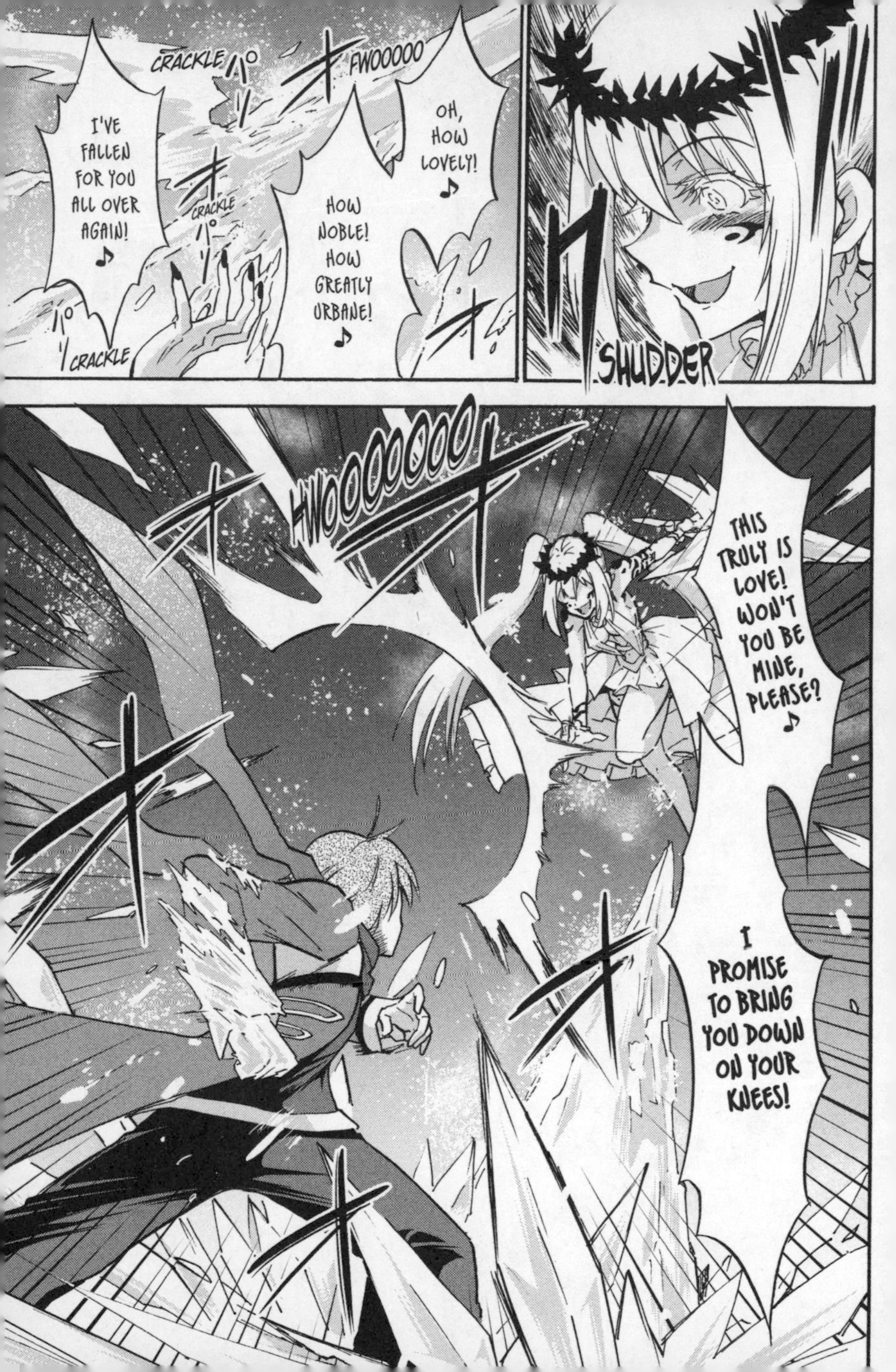

SHUDDER
FWOOOOO
CRACKLE
OH, HOW LOVELY! ♪
HOW NOBLE! HOW GREATLY URBANE! ♪
I'VE FALLEN FOR YOU ALL OVER AGAIN! ♪
CRACKLE
CRACKLE
FWOOOOOOO
THIS TRULY IS LOVE! WON'T YOU BE MINE, PLEASE? ♪
I PROMISE TO BRING YOU DOWN ON YOUR KNEES!

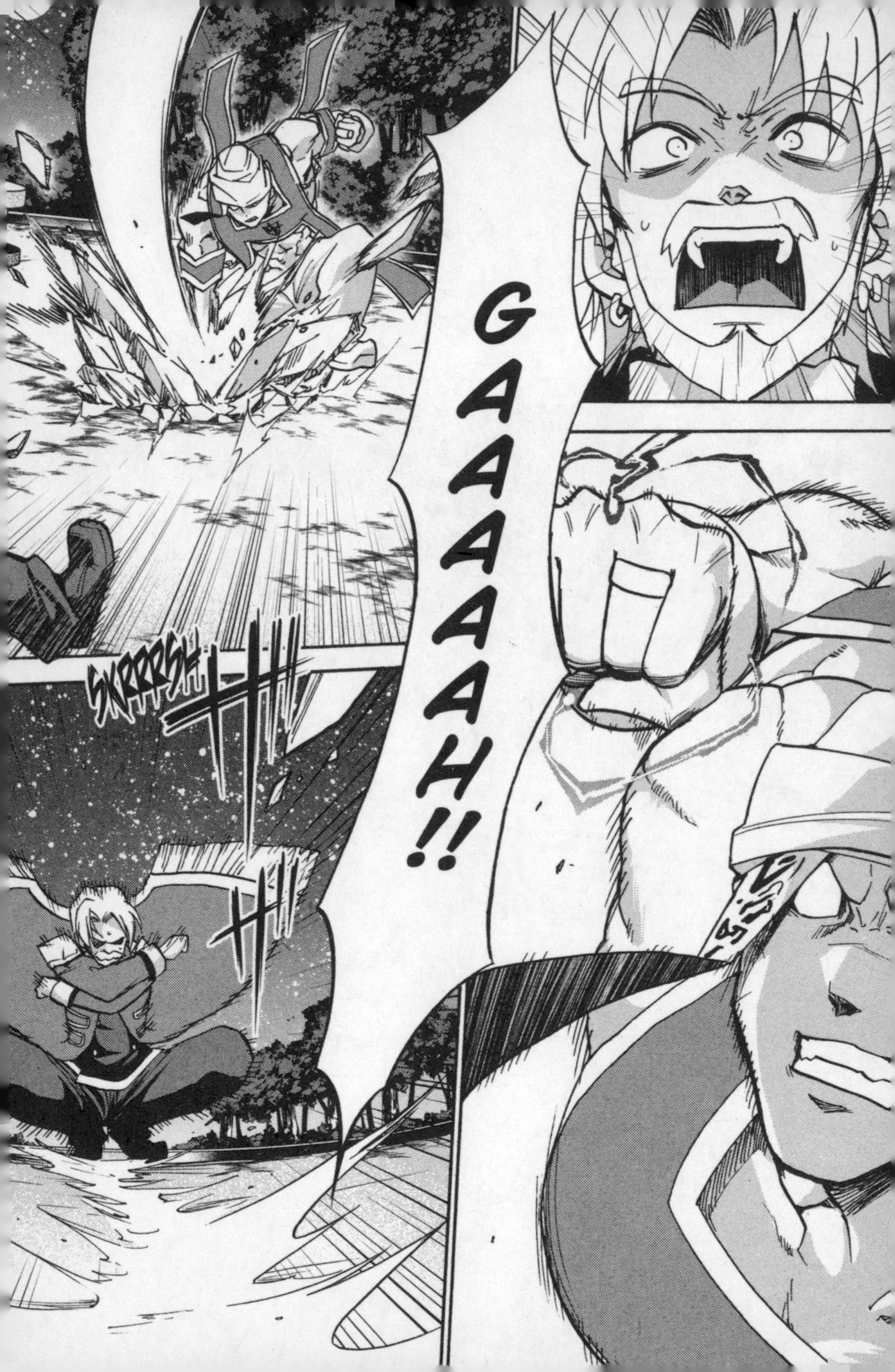
GAAAAAAH!!
SKRRRSH

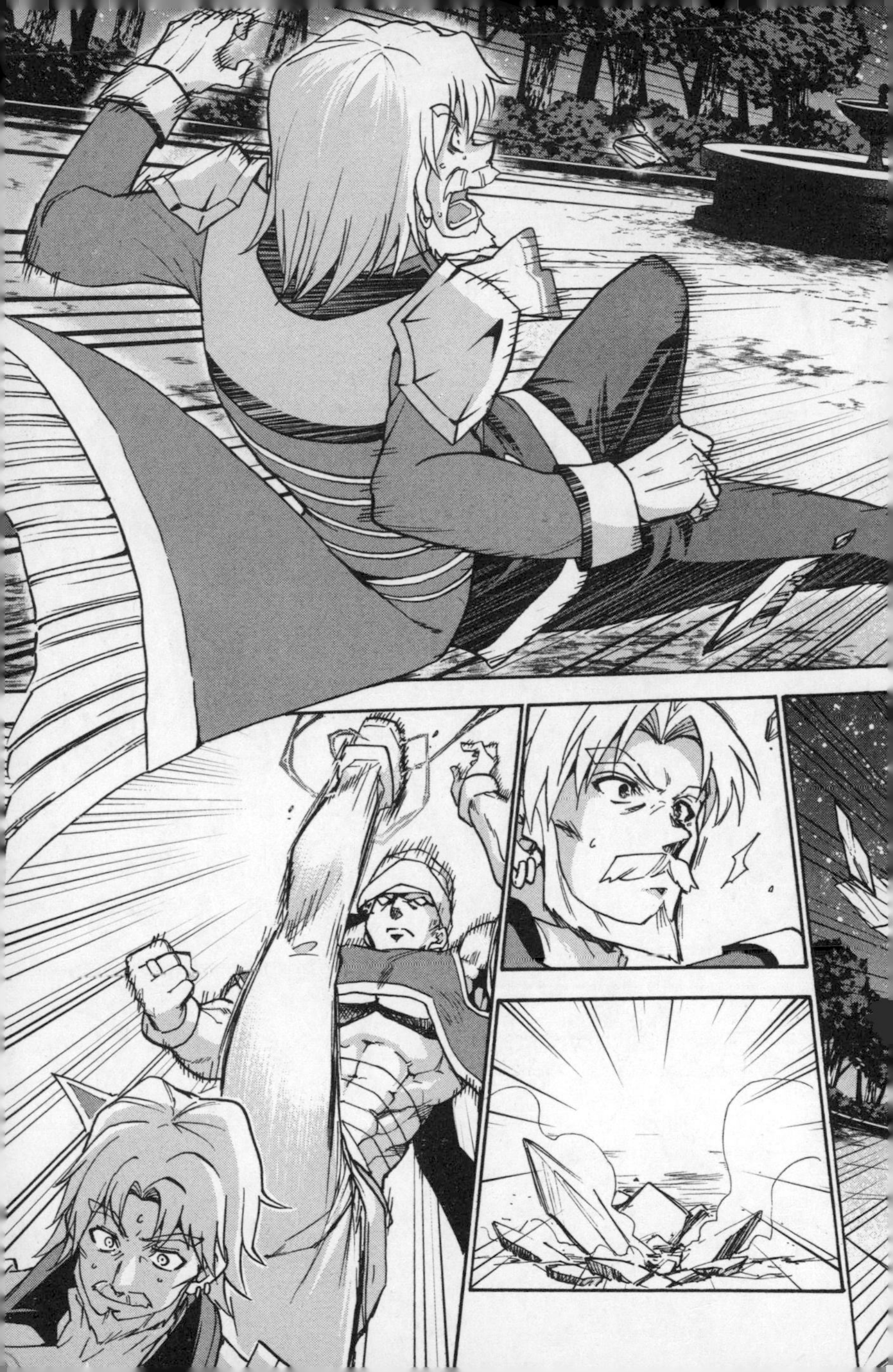

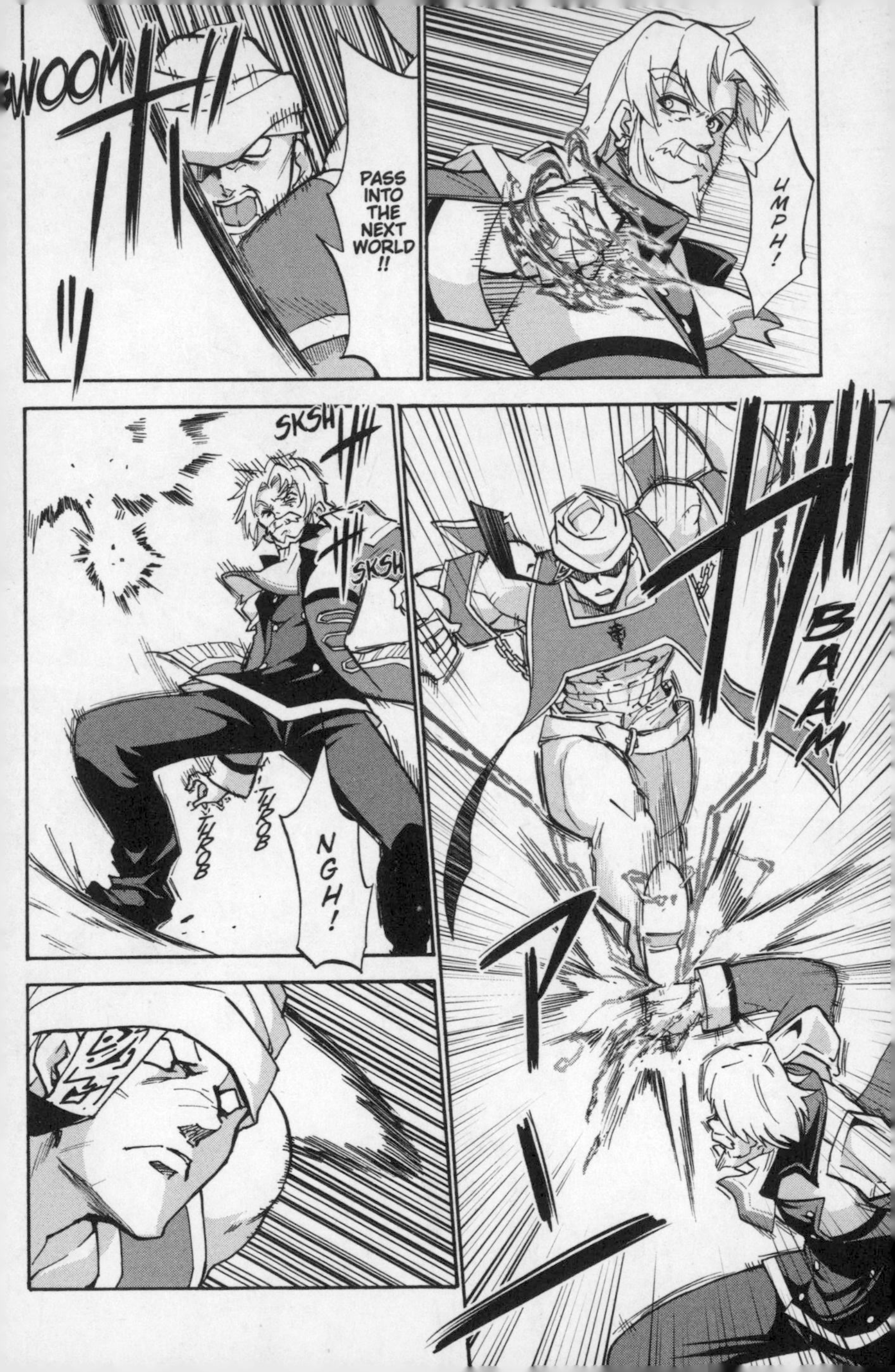

UMPH!
WOOM
PASS INTO THE NEXT WORLD!!
BAAM
SKSH
SKSH
NGH!
THROB
THROB

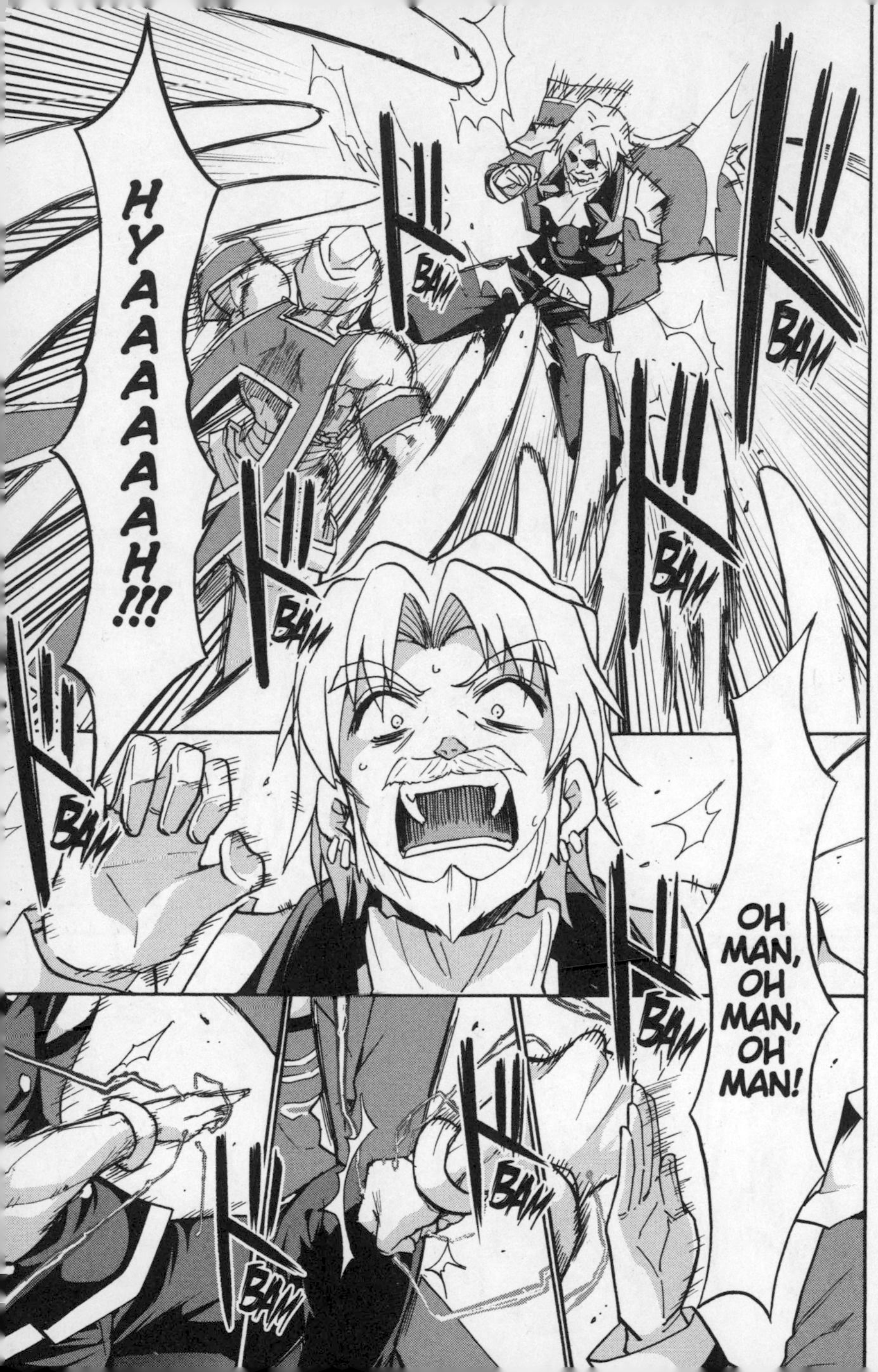
BAM
BAM
BAM
BAM
HYAAAAAAH!!!
OH MAN, OH MAN, OH MAN!
BAM
BAM
BAM
BAM

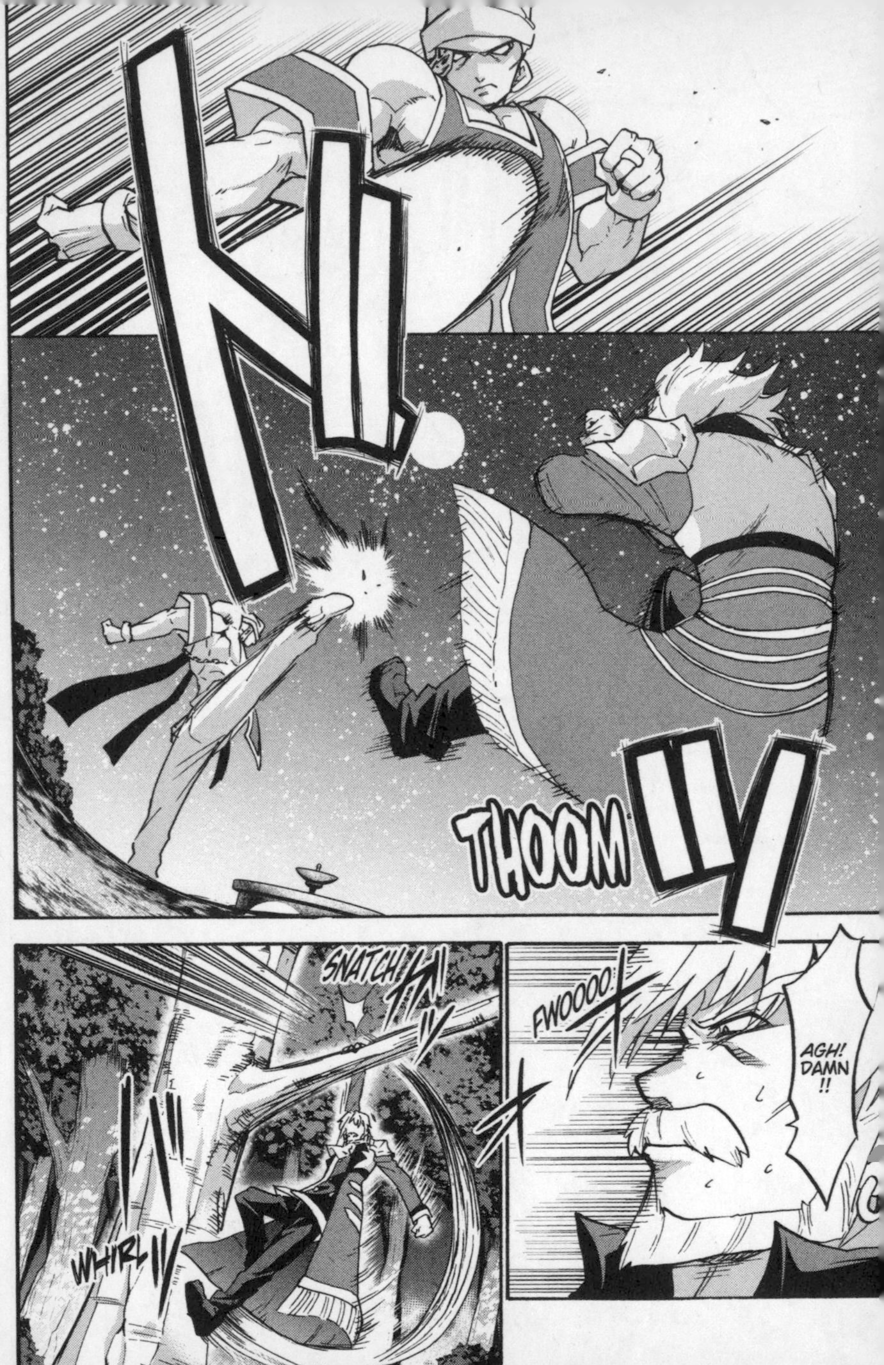
THOOM
FWOOOO
AGH! DAMN!!
SNATCH
WHIRL

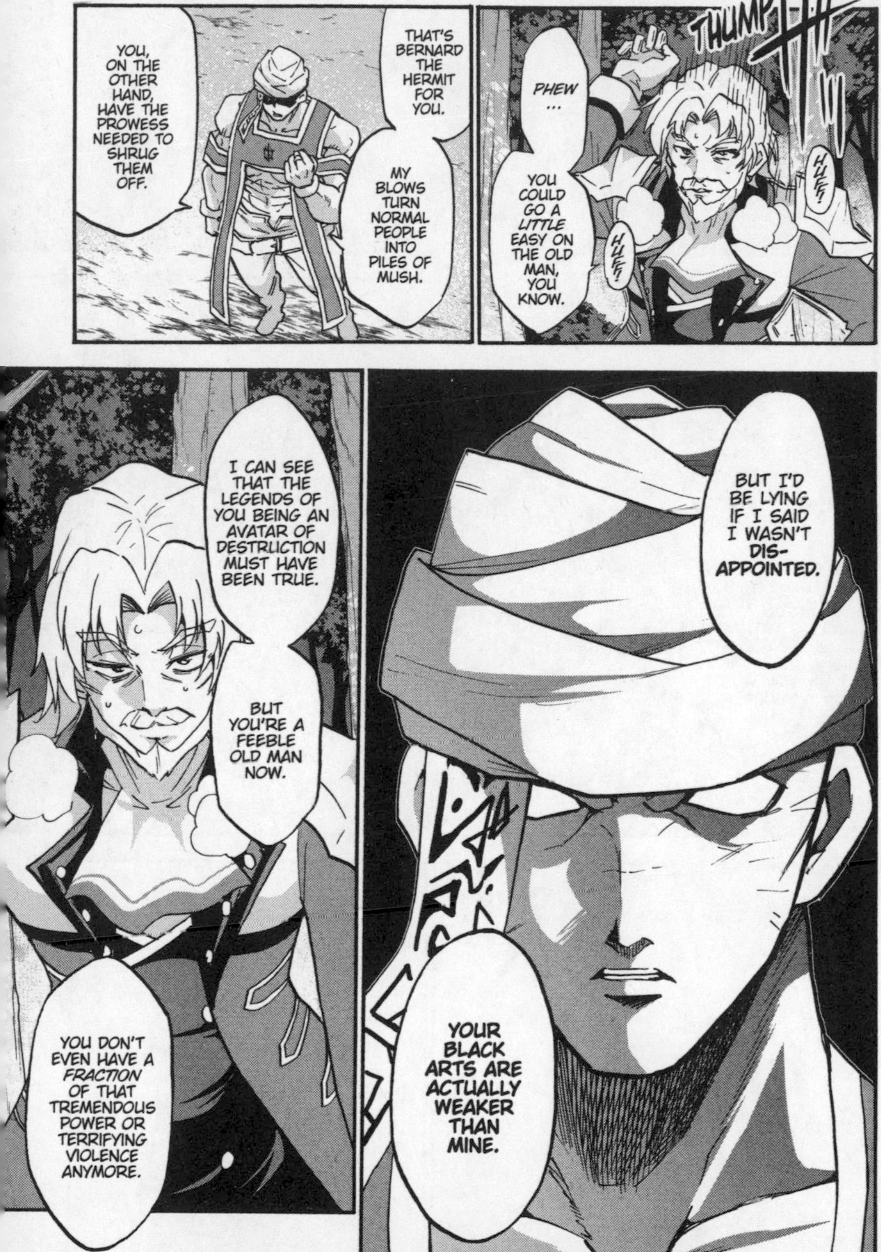
THUMP
HUFF!
PHEW...
YOU COULD GO A *LITTLE* EASY ON THE OLD MAN, YOU KNOW.
HUFF!
THAT'S BERNARD THE HERMIT FOR YOU.
MY BLOWS TURN NORMAL PEOPLE INTO PILES OF MUSH.
YOU, ON THE OTHER HAND, HAVE THE PROWESS NEEDED TO SHRUG THEM OFF.
BUT I'D BE LYING IF I SAID I WASN'T **DIS-APPOINTED.**
YOUR BLACK ARTS ARE ACTUALLY WEAKER THAN MINE.
I CAN SEE THAT THE LEGENDS OF YOU BEING AN AVATAR OF DESTRUCTION MUST HAVE BEEN TRUE.
BUT YOU'RE A FEEBLE OLD MAN NOW.
YOU DON'T EVEN HAVE A *FRACTION* OF THAT TREMENDOUS POWER OR TERRIFYING VIOLENCE ANYMORE.

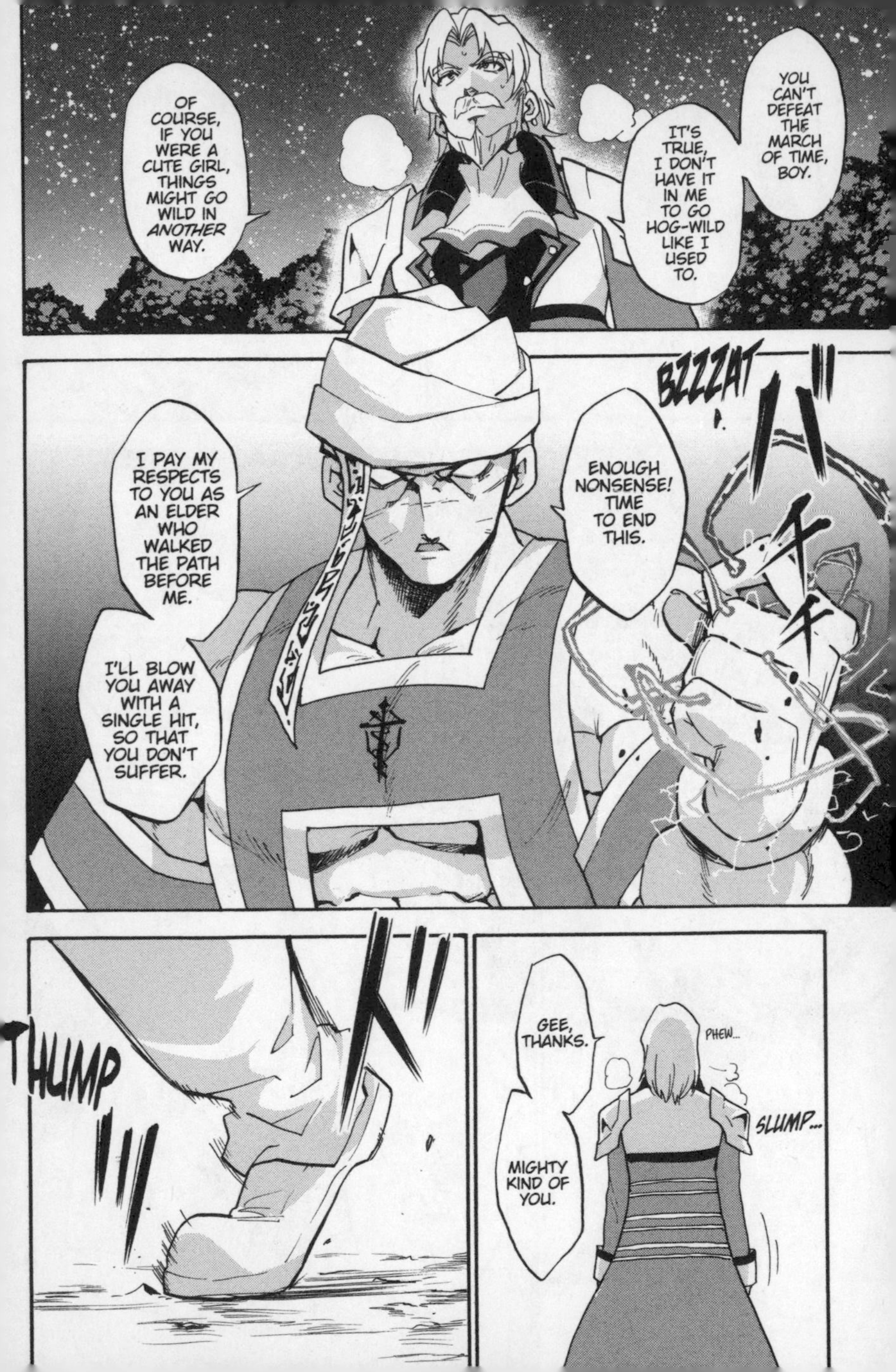
YOU CAN'T DEFEAT THE MARCH OF TIME, BOY.
IT'S TRUE, I DON'T HAVE IT IN ME TO GO HOG-WILD LIKE I USED TO.
OF COURSE, IF YOU WERE A CUTE GIRL, THINGS MIGHT GO WILD IN *ANOTHER* WAY.
BZZZAT
ENOUGH NONSENSE! TIME TO END THIS.
I PAY MY RESPECTS TO YOU AS AN ELDER WHO WALKED THE PATH BEFORE ME.
I'LL BLOW YOU AWAY WITH A SINGLE HIT, SO THAT YOU DON'T SUFFER.
GEE, THANKS.
PHEW...
SLUMP...
MIGHTY KIND OF YOU.
THUMP

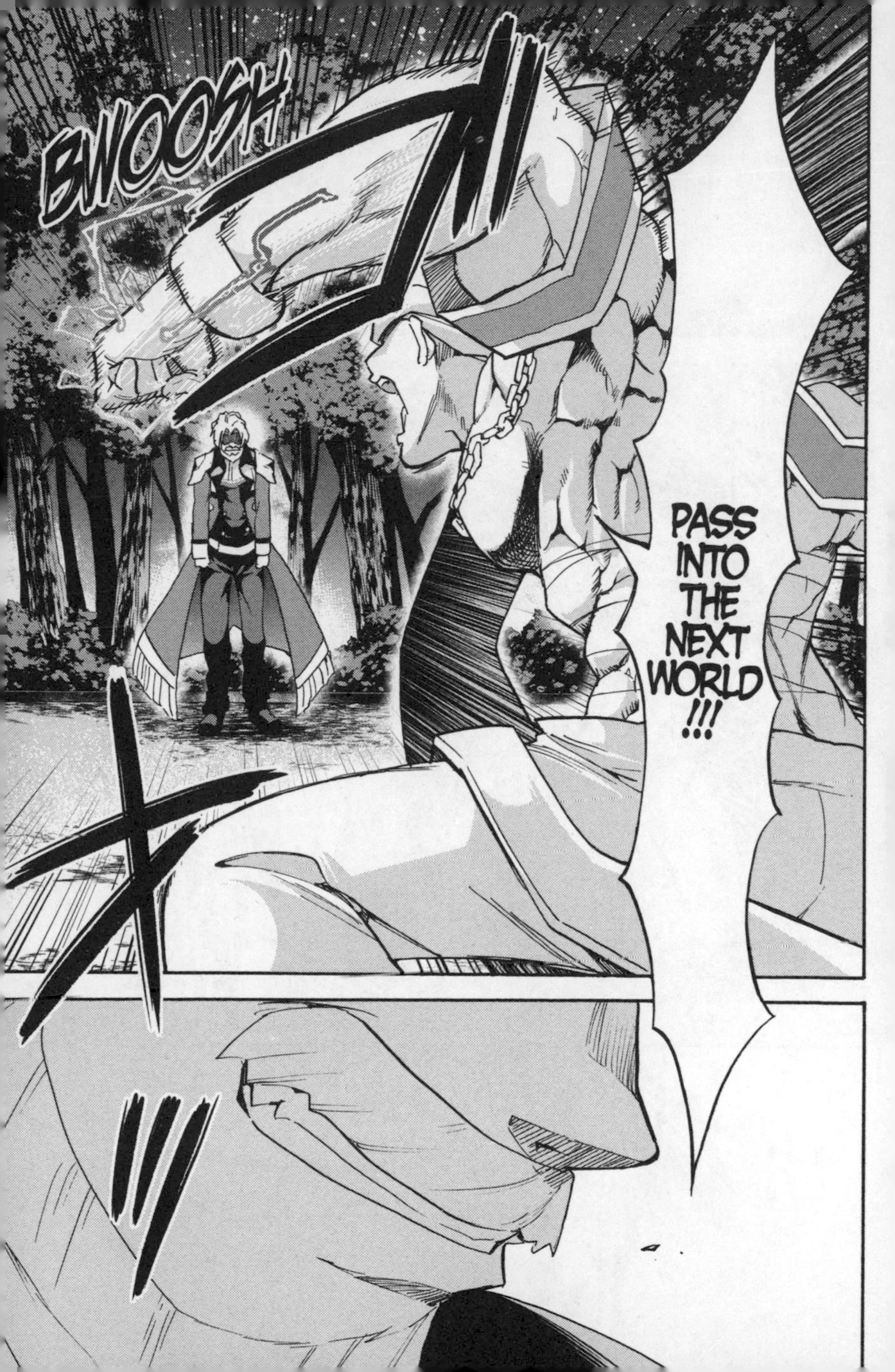

PASS INTO THE NEXT WORLD!!!
BWOOSH

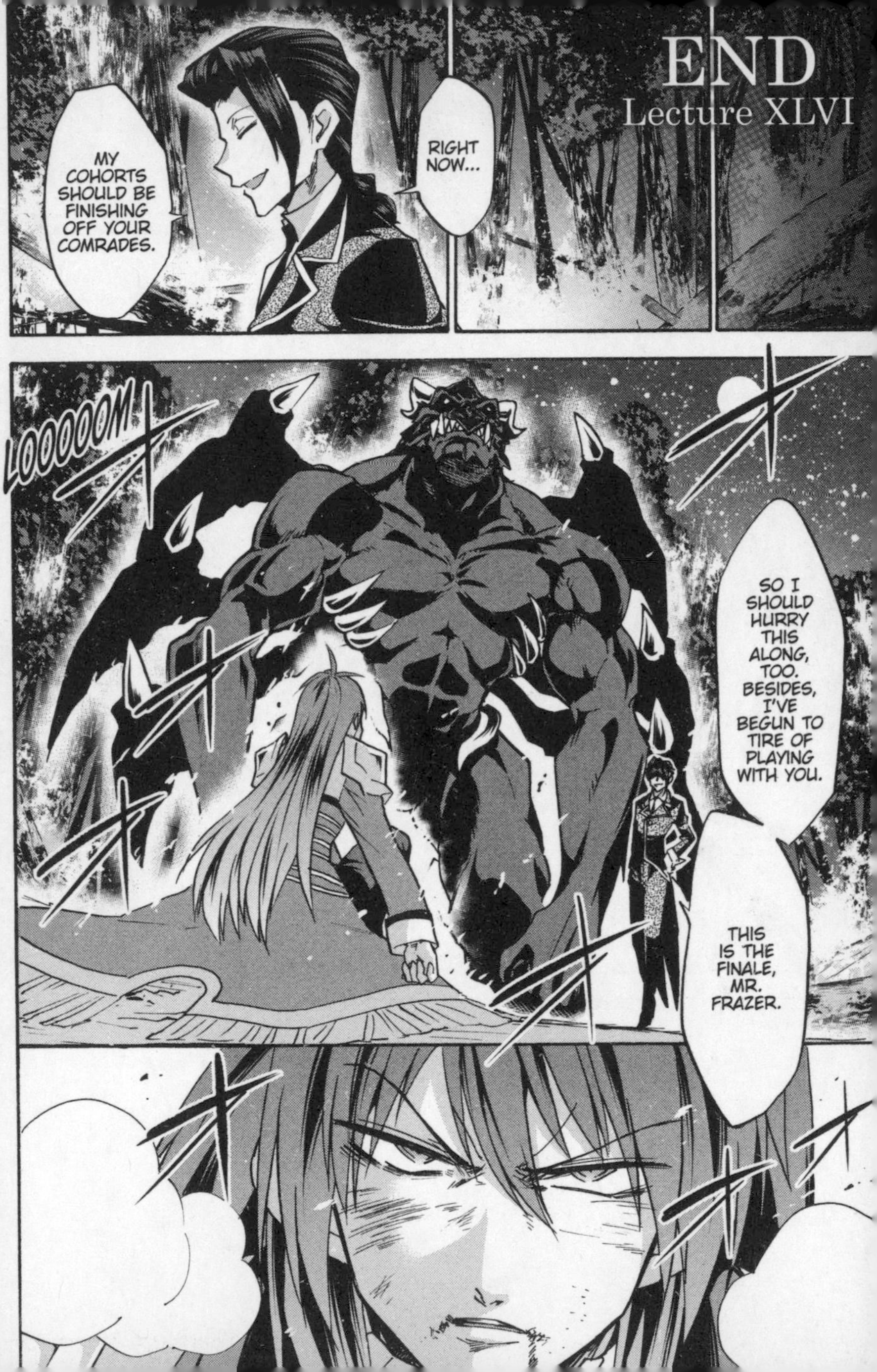
END
Lecture XLVI
RIGHT NOW...
MY COHORTS SHOULD BE FINISHING OFF YOUR COMRADES.
SO I SHOULD HURRY THIS ALONG, TOO. BESIDES, I'VE BEGUN TO TIRE OF PLAYING WITH YOU.
THIS IS THE FINALE, MR. FRAZER.
LOOOOOM

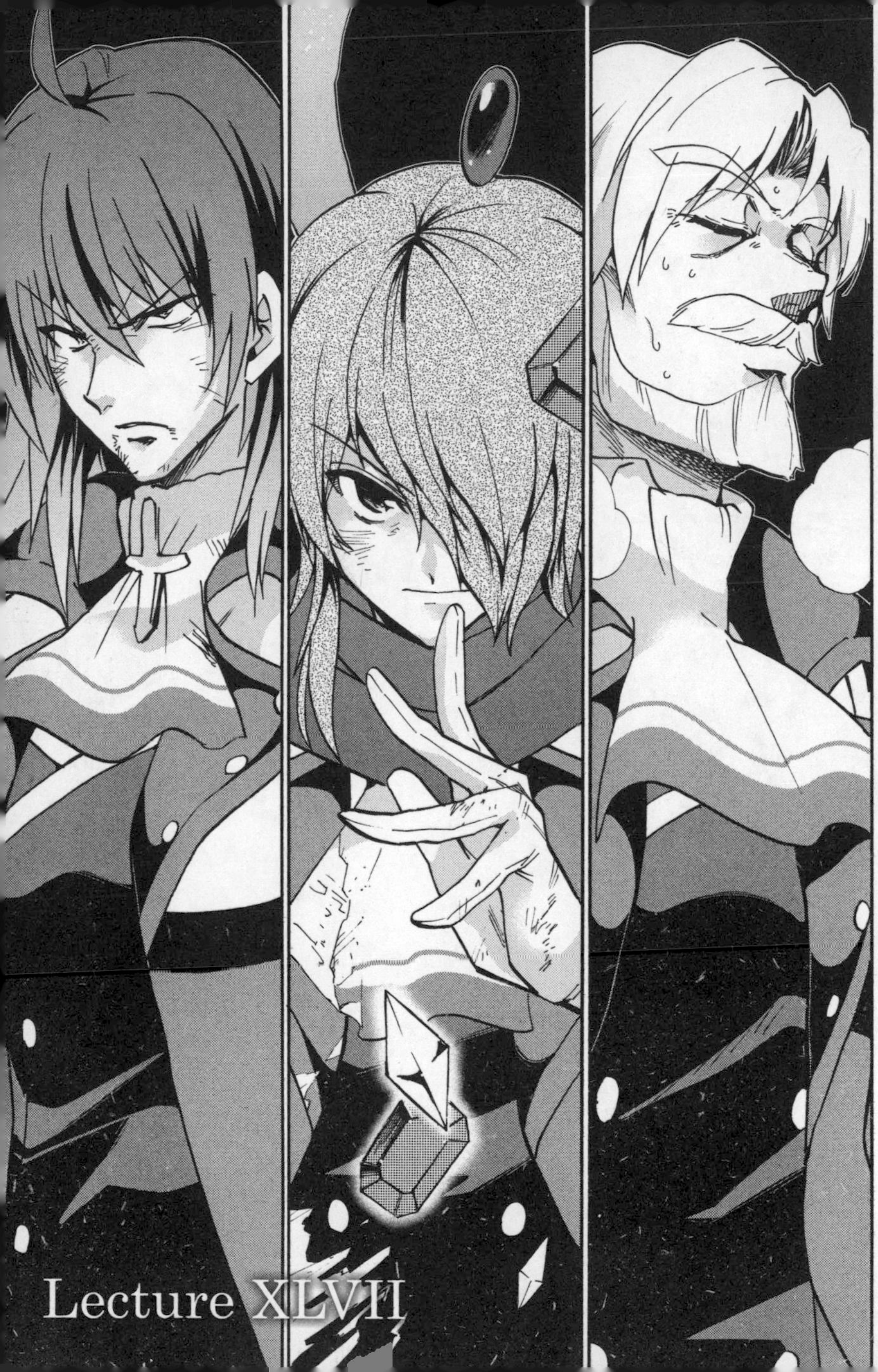
Lecture XLVII

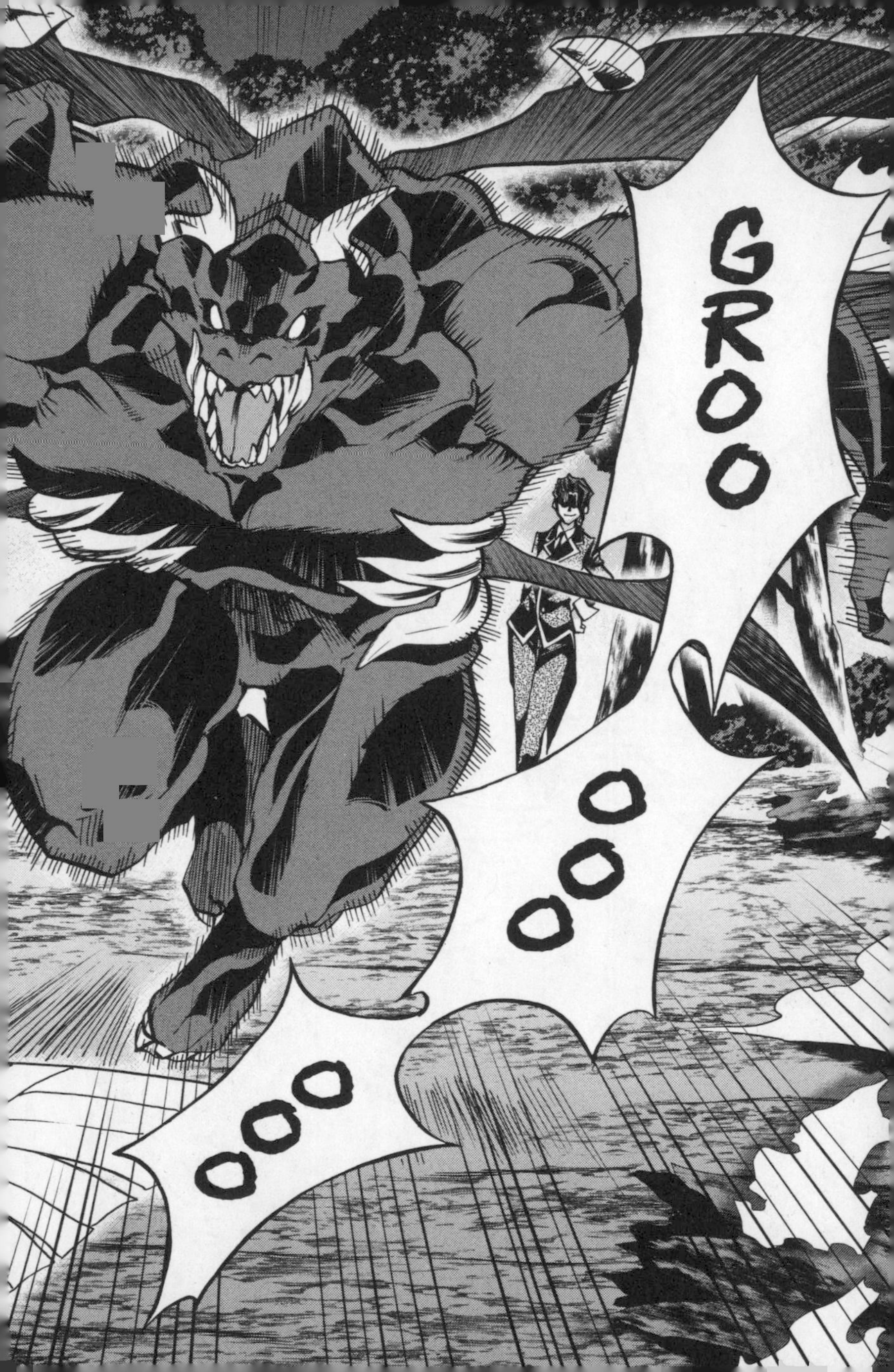
GROOOOOOOO

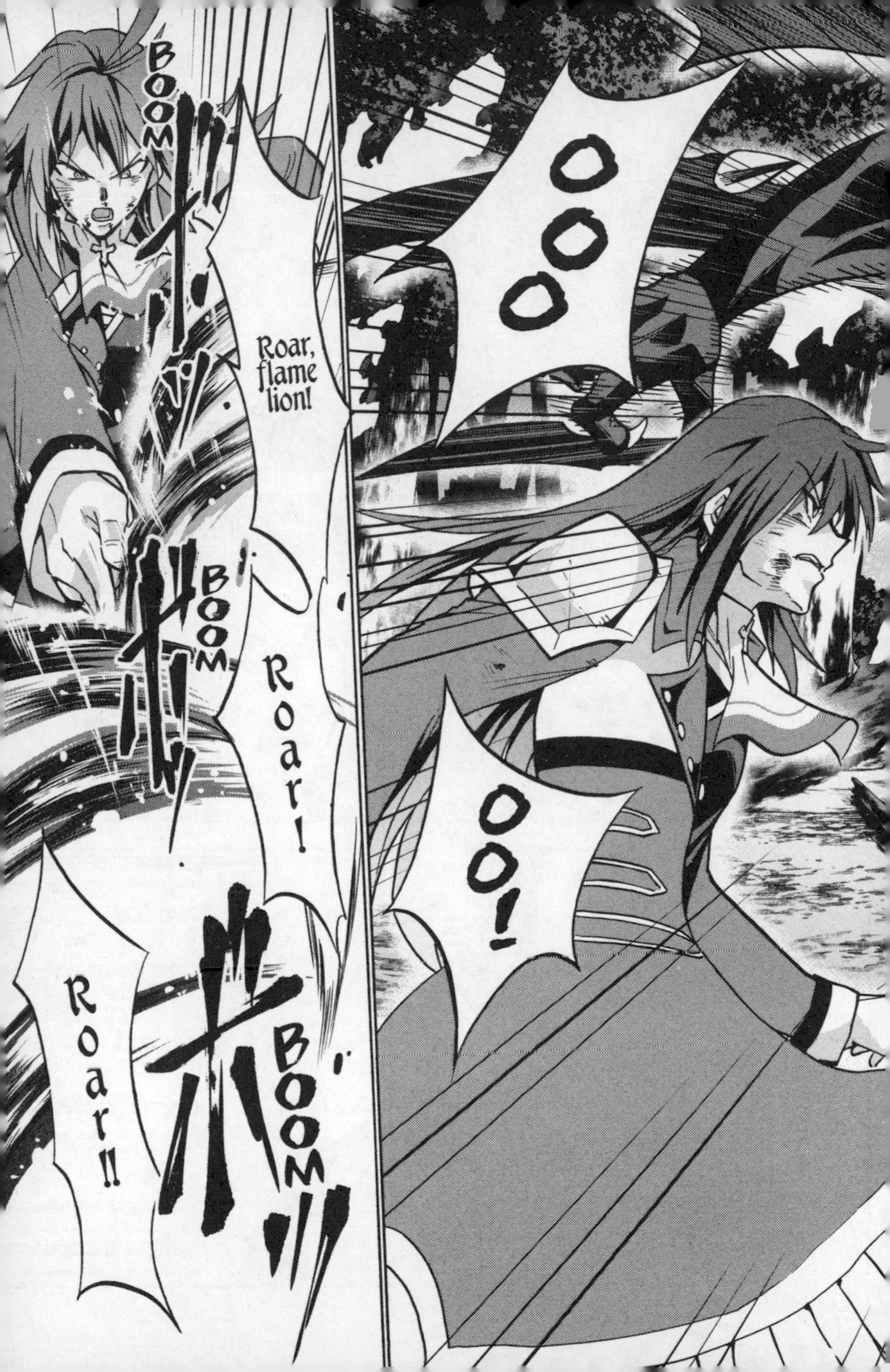
OOOO
OOO!
BOOM
Roar, flame lion!
BOOM
Roar!
BOOM!!
Roar!!

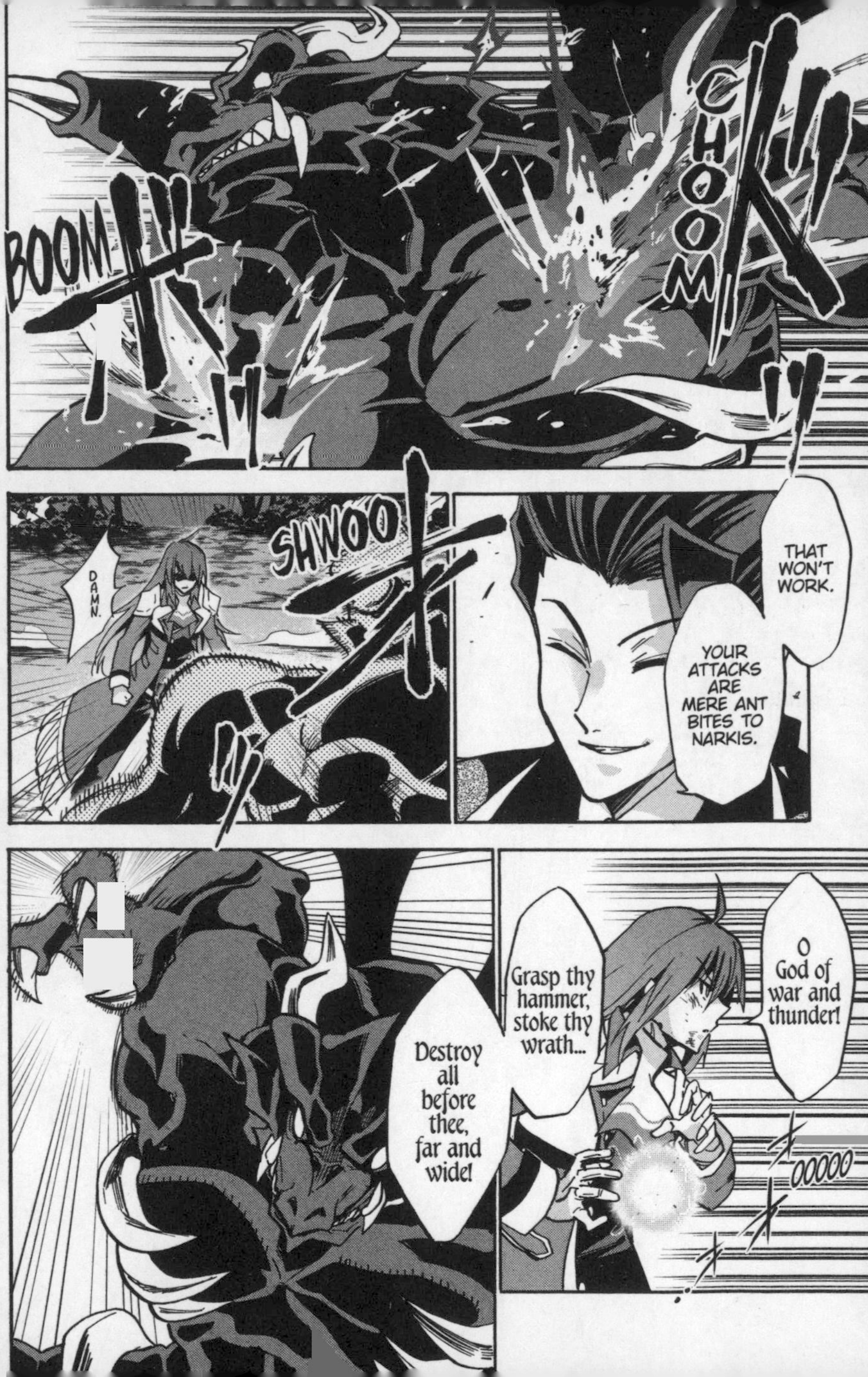
CHOOM
BOOM
THAT WON'T WORK.
YOUR ATTACKS ARE MERE ANT BITES TO NARKIS.
SHWOO
DAMN.
O God of war and thunder!
Grasp thy hammer, stoke thy wrath...
Destroy all before thee, far and wide!
OOOOO

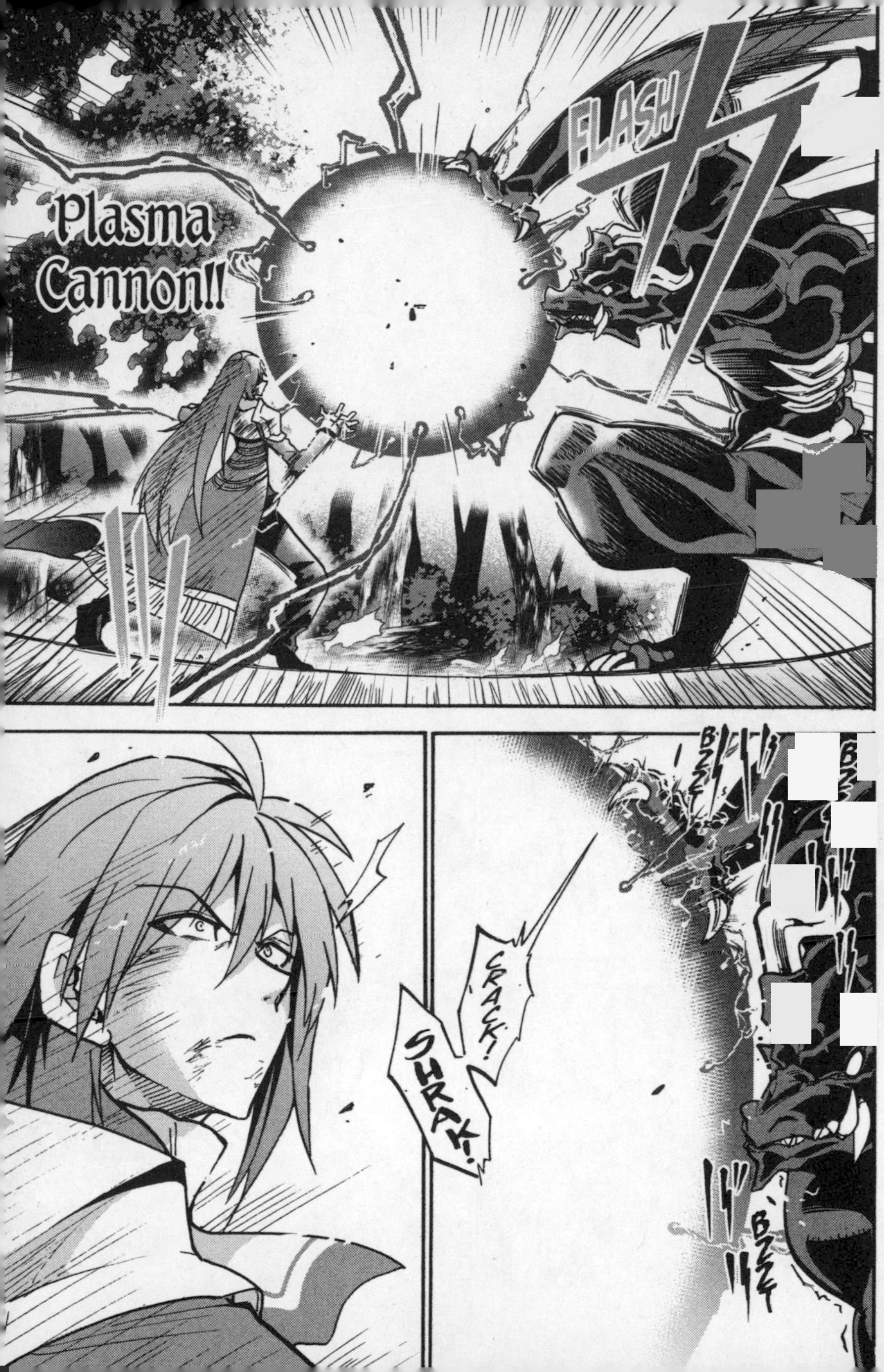
FLASH
Plasma Cannon!!
BZZT
CRACK!
SHRAK!
BZZT

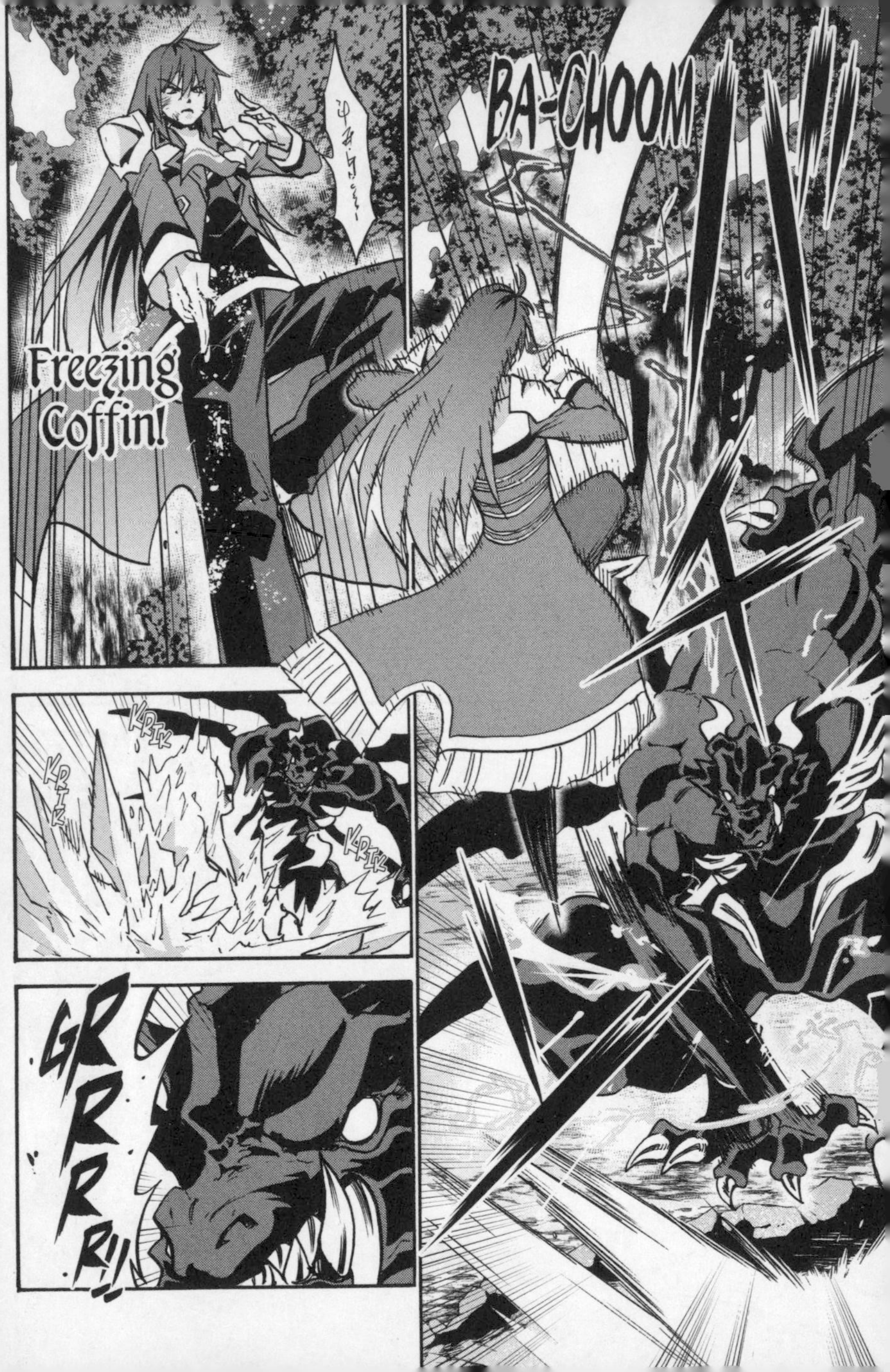
BA-CHOOM
Freezing Coffin!
KRIK
KRIK
KRIK
GRRRR!!

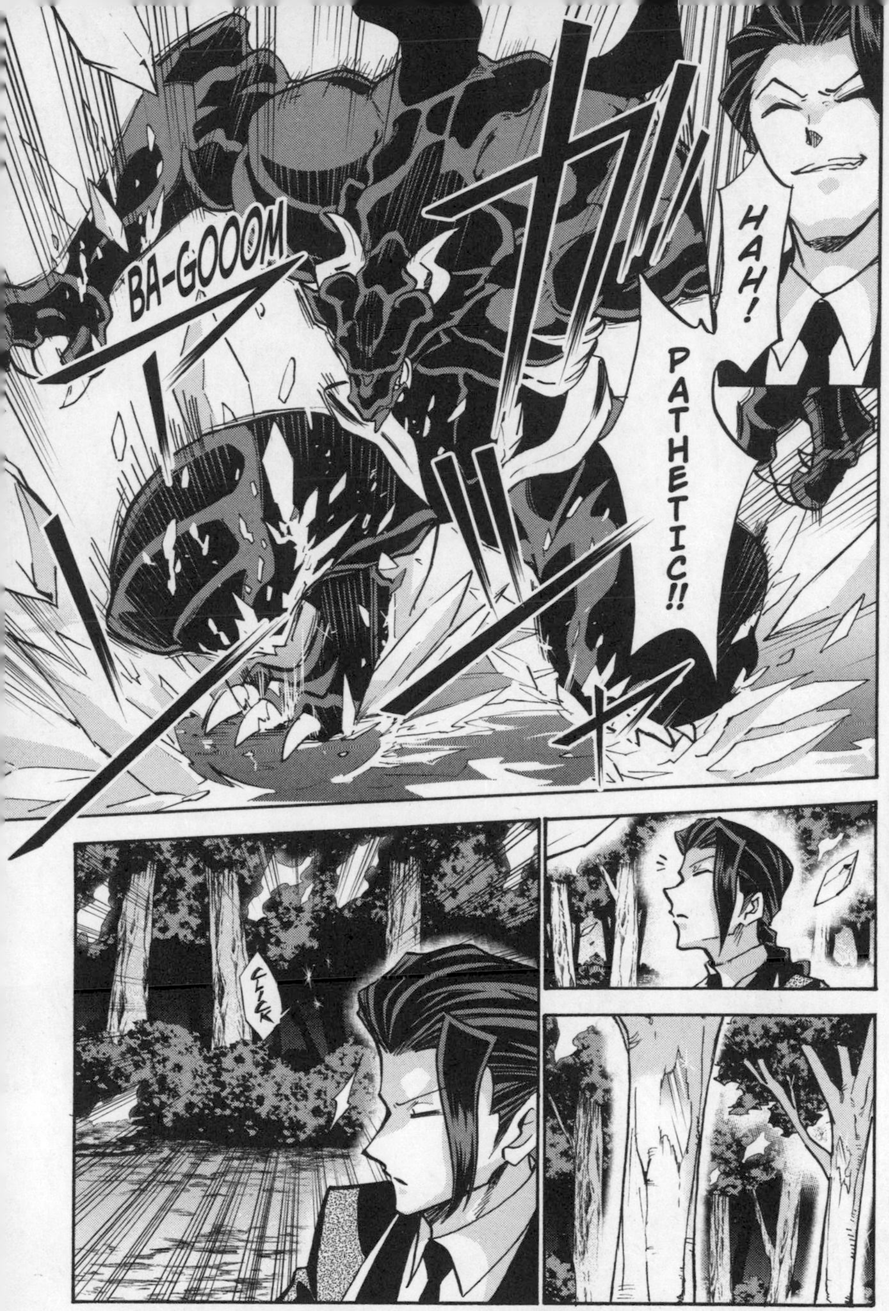
HAH! PATHETIC!!
BA-GOOOM
CLICK

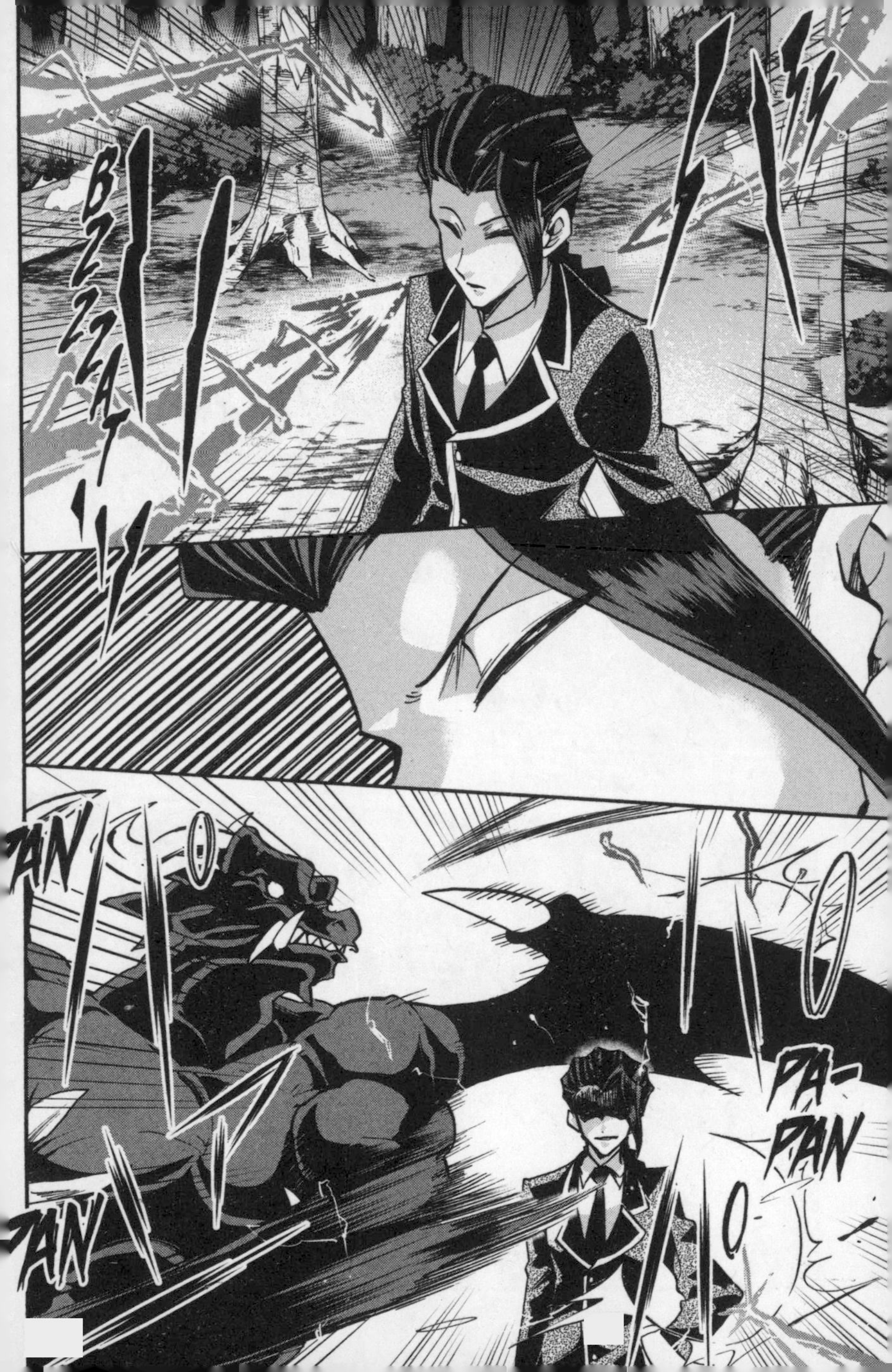
BZZZAT!!
PA-PAN
PAN
PAN

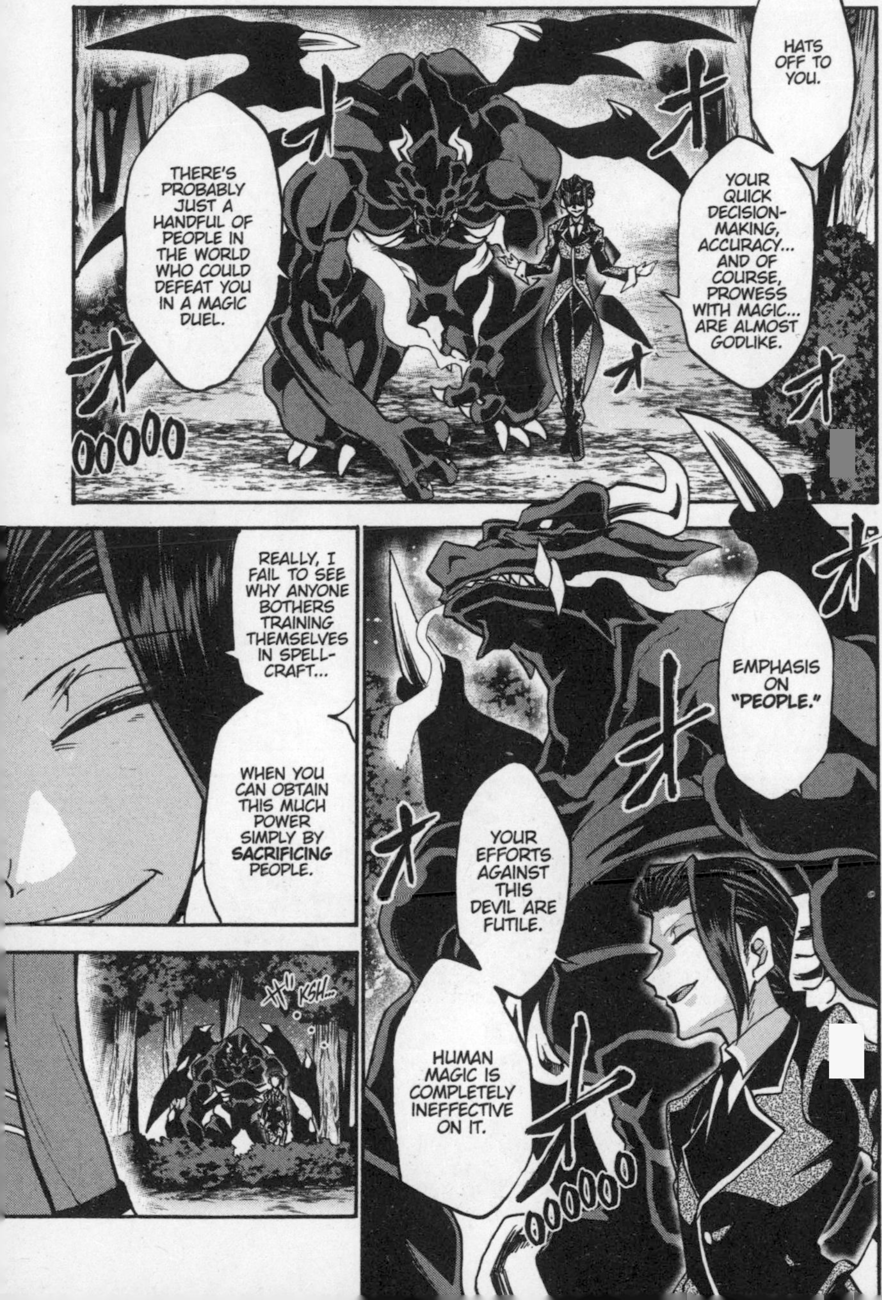

HATS OFF TO YOU.
YOUR QUICK DECISION-MAKING, ACCURACY... AND OF COURSE, PROWESS WITH MAGIC... ARE ALMOST GODLIKE.
THERE'S PROBABLY JUST A HANDFUL OF PEOPLE IN THE WORLD WHO COULD DEFEAT YOU IN A MAGIC DUEL.
OOOOO
EMPHASIS ON "PEOPLE."
YOUR EFFORTS AGAINST THIS DEVIL ARE FUTILE.
HUMAN MAGIC IS COMPLETELY INEFFECTIVE ON IT.
OOOOOO
REALLY, I FAIL TO SEE WHY ANYONE BOTHERS TRAINING THEMSELVES IN SPELL-CRAFT...
WHEN YOU CAN OBTAIN THIS MUCH POWER SIMPLY BY SACRIFICING PEOPLE.
KSH...

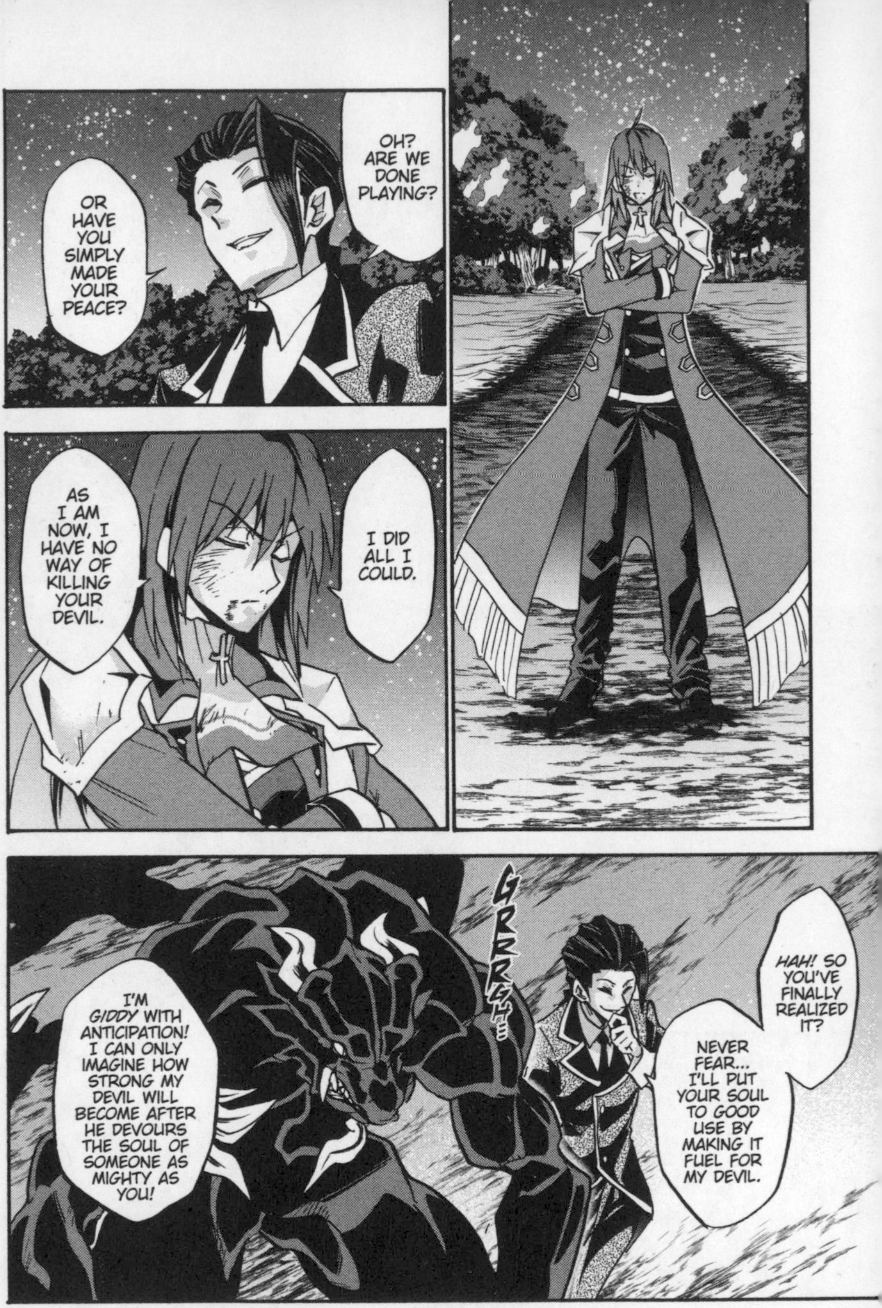
OH? ARE WE DONE PLAYING?
OR HAVE YOU SIMPLY MADE YOUR PEACE?
I DID ALL I COULD.
AS I AM NOW, I HAVE NO WAY OF KILLING YOUR DEVIL.
HAH! SO YOU'VE FINALLY REALIZED IT?
NEVER FEAR... I'LL PUT YOUR SOUL TO GOOD USE BY MAKING IT FUEL FOR MY DEVIL.
GRRRGH!!
I'M GIDDY WITH ANTICIPATION! I CAN ONLY IMAGINE HOW STRONG MY DEVIL WILL BECOME AFTER HE DEVOURS THE SOUL OF SOMEONE AS MIGHTY AS YOU!

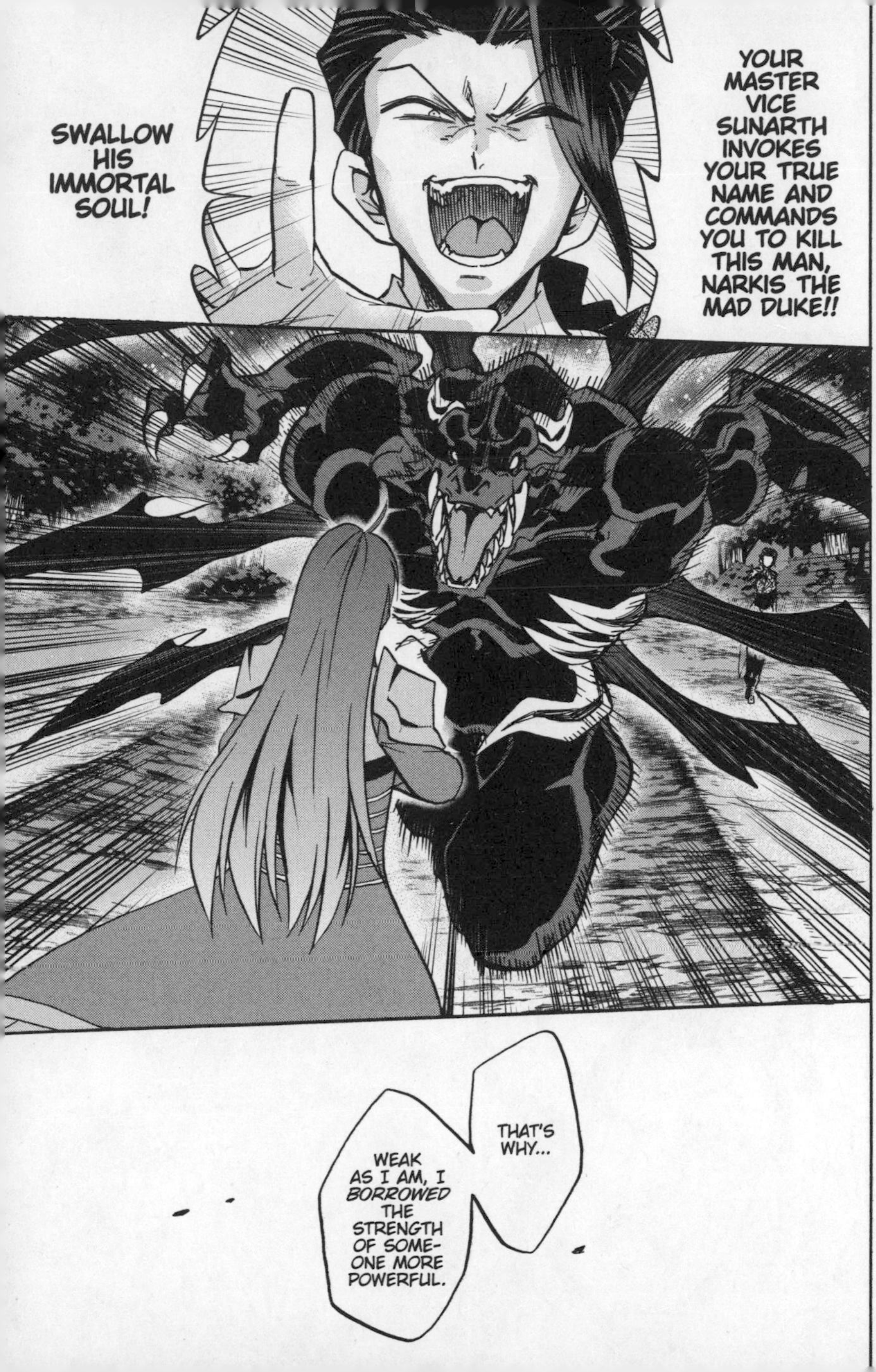
YOUR MASTER VICE SUNARTH INVOKES YOUR TRUE NAME AND COMMANDS YOU TO KILL THIS MAN, NARKIS THE MAD DUKE!!
SWALLOW HIS IMMORTAL SOUL!
THAT'S WHY...
WEAK AS I AM, I *BORROWED* THE STRENGTH OF SOME-ONE MORE POWERFUL.

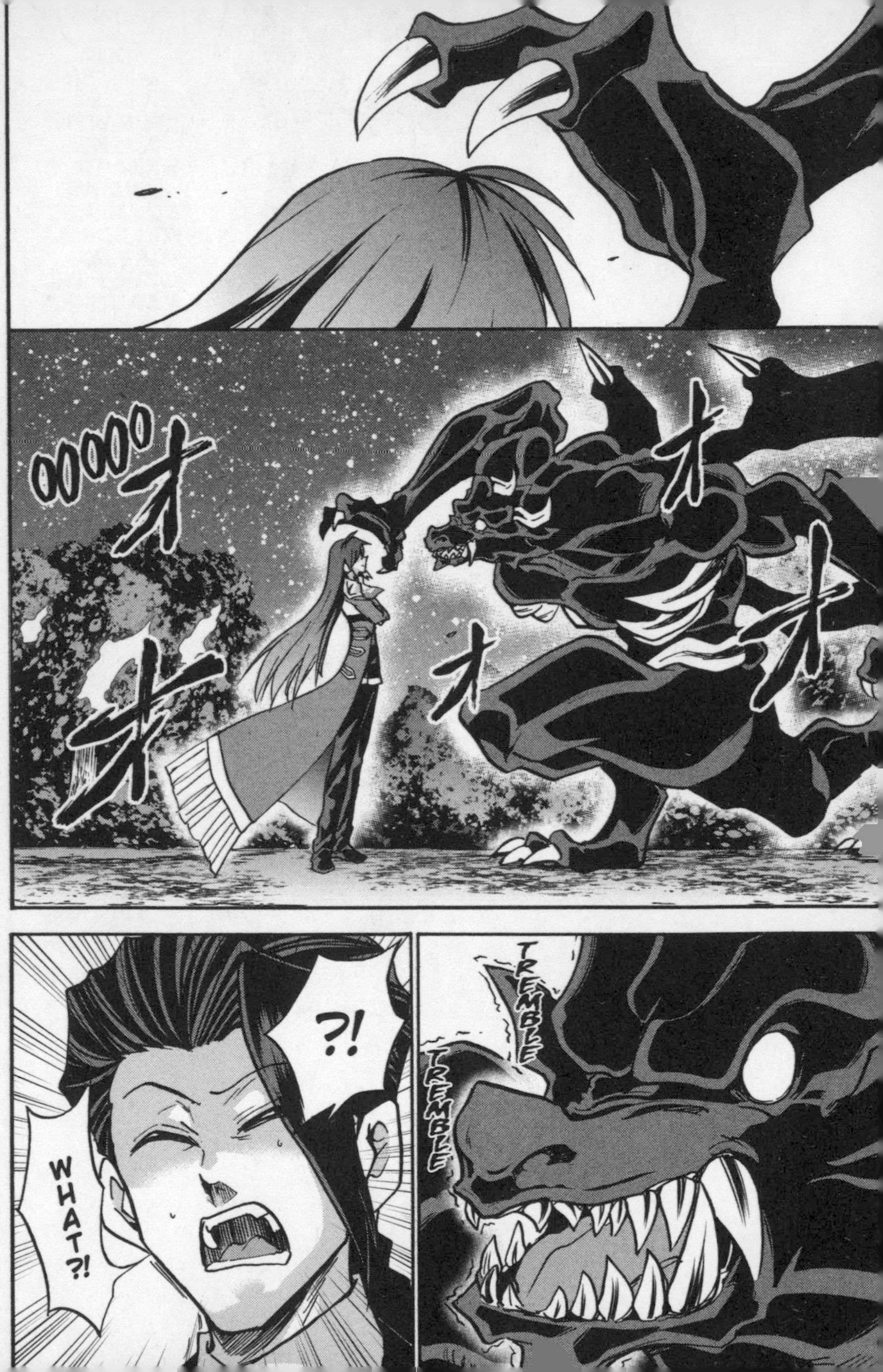
OOOOO
TREMBLE
TREMBLE
?!
WHAT?!

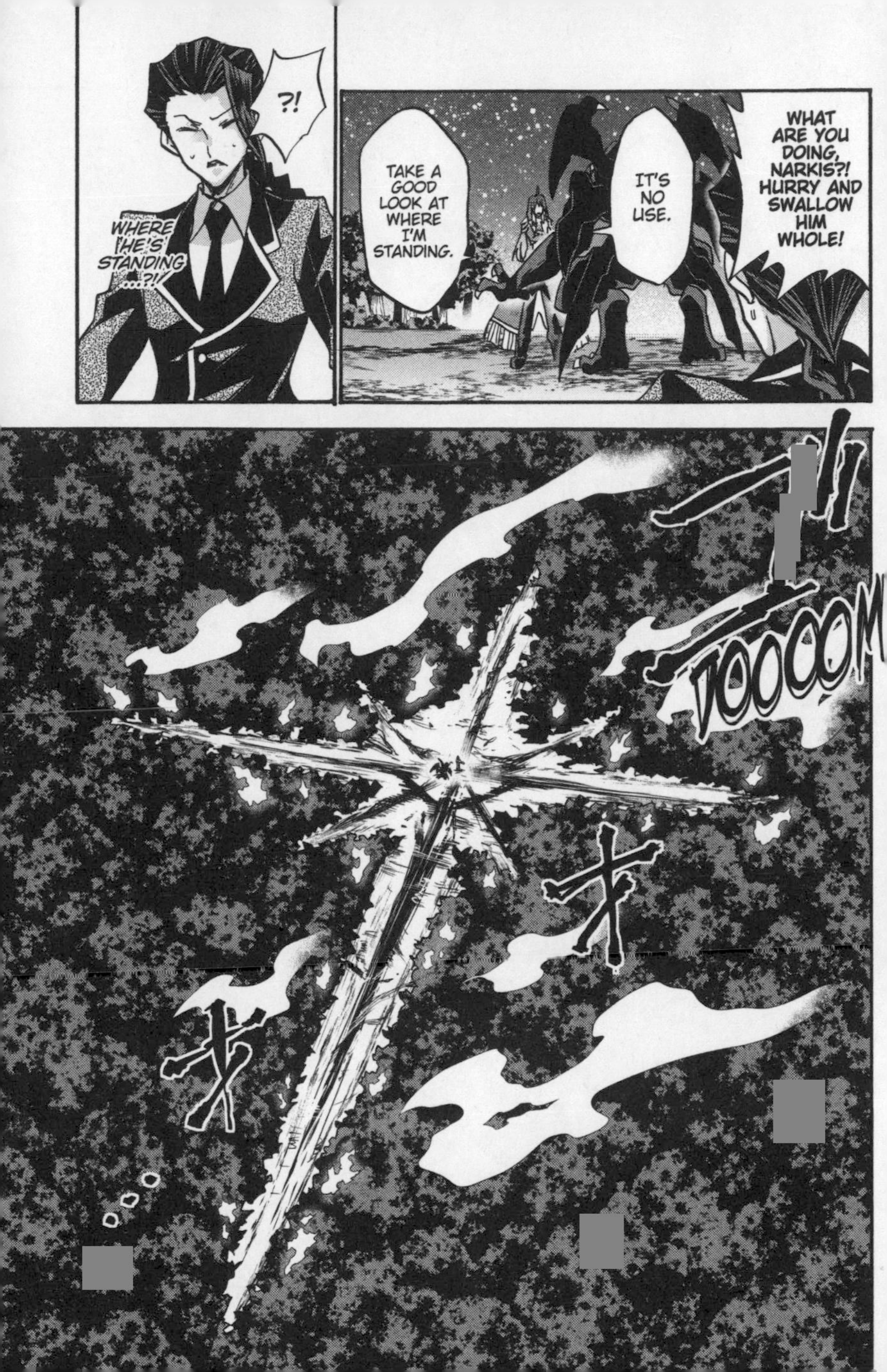
WHAT ARE YOU DOING, NARKIS?! HURRY AND SWALLOW HIM WHOLE!
IT'S NO USE.
TAKE A GOOD LOOK AT WHERE I'M STANDING.
?!
WHERE HE'S STANDING ...?!
DOOOOM

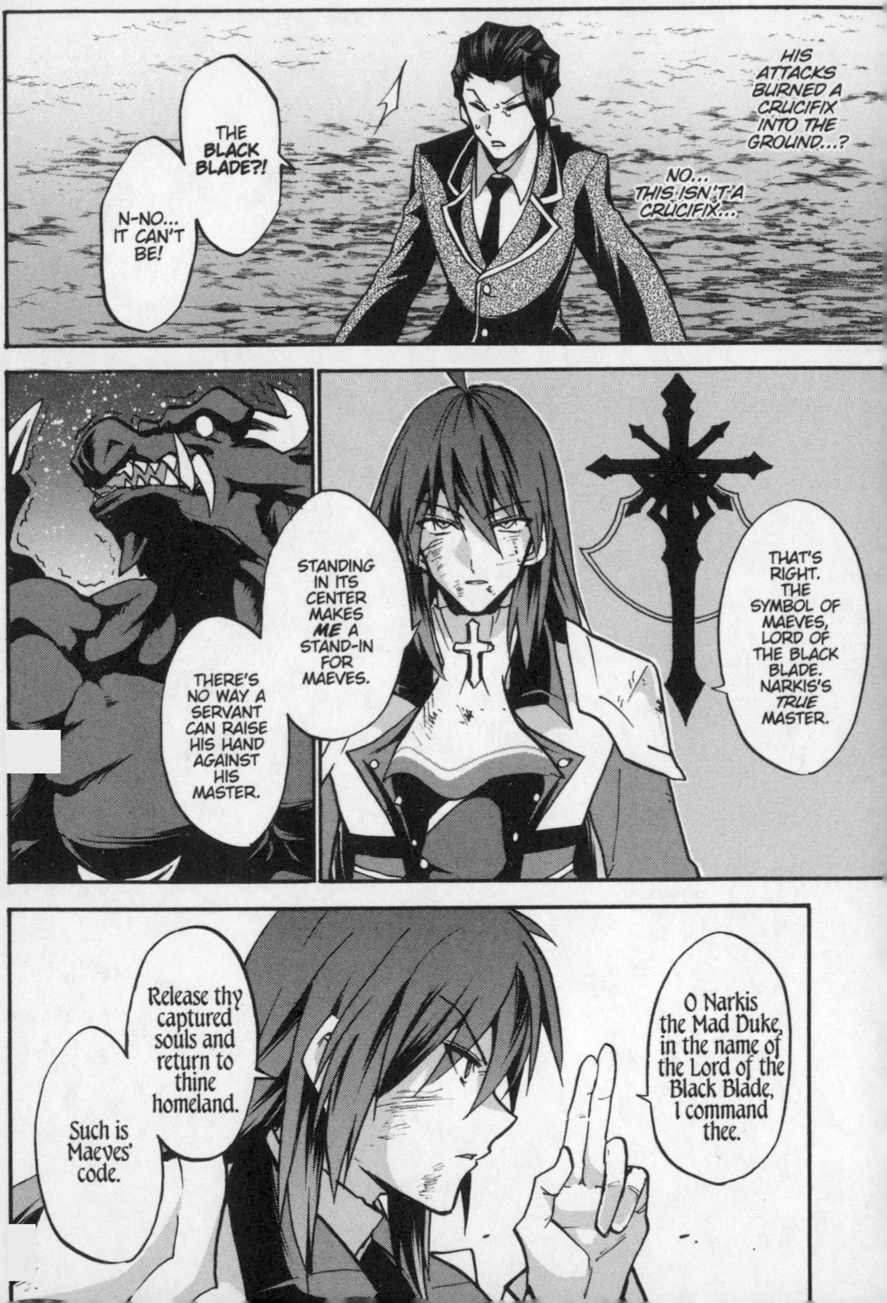
HIS ATTACKS BURNED A CRUCIFIX INTO THE GROUND...?
NO... THIS ISN'T A CRUCIFIX...
THE BLACK BLADE?!
N-NO... IT CAN'T BE!
THAT'S RIGHT. THE SYMBOL OF MAEVES, LORD OF THE BLACK BLADE. NARKIS'S *TRUE* MASTER.
STANDING IN ITS CENTER MAKES ***ME*** A STAND-IN FOR MAEVES.
THERE'S NO WAY A SERVANT CAN RAISE HIS HAND AGAINST HIS MASTER.
O Narkis the Mad Duke, in the name of the Lord of the Black Blade, I command thee.
Release thy captured souls and return to thine homeland.
Such is Maeves' code.

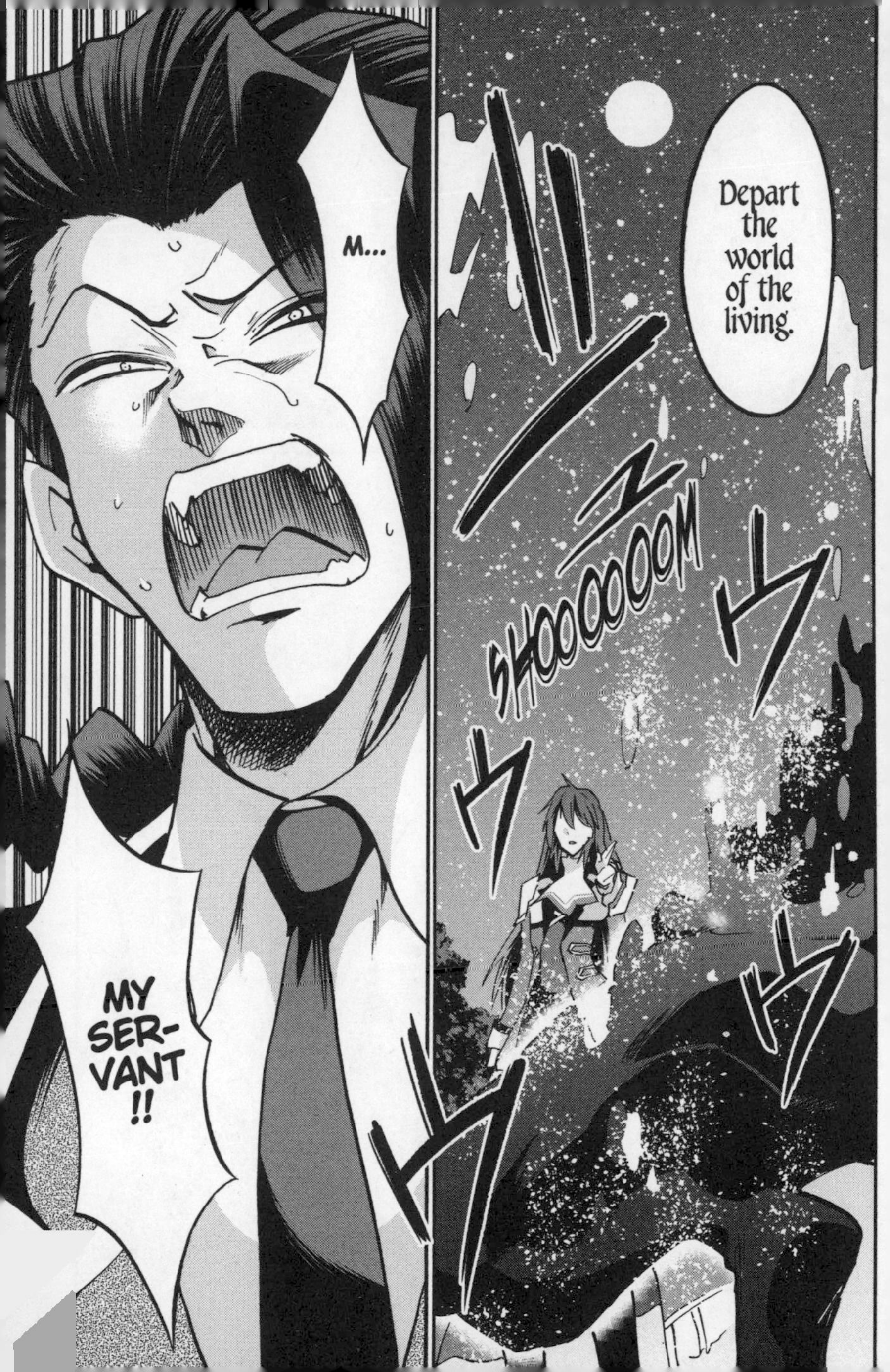
Depart the world of the living.
SHOOOOOOM
M...
MY SER-VANT!!

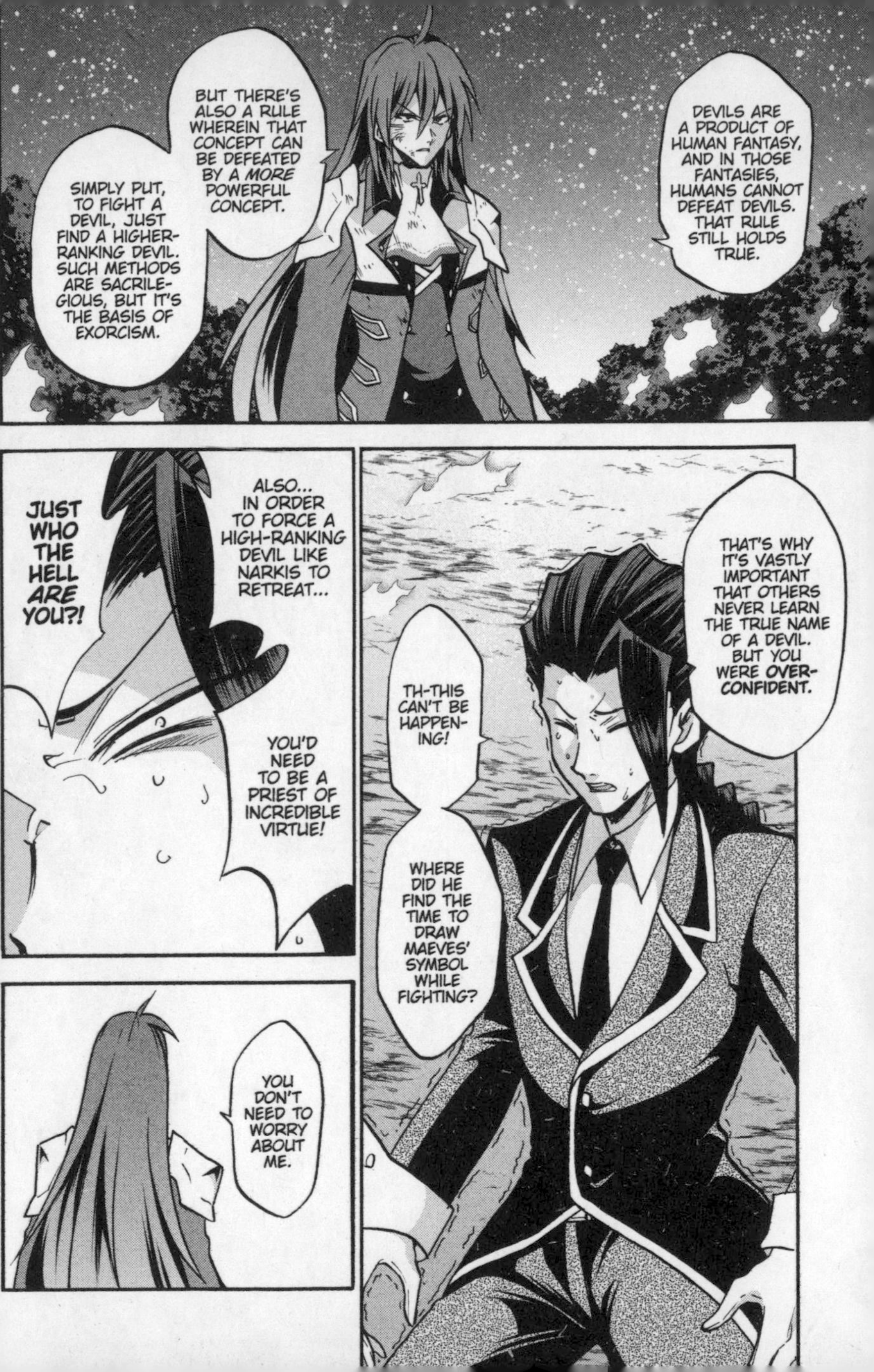
DEVILS ARE A PRODUCT OF HUMAN FANTASY, AND IN THOSE FANTASIES, HUMANS CANNOT DEFEAT DEVILS. THAT RULE STILL HOLDS TRUE.
BUT THERE'S ALSO A RULE WHEREIN THAT CONCEPT CAN BE DEFEATED BY A *MORE* POWERFUL CONCEPT.
SIMPLY PUT, TO FIGHT A DEVIL, JUST FIND A HIGHER-RANKING DEVIL. SUCH METHODS ARE SACRILEGIOUS, BUT IT'S THE BASIS OF EXORCISM.
THAT'S WHY IT'S VASTLY IMPORTANT THAT OTHERS NEVER LEARN THE TRUE NAME OF A DEVIL. BUT YOU WERE **OVER-CONFIDENT.**
TH-THIS CAN'T BE HAPPENING!
WHERE DID HE FIND THE TIME TO DRAW MAEVES' SYMBOL WHILE FIGHTING?
ALSO... IN ORDER TO FORCE A HIGH-RANKING DEVIL LIKE NARKIS TO RETREAT...
YOU'D NEED TO BE A PRIEST OF INCREDIBLE VIRTUE!
JUST WHO THE HELL *ARE* YOU?!
YOU DON'T NEED TO WORRY ABOUT ME.

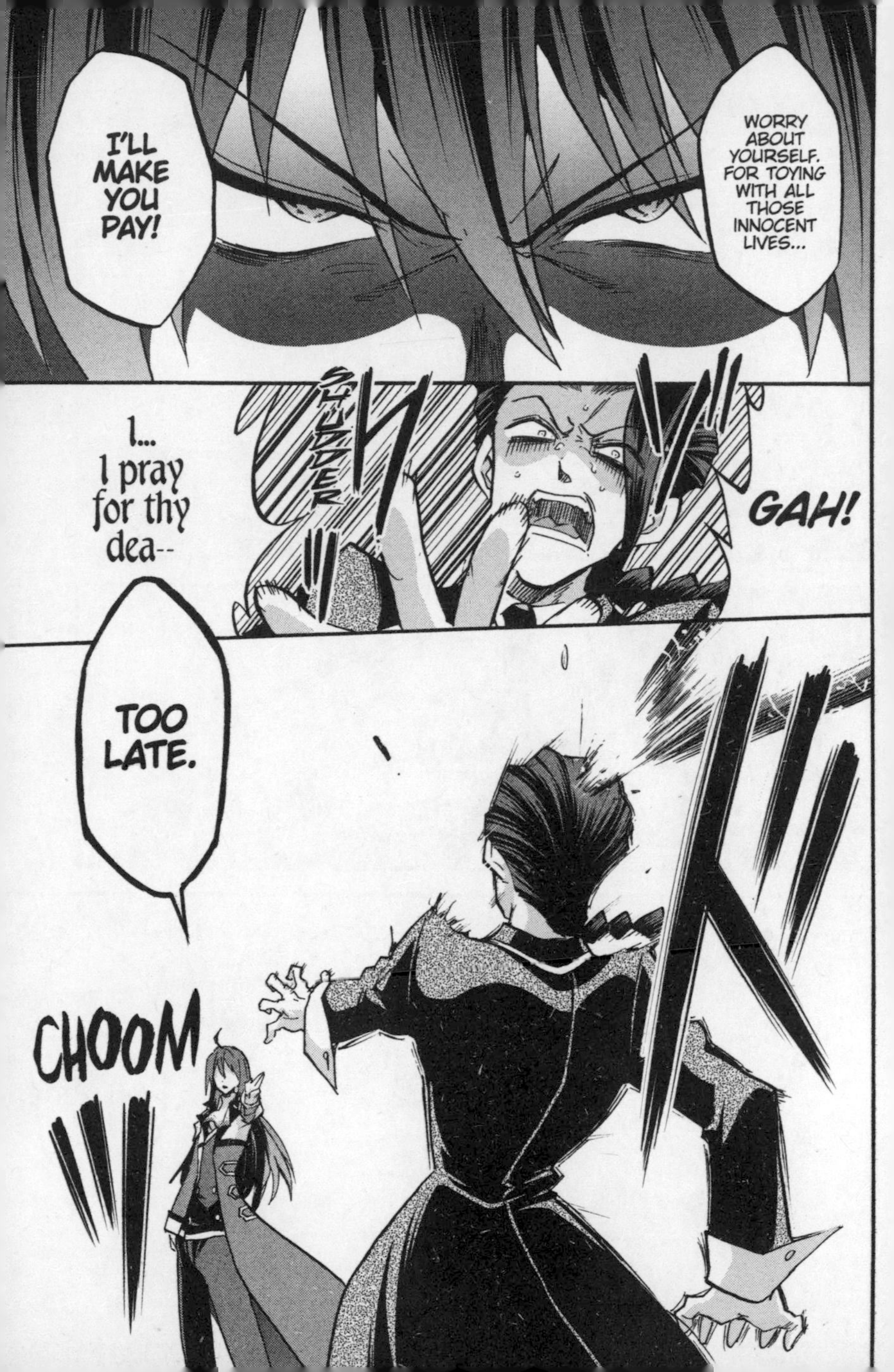

WORRY ABOUT YOURSELF. FOR TOYING WITH ALL THOSE INNOCENT LIVES...
I'LL MAKE YOU PAY!
GAH!
SHUDDER
I... I pray for thy dea--
TOO LATE.
CHOOM

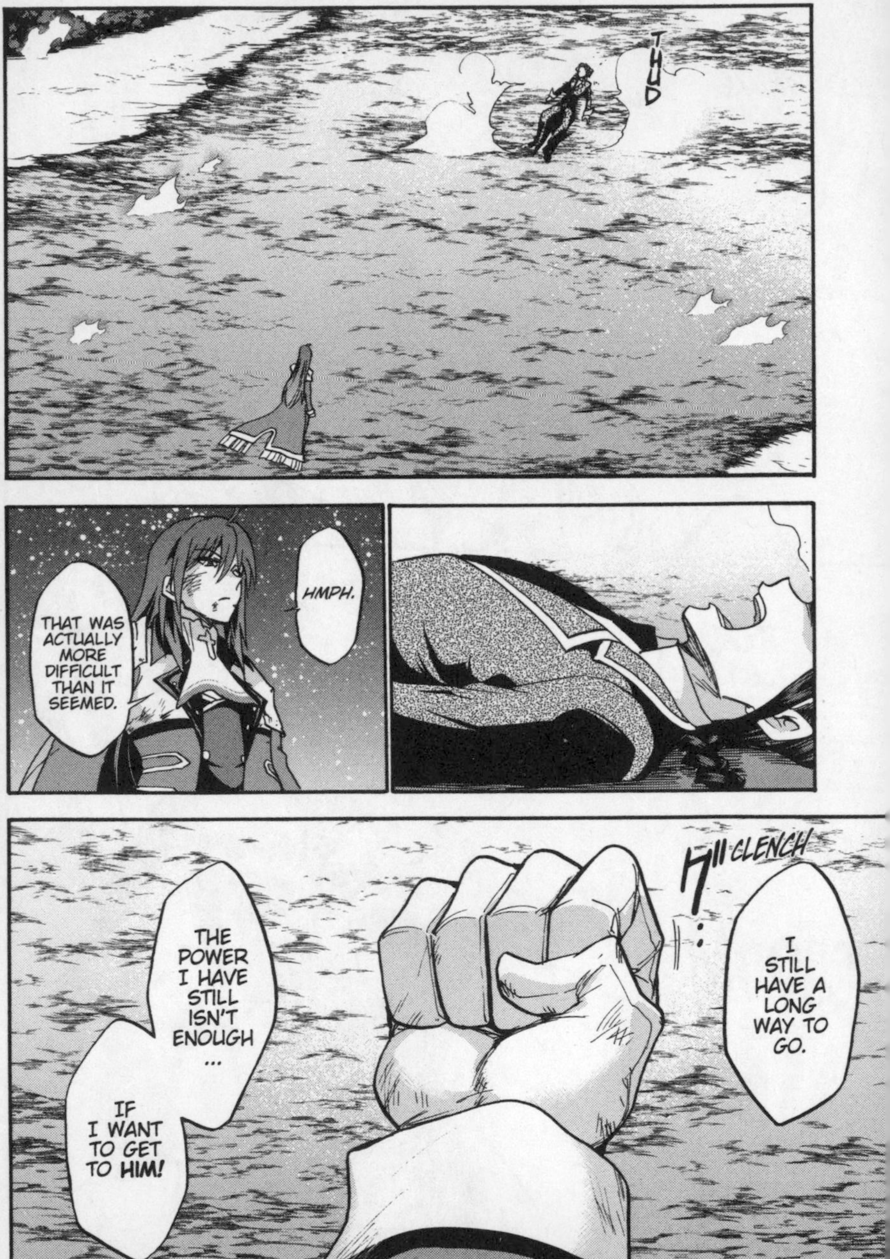
THUD
HMPH.
THAT WAS ACTUALLY MORE DIFFICULT THAN IT SEEMED.
CLENCH
I STILL HAVE A LONG WAY TO GO.
THE POWER I HAVE STILL ISN'T ENOUGH...
IF I WANT TO GET TO HIM!

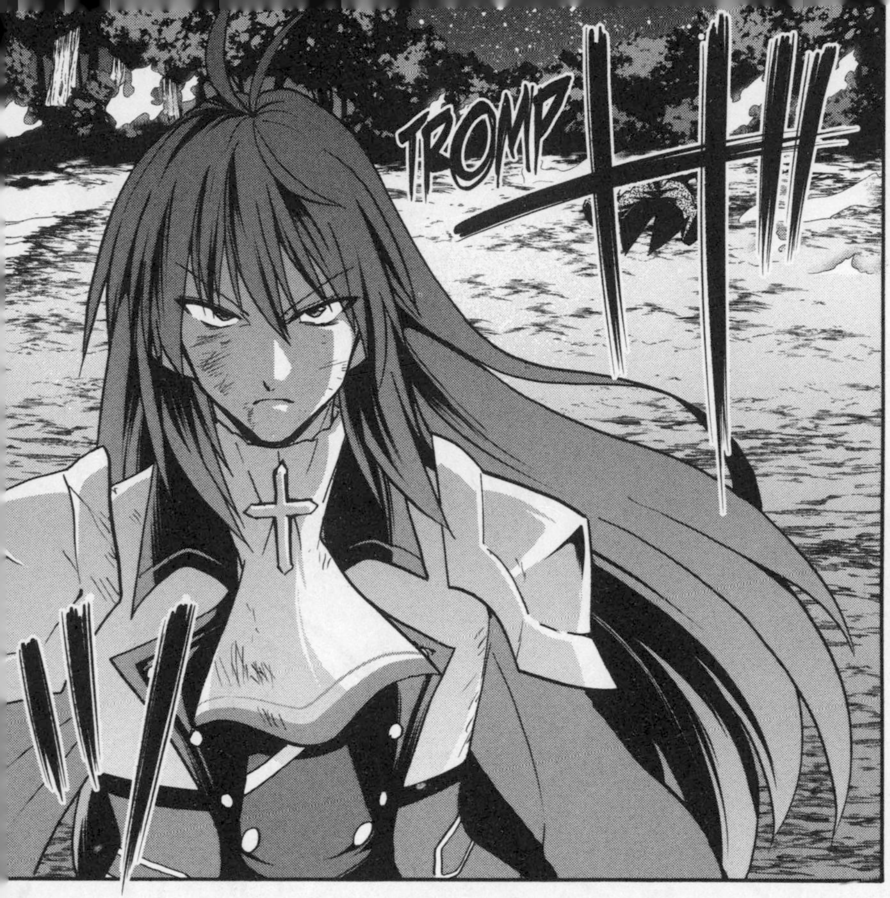
TROMP
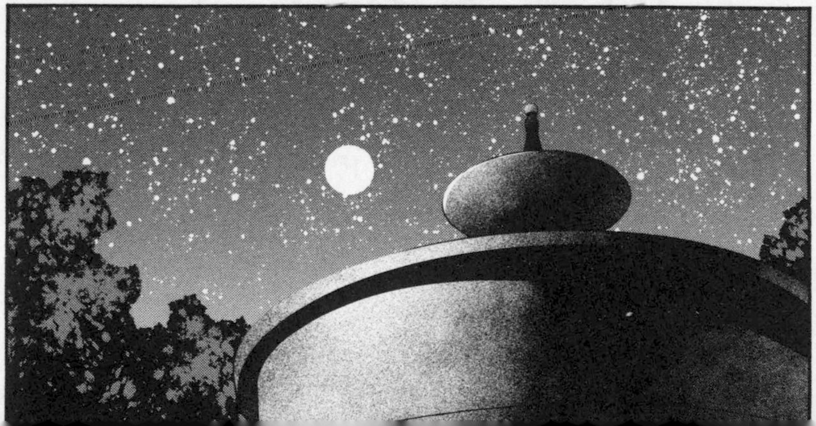

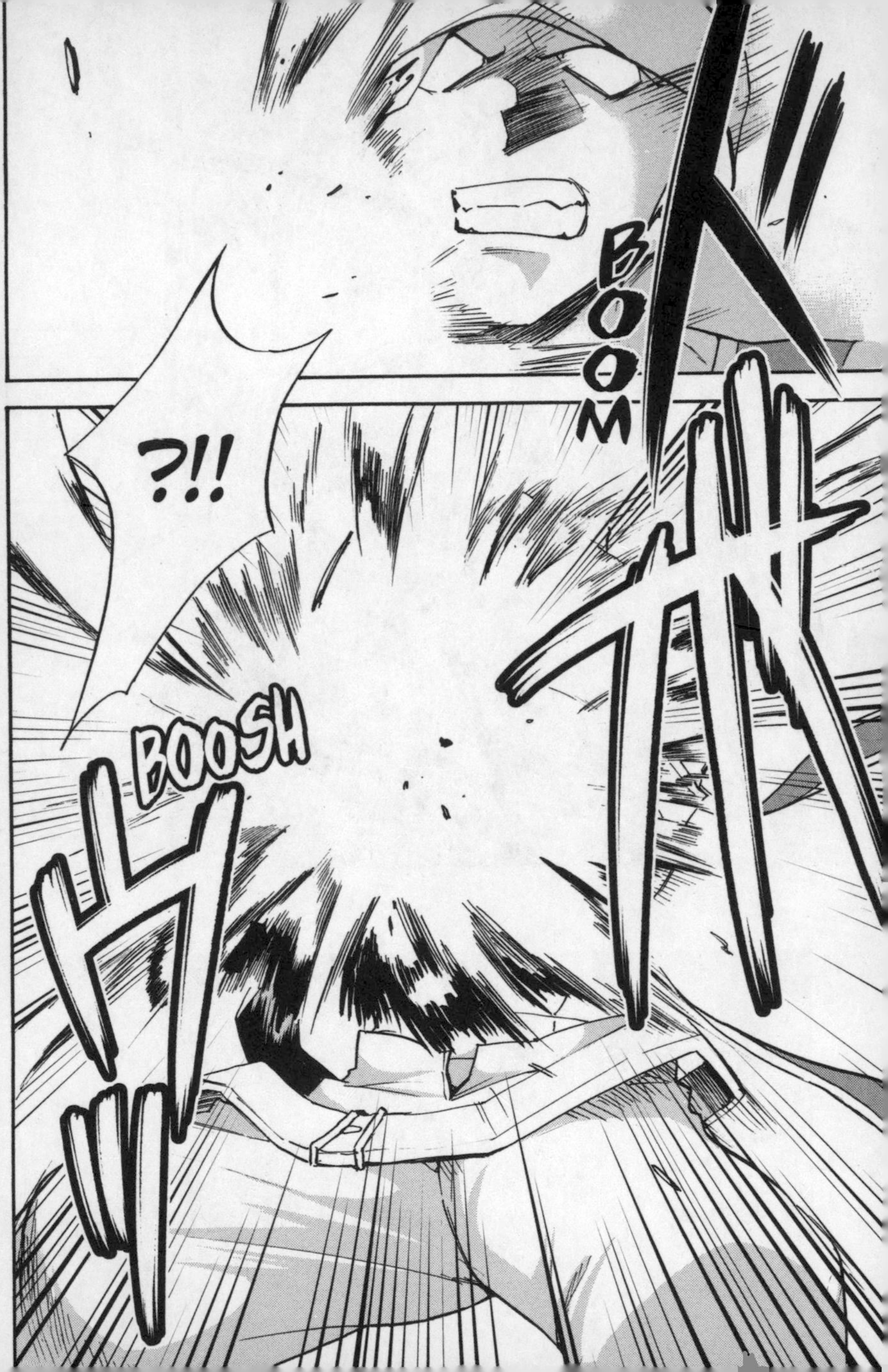
BOOM
?!!
BOOSH

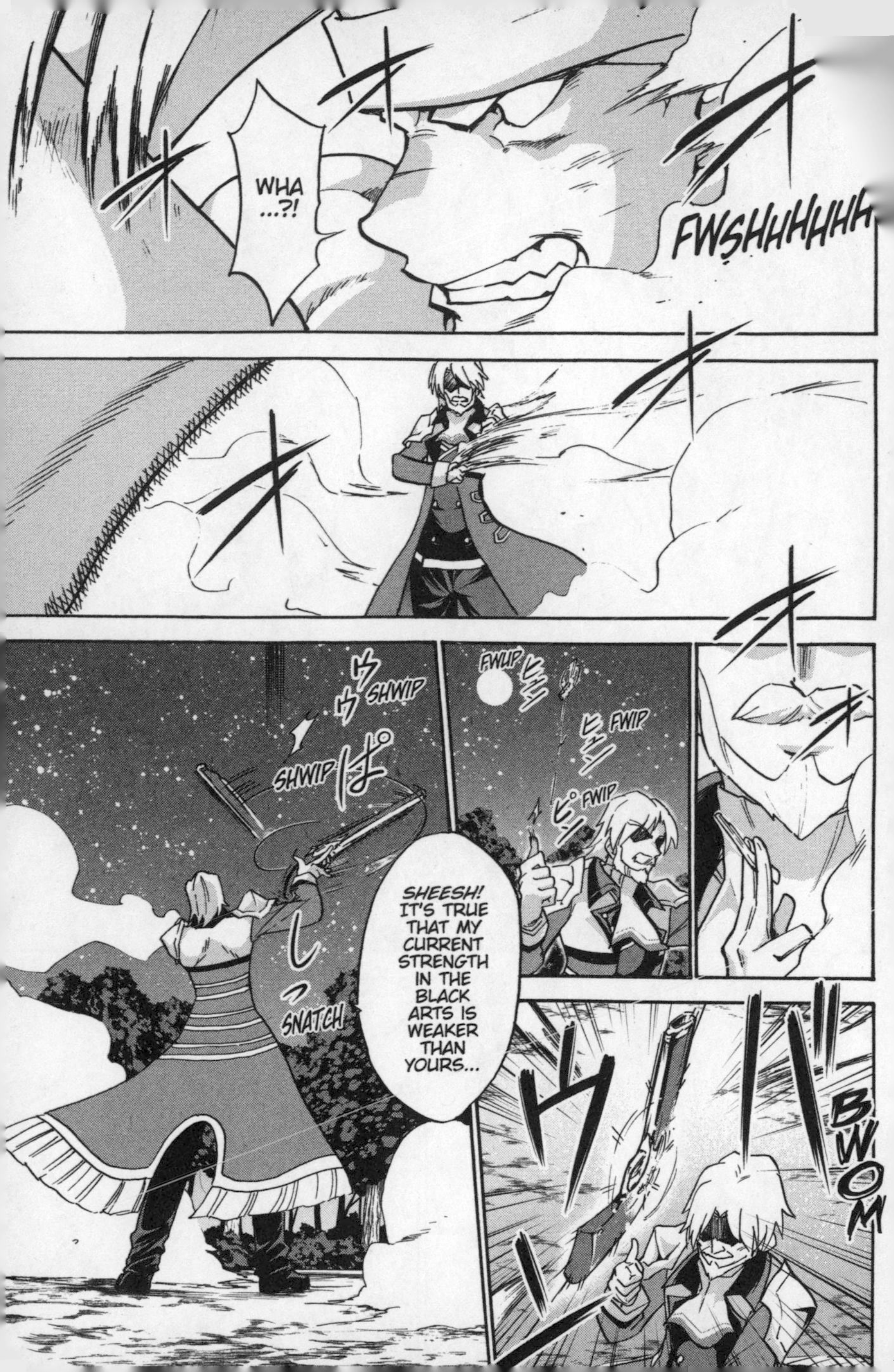
FWSHHHHHH
WHA ...?!
FWUP
FWIP
FWIP
SHWIP
SHWIP
ぱ
しっ
SNATCH
SHEESH! IT'S TRUE THAT MY CURRENT STRENGTH IN THE BLACK ARTS IS WEAKER THAN YOURS...
BWOM

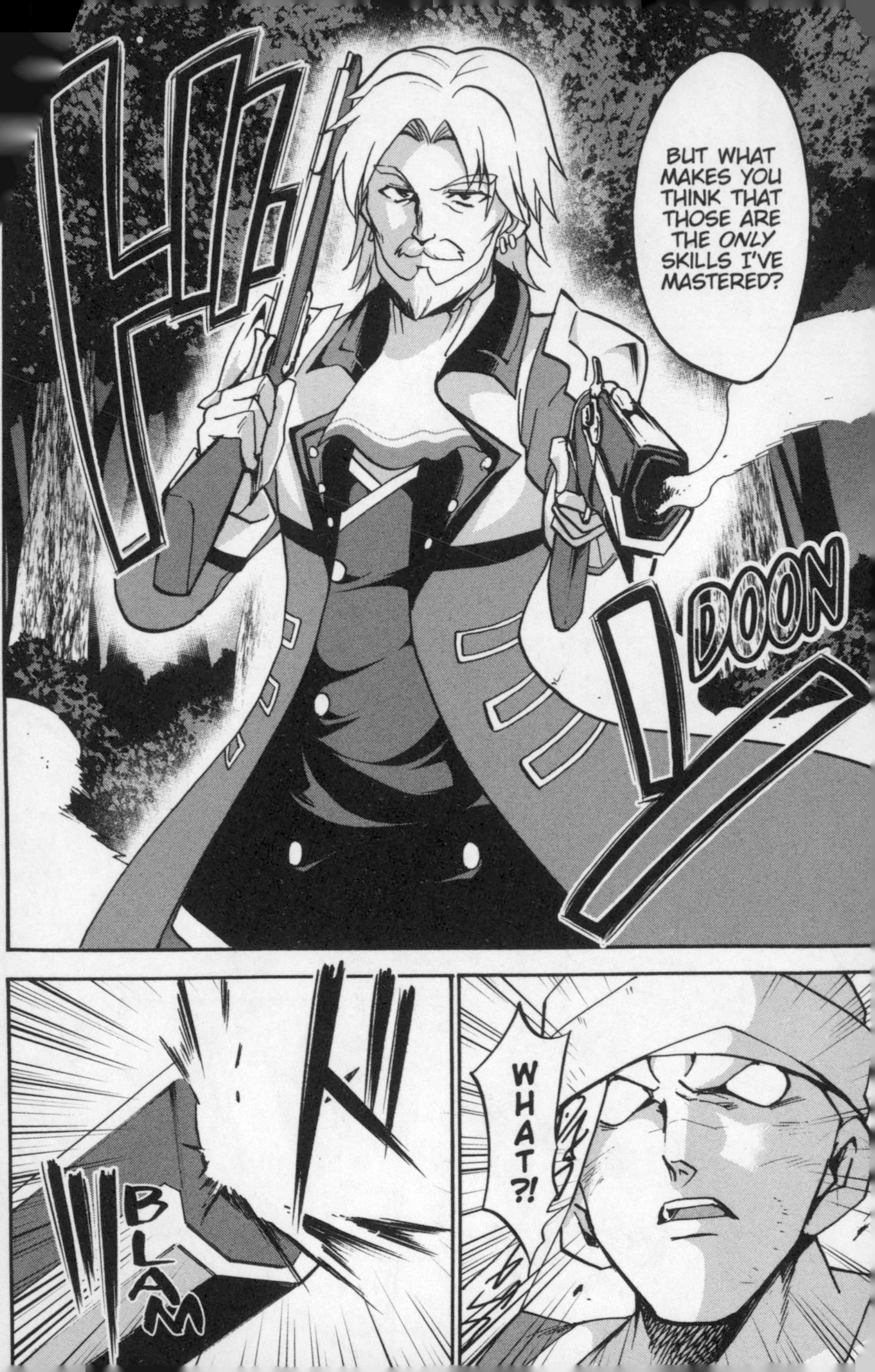
BUT WHAT MAKES YOU THINK THAT THOSE ARE THE *ONLY* SKILLS I'VE MASTERED?
DOON
WHAT?!
BLAM

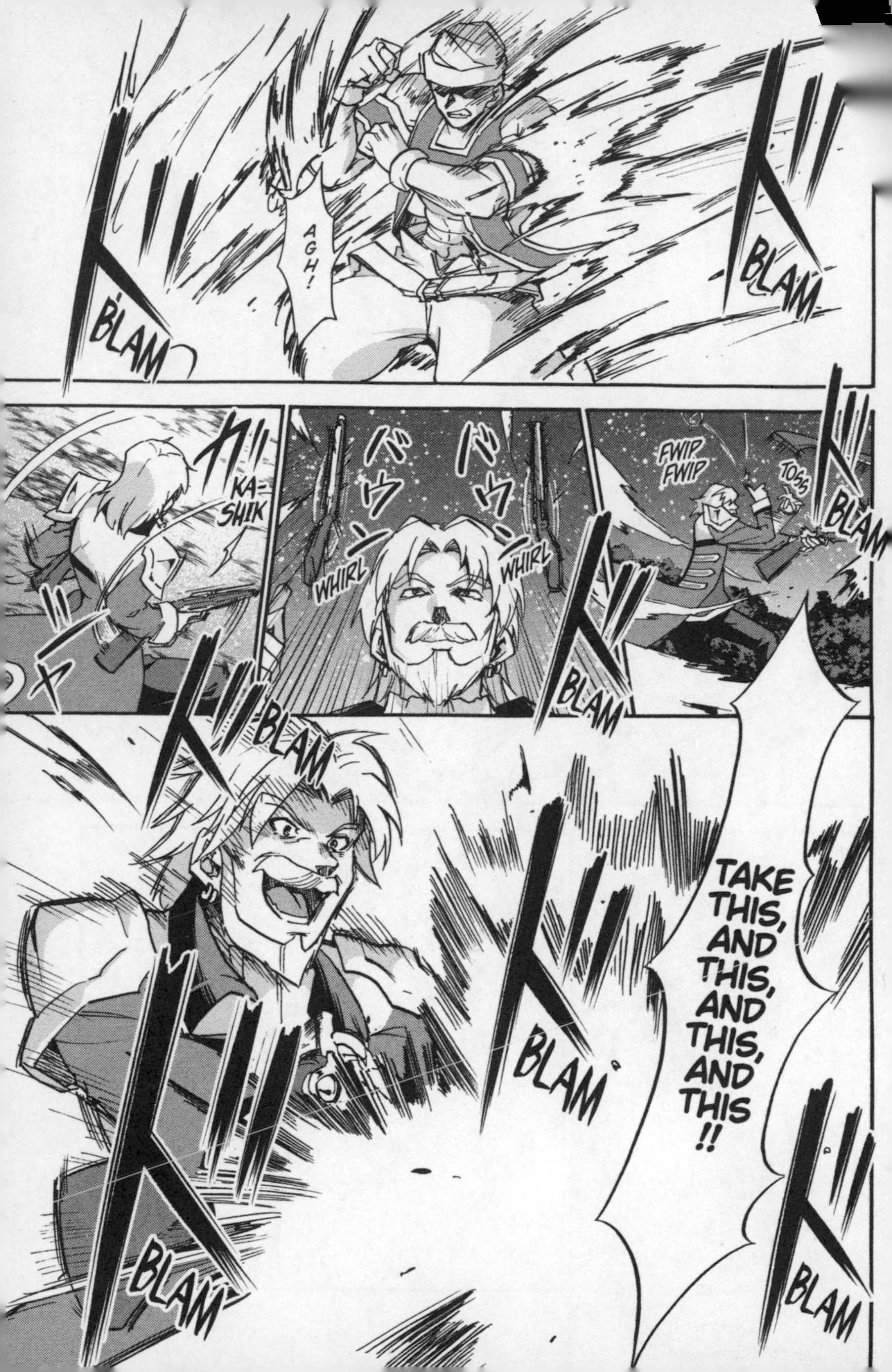
BLAM
AGH!
BLAM
BLAM
TOSS
FWIP FWIP
BLAM
バウン
バウン
WHIRL
WHIRL
KA-SHIK
TAKE THIS, AND THIS, AND THIS, AND THIS!!
BLAM
BLAM
BLAM
BLAM

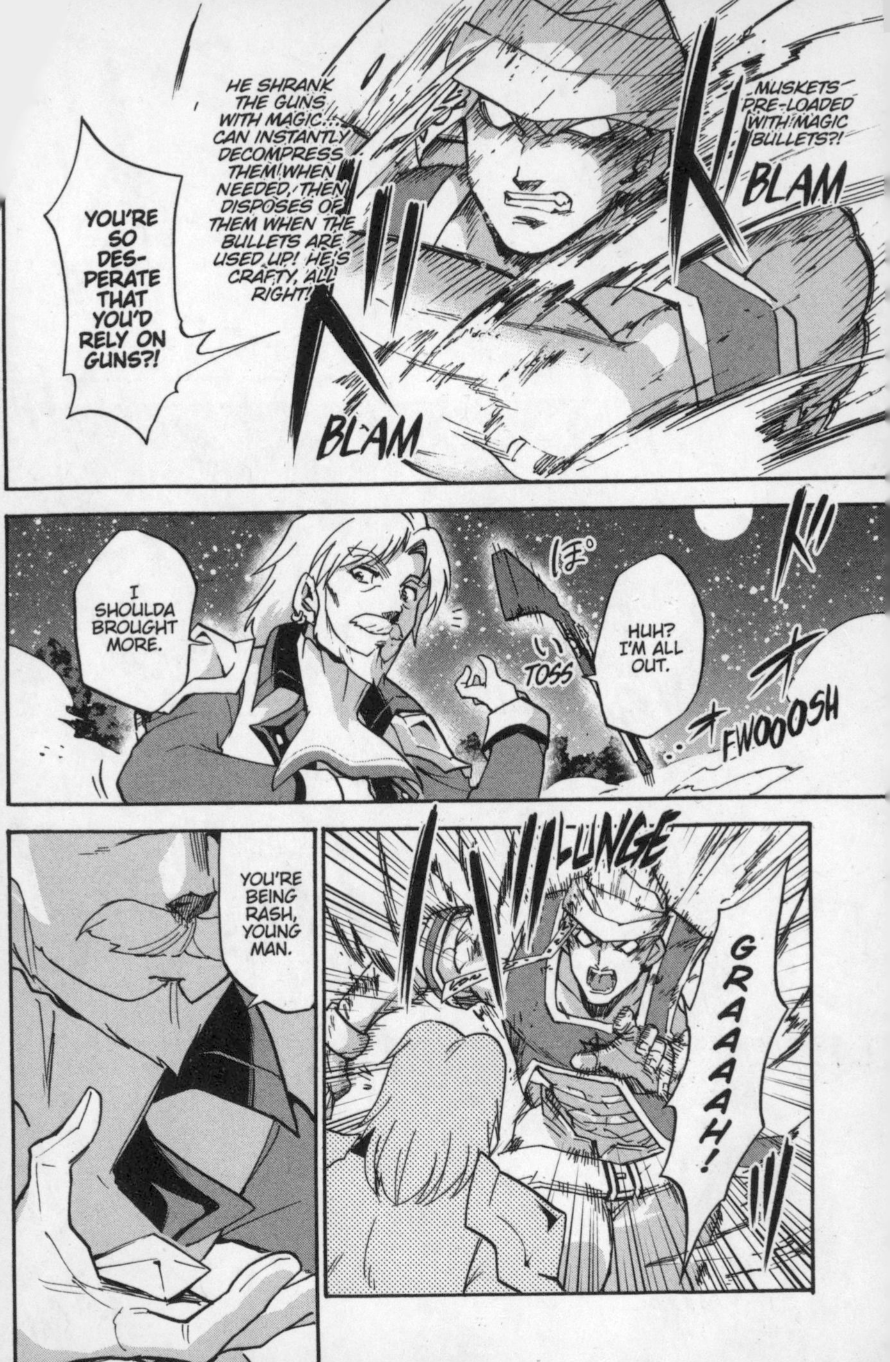
MUSKETS PRE-LOADED WITH MAGIC BULLETS?!
BLAM
HE SHRANK THE GUNS WITH MAGIC... CAN INSTANTLY DECOMPRESS THEM WHEN NEEDED, THEN DISPOSES OF THEM WHEN THE BULLETS ARE USED UP! HE'S CRAFTY, ALL RIGHT!
YOU'RE SO DES-PERATE THAT YOU'D RELY ON GUNS?!
BLAM
BLAM
FWOOOSH
HUH? I'M ALL OUT.
ぽ
い
TOSS
I SHOULDA BROUGHT MORE.
LUNGE
GRAAAAAH!
YOU'RE BEING RASH, YOUNG MAN.

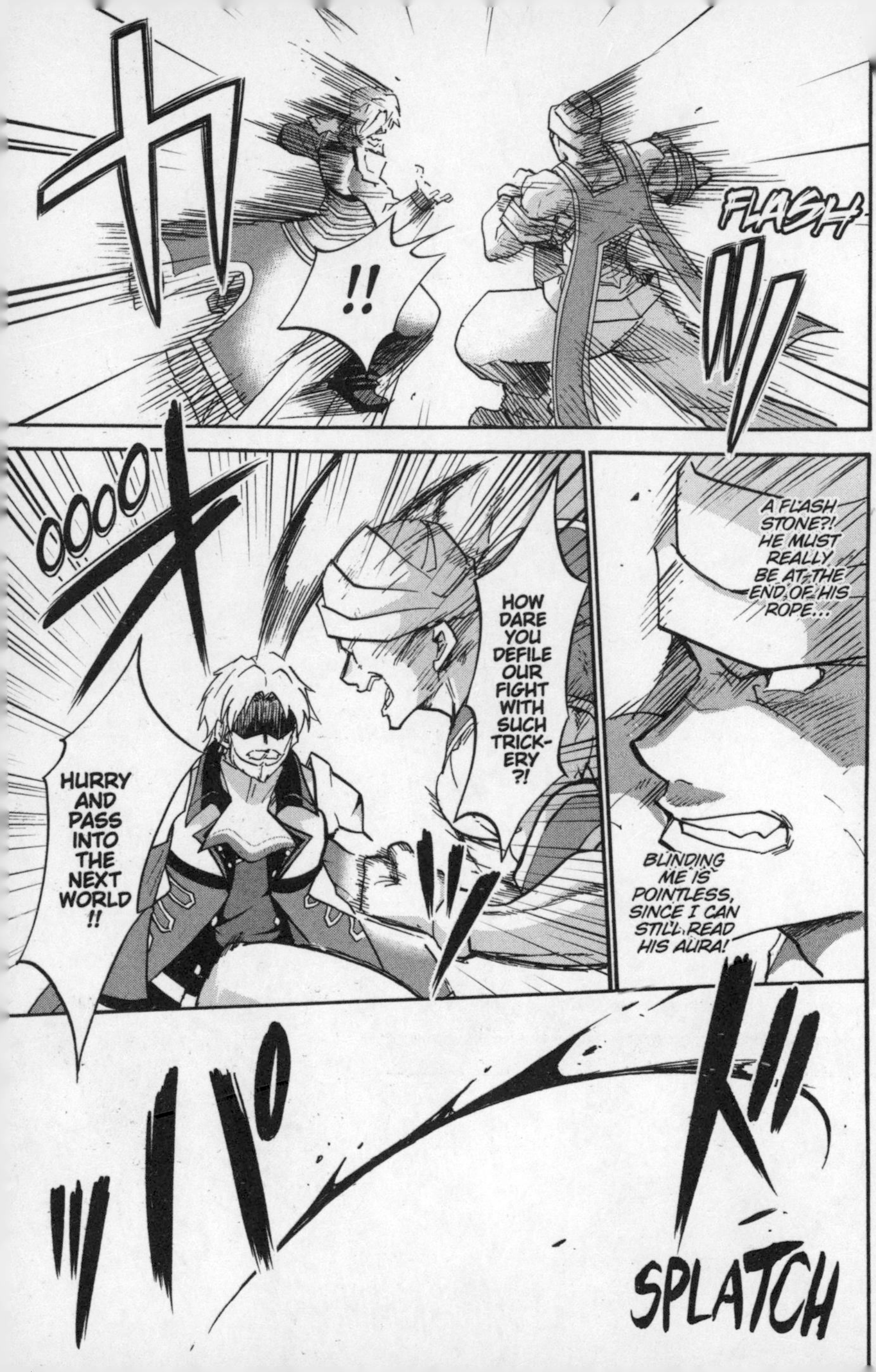
FLASH
!!
A FLASH STONE?! HE MUST REALLY BE AT THE END OF HIS ROPE...
BLINDING ME IS POINTLESS, SINCE I CAN STILL READ HIS AURA!
HOW DARE YOU DEFILE OUR FIGHT WITH SUCH TRICKERY?!
HURRY AND PASS INTO THE NEXT WORLD!!
SPLATCH

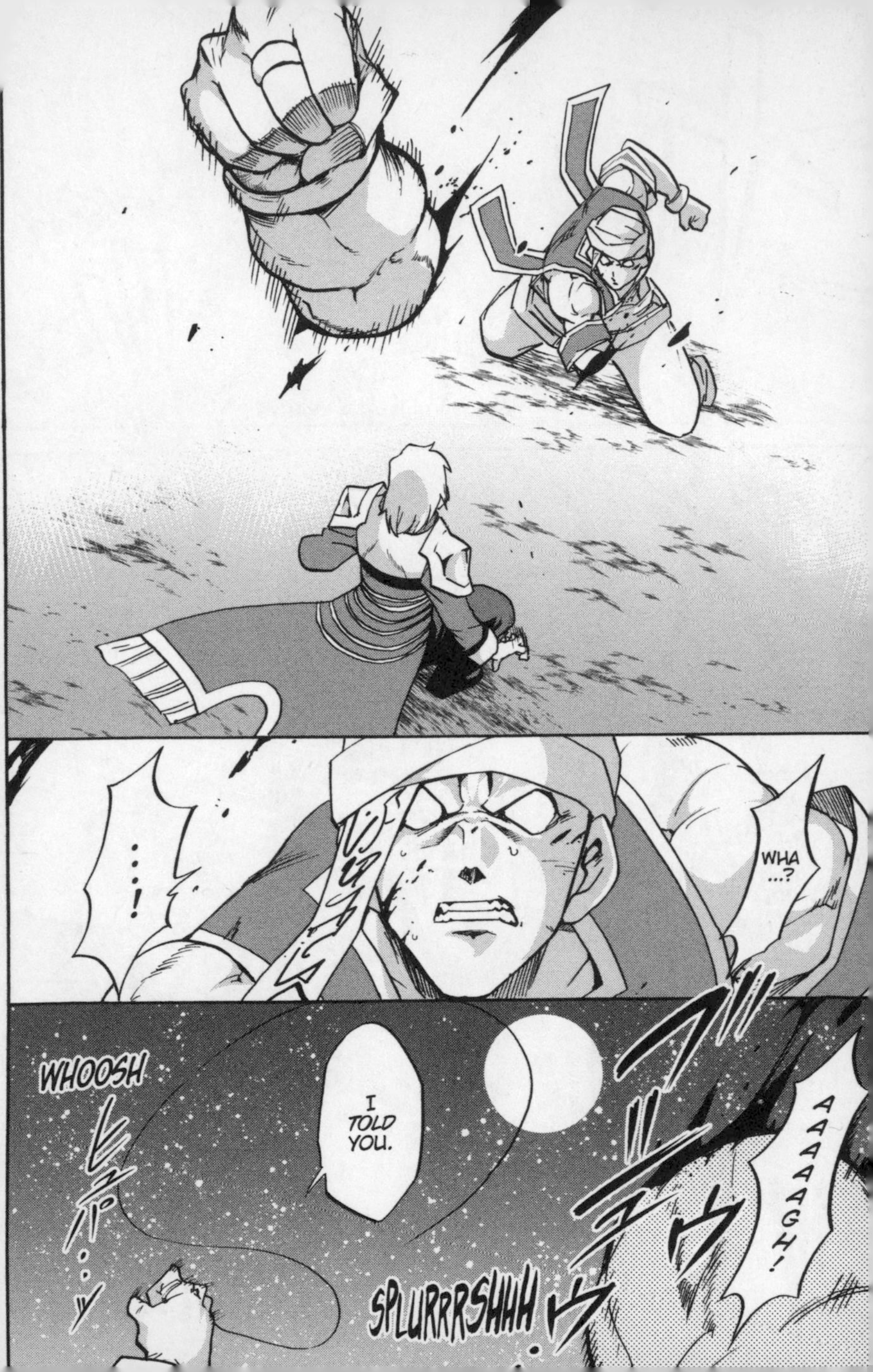
WHA ...?
...!
AAAAAAGH!
SPLURRRSHHH
I TOLD YOU.
WHOOSH

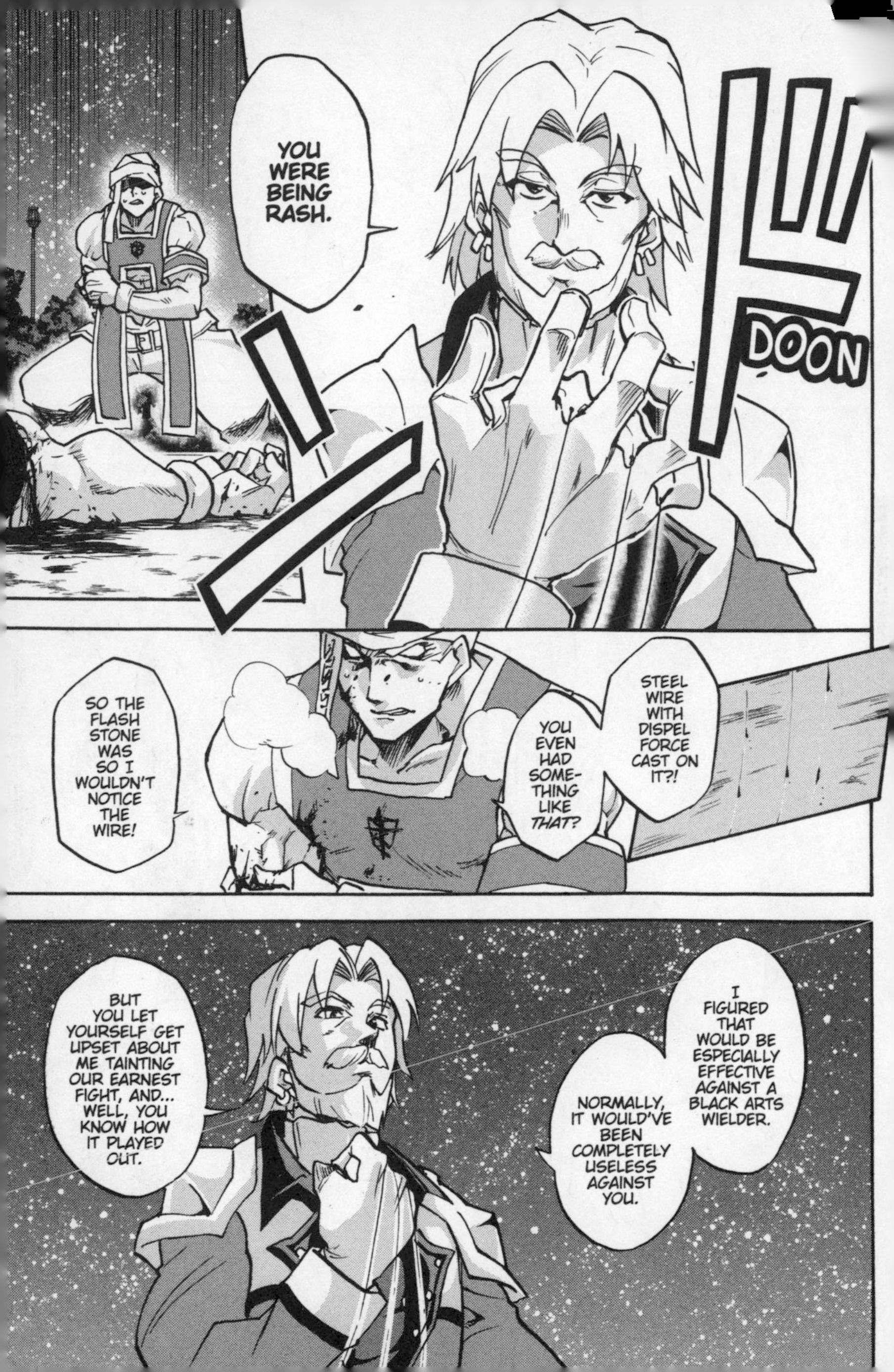
DOON
YOU WERE BEING RASH.
STEEL WIRE WITH DISPEL FORCE CAST ON IT?!
YOU EVEN HAD SOMETHING LIKE *THAT*?
SO THE FLASH STONE WAS SO I WOULDN'T NOTICE THE WIRE!
I FIGURED THAT WOULD BE ESPECIALLY EFFECTIVE AGAINST A BLACK ARTS WIELDER.
NORMALLY, IT WOULD'VE BEEN COMPLETELY USELESS AGAINST YOU.
BUT YOU LET YOURSELF GET UPSET ABOUT ME TAINTING OUR EARNEST FIGHT, AND... WELL, YOU KNOW HOW IT PLAYED OUT.

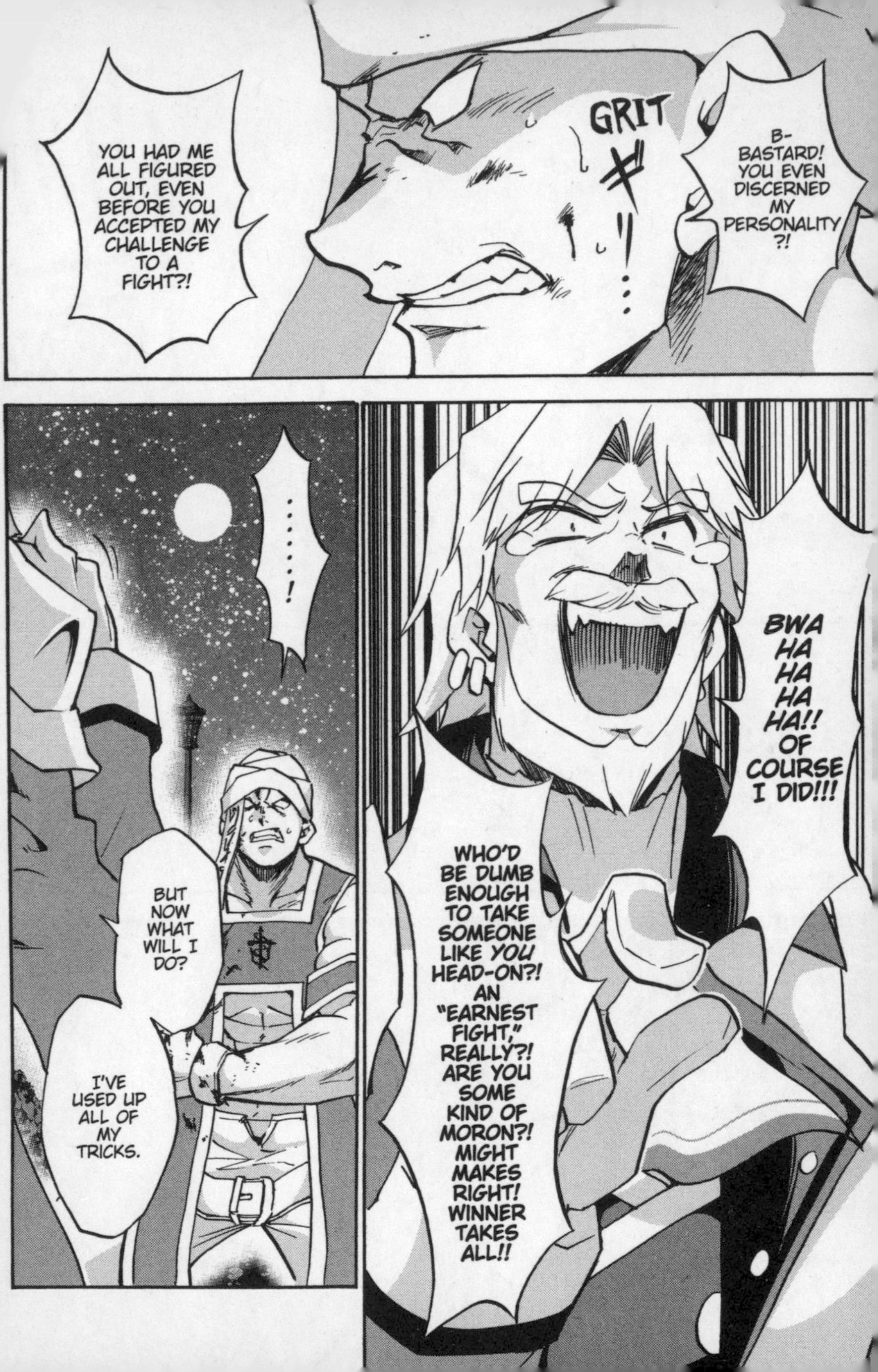
GRIT
B-BASTARD! YOU EVEN DISCERNED MY PERSONALITY?!
YOU HAD ME ALL FIGURED OUT, EVEN BEFORE YOU ACCEPTED MY CHALLENGE TO A FIGHT?!
BWA HA HA HA HA!! OF COURSE I DID!!!
WHO'D BE DUMB ENOUGH TO TAKE SOMEONE LIKE *YOU* HEAD-ON?! AN "EARNEST FIGHT," REALLY?! ARE YOU SOME KIND OF MORON?! MIGHT MAKES RIGHT! WINNER TAKES ALL!!
......!
BUT NOW WHAT WILL I DO?
I'VE USED UP ALL OF MY TRICKS.

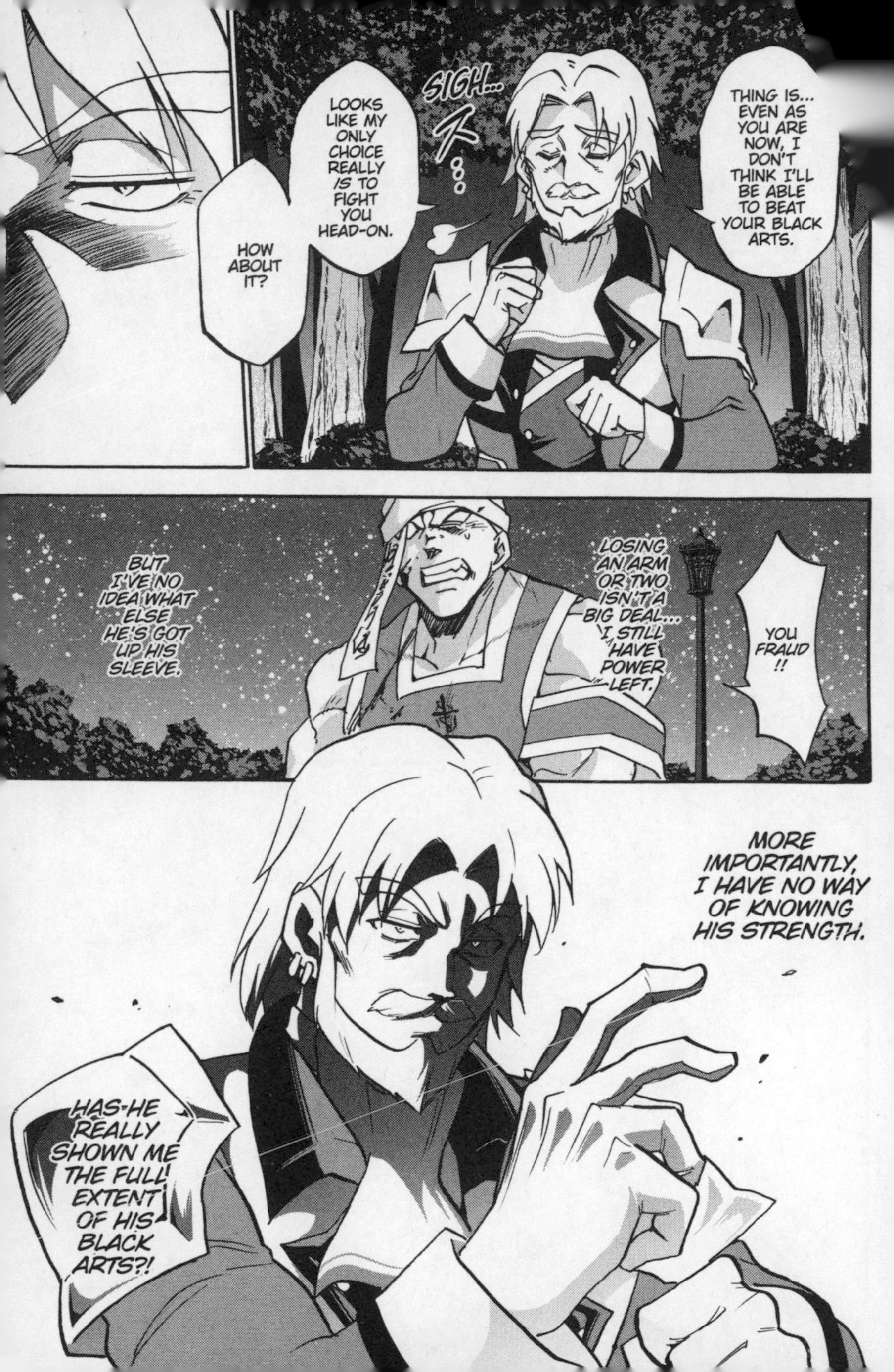
THING IS... EVEN AS YOU ARE NOW, I DON'T THINK I'LL BE ABLE TO BEAT YOUR BLACK ARTS.
SIGH...
LOOKS LIKE MY ONLY CHOICE REALLY IS TO FIGHT YOU HEAD-ON.
HOW ABOUT IT?
YOU FRAUD !!
LOSING AN ARM OR TWO ISN'T A BIG DEAL... I STILL HAVE POWER LEFT.
BUT I'VE NO IDEA WHAT ELSE HE'S GOT UP HIS SLEEVE.
MORE IMPORTANTLY, I HAVE NO WAY OF KNOWING HIS STRENGTH.
HAS HE REALLY SHOWN ME THE FULL EXTENT OF HIS BLACK ARTS?!

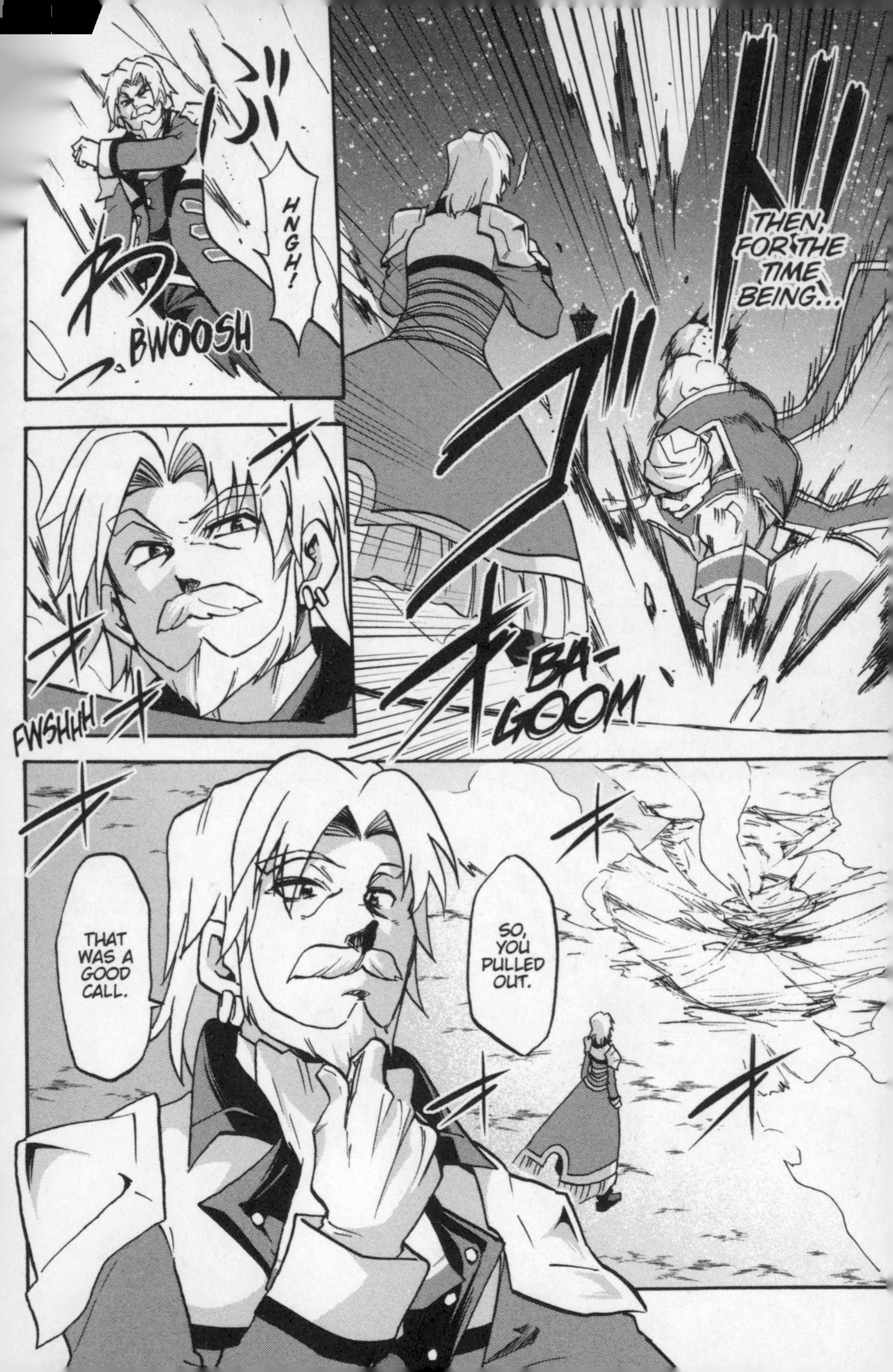
THEN, FOR THE TIME BEING...
BA-GOOM
HNGH!
BWOOSH
FWSHHH
SO, YOU PULLED OUT.
THAT WAS A GOOD CALL.

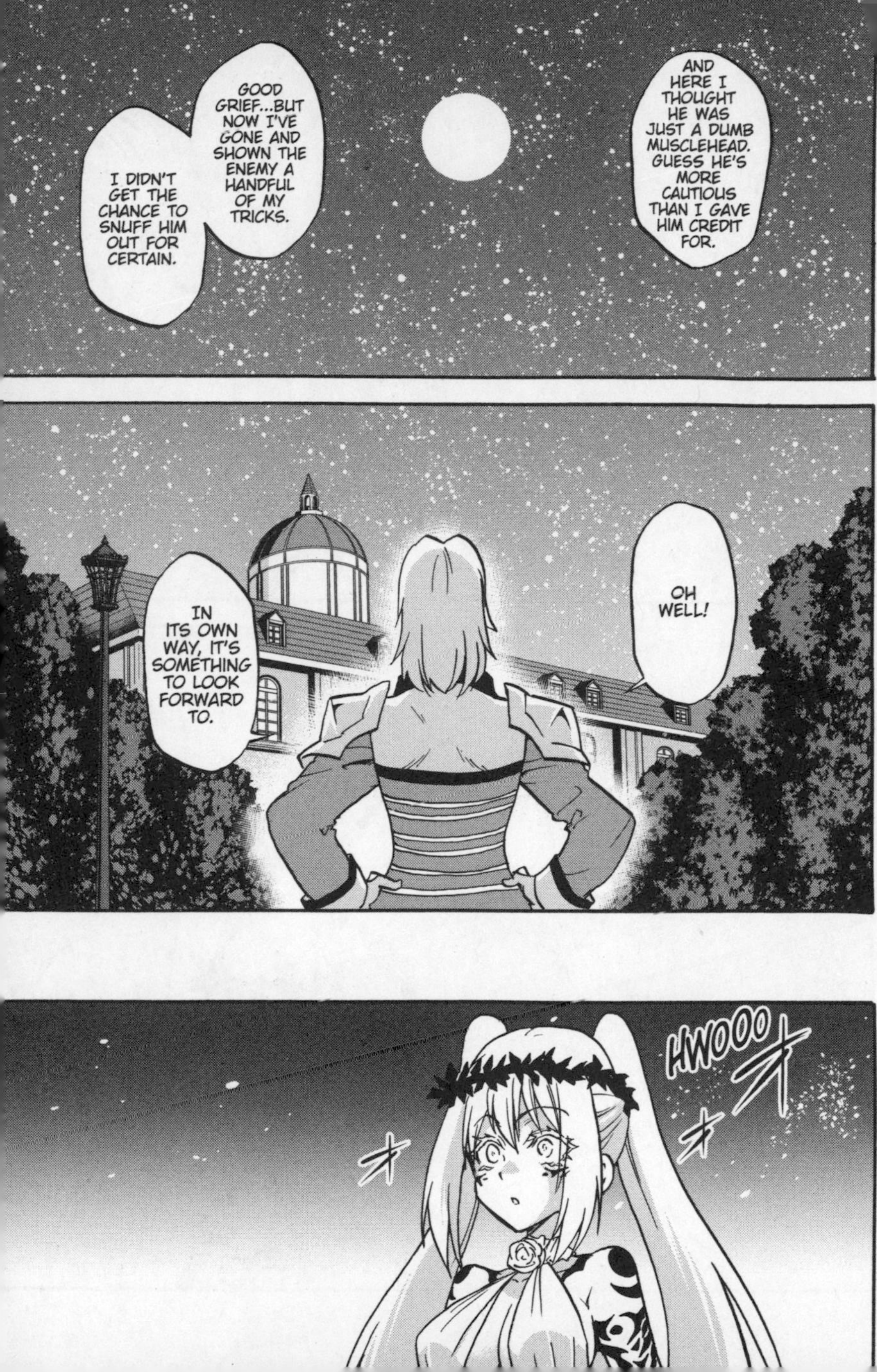
AND HERE I THOUGHT HE WAS JUST A DUMB MUSCLEHEAD. GUESS HE'S MORE CAUTIOUS THAN I GAVE HIM CREDIT FOR.
GOOD GRIEF...BUT NOW I'VE GONE AND SHOWN THE ENEMY A HANDFUL OF MY TRICKS.
I DIDN'T GET THE CHANCE TO SNUFF HIM OUT FOR CERTAIN.
OH WELL!
IN ITS OWN WAY, IT'S SOMETHING TO LOOK FORWARD TO.
HWOOO
オ
オ
オ

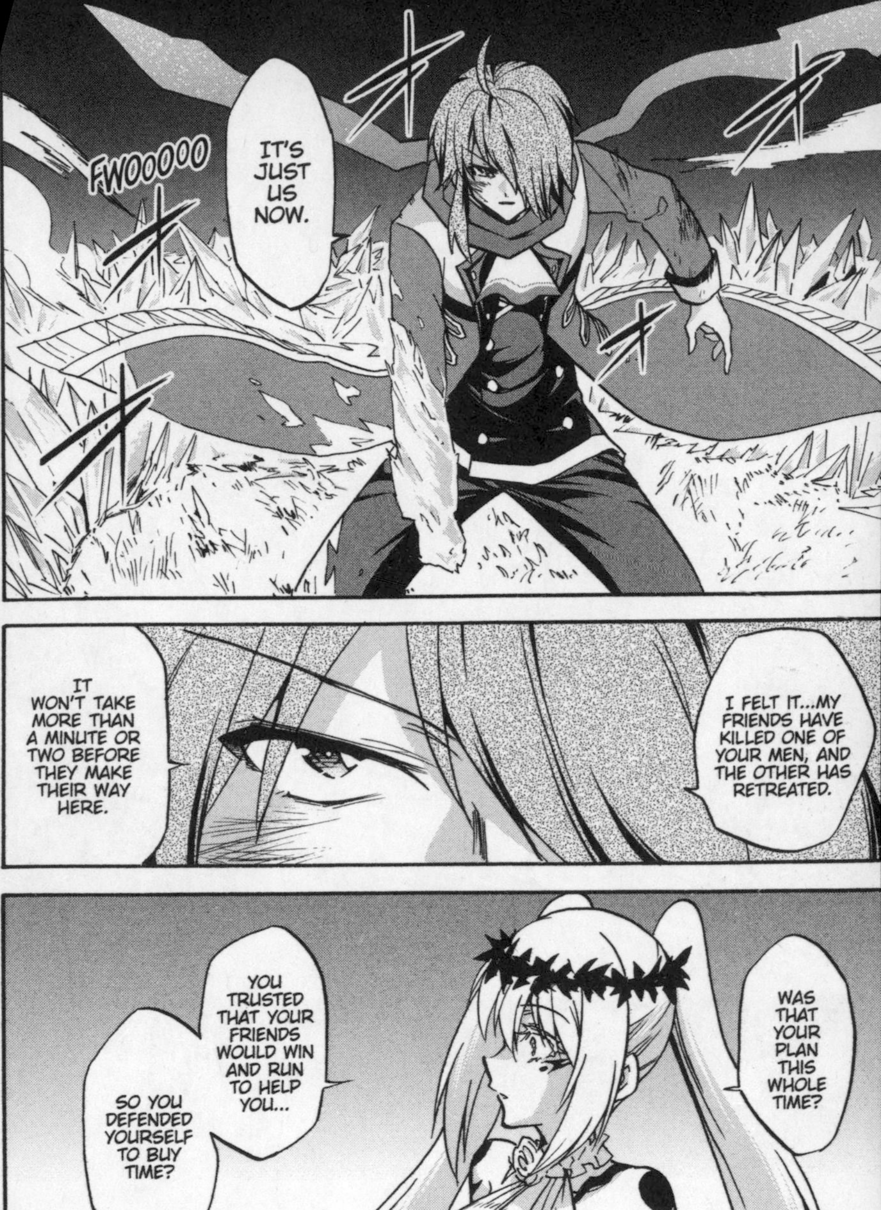
IT'S JUST US NOW.
FWOOOOO
I FELT IT...MY FRIENDS HAVE KILLED ONE OF YOUR MEN, AND THE OTHER HAS RETREATED.
IT WON'T TAKE MORE THAN A MINUTE OR TWO BEFORE THEY MAKE THEIR WAY HERE.
WAS THAT YOUR PLAN THIS WHOLE TIME?
YOU TRUSTED THAT YOUR FRIENDS WOULD WIN AND RUN TO HELP YOU...
SO YOU DEFENDED YOURSELF TO BUY TIME?

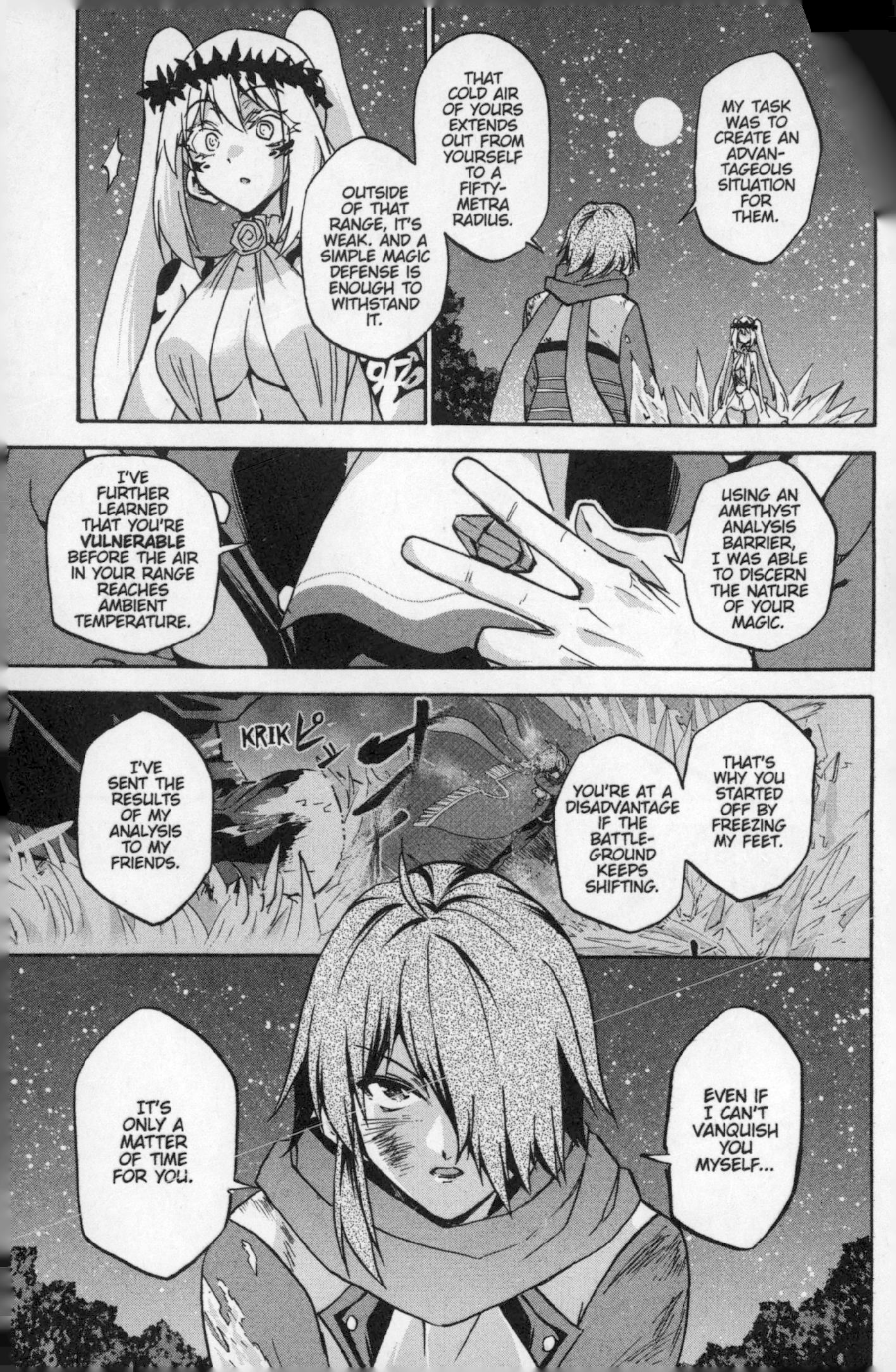
MY TASK WAS TO CREATE AN ADVANTAGEOUS SITUATION FOR THEM.
THAT COLD AIR OF YOURS EXTENDS OUT FROM YOURSELF TO A FIFTY-METRA RADIUS.
OUTSIDE OF THAT RANGE, IT'S WEAK. AND A SIMPLE MAGIC DEFENSE IS ENOUGH TO WITHSTAND IT.
USING AN AMETHYST ANALYSIS BARRIER, I WAS ABLE TO DISCERN THE NATURE OF YOUR MAGIC.
I'VE FURTHER LEARNED THAT YOU'RE **VULNERABLE** BEFORE THE AIR IN YOUR RANGE REACHES AMBIENT TEMPERATURE.
THAT'S WHY YOU STARTED OFF BY FREEZING MY FEET.
YOU'RE AT A DISADVANTAGE IF THE BATTLEGROUND KEEPS SHIFTING.
KRIK
I'VE SENT THE RESULTS OF MY ANALYSIS TO MY FRIENDS.
EVEN IF I CAN'T VANQUISH YOU MYSELF...
IT'S ONLY A MATTER OF TIME FOR YOU.

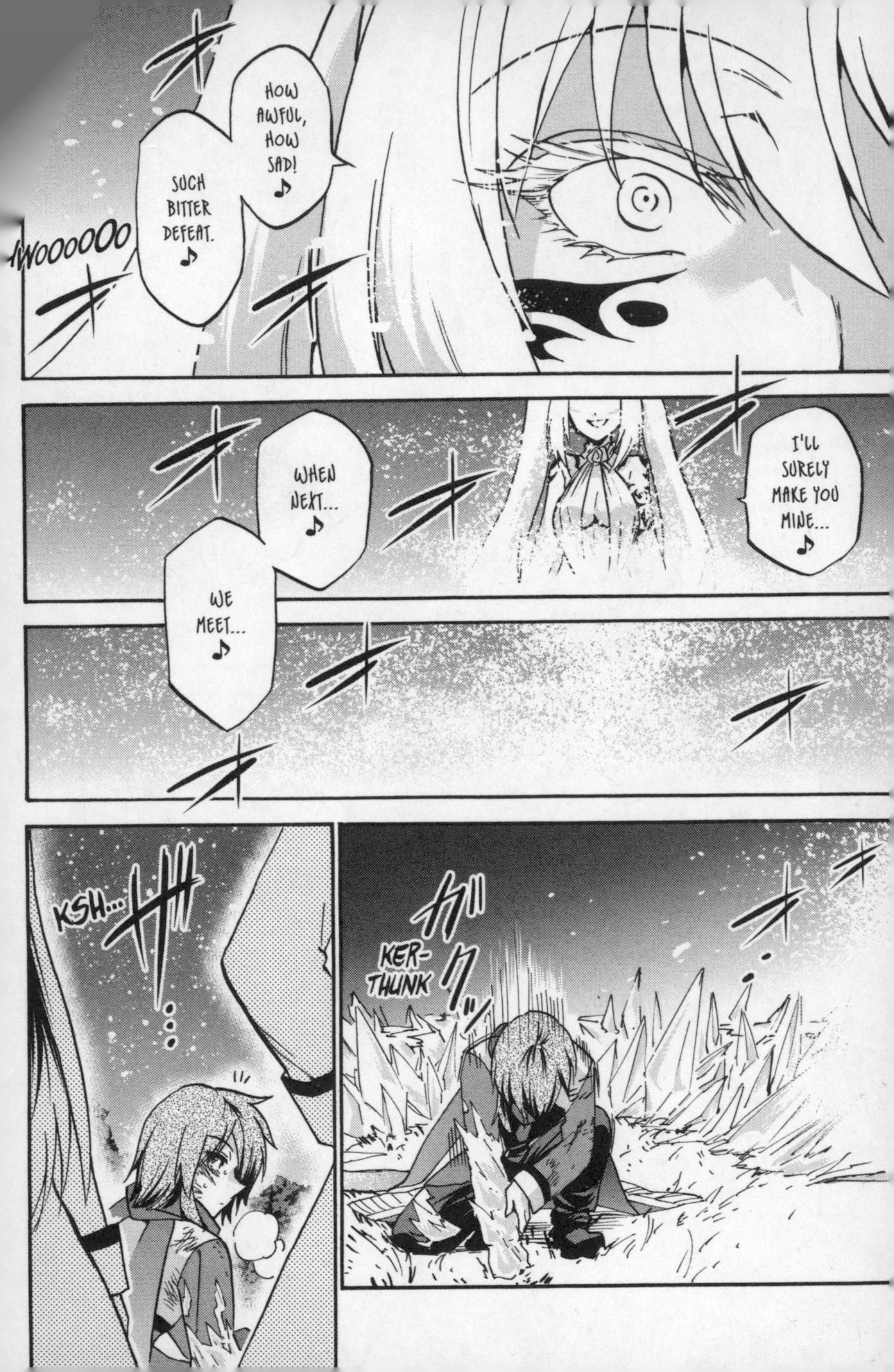

HOW AWFUL, HOW SAD! ♪
SUCH BITTER DEFEAT. ♪
WOOOOOO
I'LL SURELY MAKE YOU MINE... ♪
WHEN NEXT... ♪
WE MEET... ♪
KER-THUNK
KSH...
...

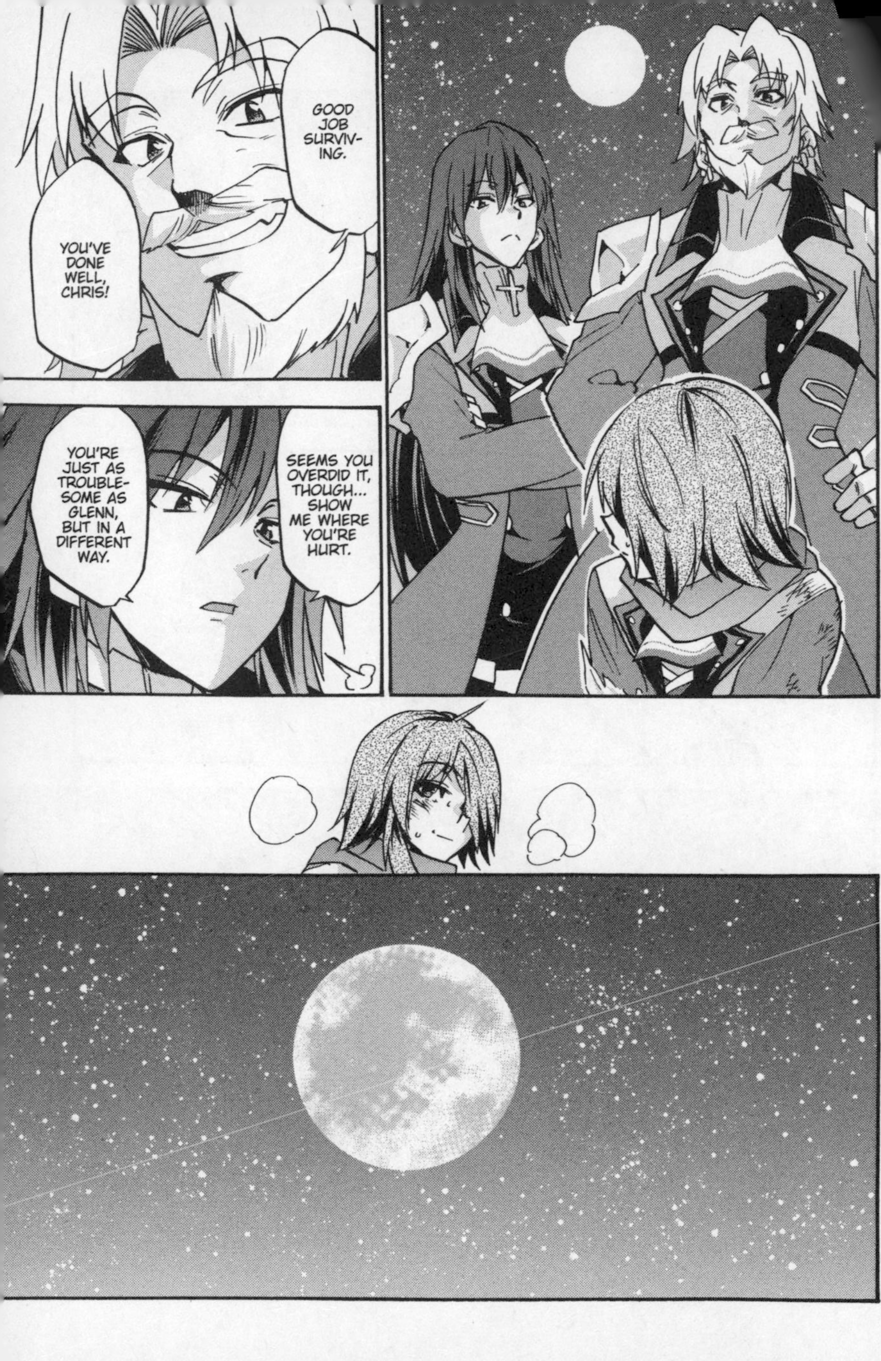
GOOD JOB SURVIV-ING.
YOU'VE DONE WELL, CHRIS!
SEEMS YOU OVERDID IT, THOUGH... SHOW ME WHERE YOU'RE HURT.
YOU'RE JUST AS TROUBLE-SOME AS GLENN, BUT IN A DIFFERENT WAY.

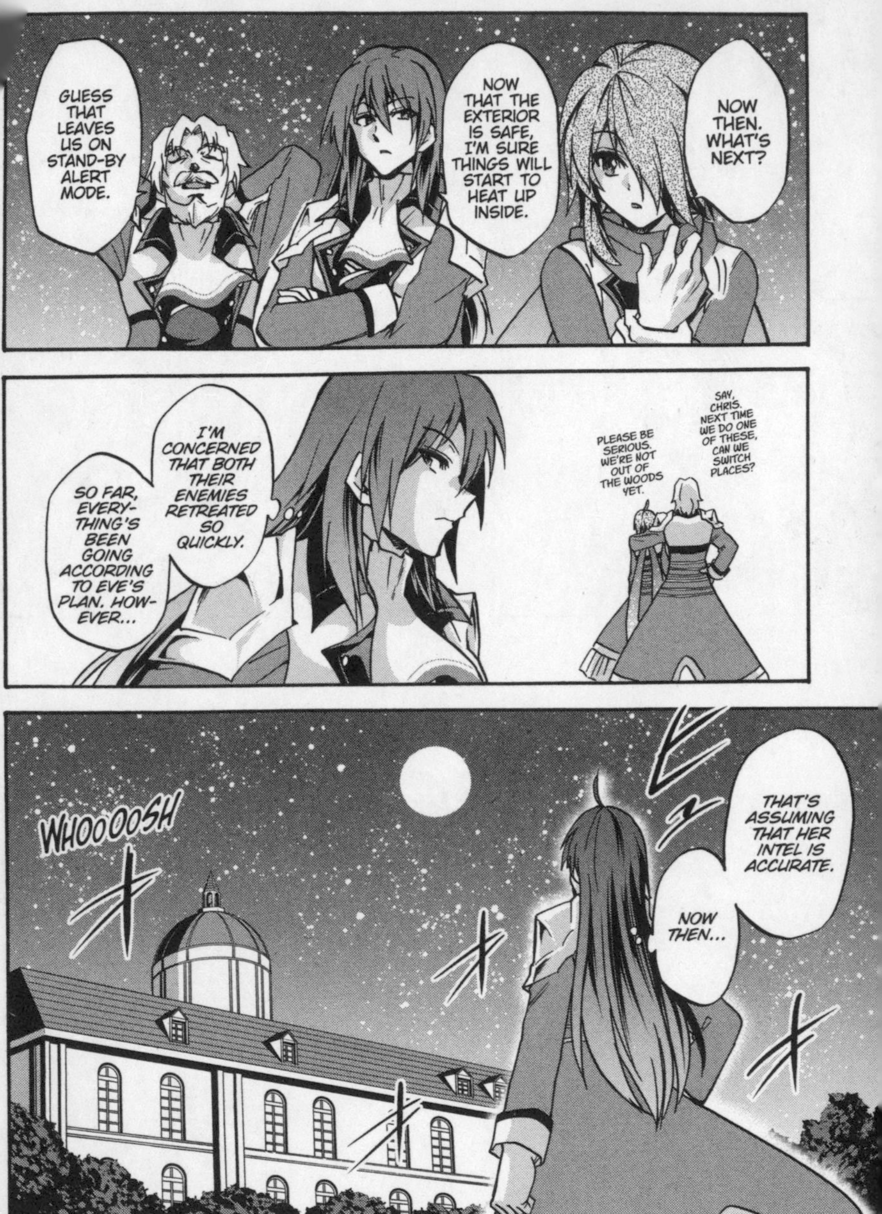
NOW THEN. WHAT'S NEXT?
NOW THAT THE EXTERIOR IS SAFE, I'M SURE THINGS WILL START TO HEAT UP INSIDE.
GUESS THAT LEAVES US ON STAND-BY ALERT MODE.
SAY, CHRIS. NEXT TIME WE DO ONE OF THESE, CAN WE SWITCH PLACES?
PLEASE BE SERIOUS. WE'RE NOT OUT OF THE WOODS YET.
SO FAR, EVERYTHING'S BEEN GOING ACCORDING TO EVE'S PLAN. HOWEVER...
I'M CONCERNED THAT BOTH THEIR ENEMIES RETREATED SO QUICKLY.
THAT'S ASSUMING THAT HER INTEL IS ACCURATE.
NOW THEN...
WHOOOOSH

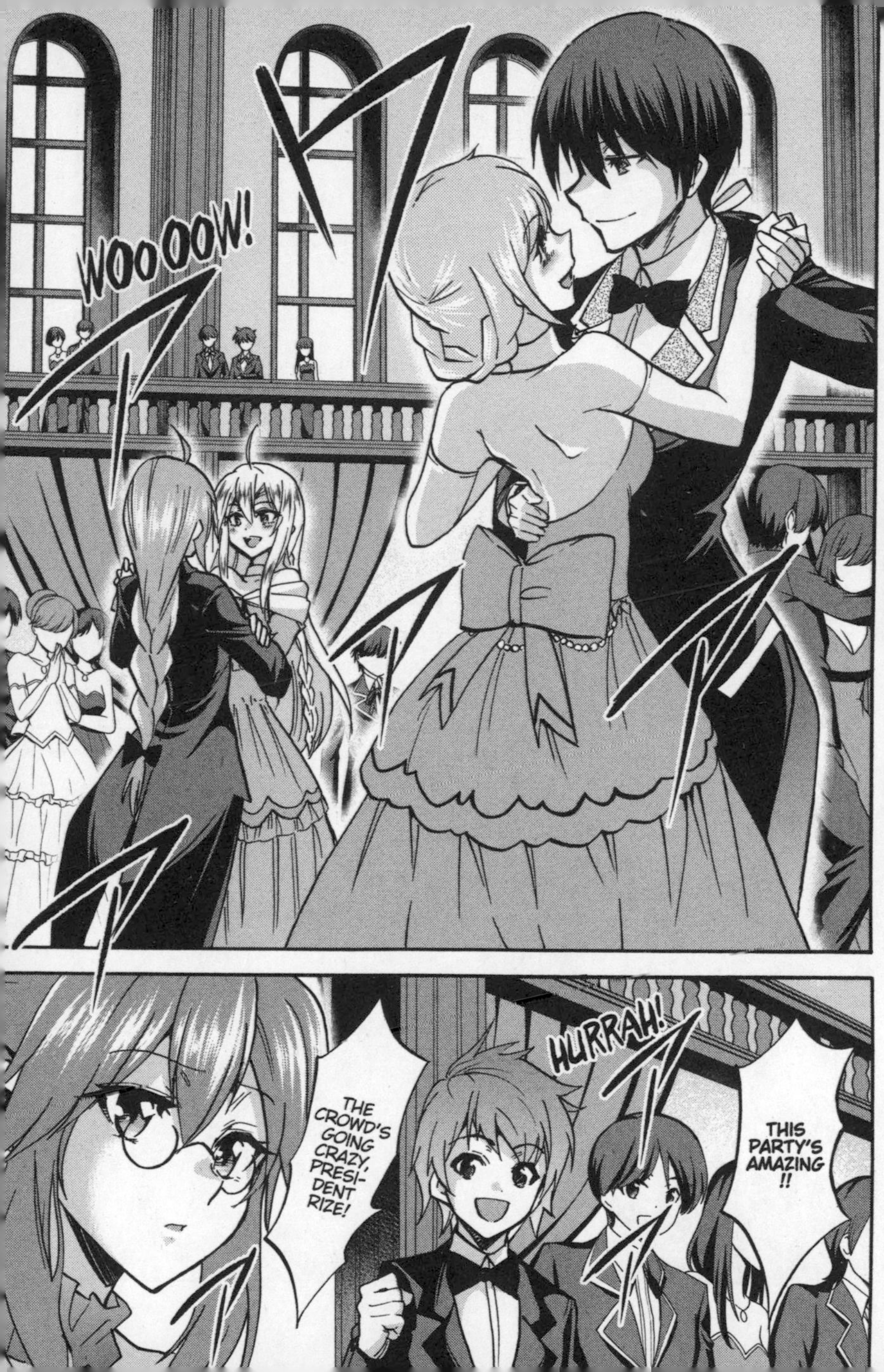
WOO OOW!
THIS PARTY'S AMAZING !!
HURRAH!
THE CROWD'S GOING CRAZY, PRESI-DENT RIZE!

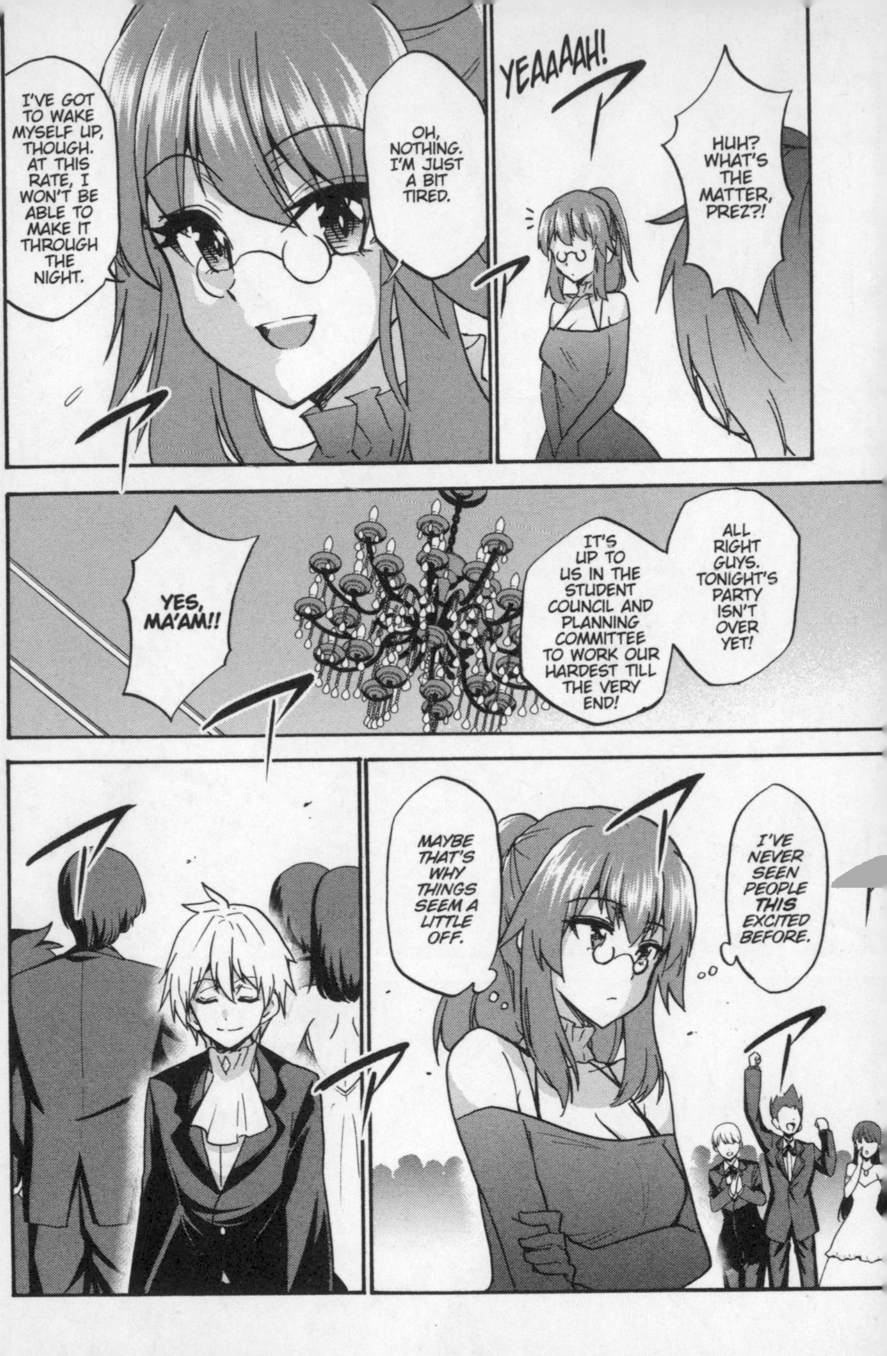
HUH? WHAT'S THE MATTER, PREZ?!
YEAAAAH!
OH, NOTHING. I'M JUST A BIT TIRED.
I'VE GOT TO WAKE MYSELF UP, THOUGH. AT THIS RATE, I WON'T BE ABLE TO MAKE IT THROUGH THE NIGHT.
ALL RIGHT GUYS. TONIGHT'S PARTY ISN'T OVER YET!
IT'S UP TO US IN THE STUDENT COUNCIL AND PLANNING COMMITTEE TO WORK OUR HARDEST TILL THE VERY END!
YES, MA'AM!!
I'VE NEVER SEEN PEOPLE THIS EXCITED BEFORE.
MAYBE THAT'S WHY THINGS SEEM A LITTLE OFF.

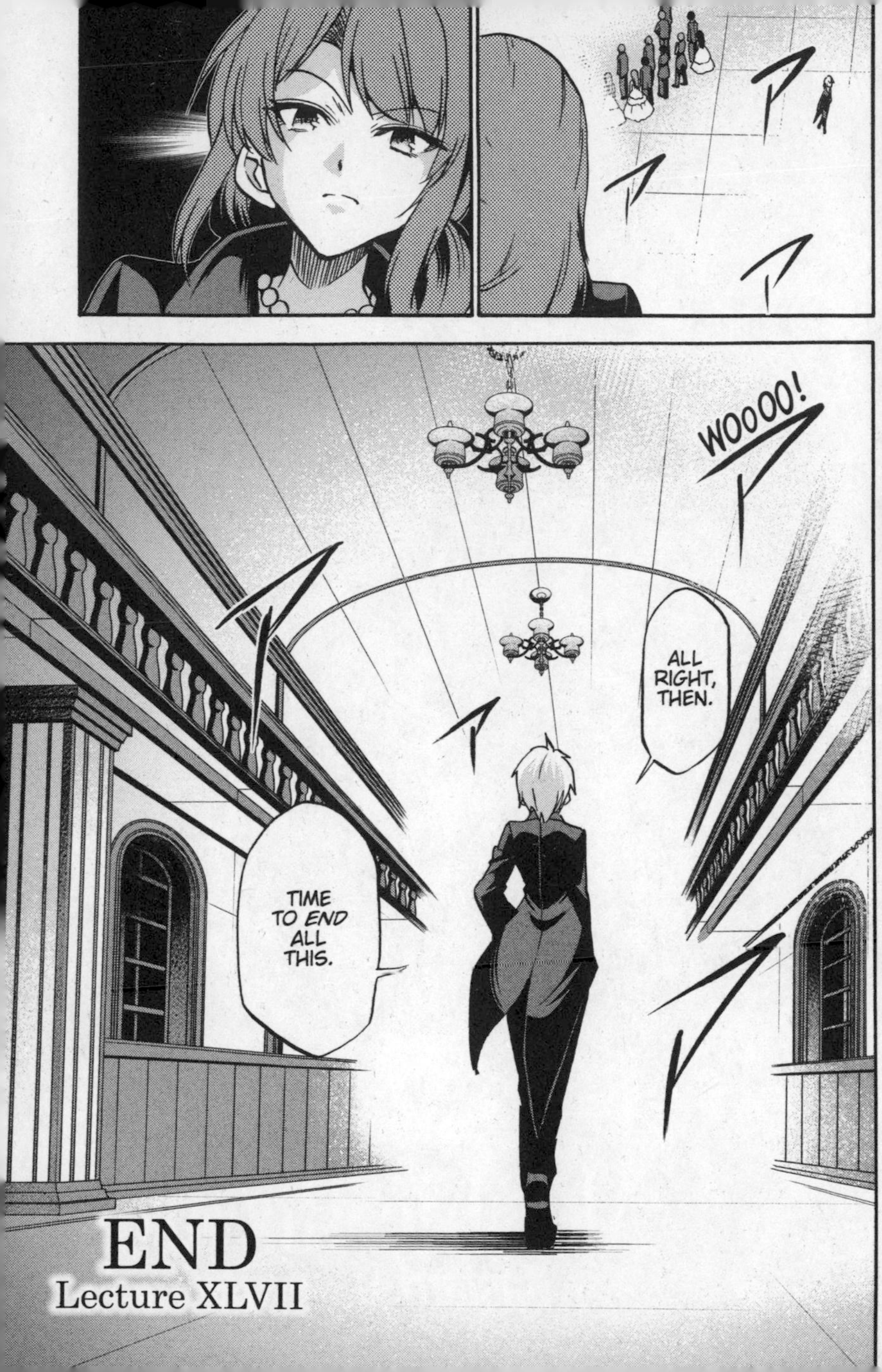
WOOOO!
ALL RIGHT, THEN.
TIME TO *END* ALL THIS.

END
Lecture XLVII

Akashic Records

of *Bastard* Magic *Instructor*

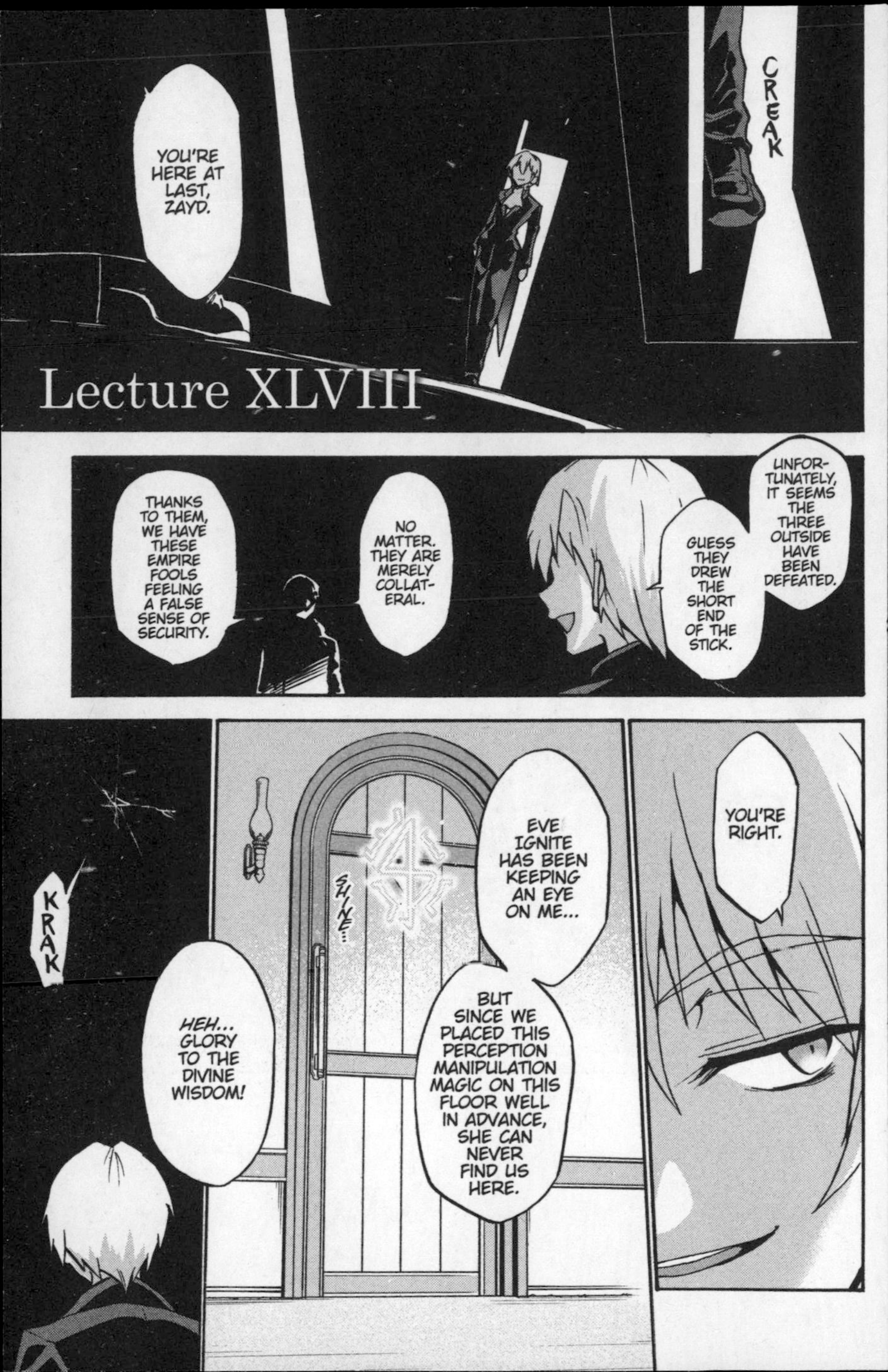
CREAK
YOU'RE HERE AT LAST, ZAYD.
Lecture XLVIII
UNFORTUNATELY, IT SEEMS THE THREE OUTSIDE HAVE BEEN DEFEATED.
GUESS THEY DREW THE SHORT END OF THE STICK.
NO MATTER. THEY ARE MERELY COLLATERAL.
THANKS TO THEM, WE HAVE THESE EMPIRE FOOLS FEELING A FALSE SENSE OF SECURITY.
YOU'RE RIGHT.
EVE IGNITE HAS BEEN KEEPING AN EYE ON ME...
BUT SINCE WE PLACED THIS PERCEPTION MANIPULATION MAGIC ON THIS FLOOR WELL IN ADVANCE, SHE CAN NEVER FIND US HERE.
SHINE...
KRAK
HEH... GLORY TO THE DIVINE WISDOM!

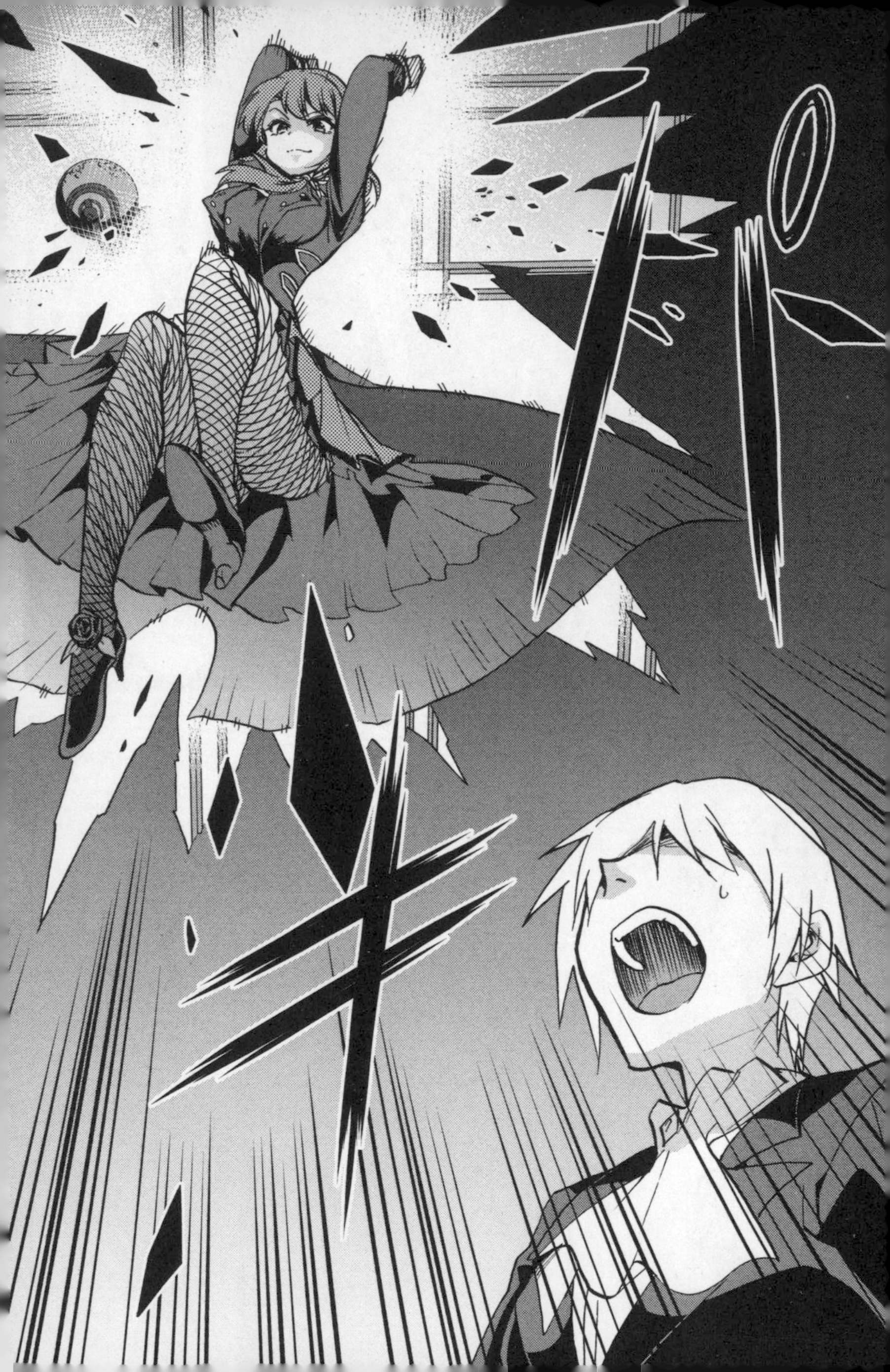
パ
キ

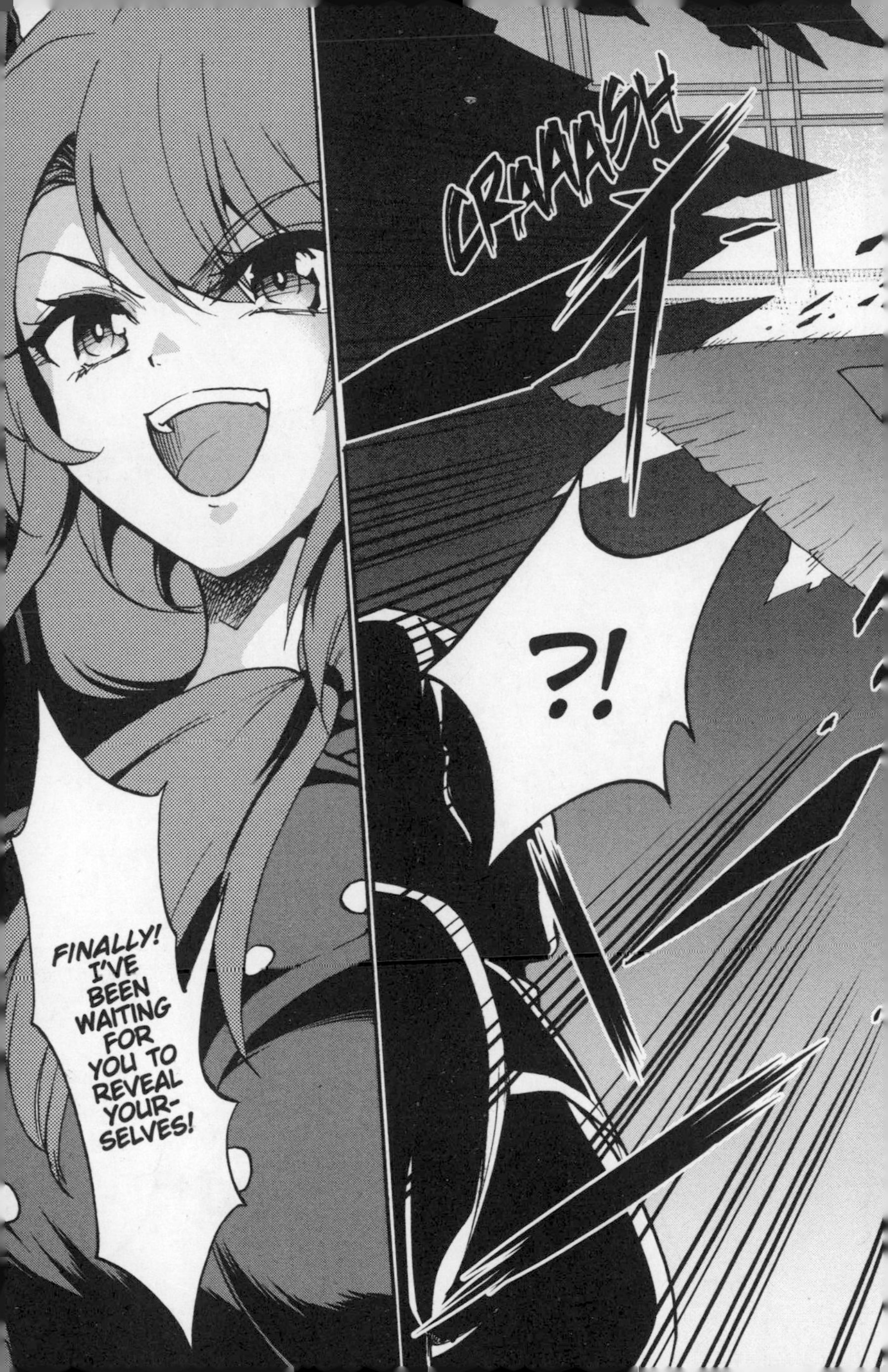
CRAAASH
?!
FINALLY! I'VE BEEN WAITING FOR YOU TO REVEAL YOUR-SELVES!

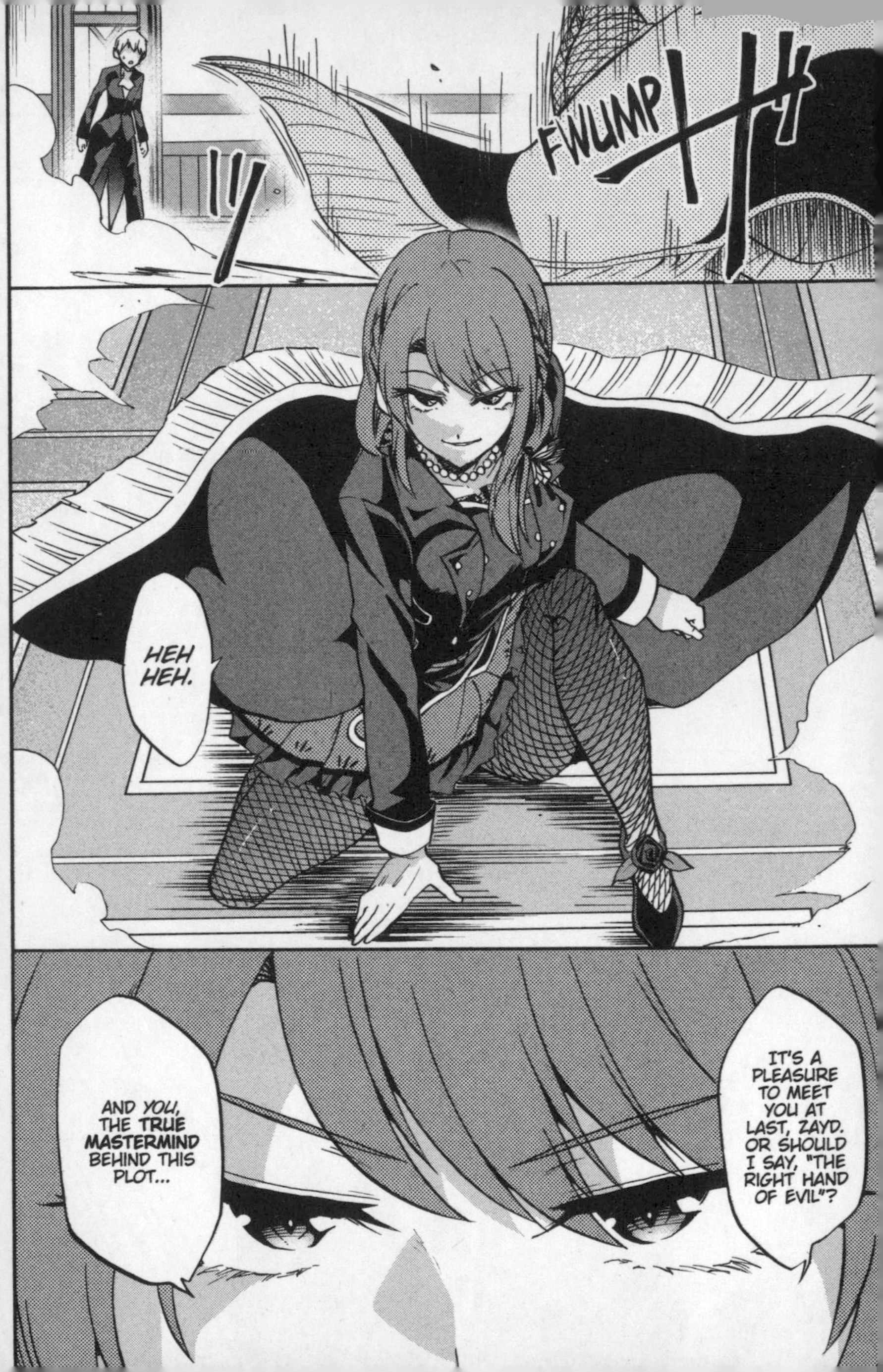
FWUMP
HEH HEH.
IT'S A PLEASURE TO MEET YOU AT LAST, ZAYD. OR SHOULD I SAY, "THE RIGHT HAND OF EVIL"?
AND *YOU*, THE **TRUE MASTERMIND** BEHIND THIS PLOT...

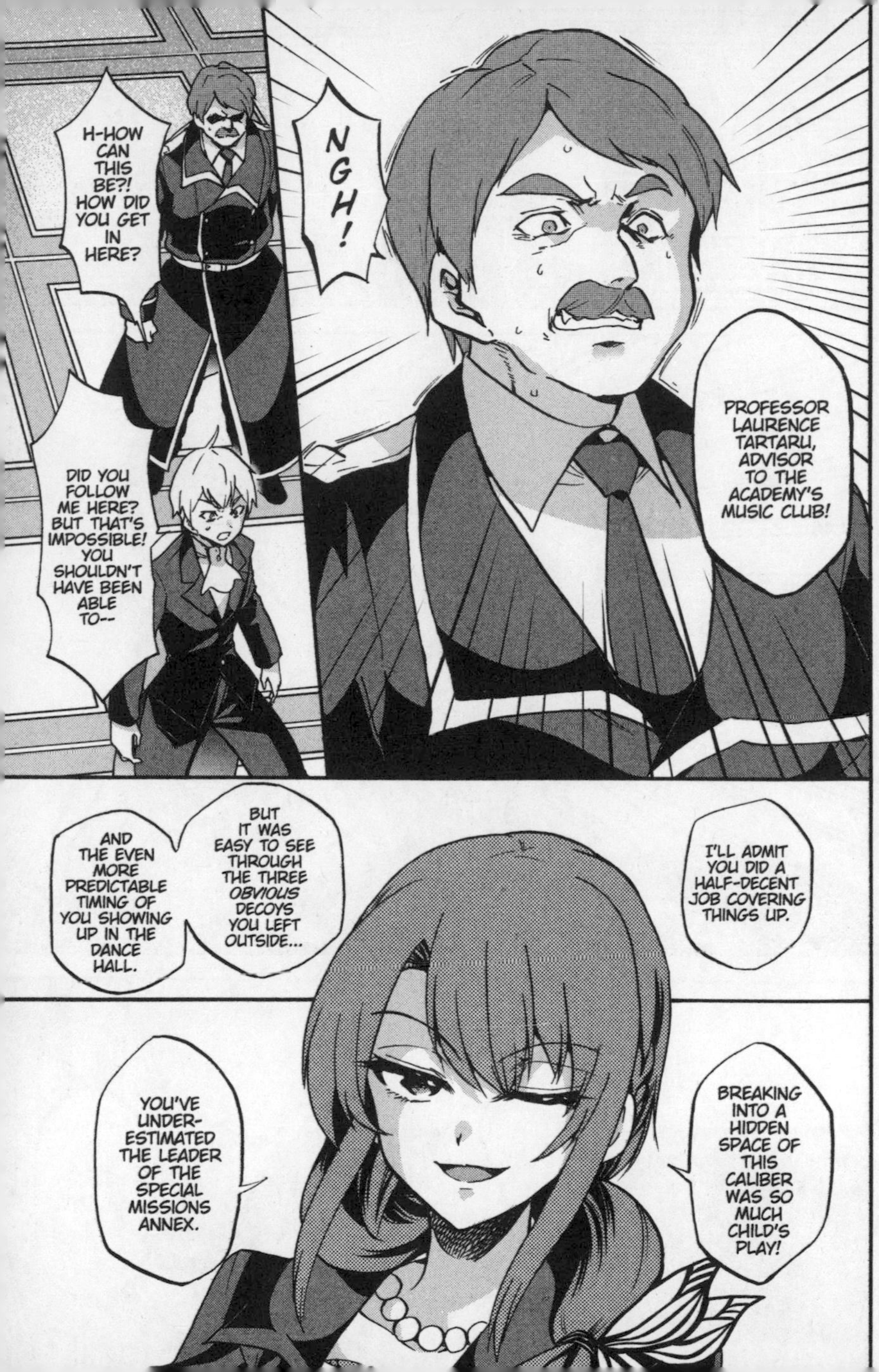
NGH!
PROFESSOR LAURENCE TARTARU, ADVISOR TO THE ACADEMY'S MUSIC CLUB!
H-HOW CAN THIS BE?! HOW DID YOU GET IN HERE?
DID YOU FOLLOW ME HERE? BUT THAT'S IMPOSSIBLE! YOU SHOULDN'T HAVE BEEN ABLE TO--
I'LL ADMIT YOU DID A HALF-DECENT JOB COVERING THINGS UP.
BUT IT WAS EASY TO SEE THROUGH THE THREE *OBVIOUS* DECOYS YOU LEFT OUTSIDE...
AND THE EVEN MORE PREDICTABLE TIMING OF YOU SHOWING UP IN THE DANCE HALL.
BREAKING INTO A HIDDEN SPACE OF THIS CALIBER WAS SO MUCH CHILD'S PLAY!
YOU'VE UNDER-ESTIMATED THE LEADER OF THE SPECIAL MISSIONS ANNEX.

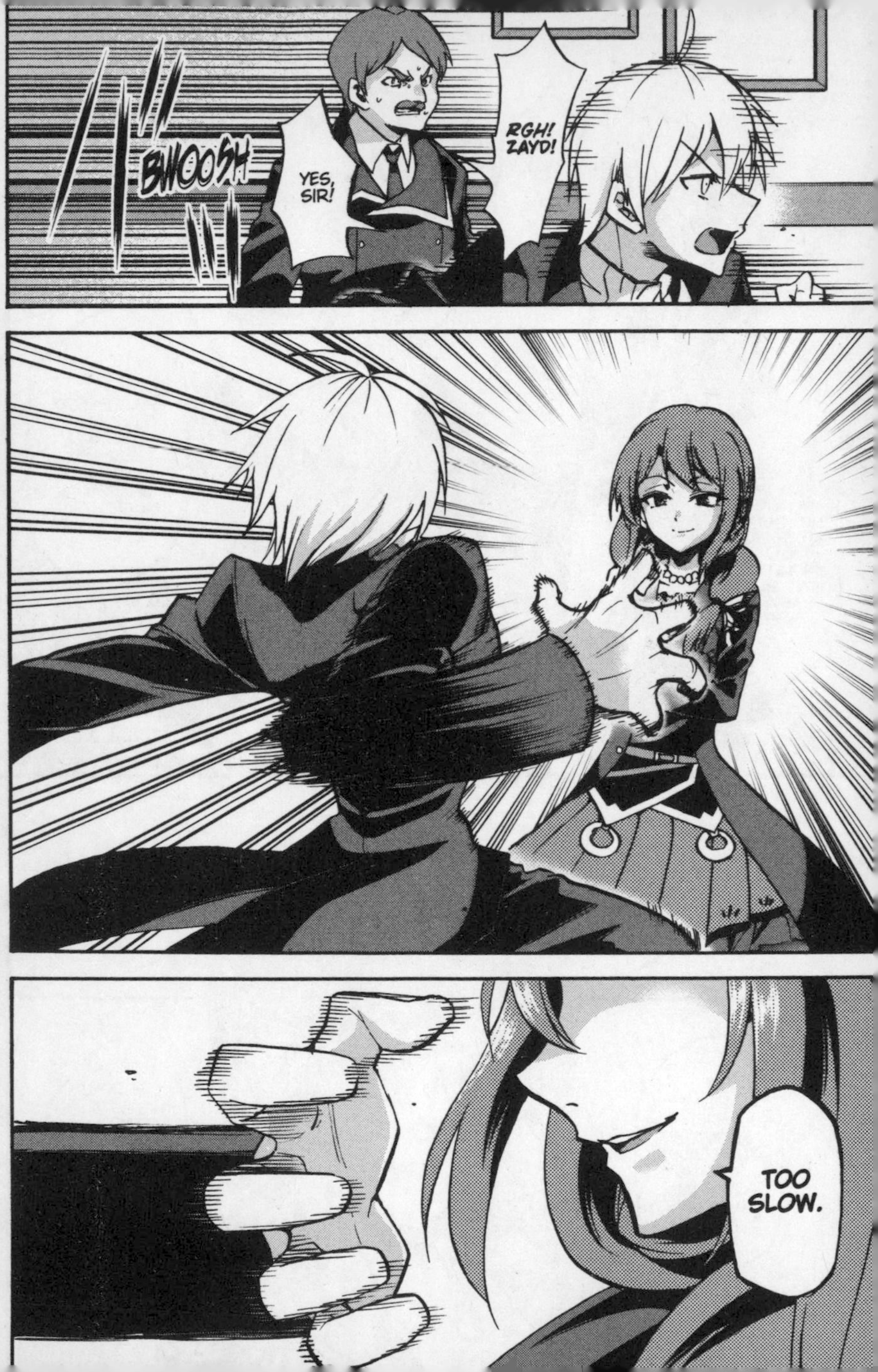
RGH! ZAYD!
YES, SIR!
BWOOSH
TOO SLOW.

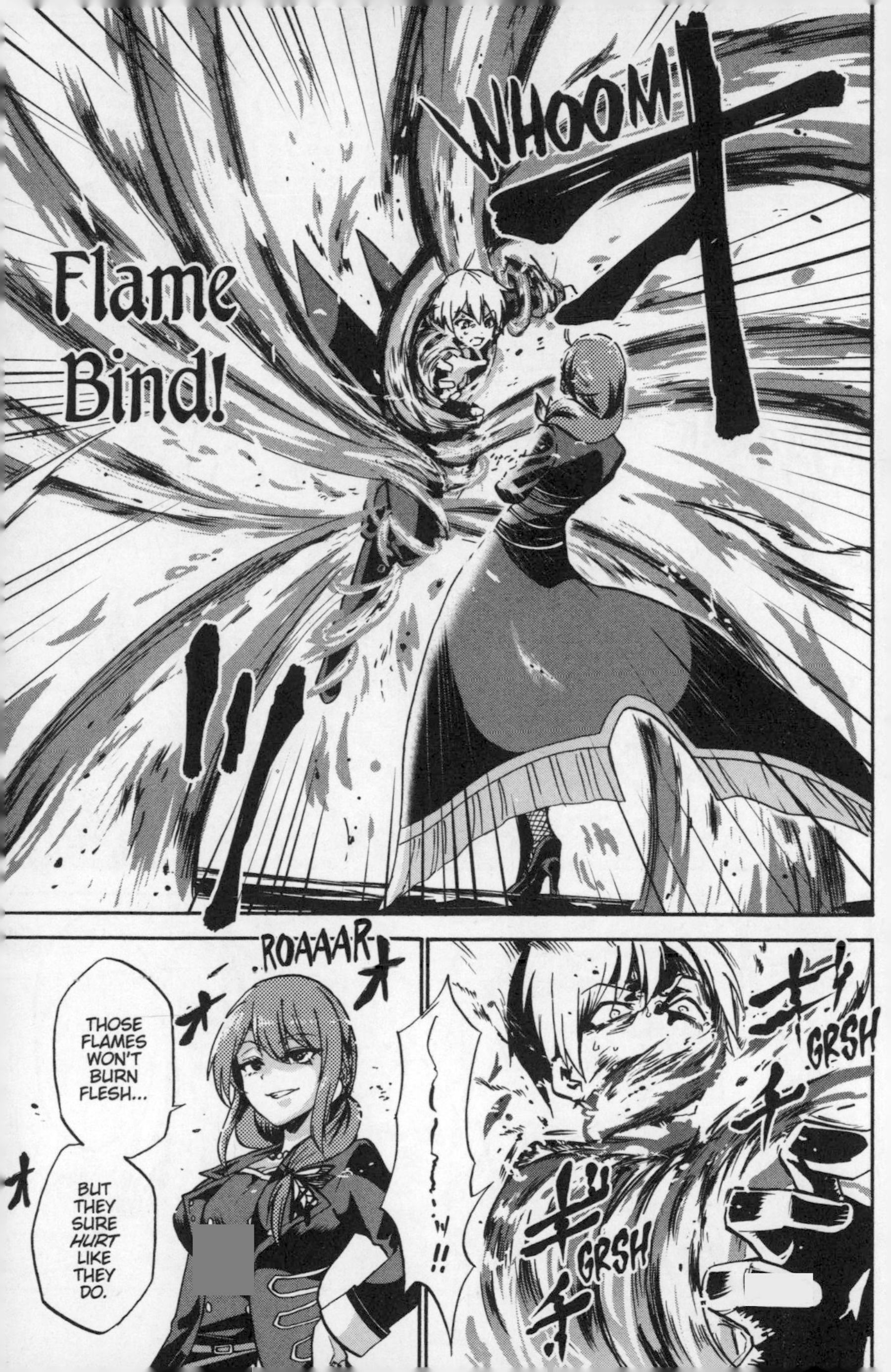

WHOOM
Flame Bind!
GRSH
GRSH
...!!
ROAAAR
THOSE FLAMES WON'T BURN FLESH...
BUT THEY SURE *HURT* LIKE THEY DO.

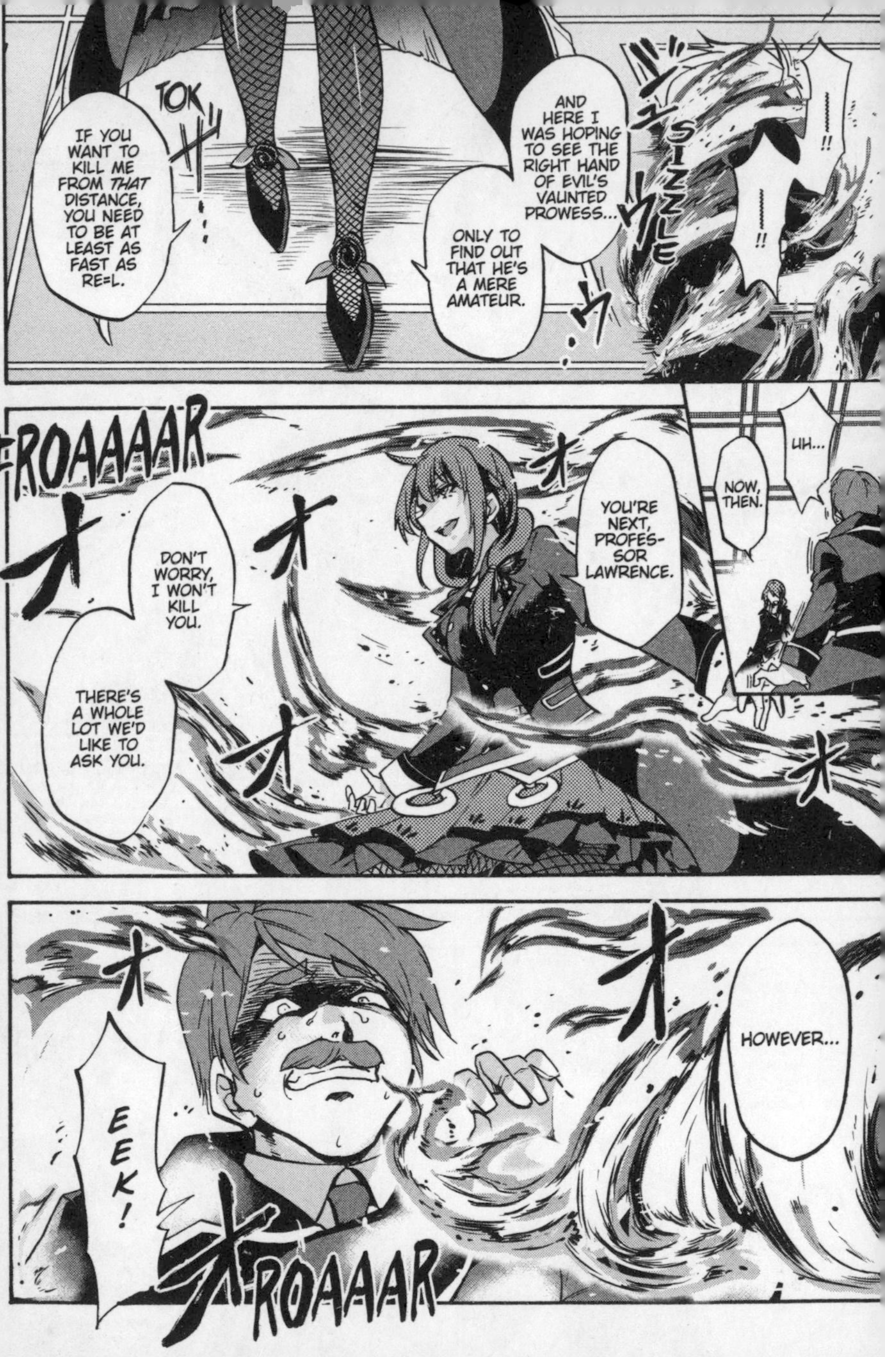

……!!
……!!
SIZZLE
AND HERE I WAS HOPING TO SEE THE RIGHT HAND OF EVIL'S VAUNTED PROWESS…
ONLY TO FIND OUT THAT HE'S A MERE AMATEUR.
TOK
IF YOU WANT TO KILL ME FROM *THAT* DISTANCE, YOU NEED TO BE AT LEAST AS FAST AS RE=L.
UH…
NOW, THEN.
YOU'RE NEXT, PROFESSOR LAWRENCE.
FROAAAAR
DON'T WORRY, I WON'T KILL YOU.
THERE'S A WHOLE LOT WE'D LIKE TO ASK YOU.
HOWEVER…
EEK!
ROAAAR

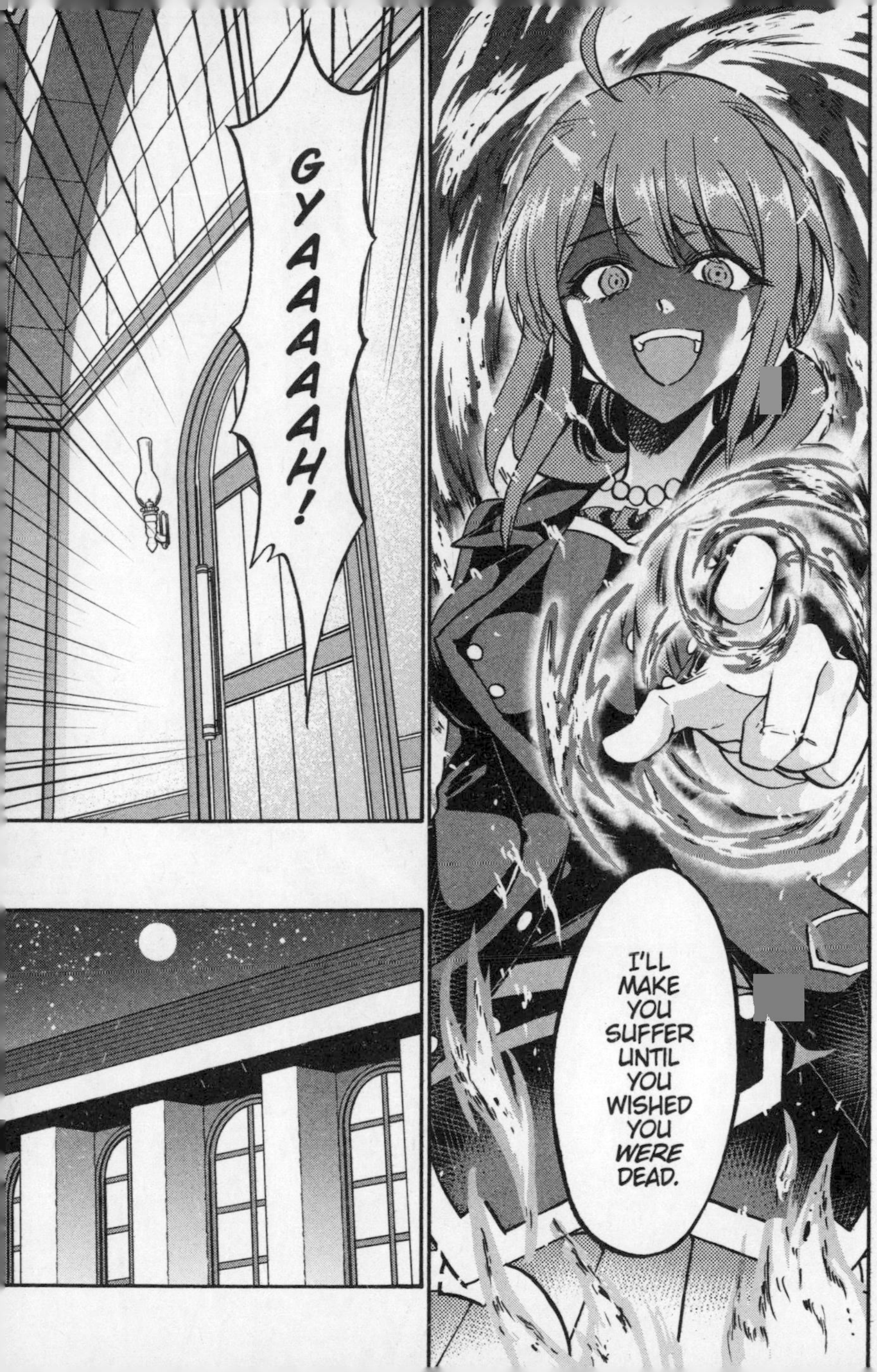
I'LL MAKE YOU SUFFER UNTIL YOU WISHED YOU *WERE* DEAD.
GYAAAAAH!

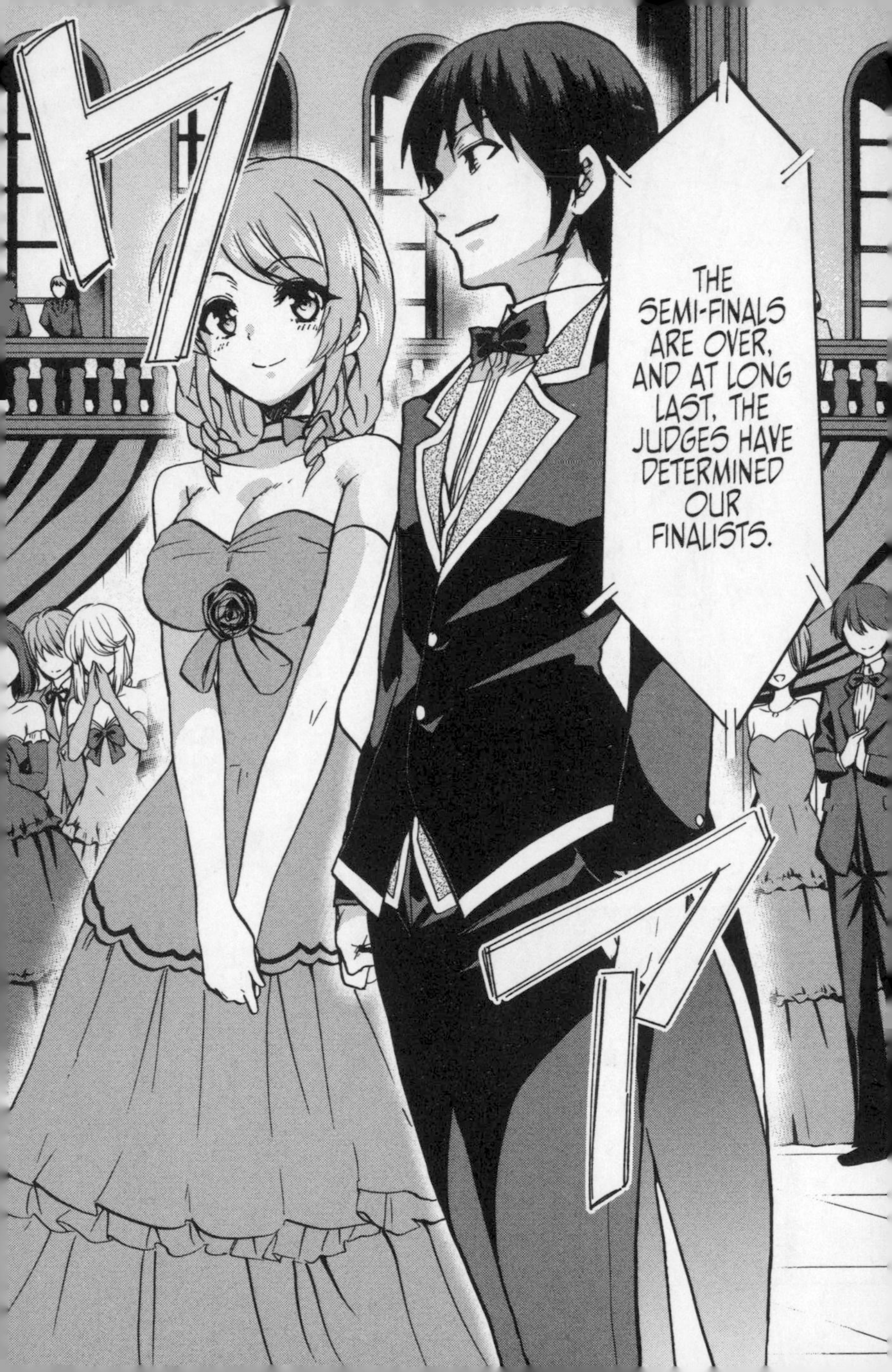
THE SEMI-FINALS ARE OVER, AND AT LONG LAST, THE JUDGES HAVE DETERMINED OUR FINALISTS.

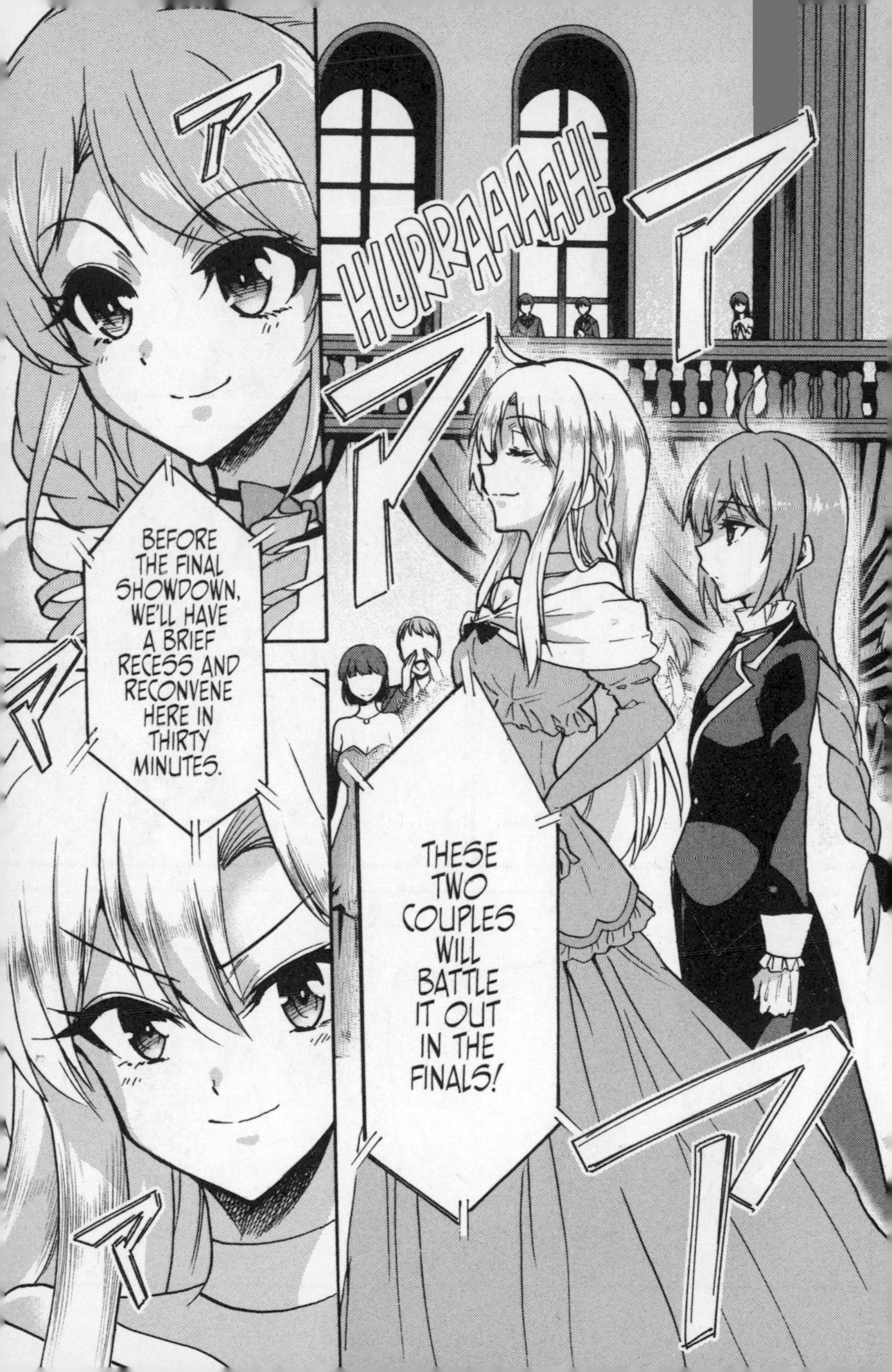
HURRAAAAH!
THESE TWO COUPLES WILL BATTLE IT OUT IN THE FINALS!
BEFORE THE FINAL SHOWDOWN, WE'LL HAVE A BRIEF RECESS AND RECONVENE HERE IN THIRTY MINUTES.

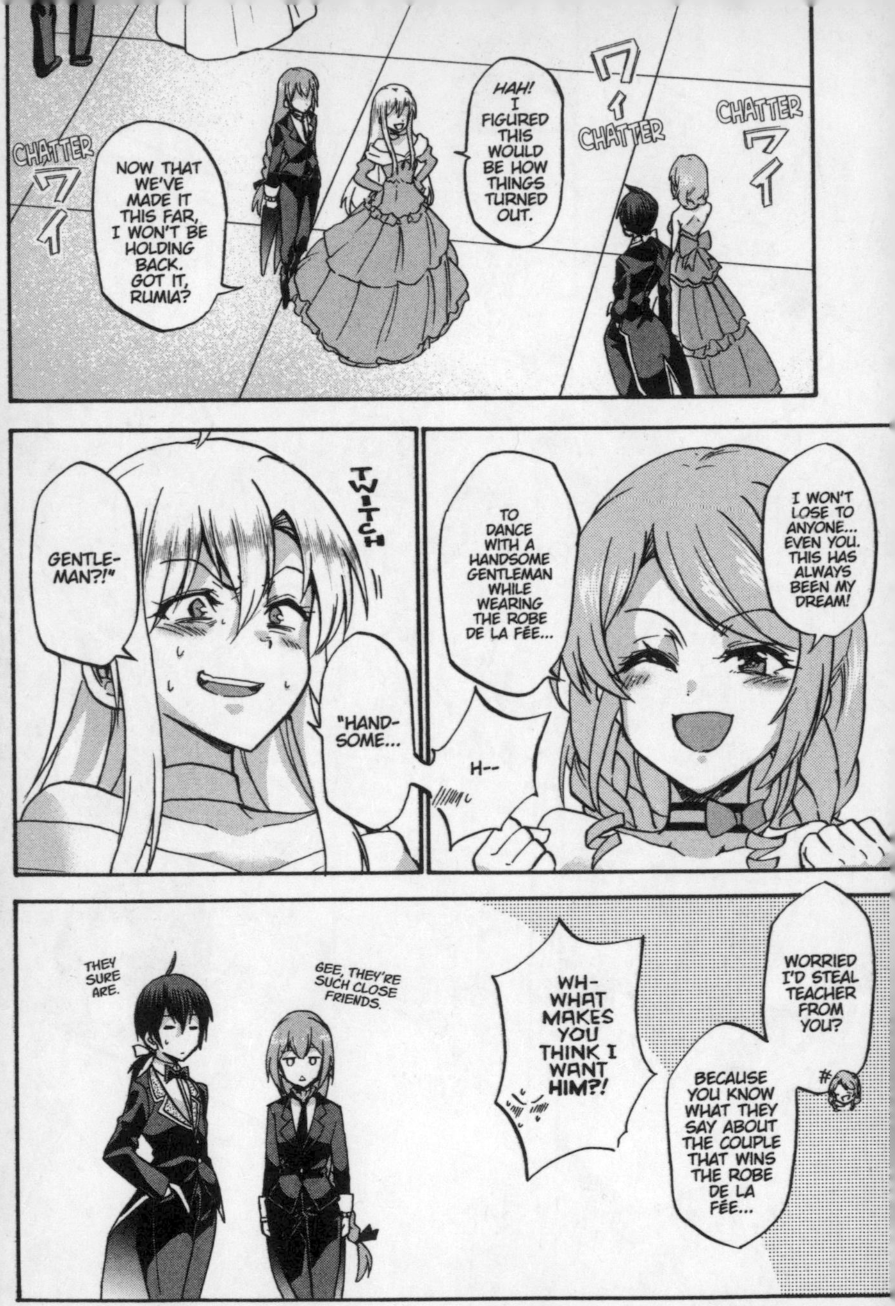
CHATTER ワイ
CHATTER ワイ
HAH! I FIGURED THIS WOULD BE HOW THINGS TURNED OUT.
NOW THAT WE'VE MADE IT THIS FAR, I WON'T BE HOLDING BACK. GOT IT, RUMIA?
CHATTER ワイ
I WON'T LOSE TO ANYONE... EVEN YOU. THIS HAS ALWAYS BEEN MY DREAM!
TO DANCE WITH A HANDSOME GENTLEMAN WHILE WEARING THE ROBE DE LA FÉE...
H--
TWITCH
"HAND-SOME...
GENTLE-MAN?!"
WORRIED I'D STEAL TEACHER FROM YOU?
BECAUSE YOU KNOW WHAT THEY SAY ABOUT THE COUPLE THAT WINS THE ROBE DE LA FÉE...
WH-WHAT MAKES YOU THINK I WANT HIM?!
GEE, THEY'RE SUCH CLOSE FRIENDS.
THEY SURE ARE.

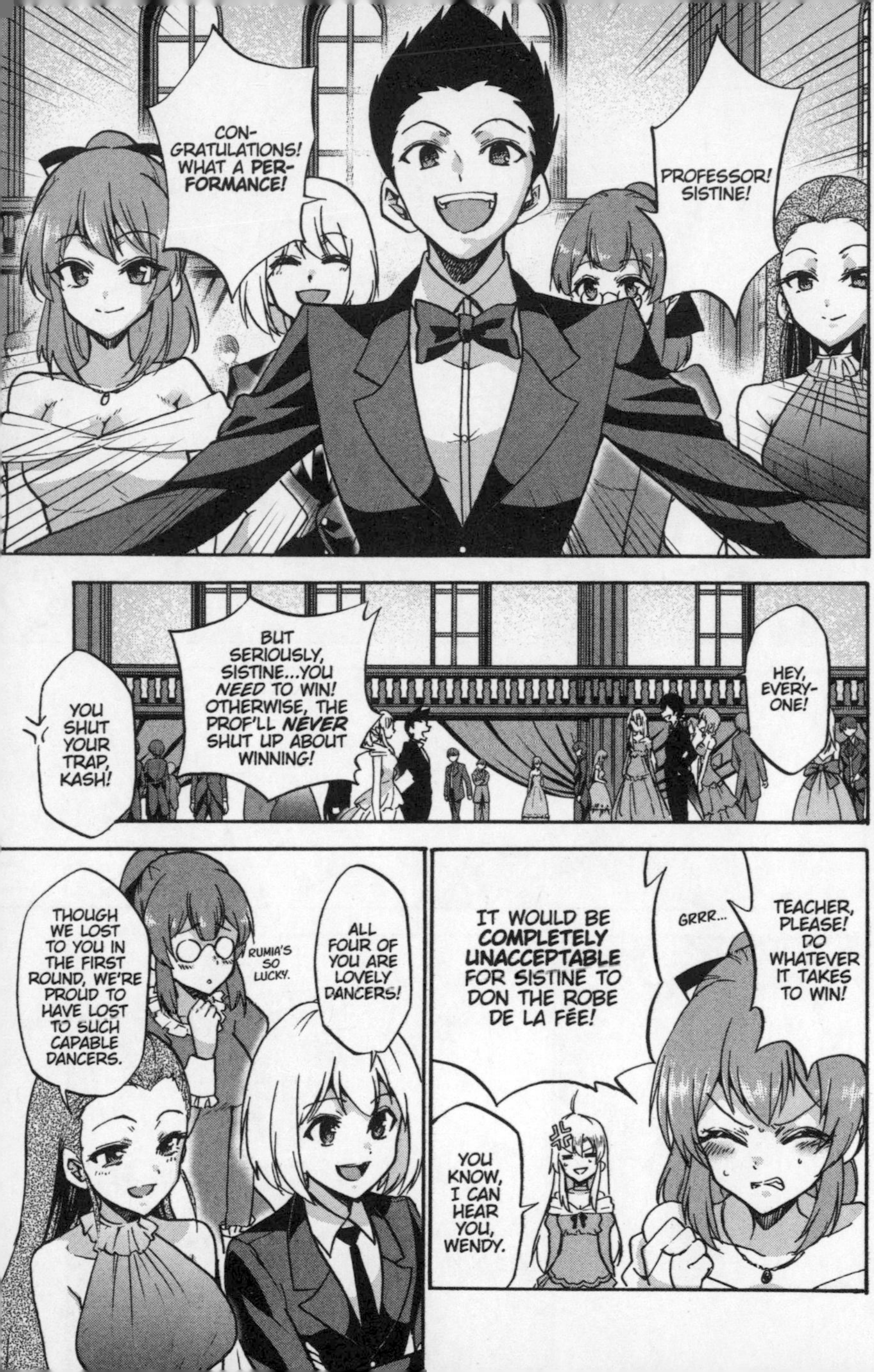
PROFESSOR! SISTINE!
CON-GRATULATIONS! WHAT A PER-FORMANCE!
HEY, EVERY-ONE!
BUT SERIOUSLY, SISTINE...YOU NEED TO WIN! OTHERWISE, THE PROF'LL NEVER SHUT UP ABOUT WINNING!
YOU SHUT YOUR TRAP, KASH!
TEACHER, PLEASE! DO WHATEVER IT TAKES TO WIN!
GRRR...
IT WOULD BE COMPLETELY UNACCEPTABLE FOR SISTINE TO DON THE ROBE DE LA FÉE!
YOU KNOW, I CAN HEAR YOU, WENDY.
ALL FOUR OF YOU ARE LOVELY DANCERS!
RUMIA'S SO LUCKY.
THOUGH WE LOST TO YOU IN THE FIRST ROUND, WE'RE PROUD TO HAVE LOST TO SUCH CAPABLE DANCERS.

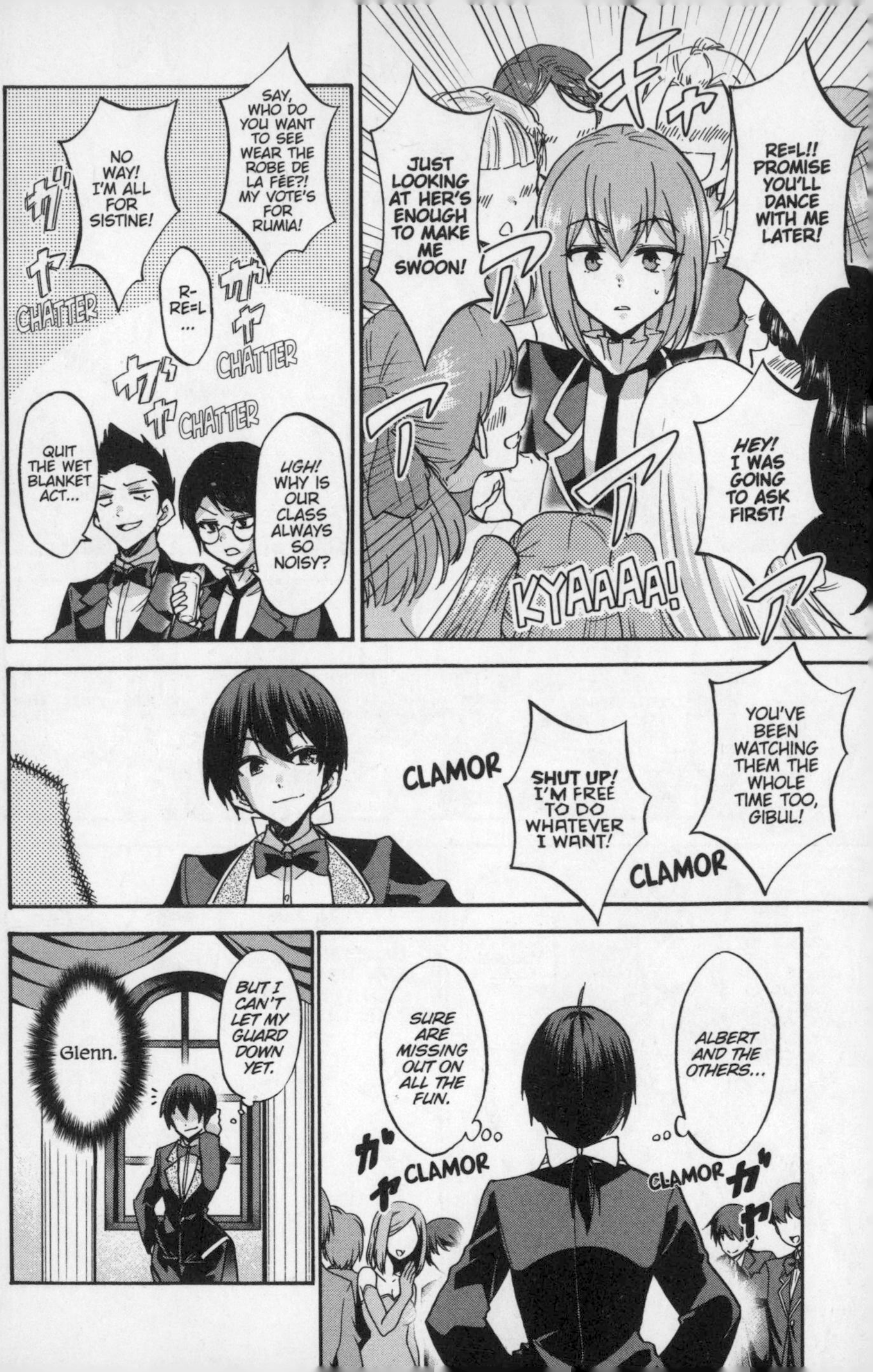
RE=L!! PROMISE YOU'LL DANCE WITH ME LATER!
JUST LOOKING AT HER'S ENOUGH TO MAKE ME SWOON!
HEY! I WAS GOING TO ASK FIRST!
KYAAAA!
SAY, WHO DO YOU WANT TO SEE WEAR THE ROBE DE LA FÉE?! MY VOTE'S FOR RUMIA!
NO WAY! I'M ALL FOR SISTINE!
CHATTER
R- RE=L ...
CHATTER
CHATTER
UGH! WHY IS OUR CLASS ALWAYS SO NOISY?
QUIT THE WET BLANKET ACT...
YOU'VE BEEN WATCHING THEM THE WHOLE TIME TOO, GIBUL!
SHUT UP! I'M FREE TO DO WHATEVER I WANT!
CLAMOR
CLAMOR
ALBERT AND THE OTHERS...
SURE ARE MISSING OUT ON ALL THE FUN.
CLAMOR
CLAMOR
BUT I CAN'T LET MY GUARD DOWN YET.
Glenn.

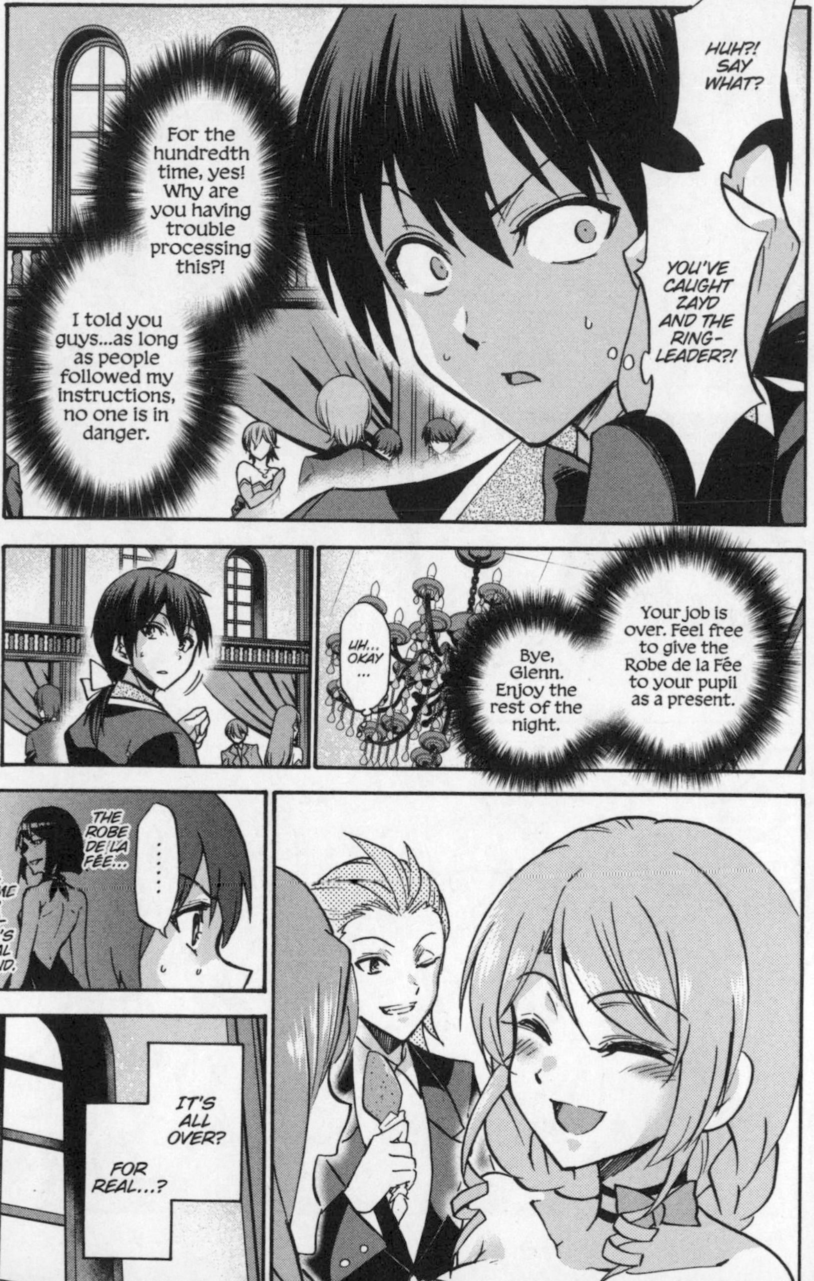
HUH?! SAY WHAT?
YOU'VE CAUGHT ZAYD AND THE RING-LEADER?!
For the hundredth time, yes! Why are you having trouble processing this?!
I told you guys...as long as people followed my instructions, no one is in danger.
Your job is over. Feel free to give the Robe de la Fée to your pupil as a present.
Bye, Glenn. Enjoy the rest of the night.
UH... OKAY ...
......
THE ROBE DE LA FÉE...
WILL BECOME HER HIGHNESS'S BURIAL SHROUD.
IT'S ALL OVER?
FOR REAL...?

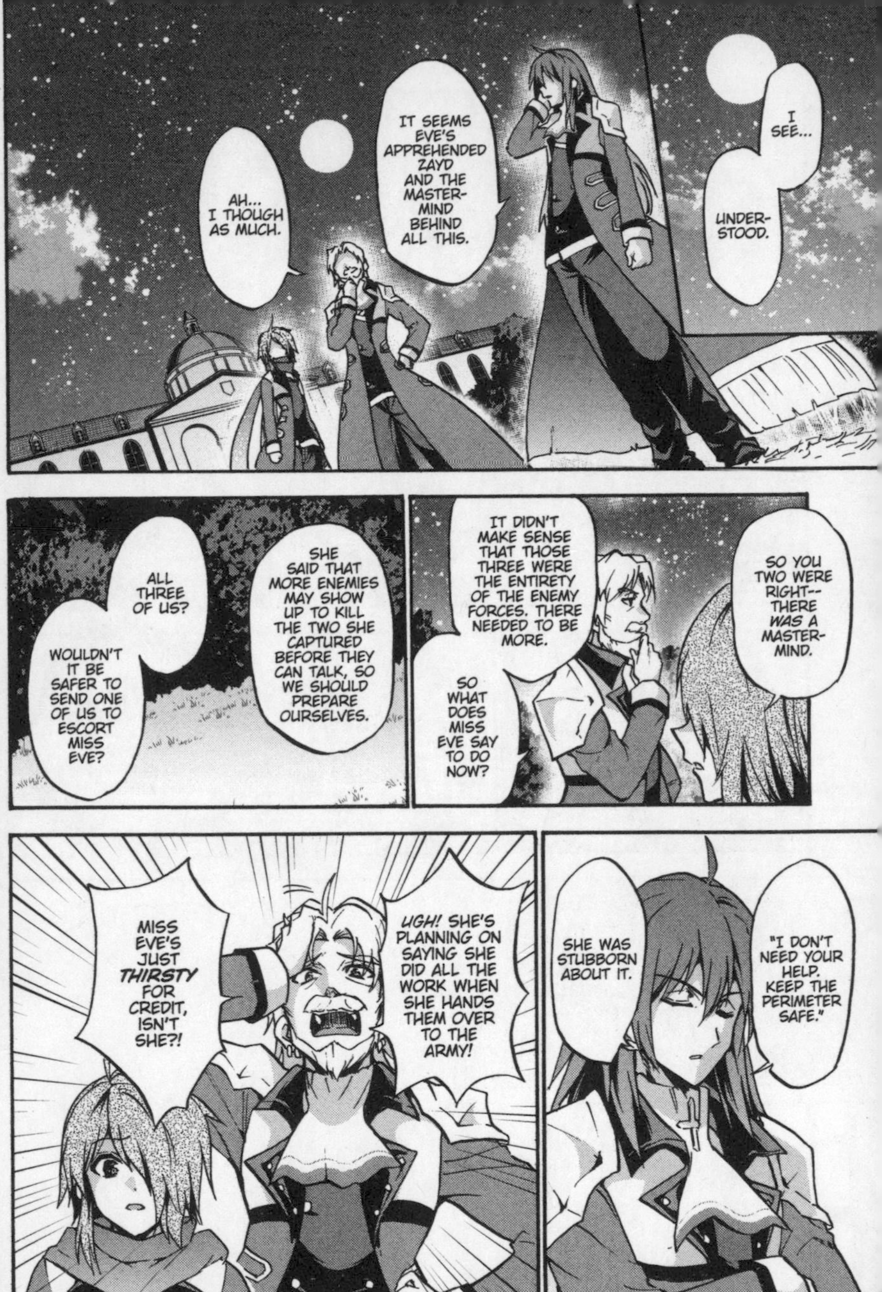
I SEE...
UNDERSTOOD.
IT SEEMS EVE'S APPREHENDED ZAYD AND THE MASTER-MIND BEHIND ALL THIS.
AH... I THOUGH AS MUCH.
SO YOU TWO WERE RIGHT-- THERE *WAS* A MASTER-MIND.
IT DIDN'T MAKE SENSE THAT THOSE THREE WERE THE ENTIRETY OF THE ENEMY FORCES. THERE NEEDED TO BE MORE.
SO WHAT DOES MISS EVE SAY TO DO NOW?
SHE SAID THAT MORE ENEMIES MAY SHOW UP TO KILL THE TWO SHE CAPTURED BEFORE THEY CAN TALK, SO WE SHOULD PREPARE OURSELVES.
ALL THREE OF US?
WOULDN'T IT BE SAFER TO SEND ONE OF US TO ESCORT MISS EVE?
"I DON'T NEED YOUR HELP. KEEP THE PERIMETER SAFE."
SHE WAS STUBBORN ABOUT IT.
UGH! SHE'S PLANNING ON SAYING SHE DID ALL THE WORK WHEN SHE HANDS THEM OVER TO THE ARMY!
MISS EVE'S JUST ***THIRSTY*** FOR CREDIT, ISN'T SHE?!

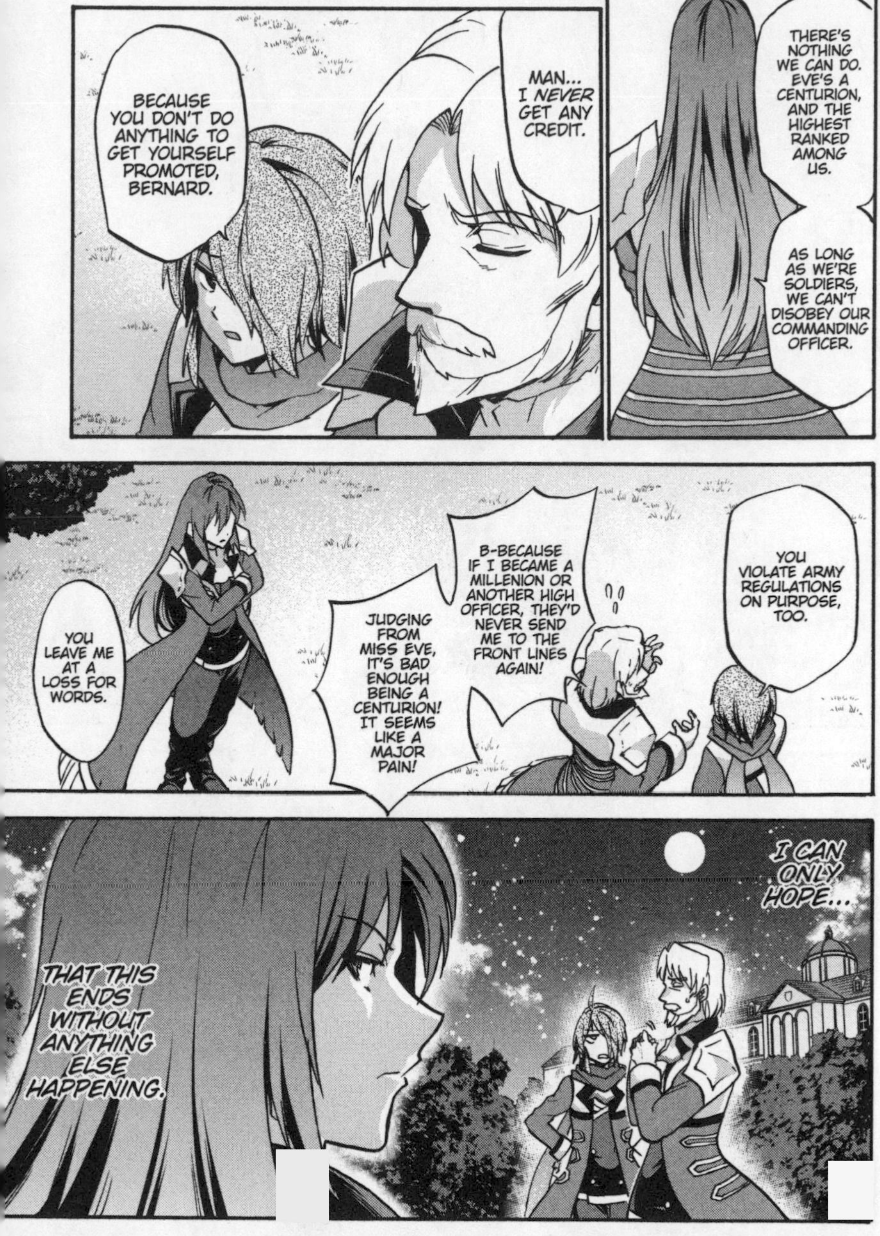
THERE'S NOTHING WE CAN DO. EVE'S A CENTURION, AND THE HIGHEST RANKED AMONG US.
AS LONG AS WE'RE SOLDIERS, WE CAN'T DISOBEY OUR COMMANDING OFFICER.
MAN... I *NEVER* GET ANY CREDIT.
BECAUSE YOU DON'T DO ANYTHING TO GET YOURSELF PROMOTED, BERNARD.
YOU VIOLATE ARMY REGULATIONS ON PURPOSE, TOO.
B-BECAUSE IF I BECAME A MILLENION OR ANOTHER HIGH OFFICER, THEY'D NEVER SEND ME TO THE FRONT LINES AGAIN!
JUDGING FROM MISS EVE, IT'S BAD ENOUGH BEING A CENTURION! IT SEEMS LIKE A MAJOR PAIN!
YOU LEAVE ME AT A LOSS FOR WORDS.
I CAN ONLY HOPE...
THAT THIS ENDS WITHOUT ANYTHING ELSE HAPPENING.

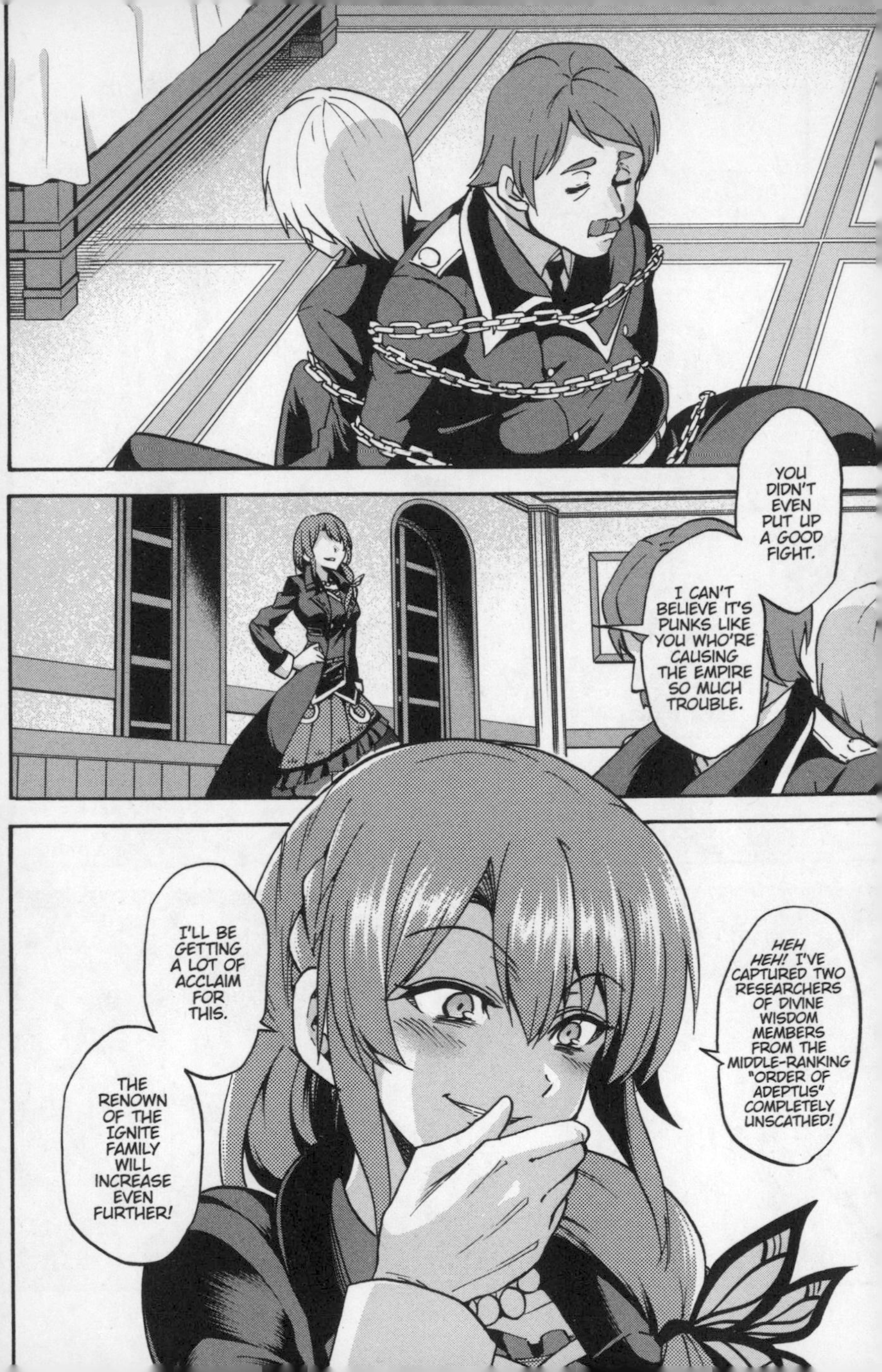
YOU DIDN'T EVEN PUT UP A GOOD FIGHT.
I CAN'T BELIEVE IT'S PUNKS LIKE YOU WHO'RE CAUSING THE EMPIRE SO MUCH TROUBLE.
HEH HEH! I'VE CAPTURED TWO RESEARCHERS OF DIVINE WISDOM MEMBERS FROM THE MIDDLE-RANKING "ORDER OF ADEPTUS" COMPLETELY UNSCATHED!
I'LL BE GETTING A LOT OF ACCLAIM FOR THIS.
THE RENOWN OF THE IGNITE FAMILY WILL INCREASE EVEN FURTHER!

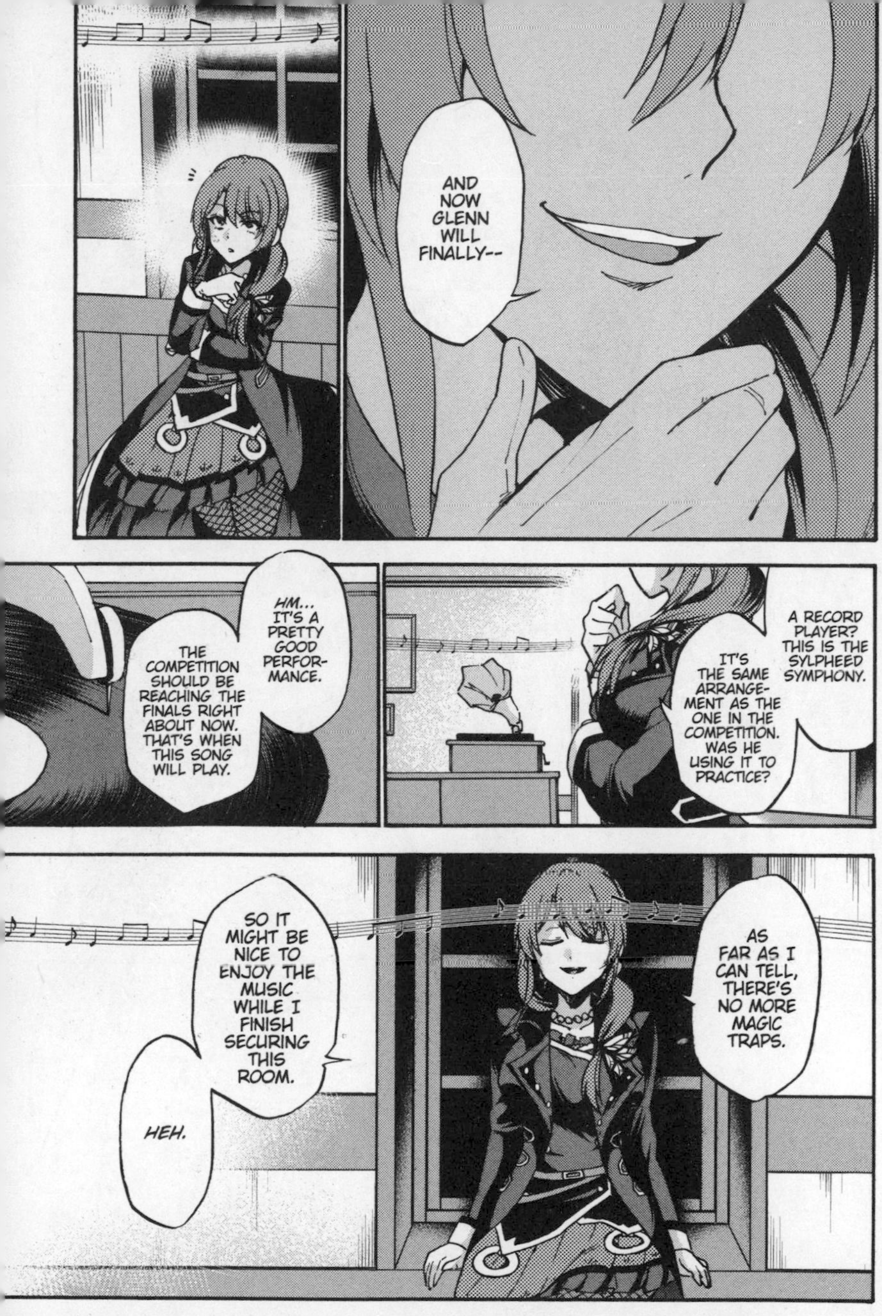
AND NOW GLENN WILL FINALLY--
A RECORD PLAYER? THIS IS THE SYLPHEED SYMPHONY.
IT'S THE SAME ARRANGEMENT AS THE ONE IN THE COMPETITION. WAS HE USING IT TO PRACTICE?
HM... IT'S A PRETTY GOOD PERFORMANCE.
THE COMPETITION SHOULD BE REACHING THE FINALS RIGHT ABOUT NOW. THAT'S WHEN THIS SONG WILL PLAY.
AS FAR AS I CAN TELL, THERE'S NO MORE MAGIC TRAPS.
SO IT MIGHT BE NICE TO ENJOY THE MUSIC WHILE I FINISH SECURING THIS ROOM.
HEH.

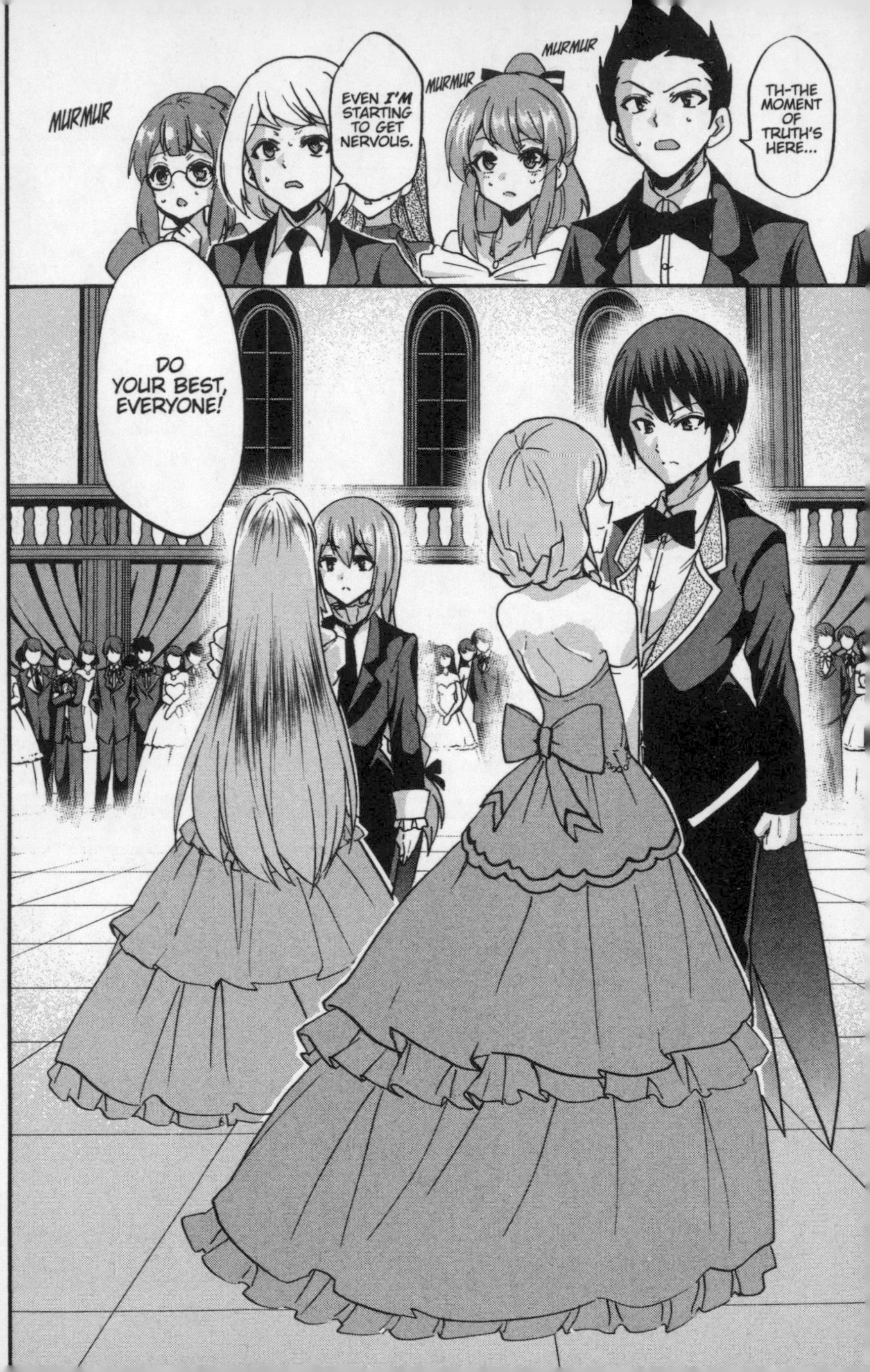
TH-THE MOMENT OF TRUTH'S HERE...
MURMUR
MURMUR
EVEN I'M STARTING TO GET NERVOUS.
MURMUR
DO YOUR BEST, EVERYONE!

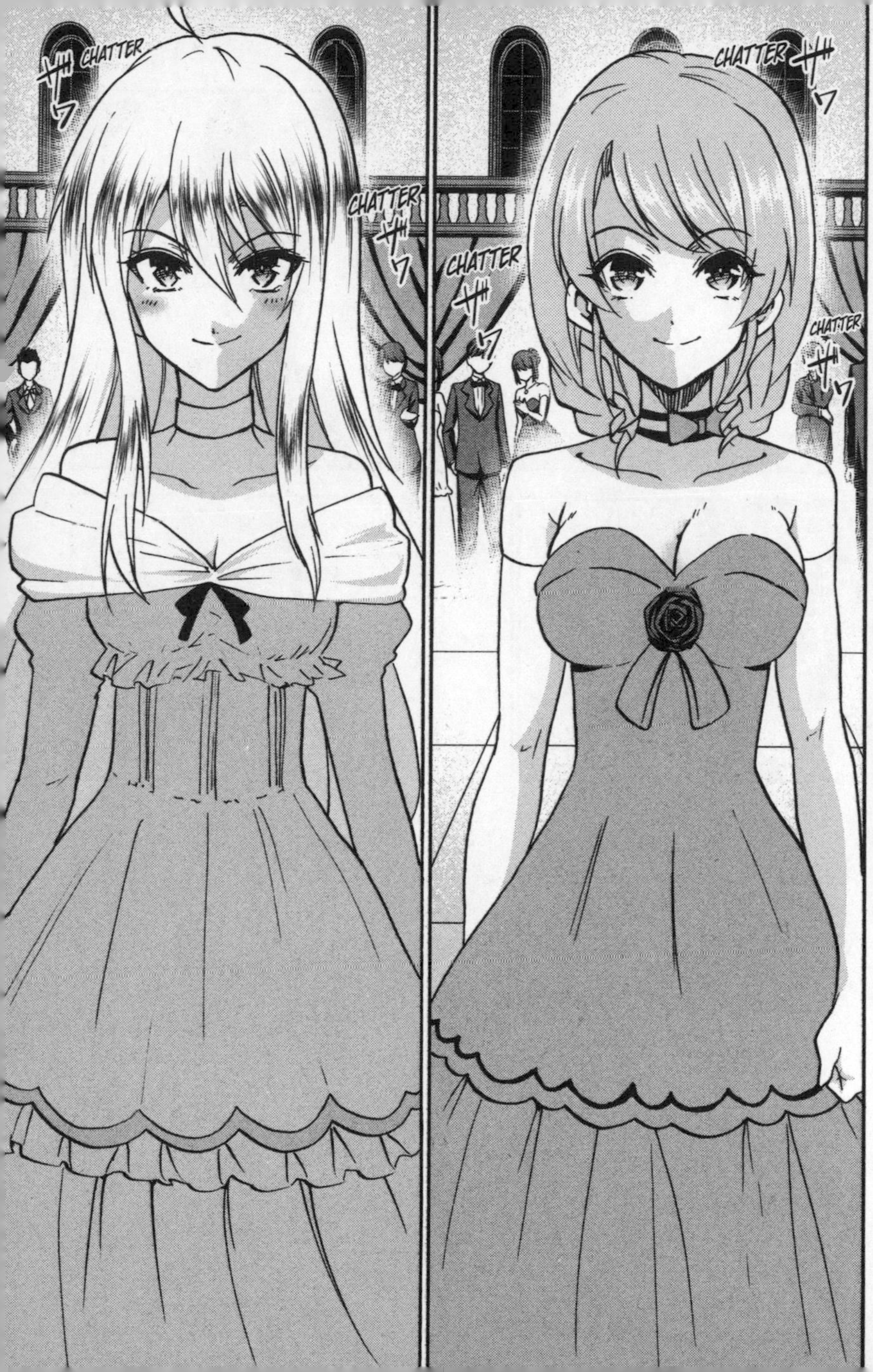
CHATTER ザワ
CHATTER ザワ
CHATTER ザワ
CHATTER ザワ
CHATTER ザワ

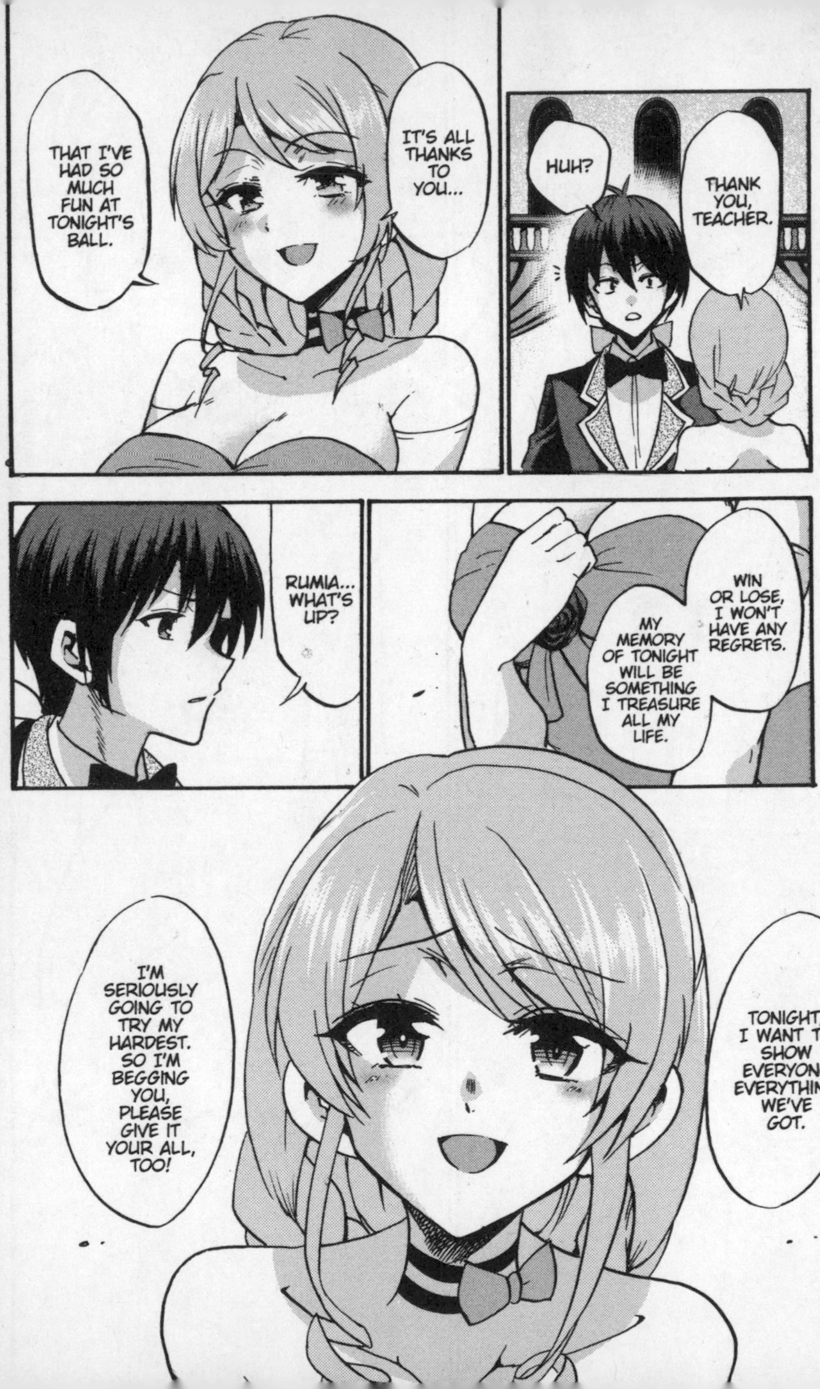
THANK YOU, TEACHER.
HUH?
IT'S ALL THANKS TO YOU...
THAT I'VE HAD SO MUCH FUN AT TONIGHT'S BALL.
WIN OR LOSE, I WON'T HAVE ANY REGRETS.
MY MEMORY OF TONIGHT WILL BE SOMETHING I TREASURE ALL MY LIFE.
RUMIA... WHAT'S UP?
TONIGHT, I WANT TO SHOW EVERYONE EVERYTHING WE'VE GOT.
I'M SERIOUSLY GOING TO TRY MY HARDEST. SO I'M BEGGING YOU, PLEASE GIVE IT YOUR ALL, TOO!

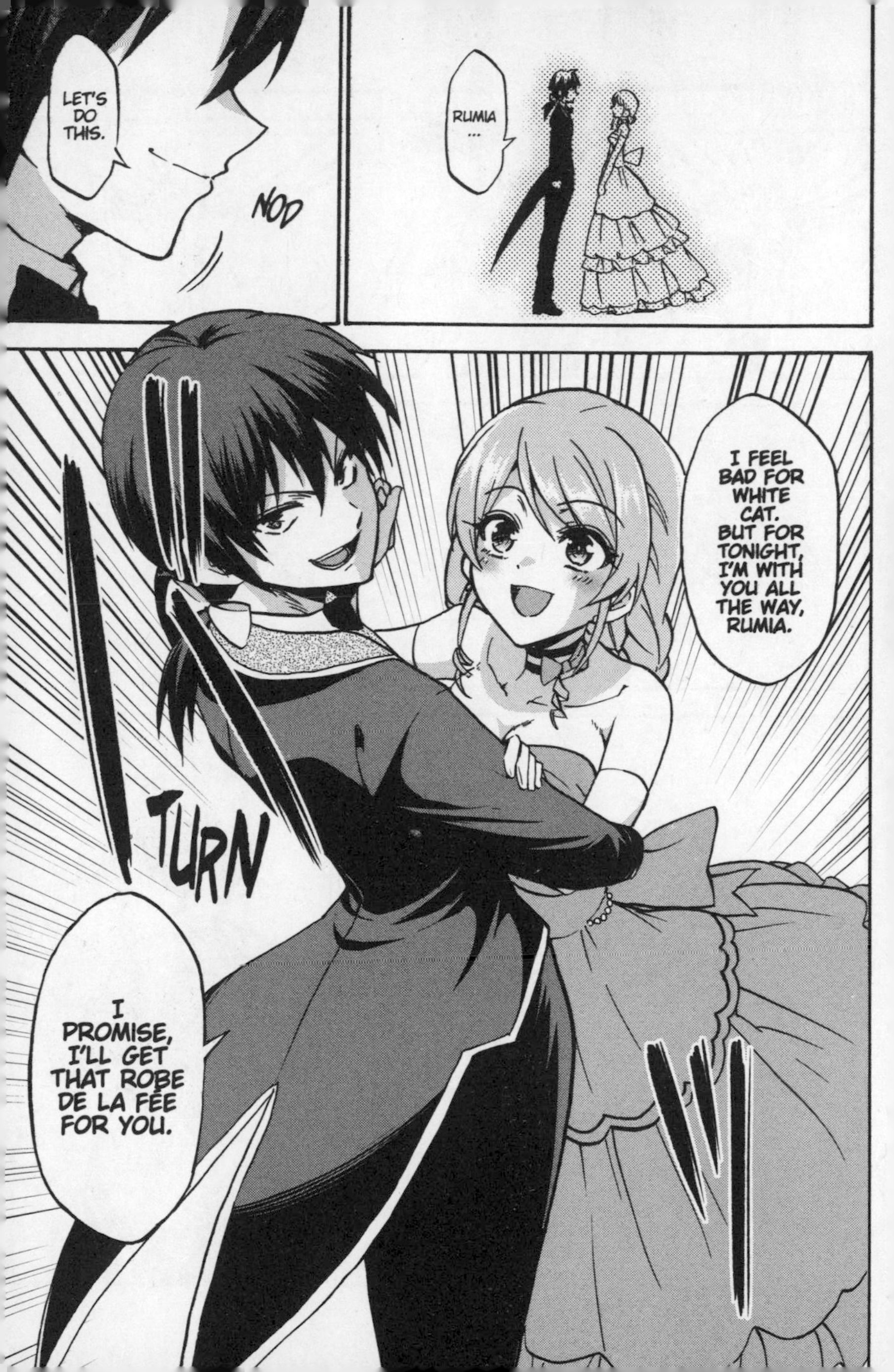
RUMIA...
LET'S DO THIS.
NOD
I FEEL BAD FOR WHITE CAT. BUT FOR TONIGHT, I'M WITH YOU ALL THE WAY, RUMIA.
TURN
I PROMISE, I'LL GET THAT ROBE DE LA FÉE FOR YOU.

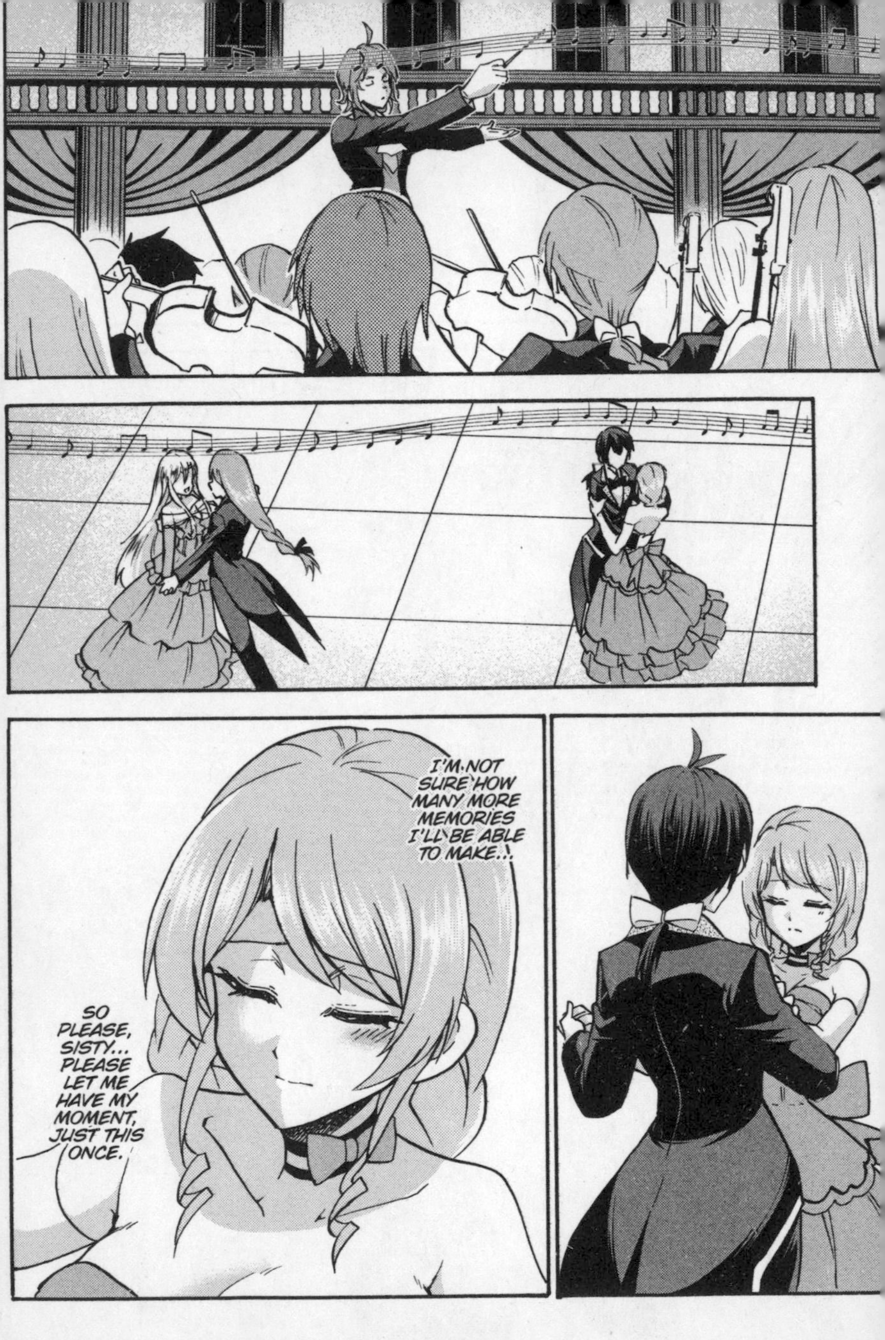
I'M NOT SURE HOW MANY MORE MEMORIES I'LL BE ABLE TO MAKE...
SO PLEASE, SISTY... PLEASE LET ME HAVE MY MOMENT, JUST THIS ONCE.

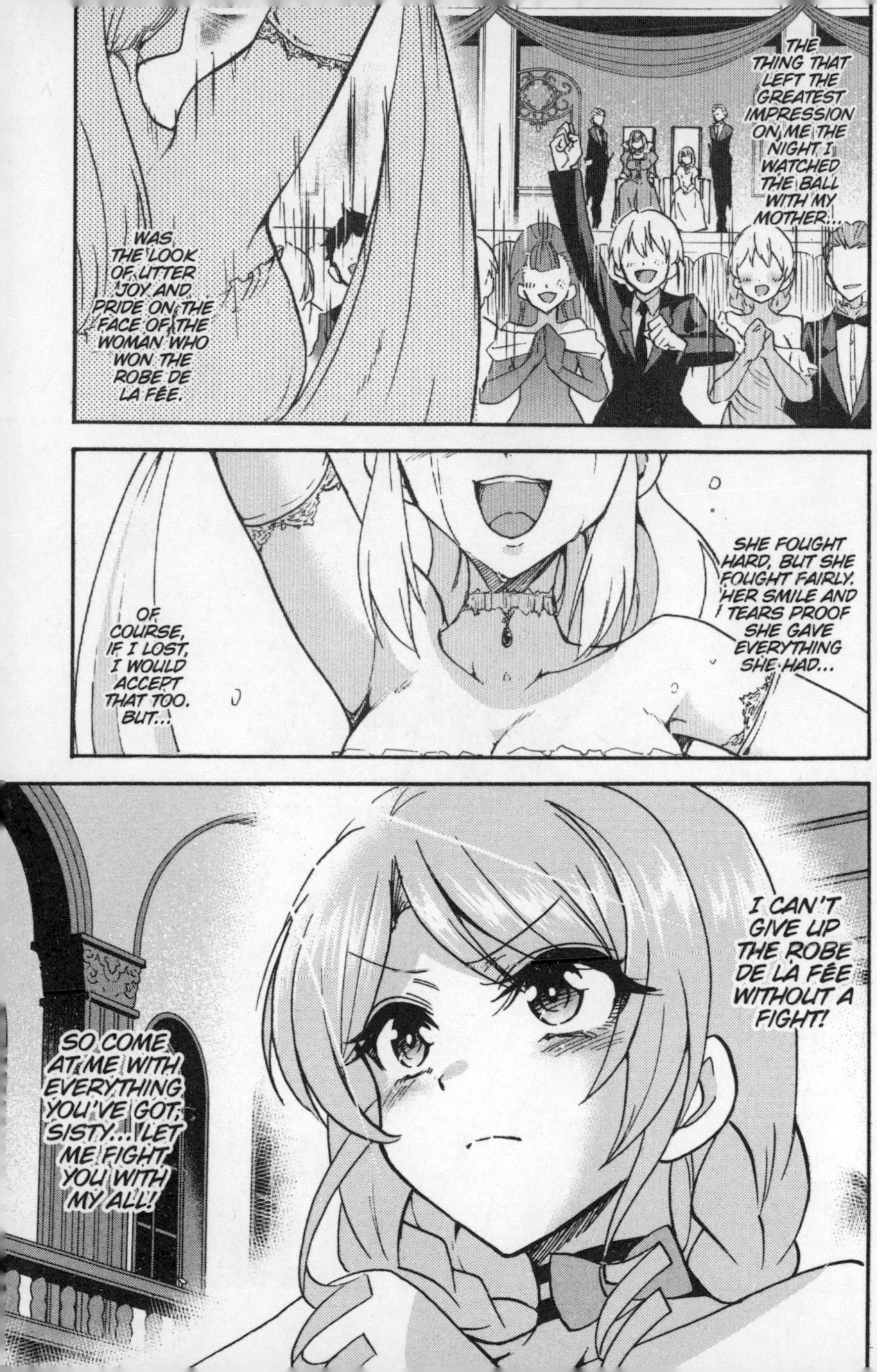
THE THING THAT LEFT THE GREATEST IMPRESSION ON ME THE NIGHT I WATCHED THE BALL WITH MY MOTHER...
WAS THE LOOK OF UTTER JOY AND PRIDE ON THE FACE OF THE WOMAN WHO WON THE ROBE DE LA FÉE.
SHE FOUGHT HARD, BUT SHE FOUGHT FAIRLY. HER SMILE AND TEARS PROOF SHE GAVE EVERYTHING SHE HAD...
OF COURSE, IF I LOST, I WOULD ACCEPT THAT TOO. BUT...
I CAN'T GIVE UP THE ROBE DE LA FÉE WITHOUT A FIGHT!
SO COME AT ME WITH EVERYTHING YOU'VE GOT, SISTY... LET ME FIGHT YOU WITH MY ALL!

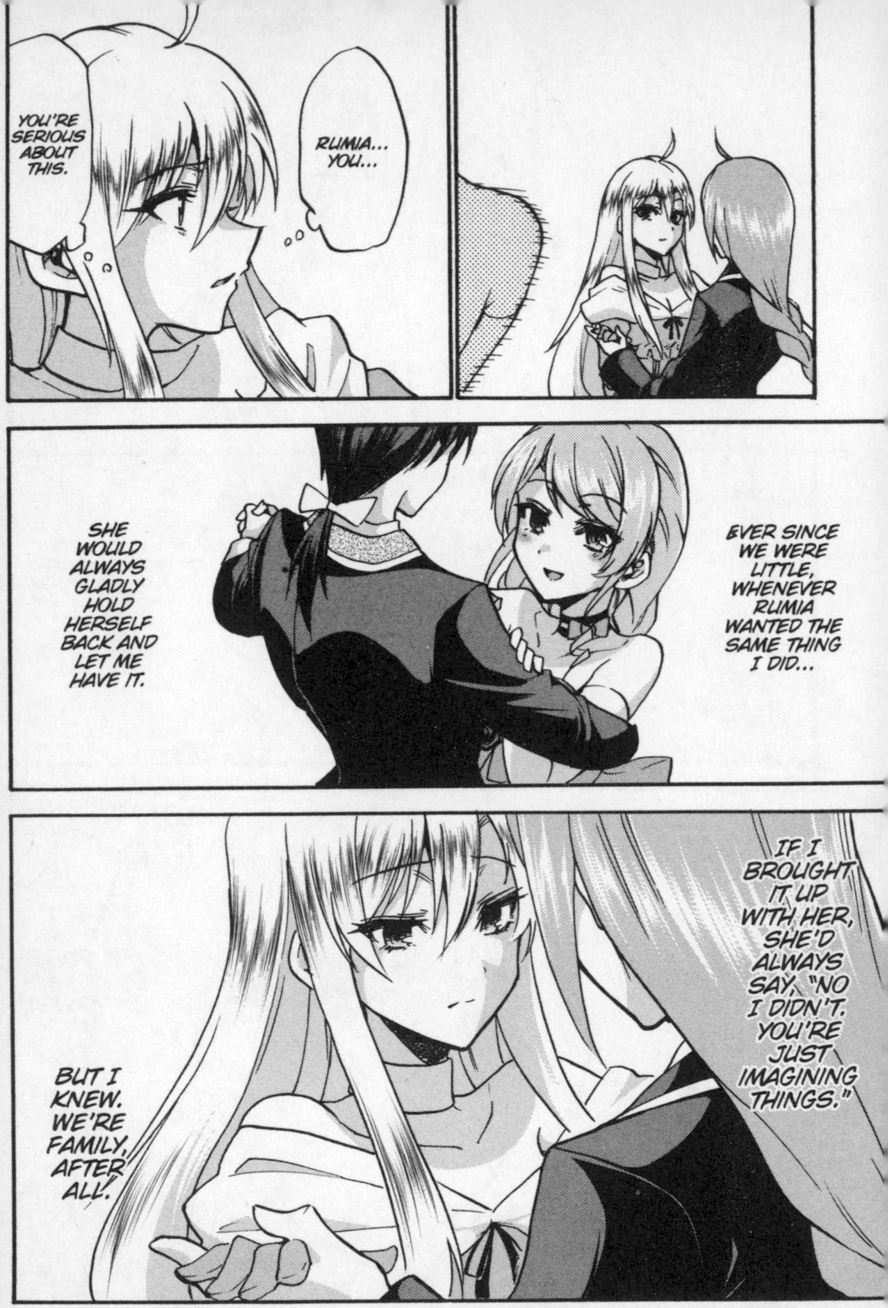
RUMIA... YOU...
YOU'RE SERIOUS ABOUT THIS.
EVER SINCE WE WERE LITTLE, WHENEVER RUMIA WANTED THE SAME THING I DID...
SHE WOULD ALWAYS GLADLY HOLD HERSELF BACK AND LET ME HAVE IT.
IF I BROUGHT IT UP WITH HER, SHE'D ALWAYS SAY, "NO I DIDN'T. YOU'RE JUST IMAGINING THINGS."
BUT I KNEW. WE'RE FAMILY, AFTER ALL.

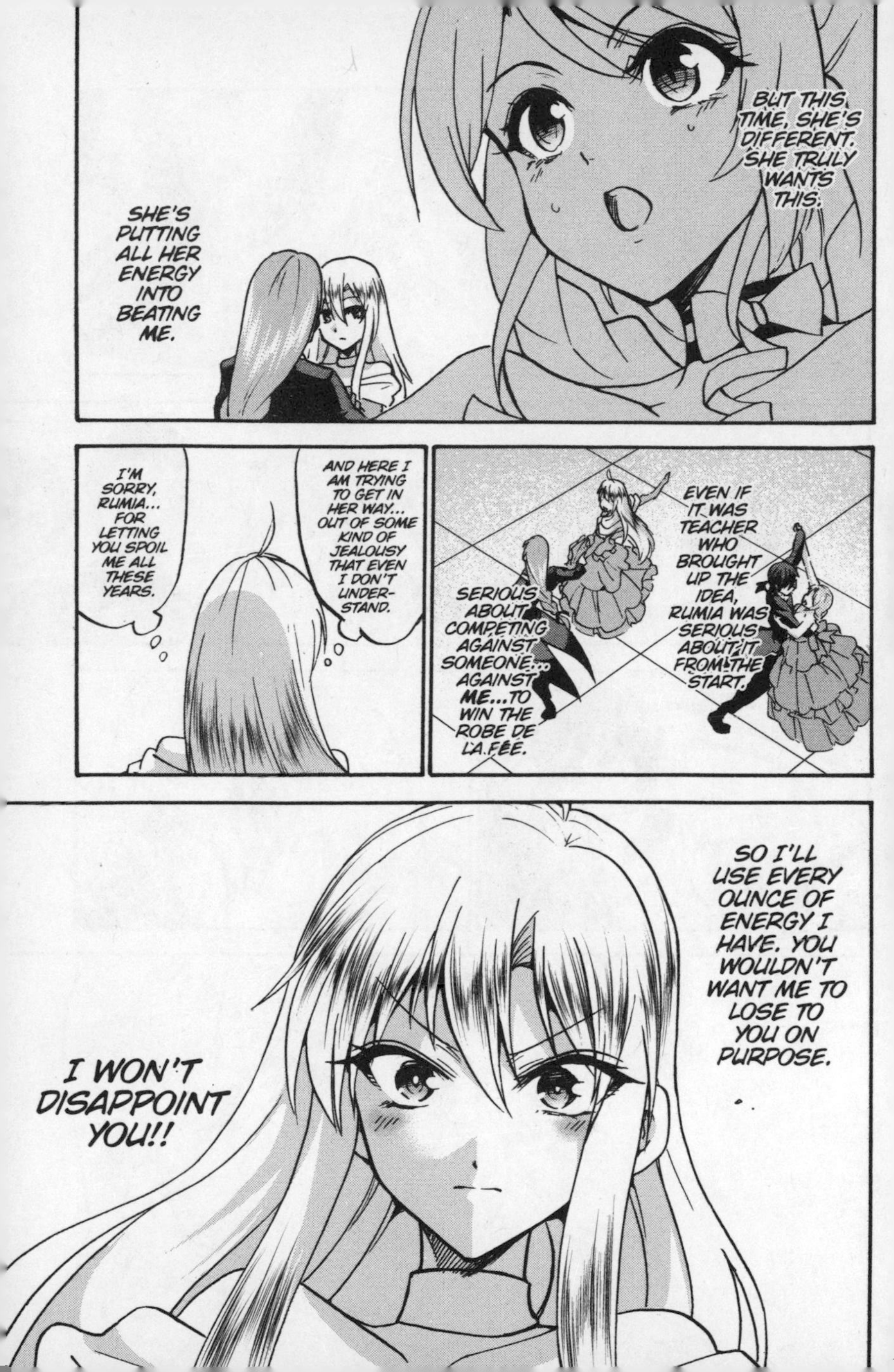
BUT THIS TIME, SHE'S DIFFERENT. SHE TRULY WANTS THIS.
SHE'S PUTTING ALL HER ENERGY INTO BEATING ME.
EVEN IF IT WAS TEACHER WHO BROUGHT UP THE IDEA, RUMIA WAS SERIOUS ABOUT IT FROM THE START.
SERIOUS ABOUT COMPETING AGAINST SOMEONE... AGAINST ME...TO WIN THE ROBE DE LA FÉE.
AND HERE I AM TRYING TO GET IN HER WAY... OUT OF SOME KIND OF JEALOUSY THAT EVEN I DON'T UNDER-STAND.
I'M SORRY, RUMIA... FOR LETTING YOU SPOIL ME ALL THESE YEARS.
SO I'LL USE EVERY OUNCE OF ENERGY I HAVE. YOU WOULDN'T WANT ME TO LOSE TO YOU ON PURPOSE.
I WON'T DISAPPOINT YOU!!

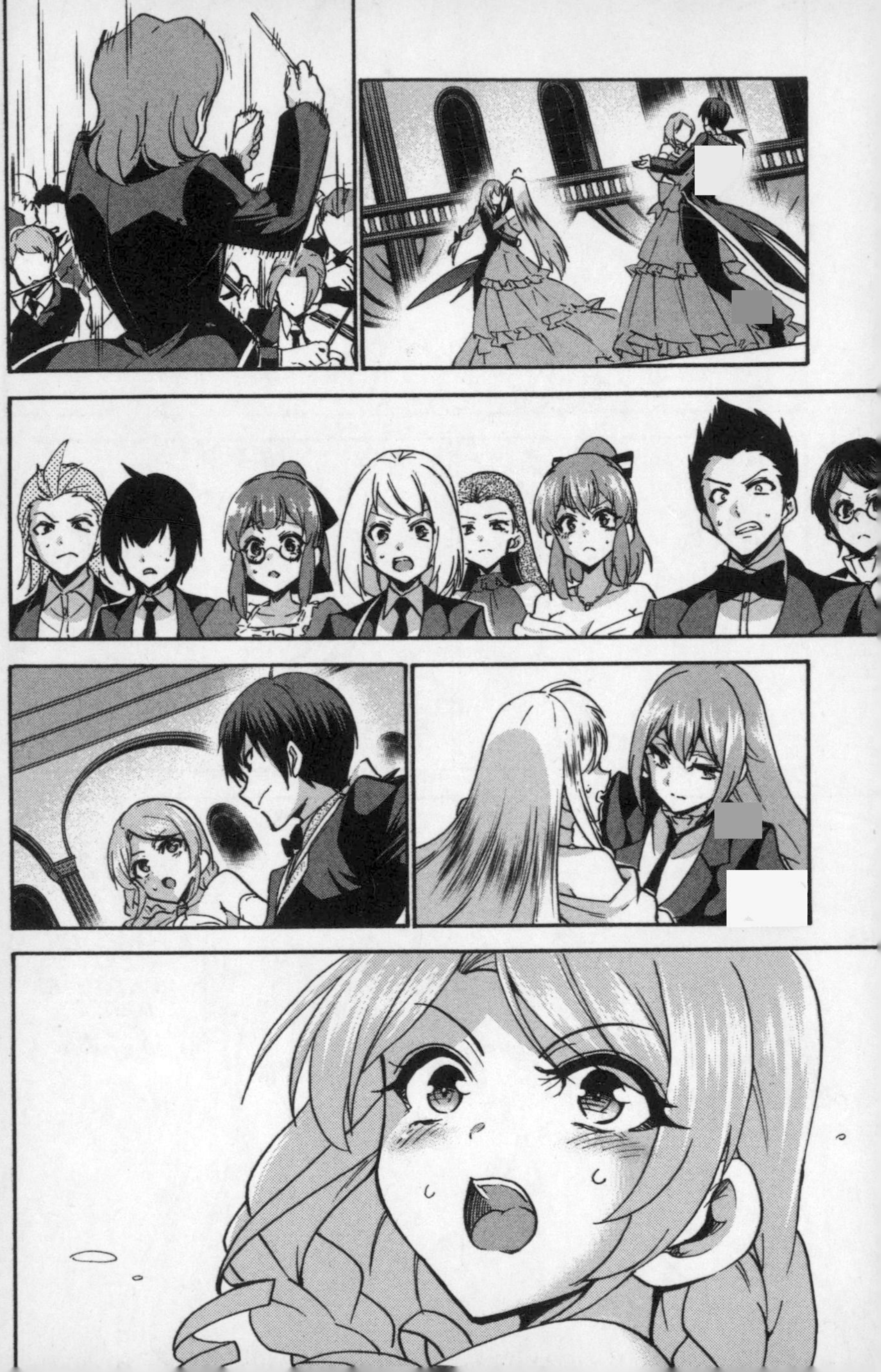

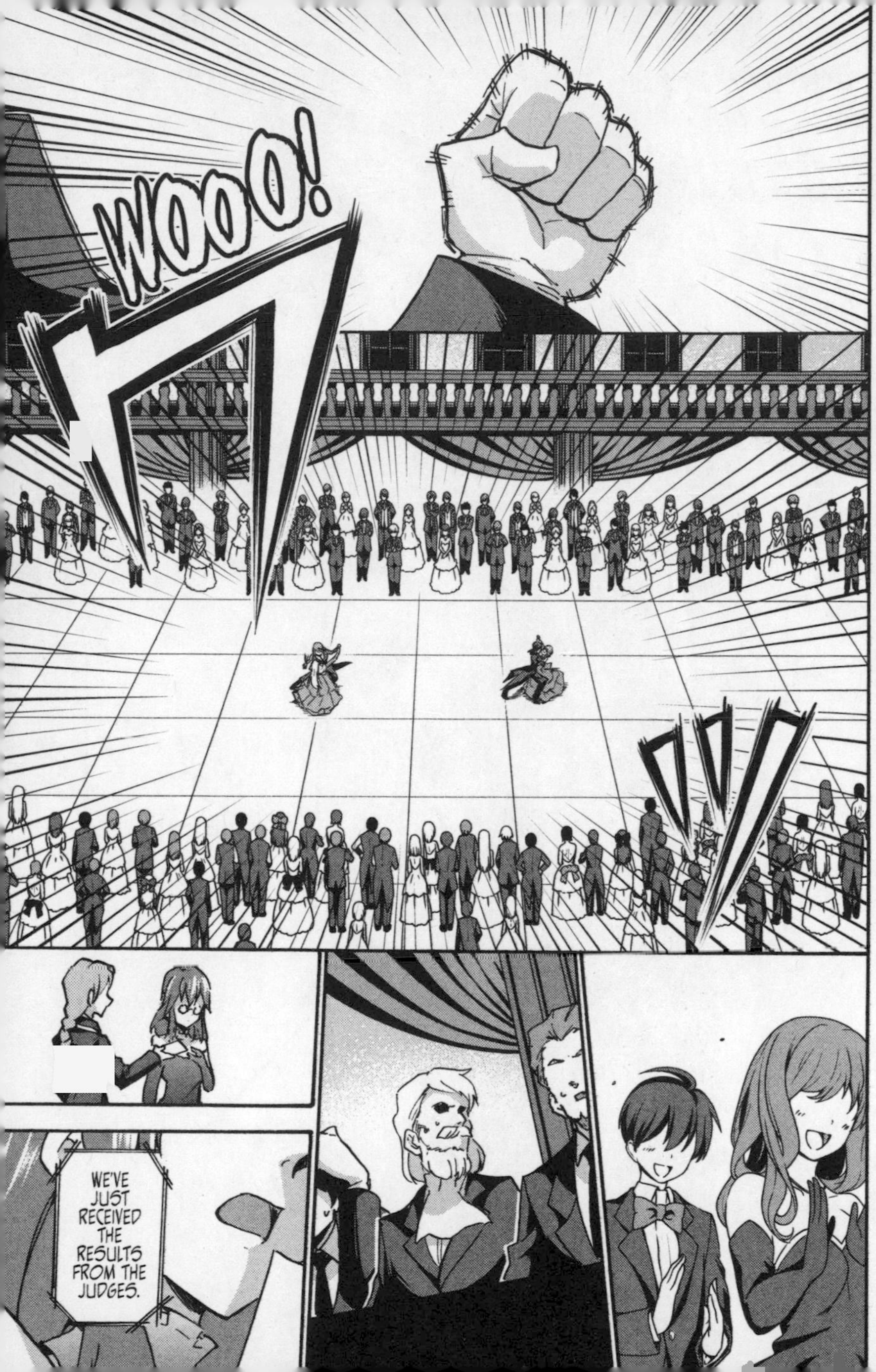
WOOO!
WE'VE JUST RECEIVED THE RESULTS FROM THE JUDGES.

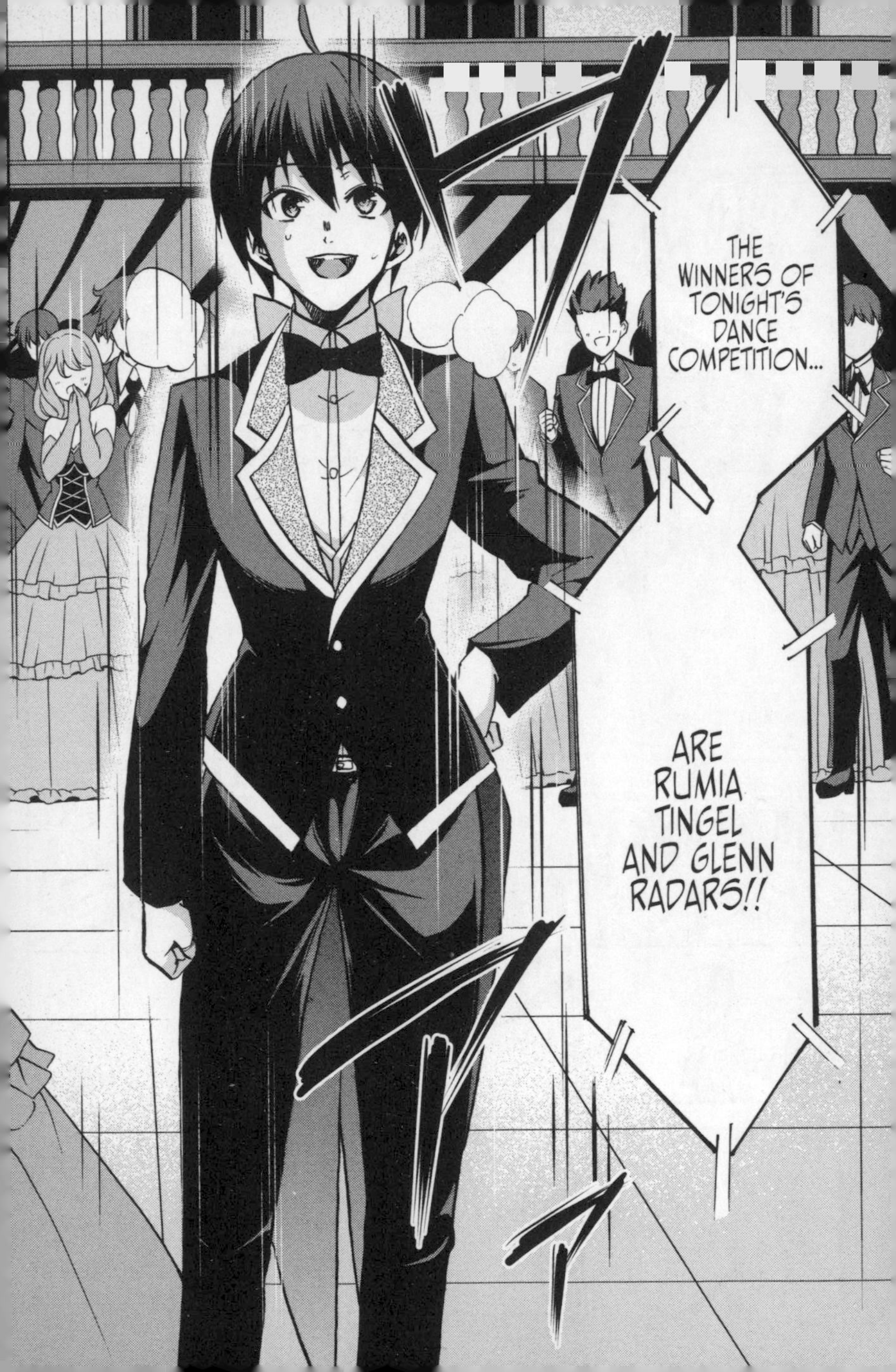
THE WINNERS OF TONIGHT'S DANCE COMPETITION...
ARE RUMIA TINGEL AND GLENN RADARS!!

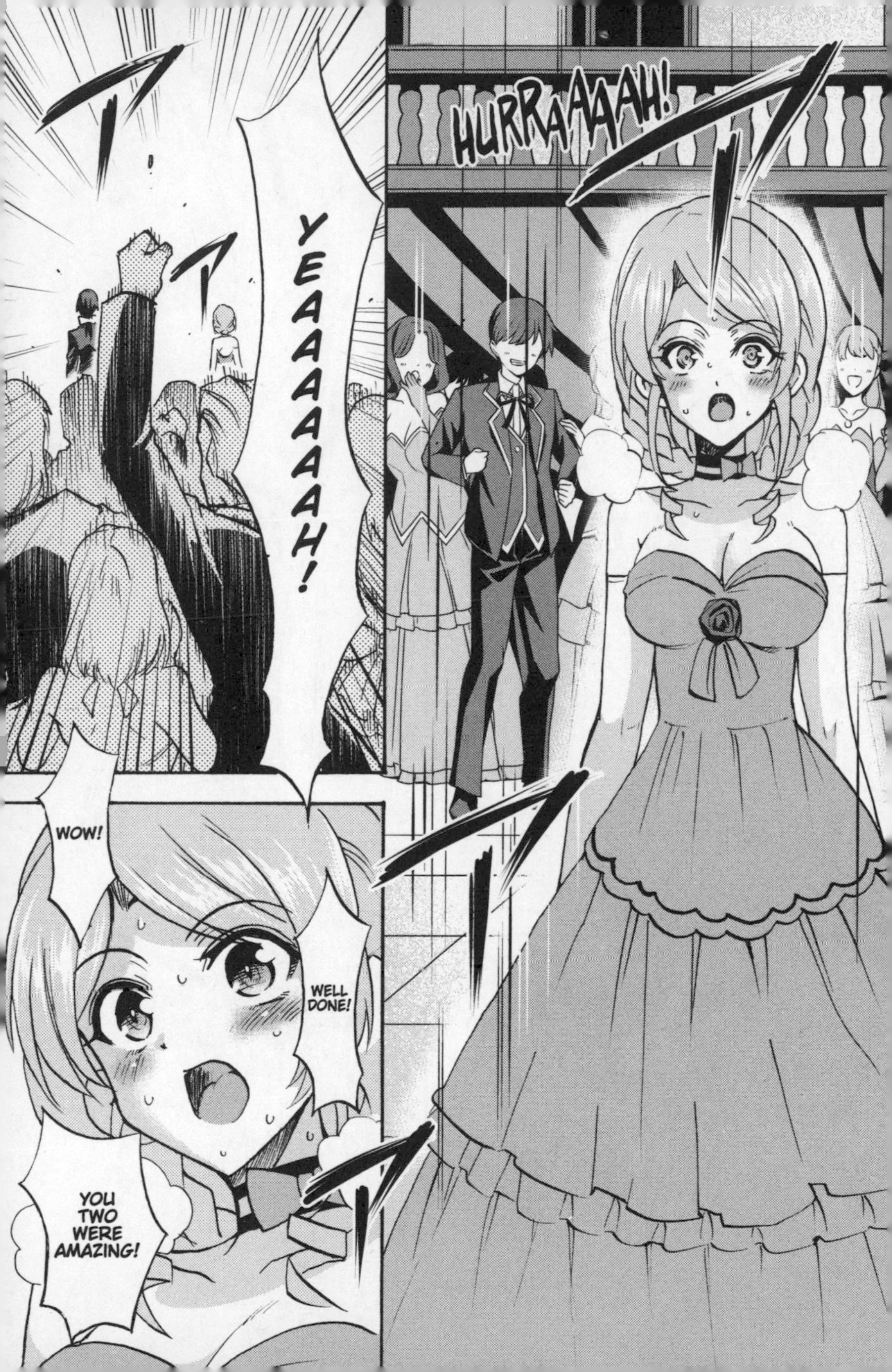
HURRAAAAH!
YEAAAAAAH!
WELL DONE!
WOW!
YOU TWO WERE AMAZING!

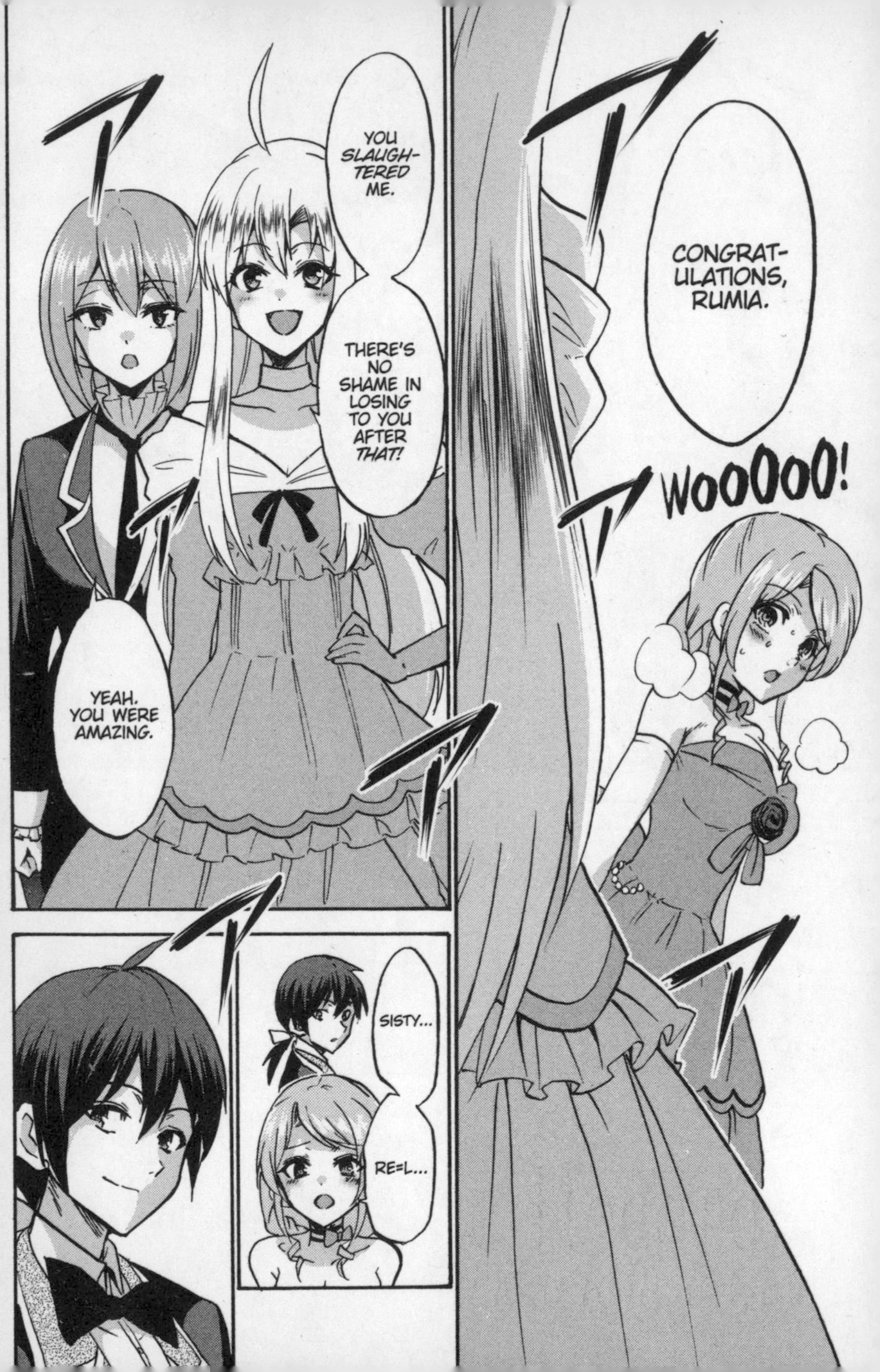
CONGRAT-ULATIONS, RUMIA.
WOOOOO!
YOU SLAUGH-TERED ME.
THERE'S NO SHAME IN LOSING TO YOU AFTER *THAT!*
YEAH. YOU WERE AMAZING.
SISTY...
RE=L...

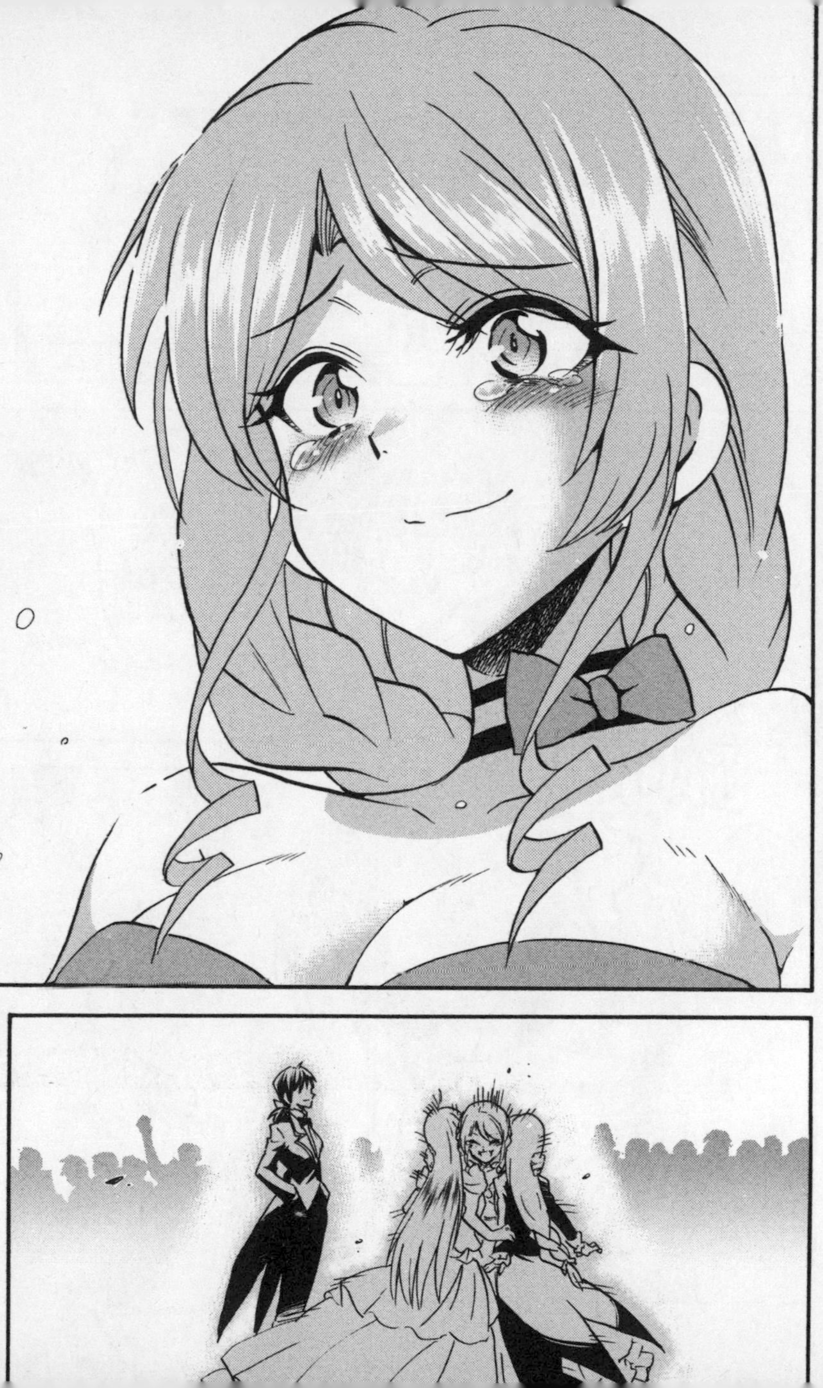

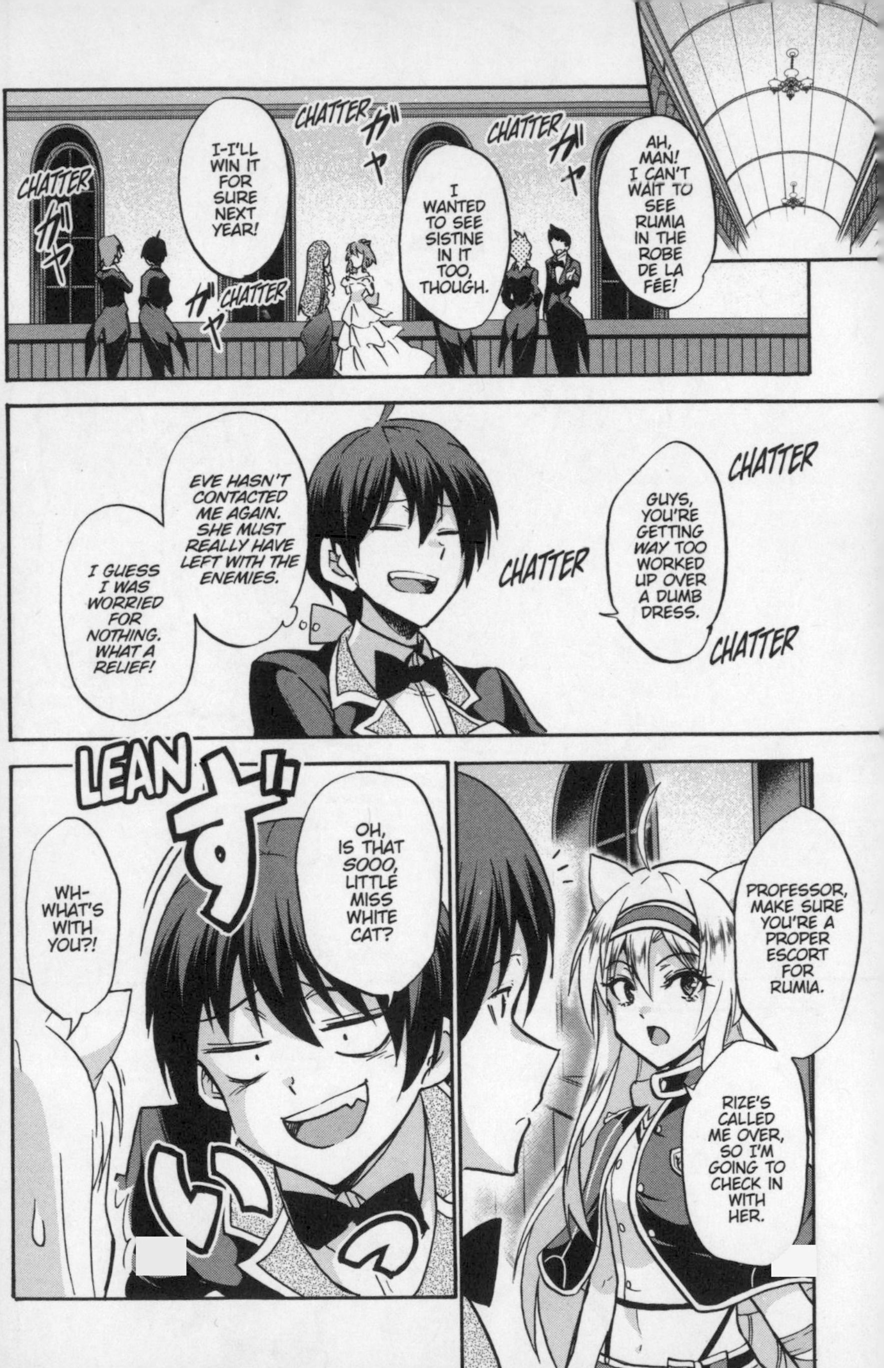
AH, MAN! I CAN'T WAIT TO SEE RUMIA IN THE ROBE DE LA FÉE!
CHATTER
I WANTED TO SEE SISTINE IN IT TOO, THOUGH.
CHATTER
I-I'LL WIN IT FOR SURE NEXT YEAR!
CHATTER
CHATTER
CHATTER
GUYS, YOU'RE GETTING WAY TOO WORKED UP OVER A DUMB DRESS.
CHATTER
CHATTER
EVE HASN'T CONTACTED ME AGAIN. SHE MUST REALLY HAVE LEFT WITH THE ENEMIES.
I GUESS I WAS WORRIED FOR NOTHING. WHAT A RELIEF!
PROFESSOR, MAKE SURE YOU'RE A PROPER ESCORT FOR RUMIA.
RIZE'S CALLED ME OVER, SO I'M GOING TO CHECK IN WITH HER.
LEAN
OH, IS THAT SOOO, LITTLE MISS WHITE CAT?
WH-WHAT'S WITH YOU?!

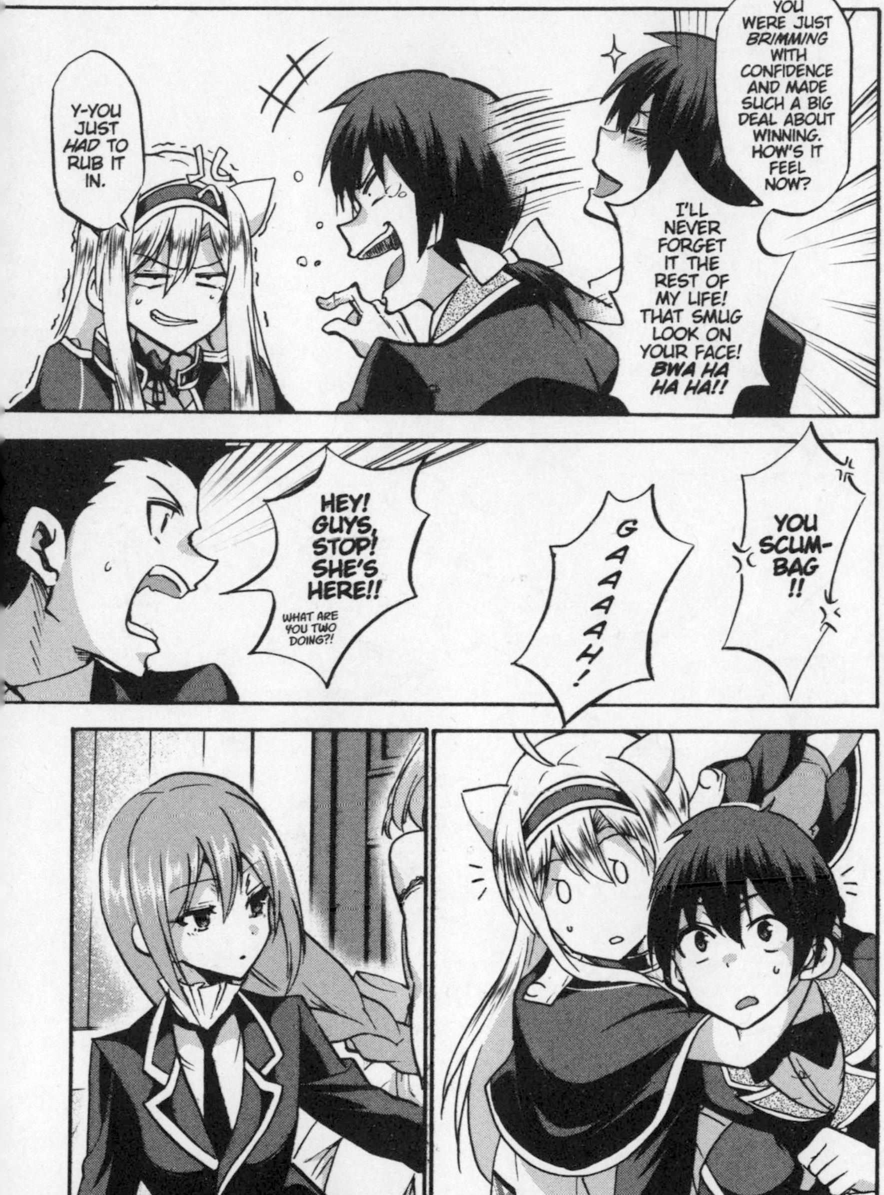
YOU WERE JUST *BRIMMING* WITH CONFIDENCE AND MADE SUCH A BIG DEAL ABOUT WINNING. HOW'S IT FEEL NOW?
I'LL NEVER FORGET IT THE REST OF MY LIFE! THAT SMUG LOOK ON YOUR FACE! ***BWA HA HA HA!!***
Y-YOU JUST *HAD* TO RUB IT IN.
YOU SCUMBAG!!
GAAAAAH!
HEY! GUYS, STOP! SHE'S HERE!!
WHAT ARE YOU TWO DOING?!

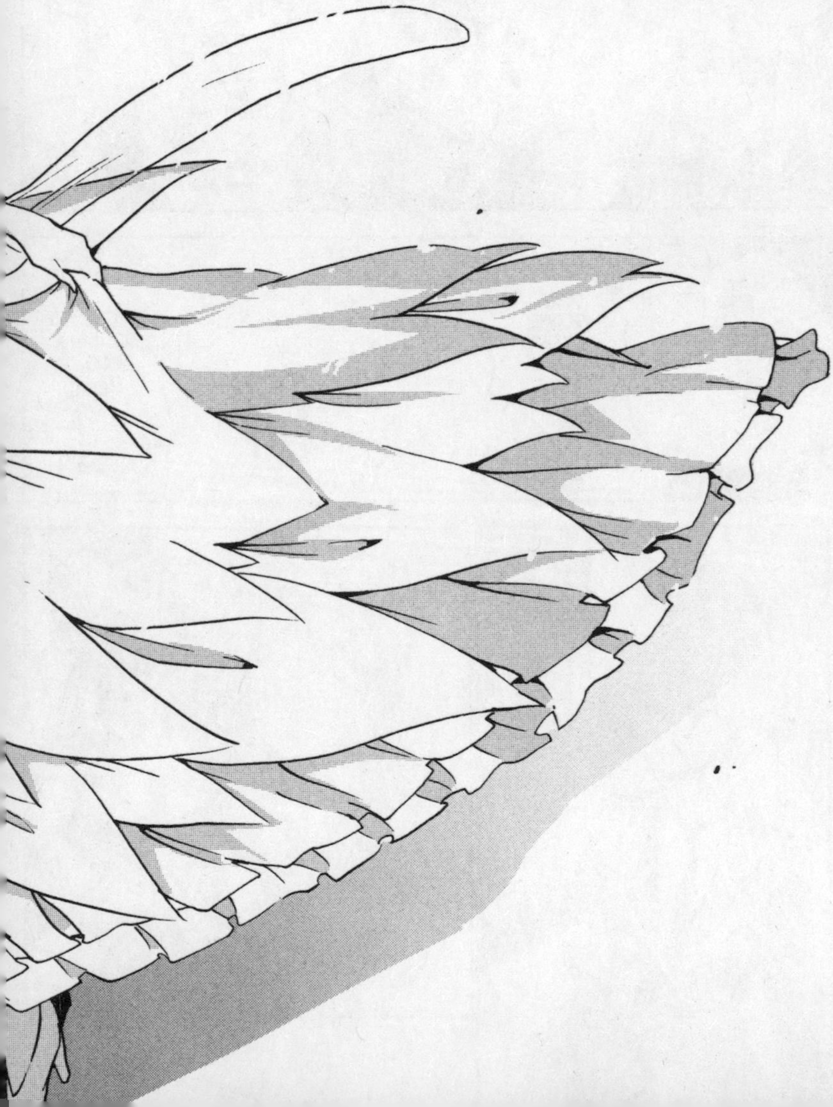

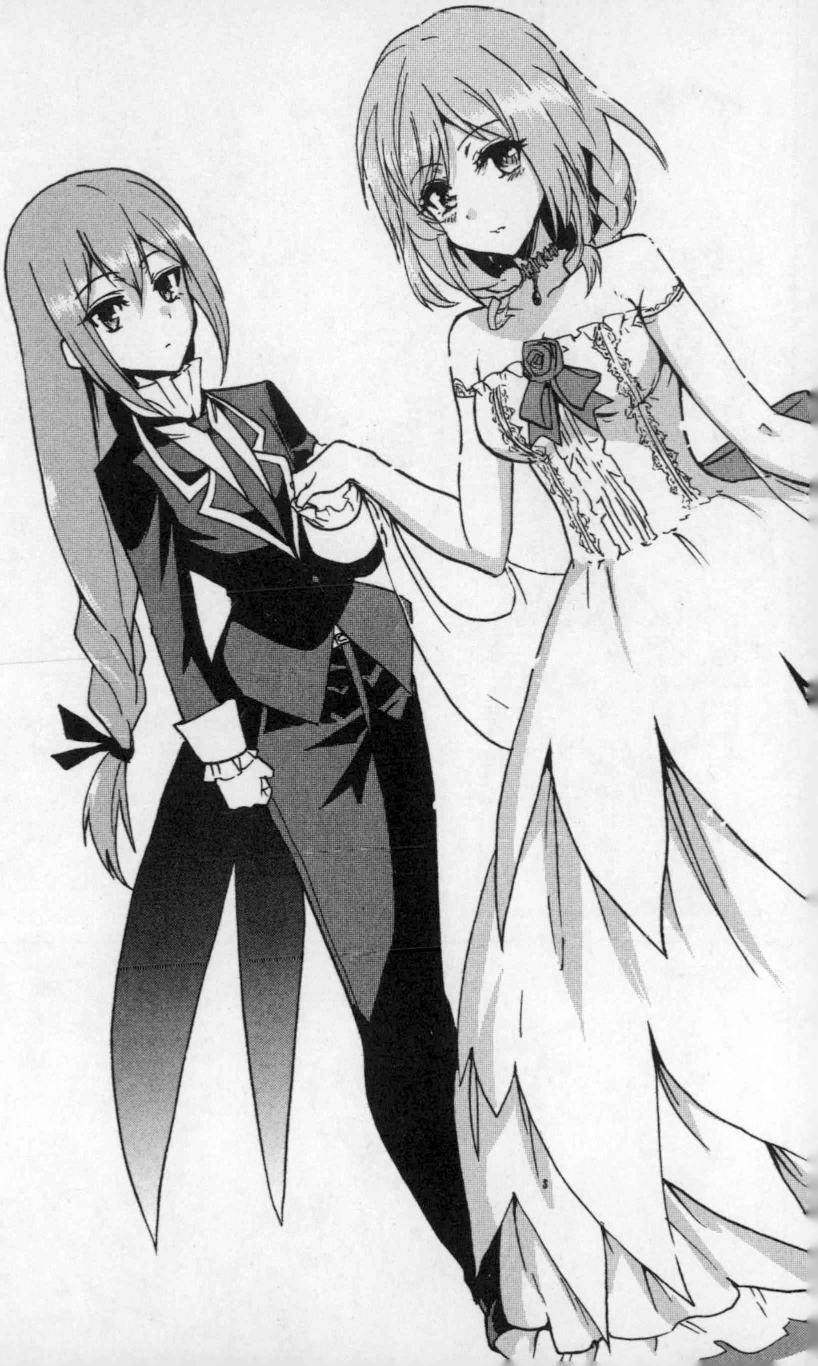

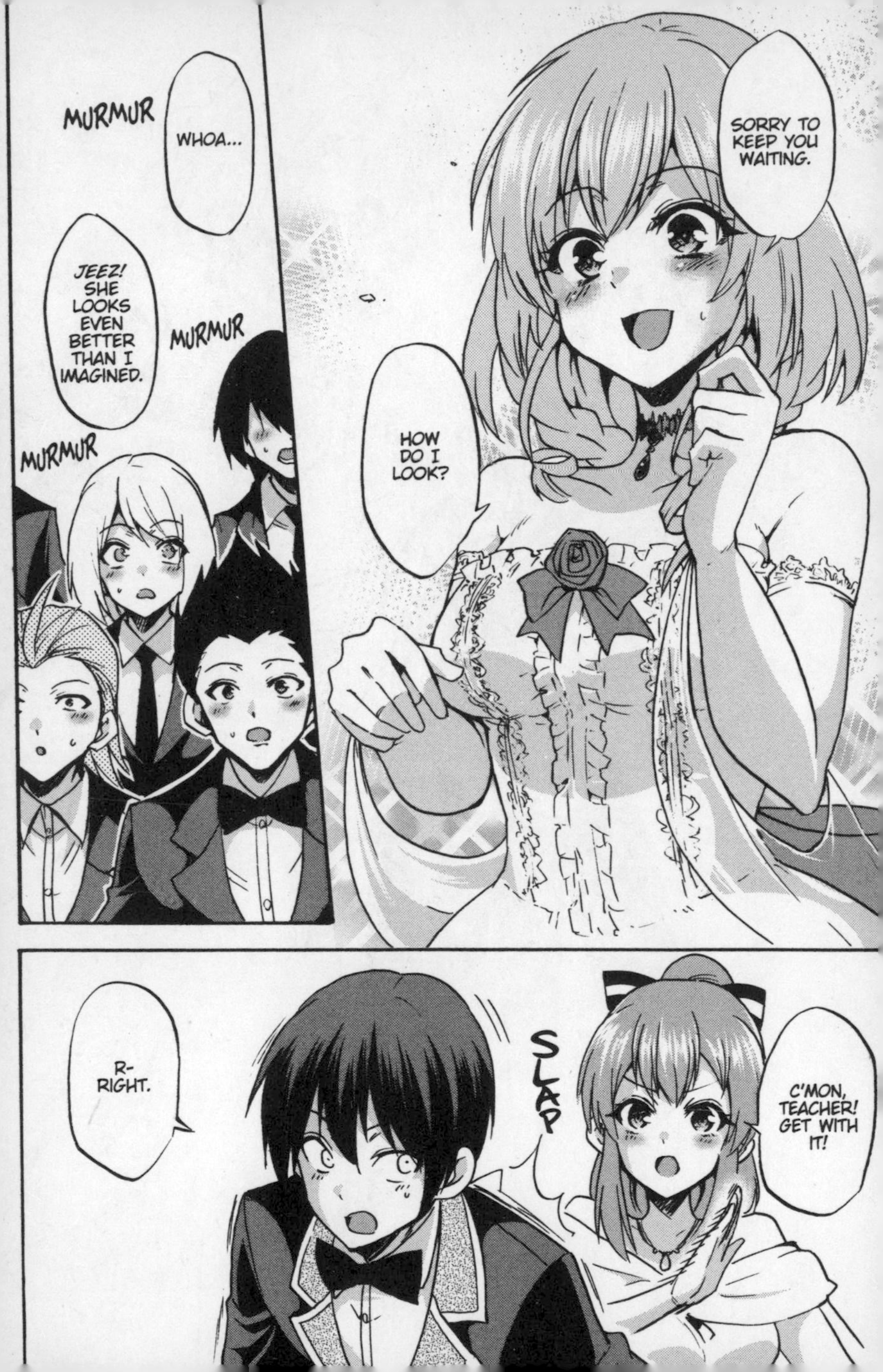
SORRY TO KEEP YOU WAITING.
HOW DO I LOOK?
MURMUR
WHOA...
JEEZ! SHE LOOKS EVEN BETTER THAN I IMAGINED.
MURMUR
MURMUR
C'MON, TEACHER! GET WITH IT!
SLAP
R-RIGHT.

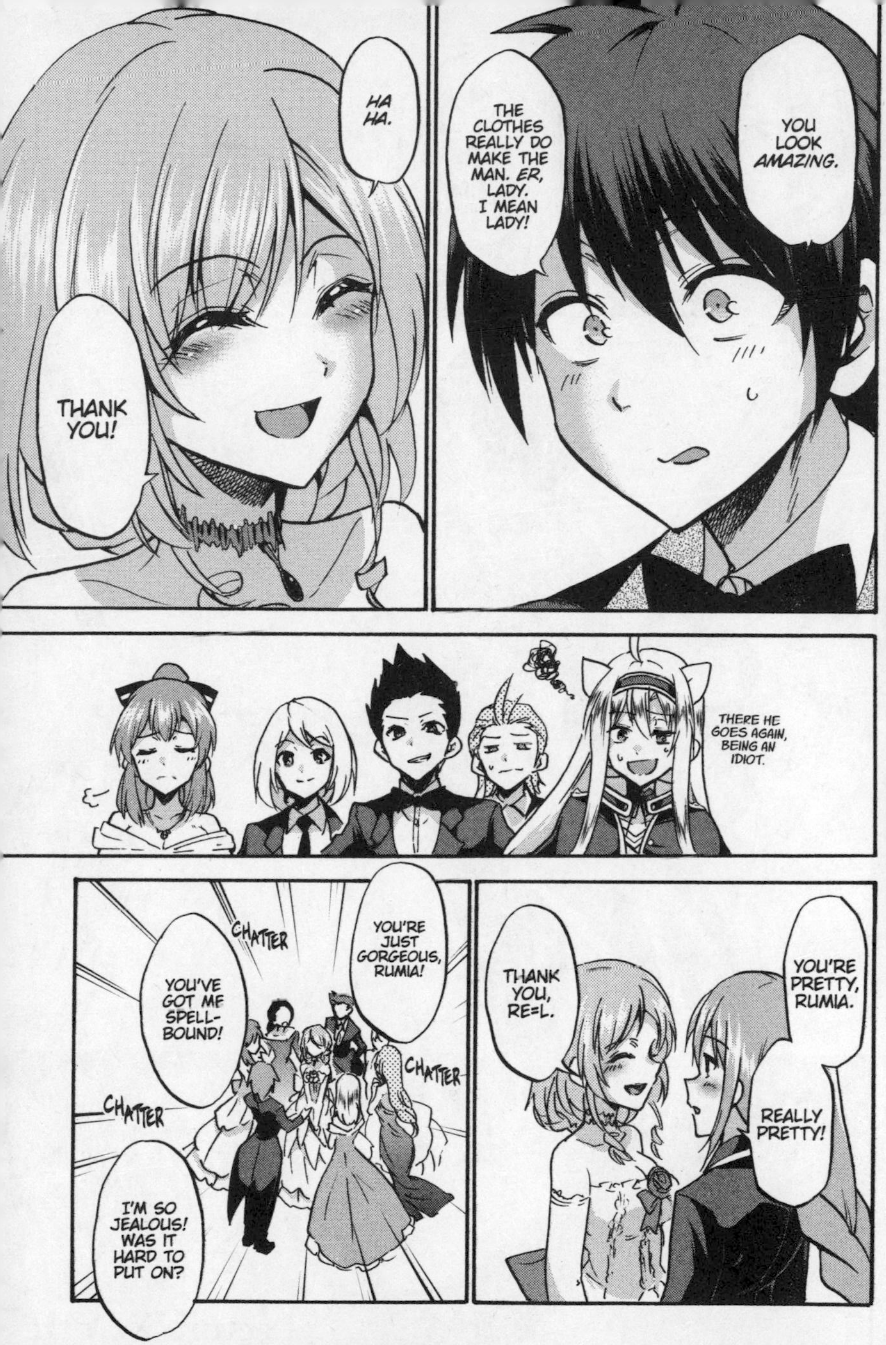
YOU LOOK AMAZING.
THE CLOTHES REALLY DO MAKE THE MAN. ER, LADY. I MEAN LADY!
HA HA.
THANK YOU!
THERE HE GOES AGAIN, BEING AN IDIOT.
YOU'RE PRETTY, RUMIA.
REALLY PRETTY!
THANK YOU, RE=L.
YOU'RE JUST GORGEOUS, RUMIA!
CHATTER
YOU'VE GOT ME SPELL-BOUND!
CHATTER
CHATTER
I'M SO JEALOUS! WAS IT HARD TO PUT ON?

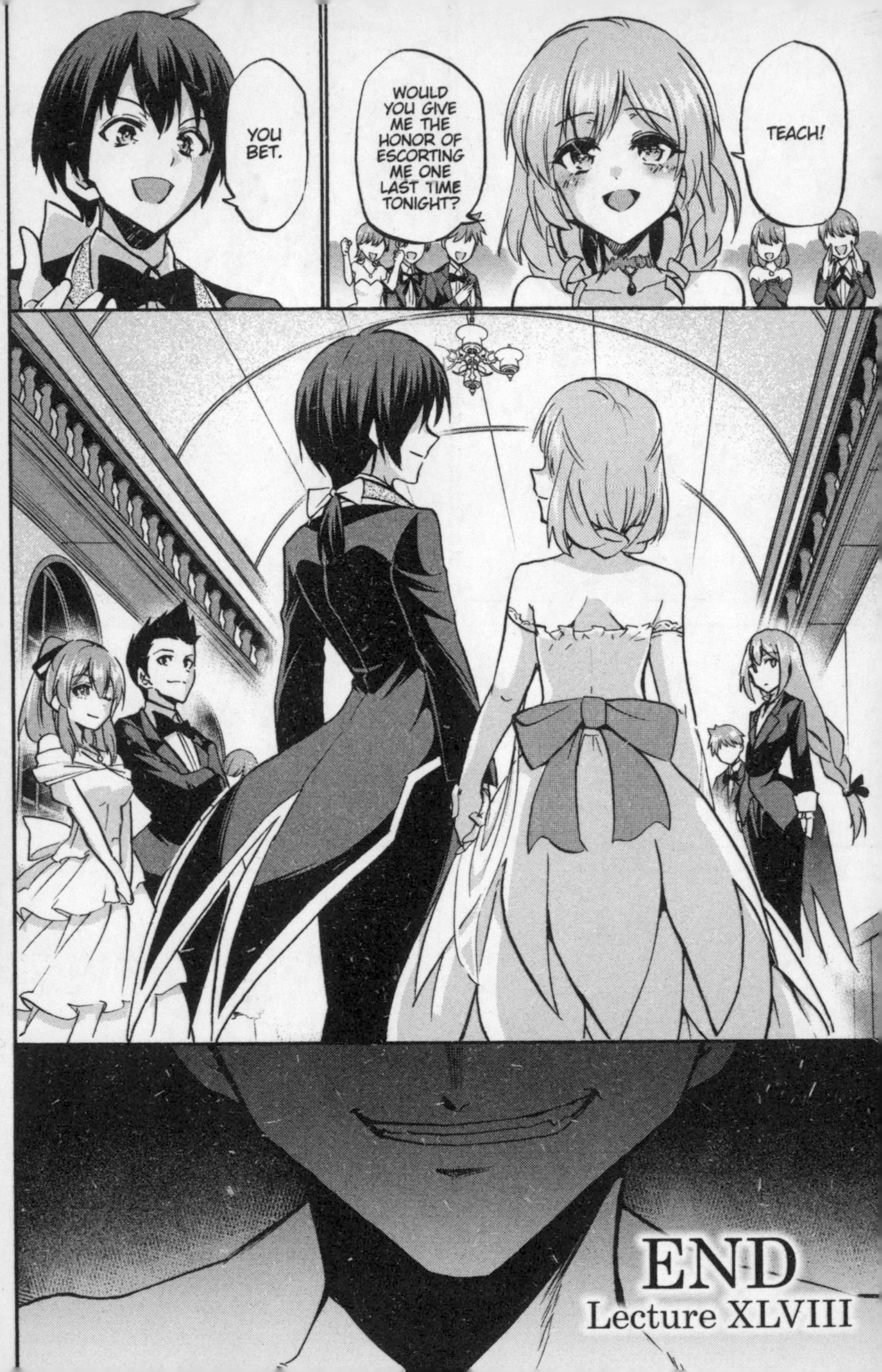
TEACH!
WOULD YOU GIVE ME THE HONOR OF ESCORTING ME ONE LAST TIME TONIGHT?
YOU BET.
END
Lecture XLVIII

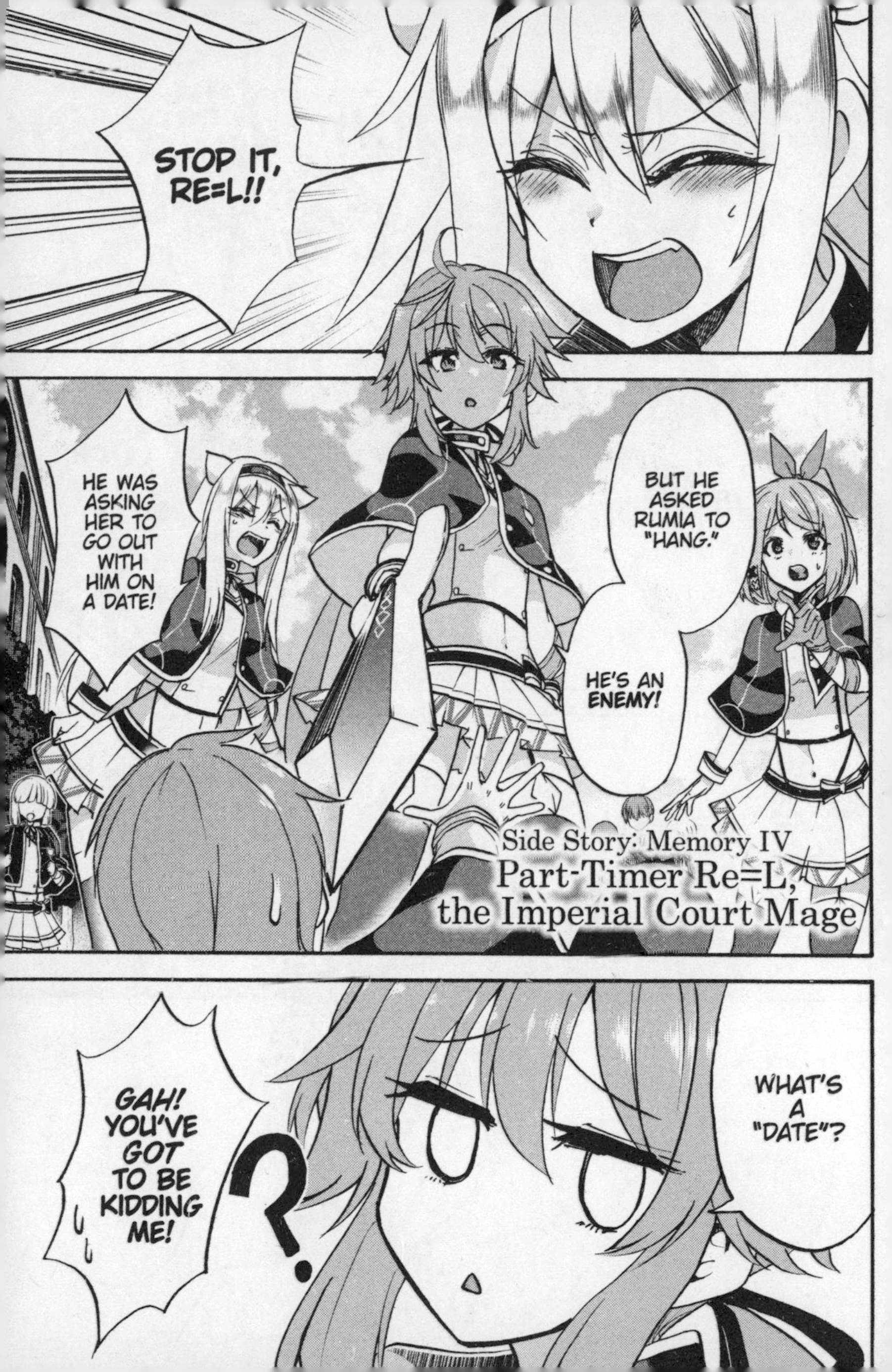
STOP IT, RE=L!!
BUT HE ASKED RUMIA TO "HANG."
HE'S AN ENEMY!
HE WAS ASKING HER TO GO OUT WITH HIM ON A DATE!
Side Story: Memory IV
Part-Timer Re=L, the Imperial Court Mage
WHAT'S A "DATE"?
GAH! YOU'VE GOT TO BE KIDDING ME!

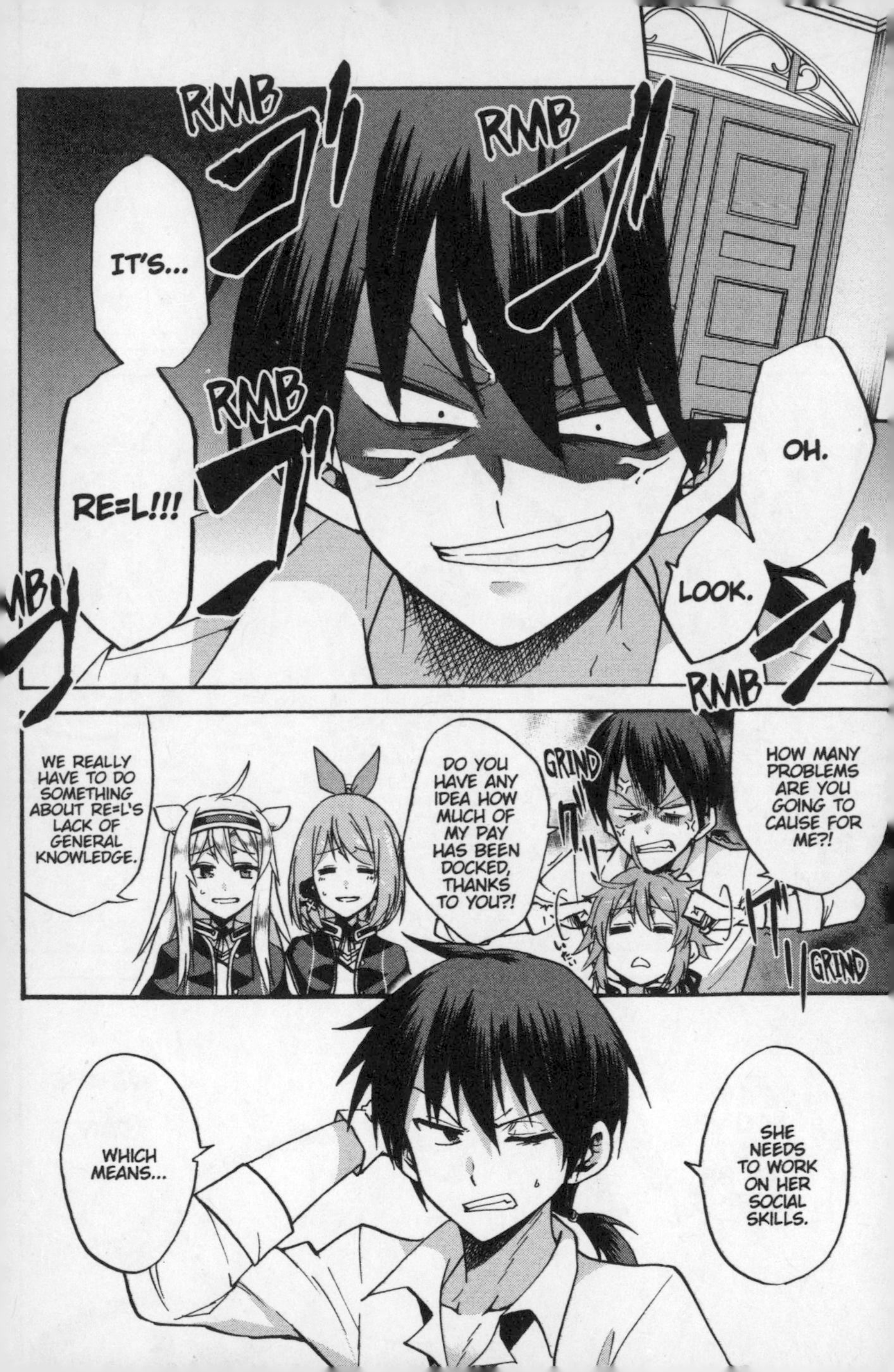
RMB
RMB
OH.
LOOK.
RMB
RMB
IT'S...
RE=L!!!
HOW MANY PROBLEMS ARE YOU GOING TO CAUSE FOR ME?!
GRIND
GRIND
DO YOU HAVE ANY IDEA HOW MUCH OF MY PAY HAS BEEN DOCKED, THANKS TO YOU?!
WE REALLY HAVE TO DO SOMETHING ABOUT RE=L'S LACK OF GENERAL KNOWLEDGE.
SHE NEEDS TO WORK ON HER SOCIAL SKILLS.
WHICH MEANS...

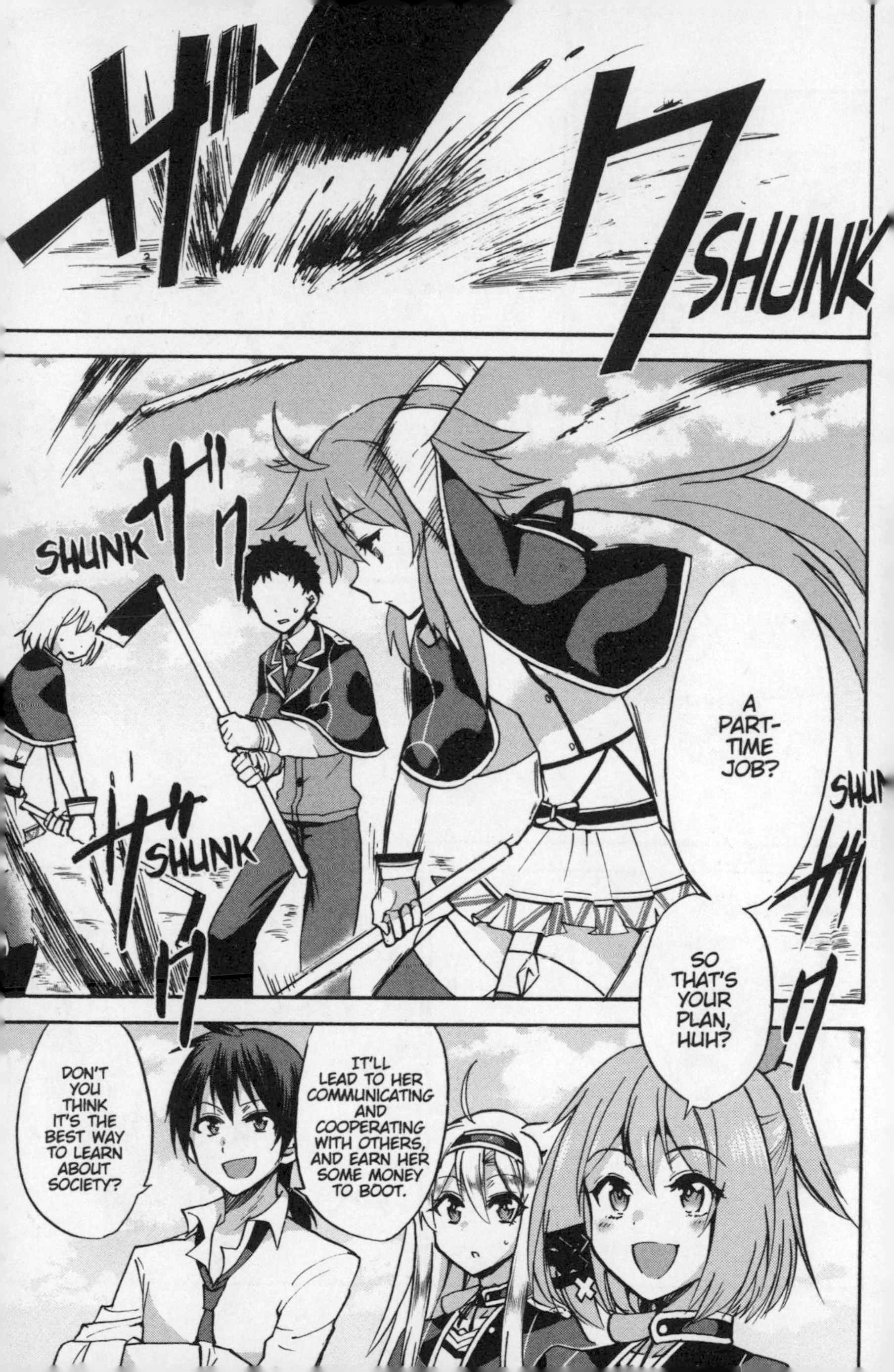

SHUNK
A PART-TIME JOB?
SHUNK
SHUNK
SO THAT'S YOUR PLAN, HUH?
IT'LL LEAD TO HER COMMUNICATING AND COOPERATING WITH OTHERS, AND EARN HER SOME MONEY TO BOOT.
DON'T YOU THINK IT'S THE BEST WAY TO LEARN ABOUT SOCIETY?

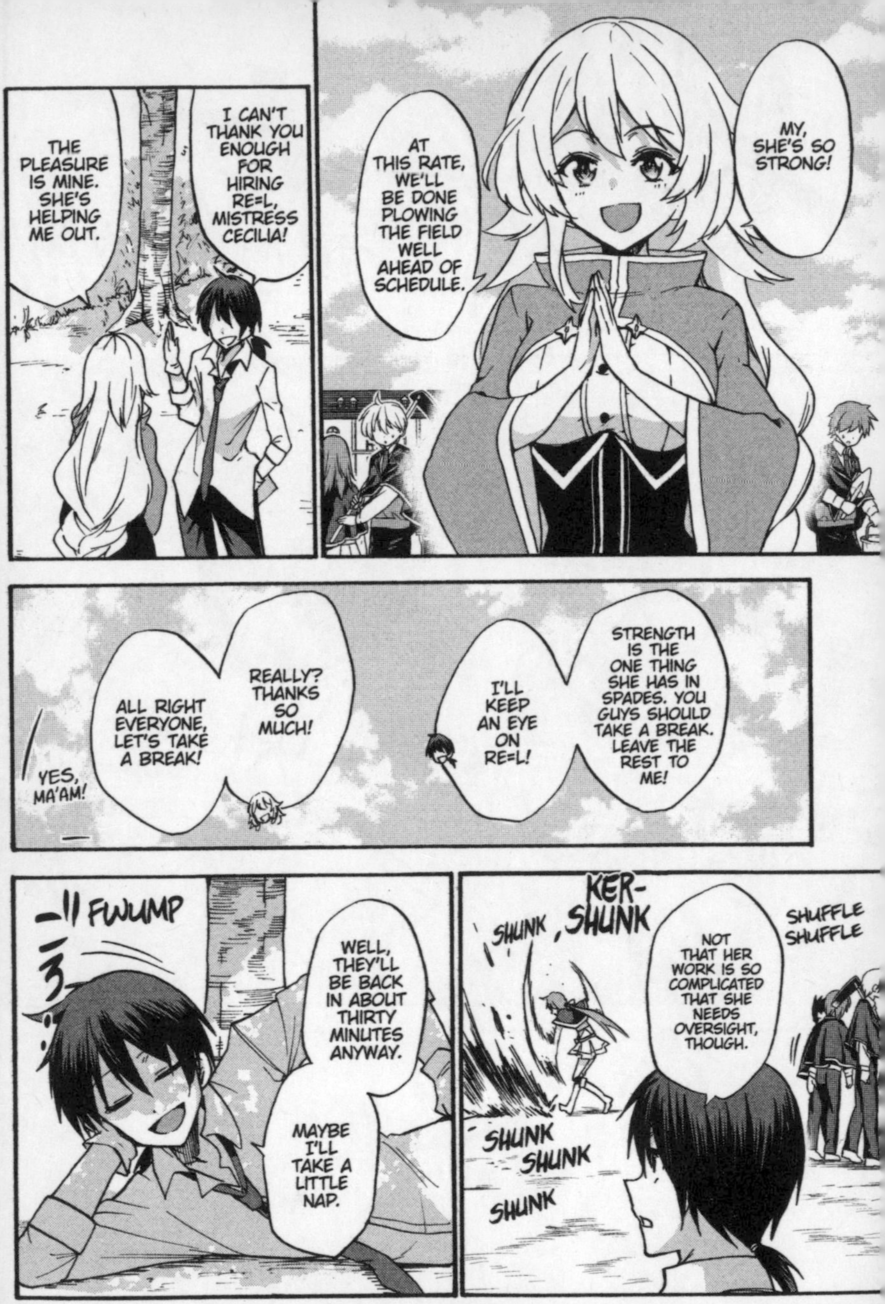
MY, SHE'S SO STRONG!
AT THIS RATE, WE'LL BE DONE PLOWING THE FIELD WELL AHEAD OF SCHEDULE.
I CAN'T THANK YOU ENOUGH FOR HIRING RE=L, MISTRESS CECILIA!
THE PLEASURE IS MINE. SHE'S HELPING ME OUT.
STRENGTH IS THE ONE THING SHE HAS IN SPADES. YOU GUYS SHOULD TAKE A BREAK. LEAVE THE REST TO ME!
I'LL KEEP AN EYE ON RE=L!
REALLY? THANKS SO MUCH!
ALL RIGHT EVERYONE, LET'S TAKE A BREAK!
YES, MA'AM!
SHUFFLE SHUFFLE
NOT THAT HER WORK IS SO COMPLICATED THAT SHE NEEDS OVERSIGHT, THOUGH.
KER-SHUNK
SHUNK
SHUNK
SHUNK
SHUNK
FWUMP
WELL, THEY'LL BE BACK IN ABOUT THIRTY MINUTES ANYWAY.
MAYBE I'LL TAKE A LITTLE NAP.

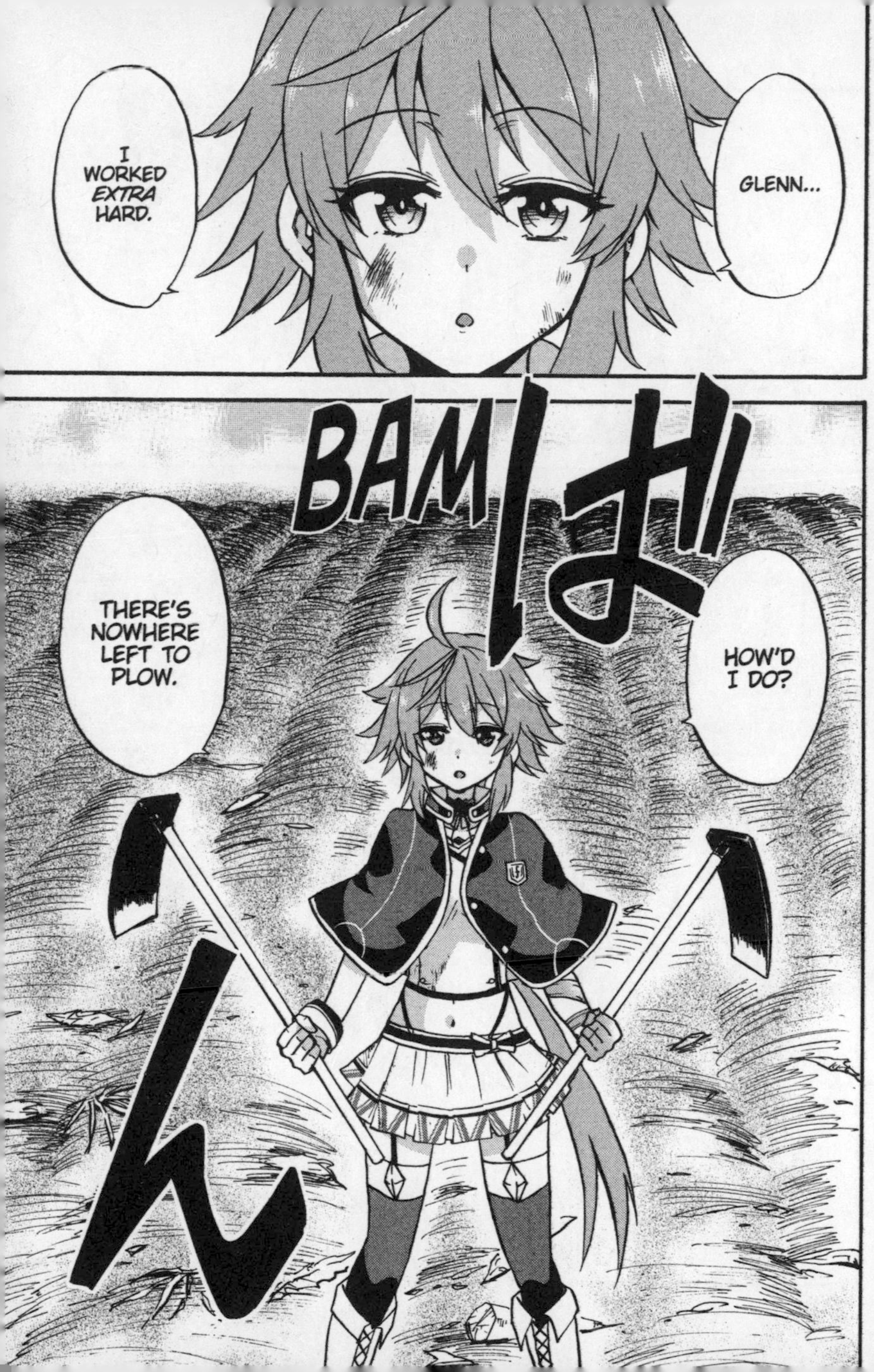
GLENN...
I WORKED *EXTRA* HARD.
BAM
ばん
HOW'D I DO?
THERE'S NOWHERE LEFT TO PLOW.

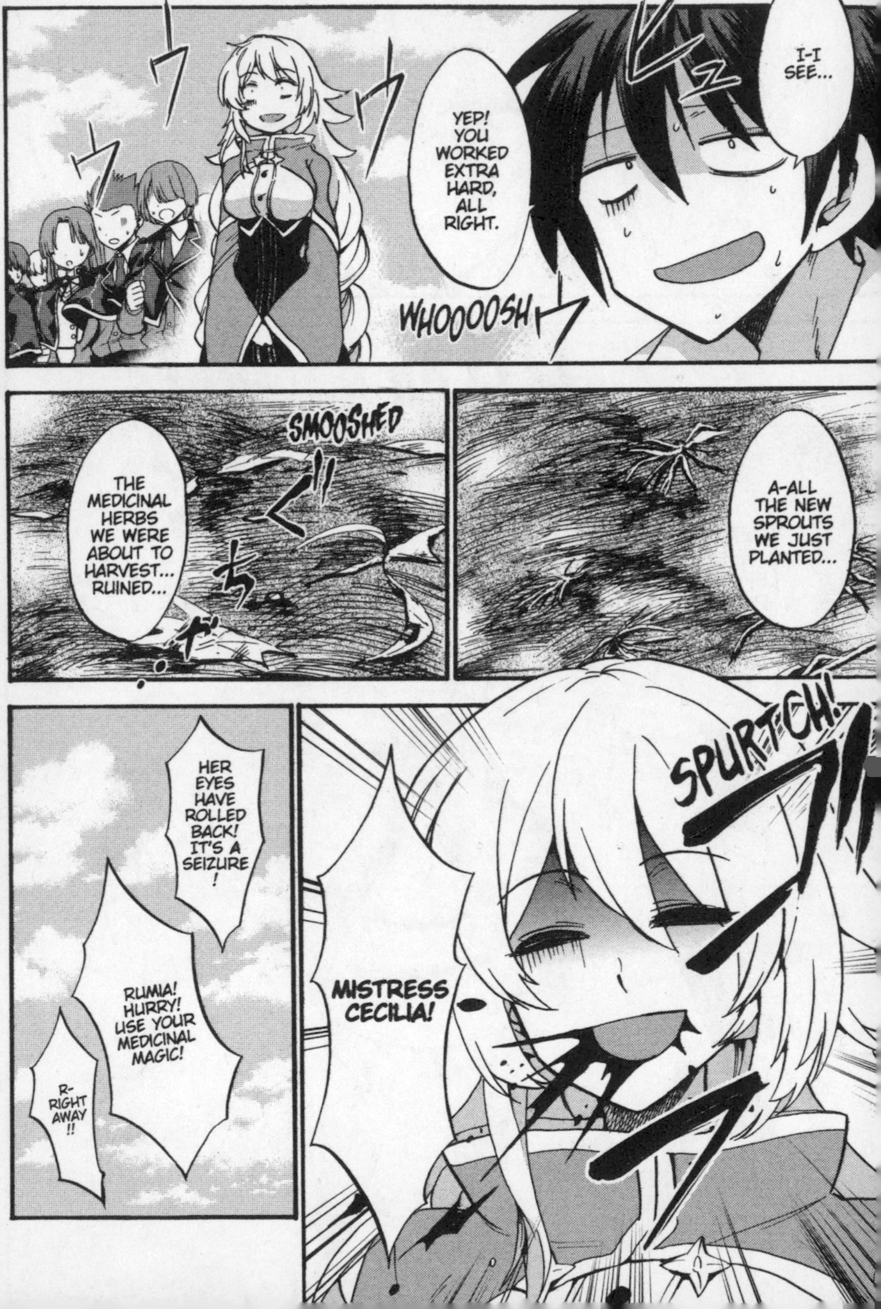
I-I SEE...
YEP! YOU WORKED EXTRA HARD, ALL RIGHT.
WHOOOOSH
A-ALL THE NEW SPROUTS WE JUST PLANTED...
SMOOSHED
THE MEDICINAL HERBS WE WERE ABOUT TO HARVEST... RUINED...
SPURTCH!
MISTRESS CECILIA!
HER EYES HAVE ROLLED BACK! IT'S A SEIZURE!
RUMIA! HURRY! USE YOUR MEDICINAL MAGIC!
R-RIGHT AWAY!!

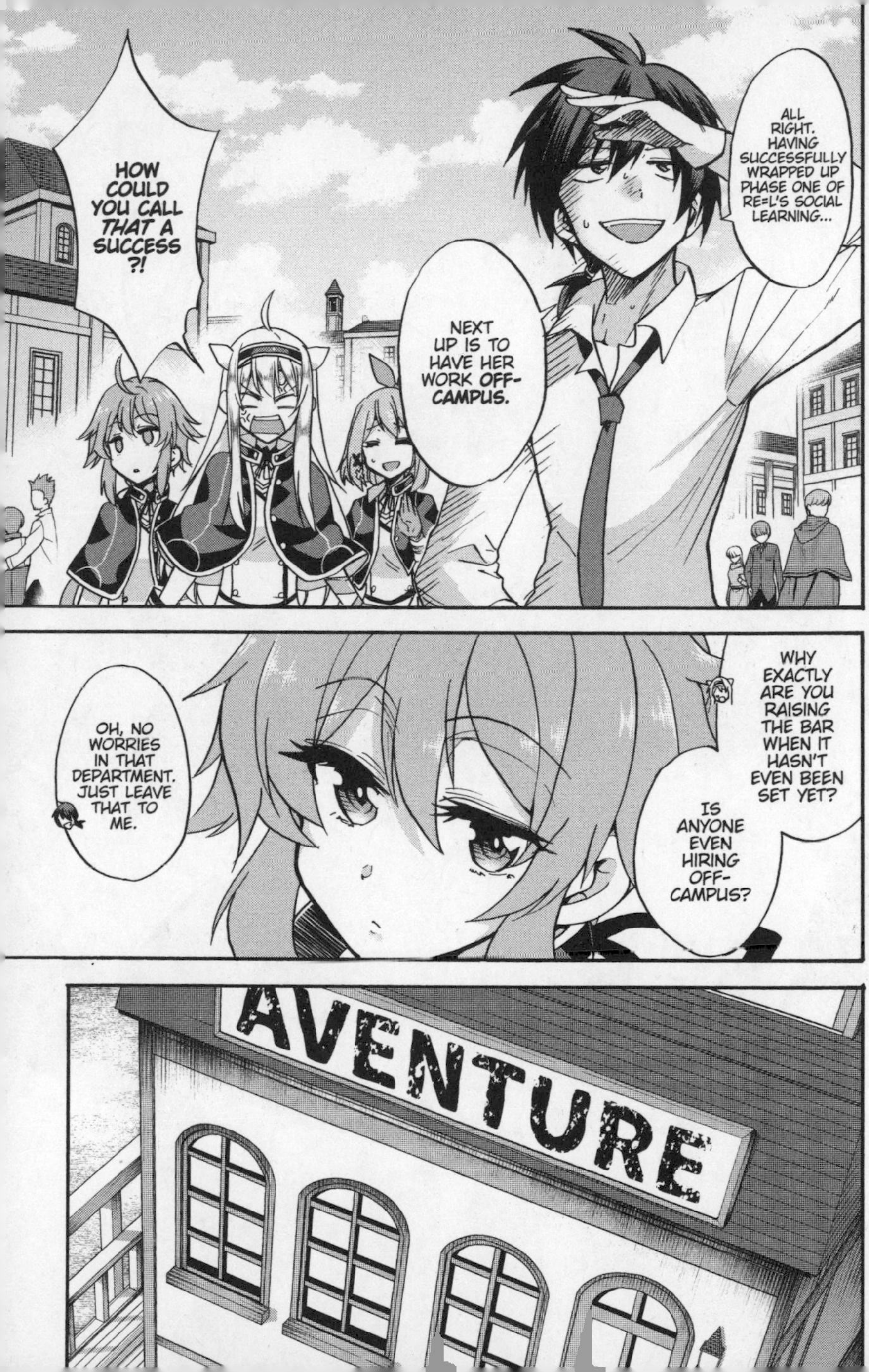
ALL RIGHT. HAVING SUCCESSFULLY WRAPPED UP PHASE ONE OF RE=L'S SOCIAL LEARNING...
NEXT UP IS TO HAVE HER WORK OFF-CAMPUS.
HOW COULD YOU CALL THAT A SUCCESS ?!
WHY EXACTLY ARE YOU RAISING THE BAR WHEN IT HASN'T EVEN BEEN SET YET?
IS ANYONE EVEN HIRING OFF-CAMPUS?
OH, NO WORRIES IN THAT DEPARTMENT. JUST LEAVE THAT TO ME.
AVENTURE

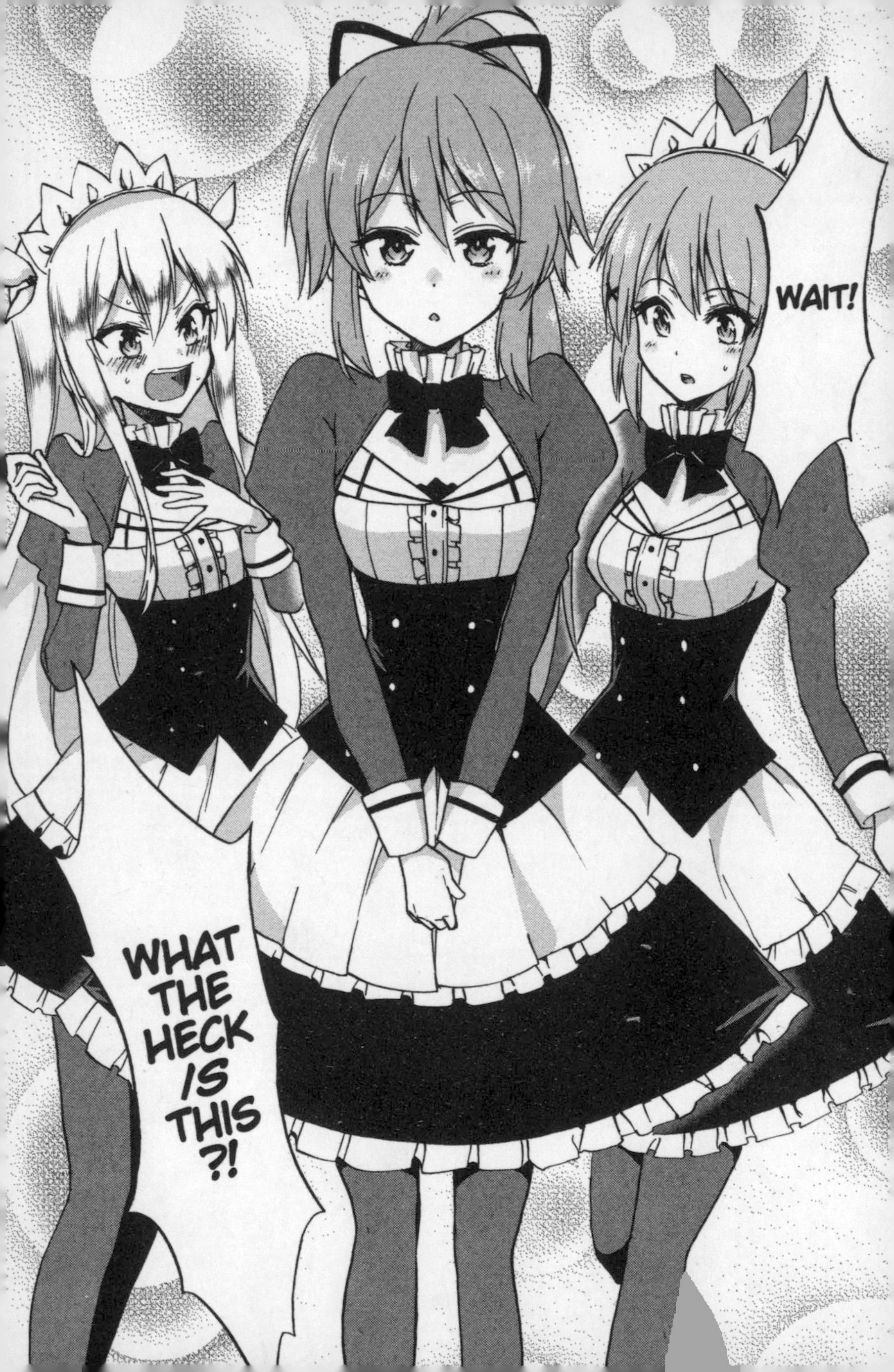
WAIT!
WHAT THE HECK IS THIS?!

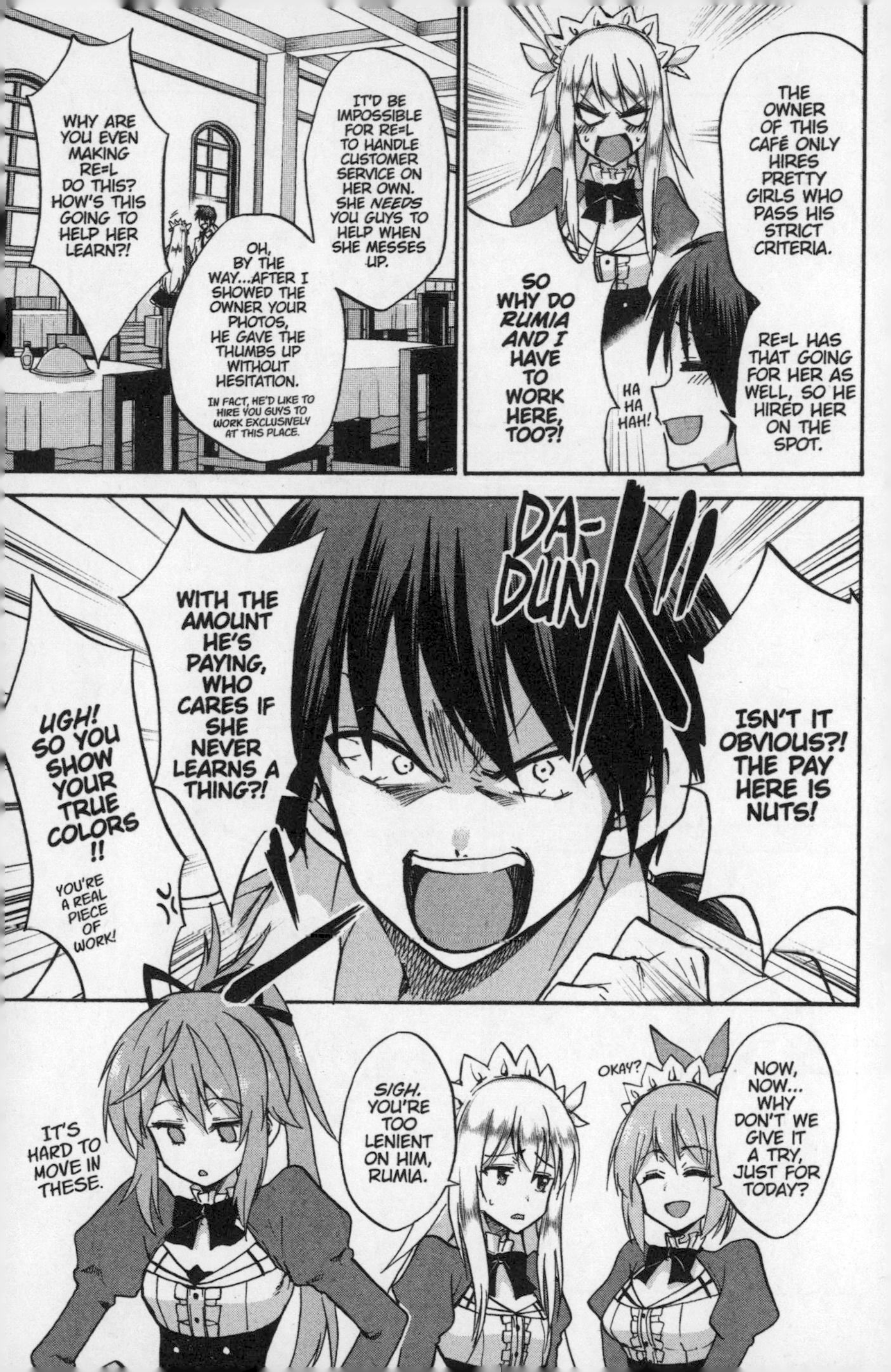
THE OWNER OF THIS CAFÉ ONLY HIRES PRETTY GIRLS WHO PASS HIS STRICT CRITERIA.
RE=L HAS THAT GOING FOR HER AS WELL, SO HE HIRED HER ON THE SPOT.
HA HA HAH!
SO WHY DO *RUMIA* AND *I* HAVE TO WORK HERE, TOO?!
IT'D BE IMPOSSIBLE FOR RE=L TO HANDLE CUSTOMER SERVICE ON HER OWN. SHE *NEEDS* YOU GUYS TO HELP WHEN SHE MESSES UP.
OH, BY THE WAY...AFTER I SHOWED THE OWNER YOUR PHOTOS, HE GAVE THE THUMBS UP WITHOUT HESITATION.
IN FACT, HE'D LIKE TO HIRE YOU GUYS TO WORK EXCLUSIVELY AT THIS PLACE.
WHY ARE YOU EVEN MAKING RE=L DO THIS? HOW'S THIS GOING TO HELP HER LEARN?!
DA-DUNK!!
ISN'T IT OBVIOUS?! THE PAY HERE IS NUTS!
WITH THE AMOUNT HE'S PAYING, WHO CARES IF SHE NEVER LEARNS A THING?!
UGH! SO YOU SHOW YOUR TRUE COLORS!!
YOU'RE A REAL PIECE OF WORK!
NOW, NOW... WHY DON'T WE GIVE IT A TRY, JUST FOR TODAY?
OKAY?
SIGH. YOU'RE TOO LENIENT ON HIM, RUMIA.
IT'S HARD TO MOVE IN THESE.

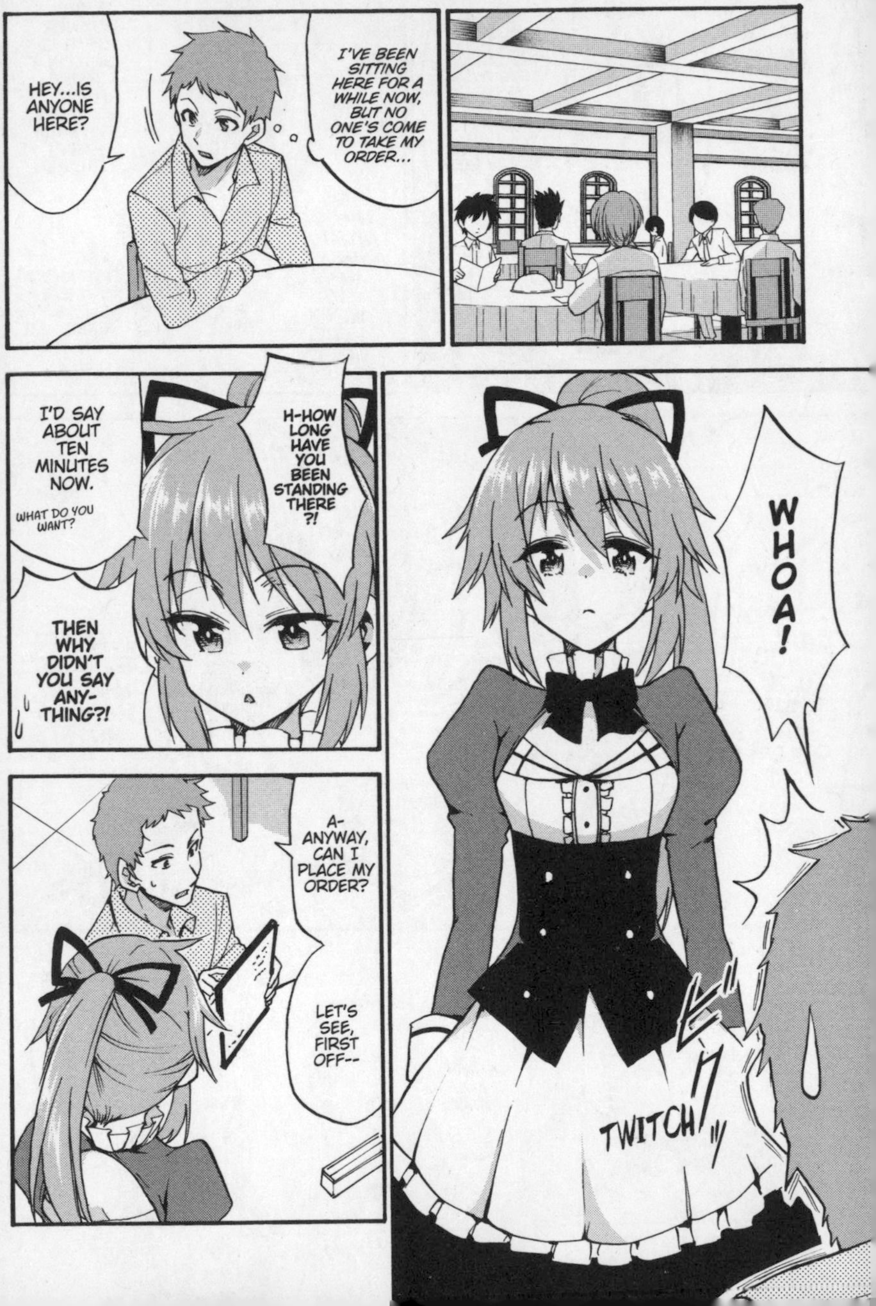
I'VE BEEN SITTING HERE FOR A WHILE NOW, BUT NO ONE'S COME TO TAKE MY ORDER...
HEY...IS ANYONE HERE?
WHOA!
TWITCH
H-HOW LONG HAVE YOU BEEN STANDING THERE?!
I'D SAY ABOUT TEN MINUTES NOW.
WHAT DO YOU WANT?
THEN WHY DIDN'T YOU SAY ANY-THING?!
A-ANYWAY, CAN I PLACE MY ORDER?
LET'S SEE, FIRST OFF--

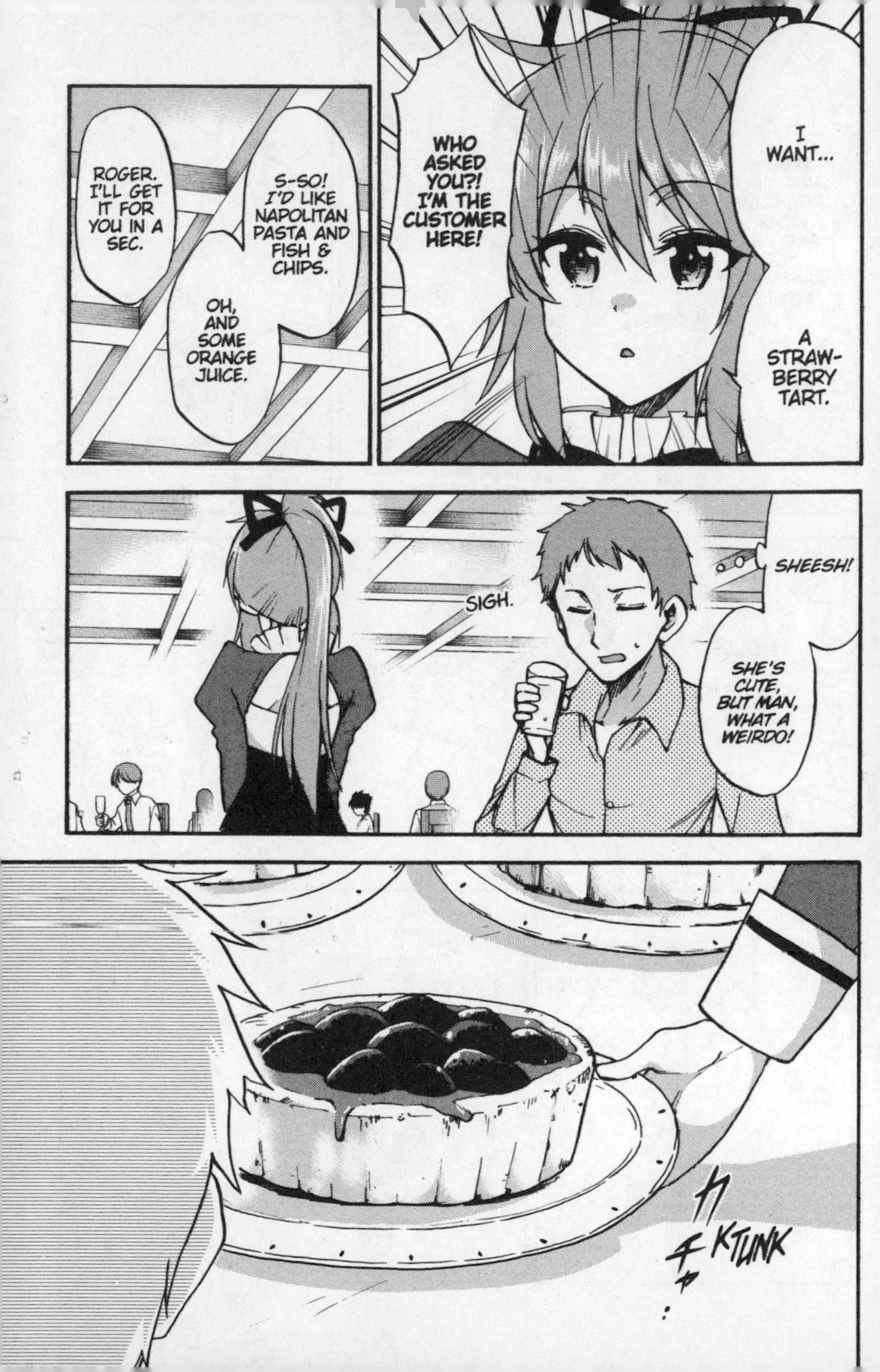
I WANT...
A STRAWBERRY TART.
WHO ASKED YOU?! I'M THE CUSTOMER HERE!
S-SO! I'D LIKE NAPOLITAN PASTA AND FISH & CHIPS.
OH, AND SOME ORANGE JUICE.
ROGER. I'LL GET IT FOR YOU IN A SEC.
SHEESH!
SHE'S CUTE, BUT MAN, WHAT A WEIRDO!
SIGH.
KTUNK

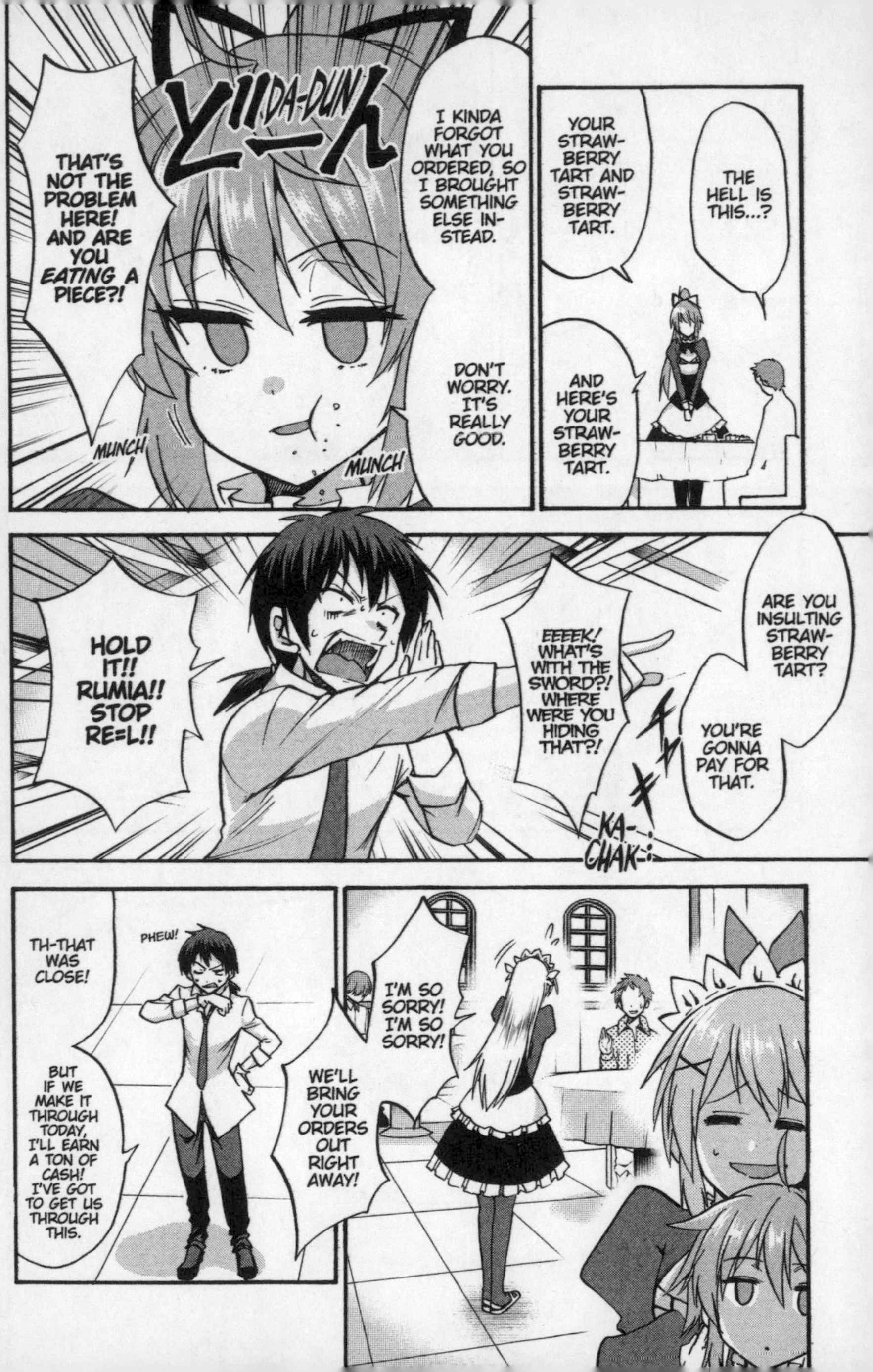

THE HELL IS THIS...?
YOUR STRAWBERRY TART AND STRAWBERRY TART.
AND HERE'S YOUR STRAWBERRY TART.
I KINDA FORGOT WHAT YOU ORDERED, SO I BROUGHT SOMETHING ELSE INSTEAD.
YIIDA-DUNK
THAT'S NOT THE PROBLEM HERE! AND ARE YOU EATING A PIECE?!
DON'T WORRY. IT'S REALLY GOOD.
MUNCH
MUNCH
ARE YOU INSULTING STRAWBERRY TART?
YOU'RE GONNA PAY FOR THAT.
KA-CHAK
EEEEK! WHAT'S WITH THE SWORD?! WHERE WERE YOU HIDING THAT?!
HOLD IT!! RUMIA!! STOP RE=L!!
I'M SO SORRY! I'M SO SORRY!
WE'LL BRING YOUR ORDERS OUT RIGHT AWAY!
PHEW!
TH-THAT WAS CLOSE!
BUT IF WE MAKE IT THROUGH TODAY, I'LL EARN A TON OF CASH! I'VE GOT TO GET US THROUGH THIS.

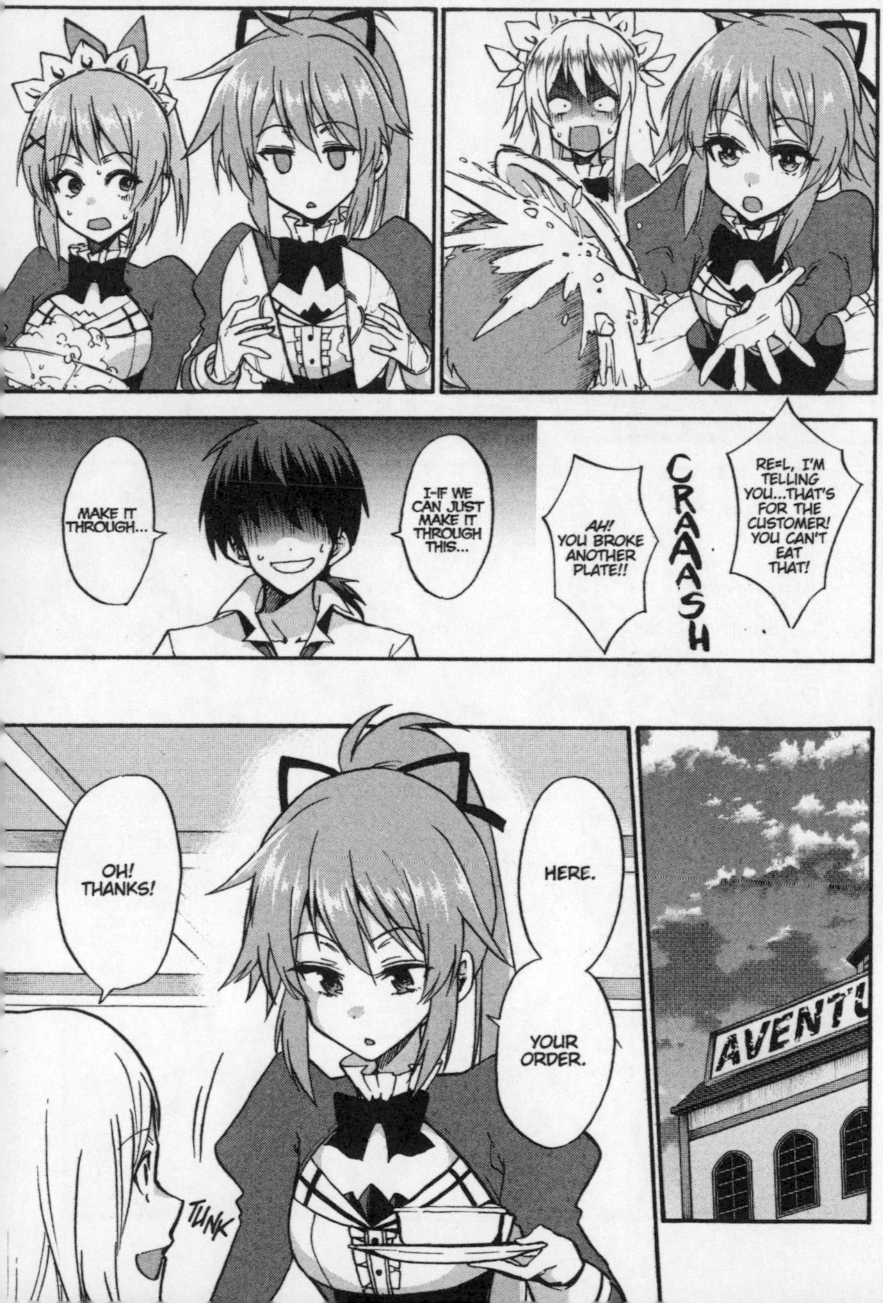
RE=L, I'M TELLING YOU...THAT'S FOR THE CUSTOMER! YOU CAN'T EAT THAT!
CRAAASH
AH! YOU BROKE ANOTHER PLATE!!
I-IF WE CAN JUST MAKE IT THROUGH THIS...
MAKE IT THROUGH...
AVENTU
HERE.
YOUR ORDER.
TUNK
OH! THANKS!

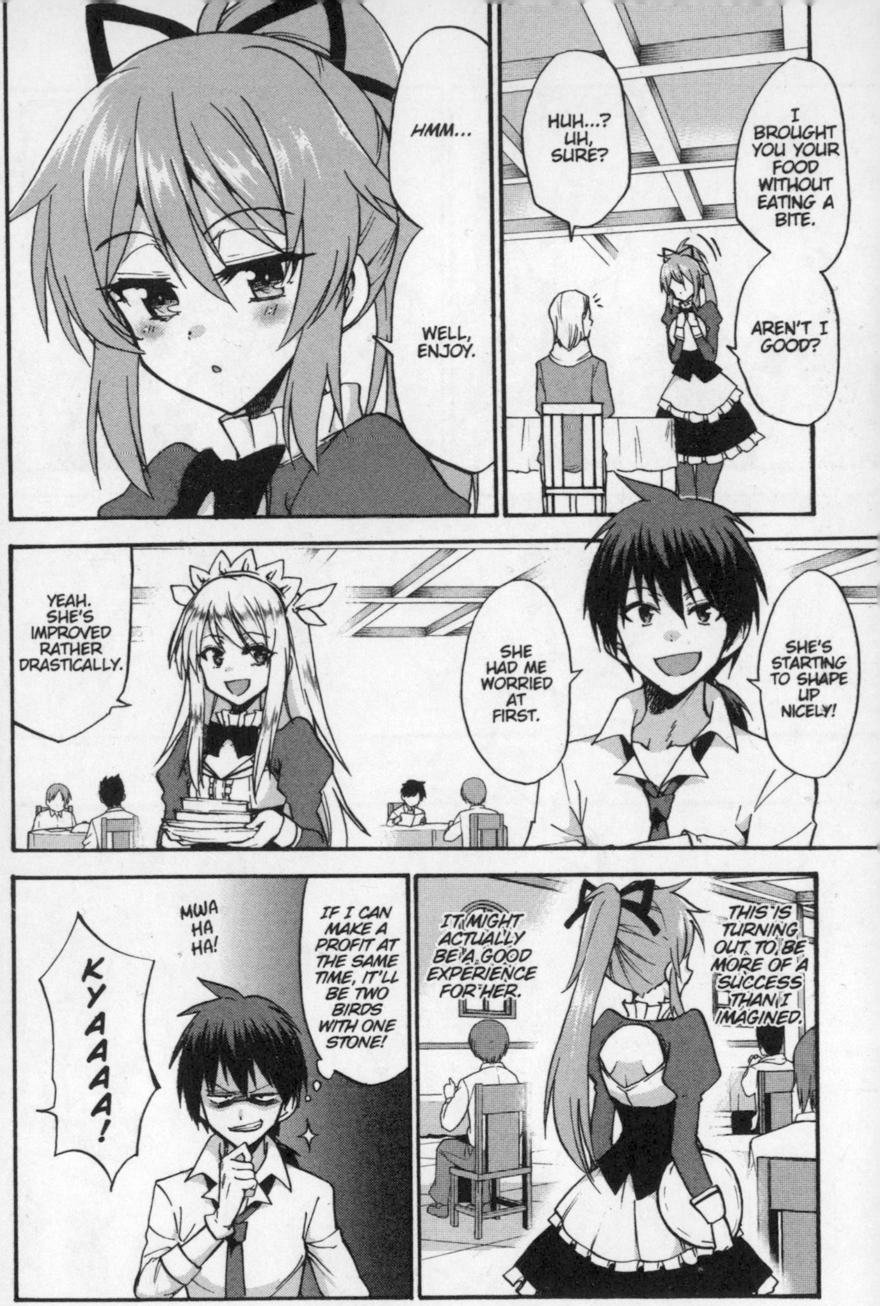
I BROUGHT YOU YOUR FOOD WITHOUT EATING A BITE.
AREN'T I GOOD?
HUH...? UH, SURE?
HMM...
WELL, ENJOY.
SHE'S STARTING TO SHAPE UP NICELY!
SHE HAD ME WORRIED AT FIRST.
YEAH. SHE'S IMPROVED RATHER DRASTICALLY.
THIS IS TURNING OUT TO BE MORE OF A SUCCESS THAN I IMAGINED.
IT MIGHT ACTUALLY BE A GOOD EXPERIENCE FOR HER.
IF I CAN MAKE A PROFIT AT THE SAME TIME, IT'LL BE TWO BIRDS WITH ONE STONE!
MWA HA HA!
KYAAAAA!

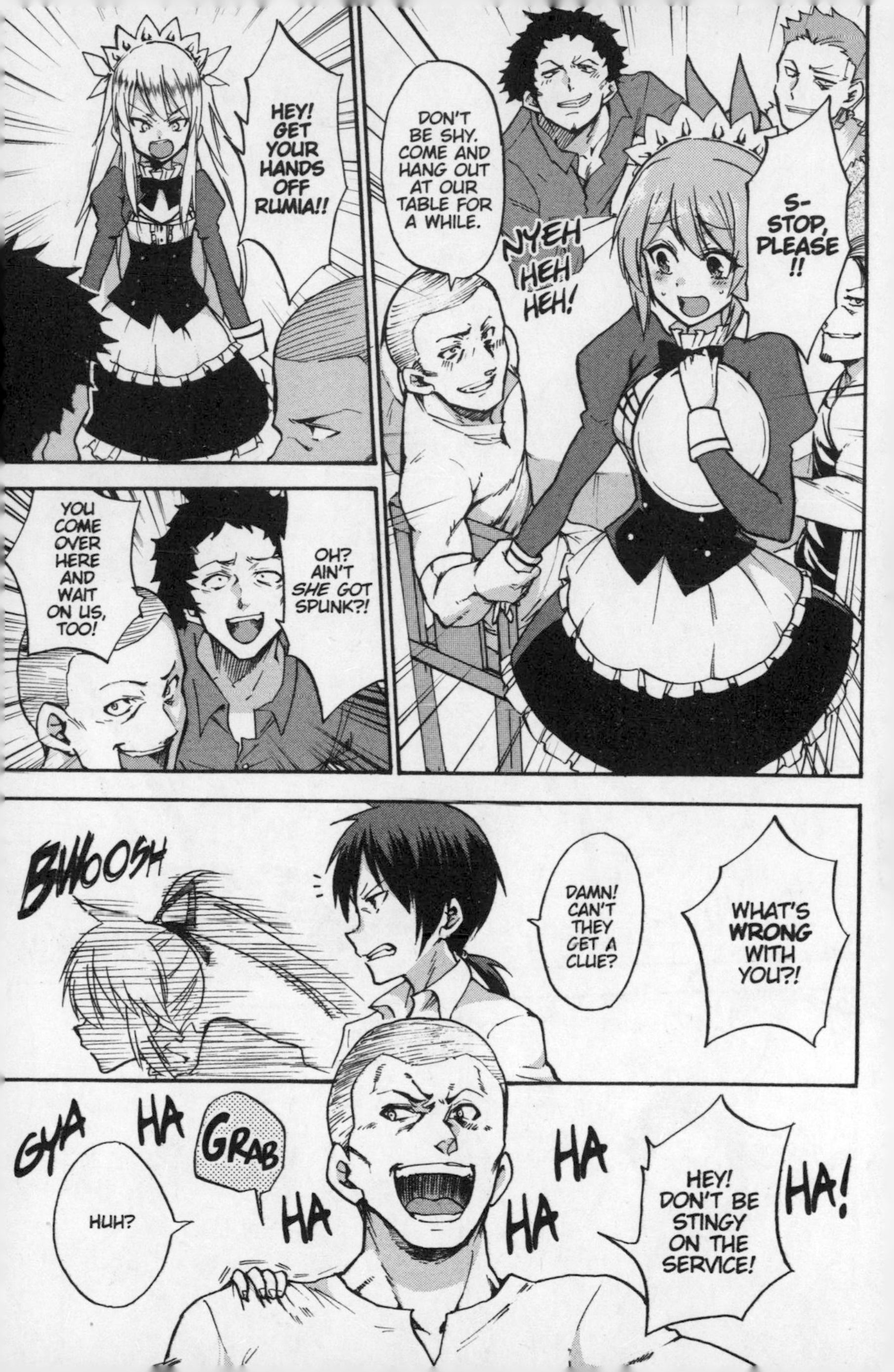
DON'T BE SHY. COME AND HANG OUT AT OUR TABLE FOR A WHILE.
NYEH HEH HEH!
S-STOP, PLEASE!!
HEY! GET YOUR HANDS OFF RUMIA!!
OH? AIN'T SHE GOT SPUNK?!
YOU COME OVER HERE AND WAIT ON US, TOO!
WHAT'S WRONG WITH YOU?!
DAMN! CAN'T THEY GET A CLUE?
BWOOSH
HEY! DON'T BE STINGY ON THE SERVICE!
GYA HA HA HA HA HA!
GRAB
HUH?

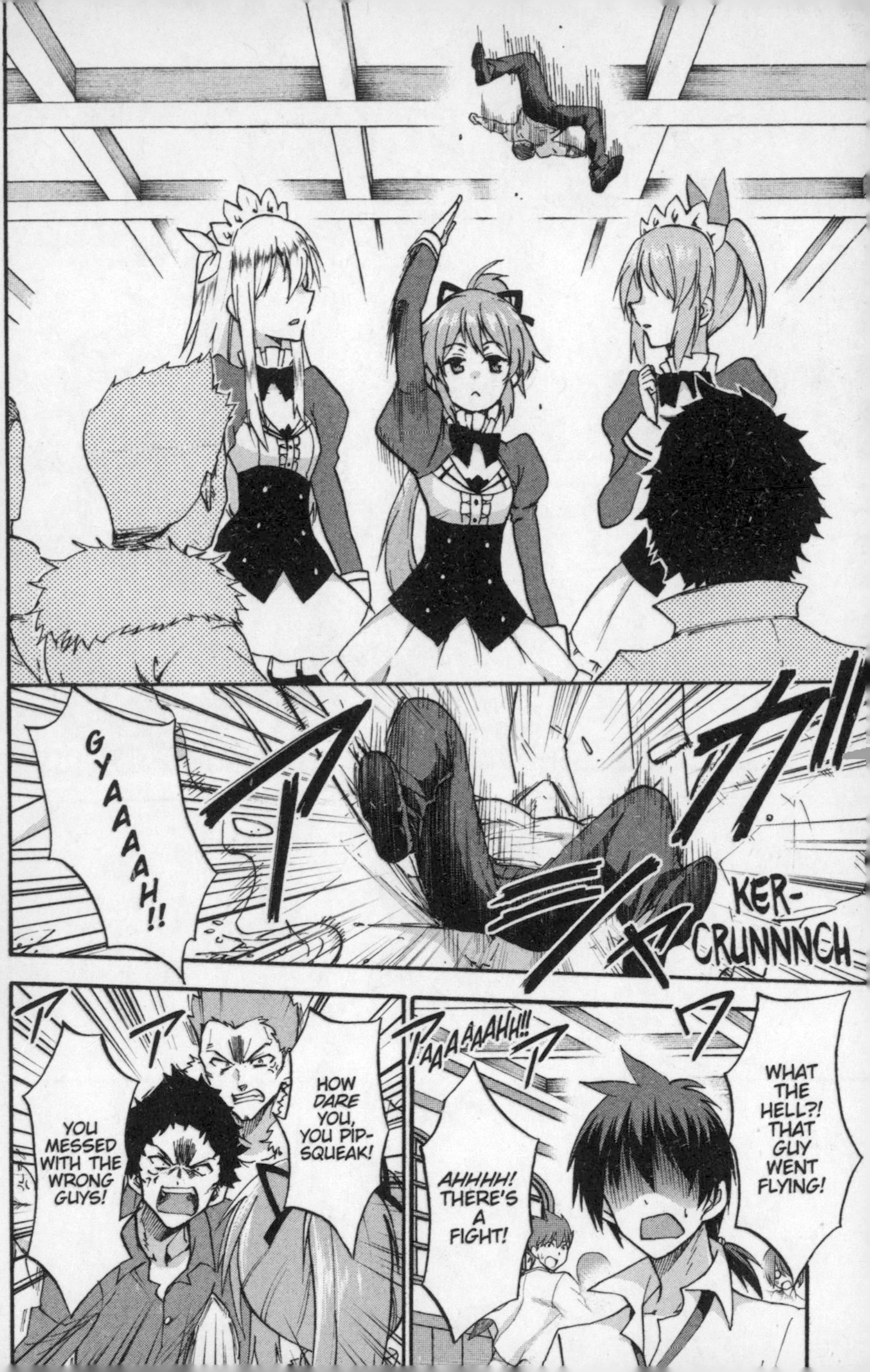
KER-CRUNNNCH
GYAAAAAH!!
WHAT THE HELL?! THAT GUY WENT FLYING!
AHHHH! THERE'S A FIGHT!
AAAAAAHH!!
HOW DARE YOU, YOU PIP-SQUEAK!
YOU MESSED WITH THE WRONG GUYS!

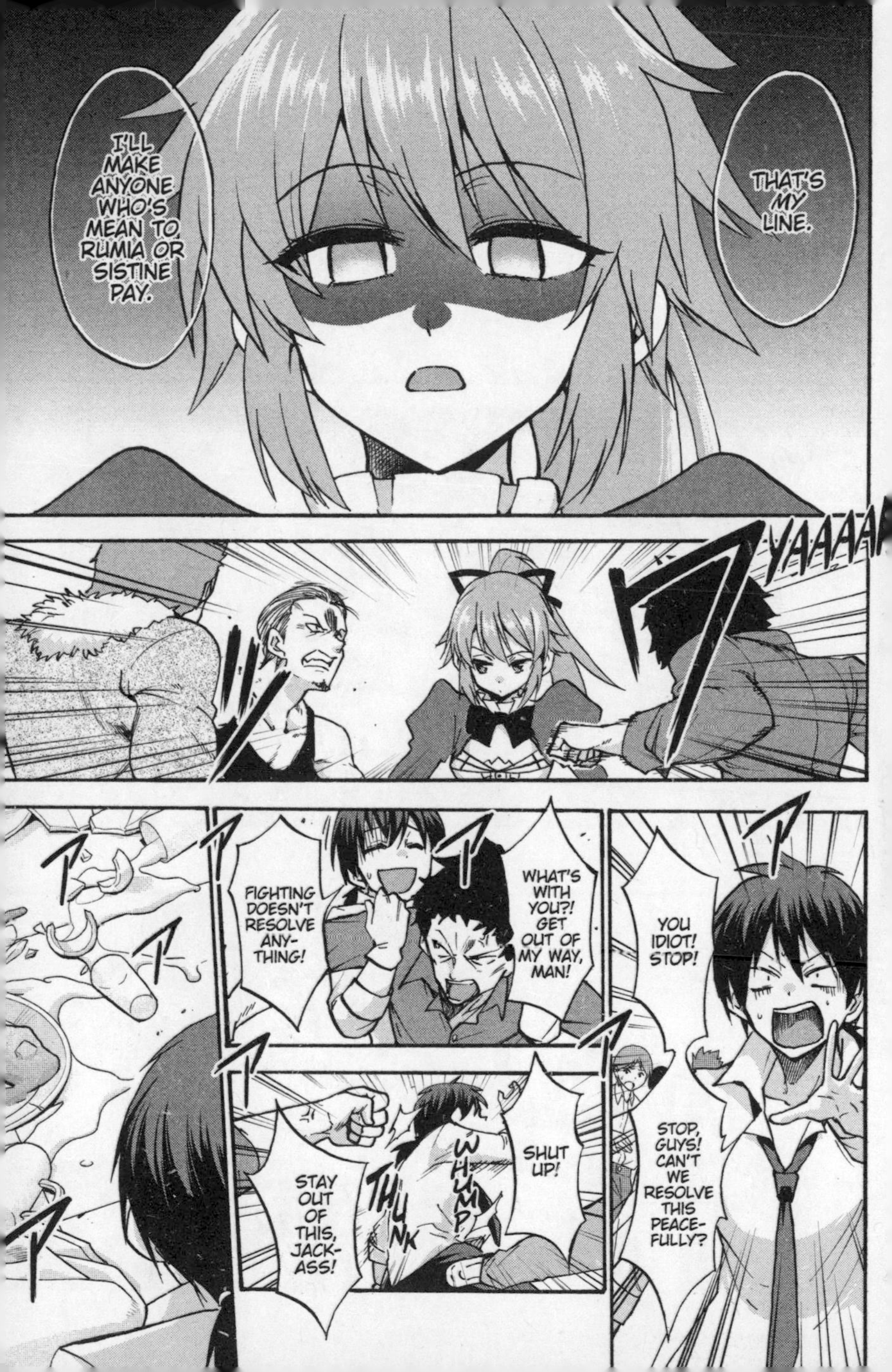
THAT'S MY LINE.
I'LL MAKE ANYONE WHO'S MEAN TO RUMIA OR SISTINE PAY.
YAAAAA
YOU IDIOT! STOP!
STOP, GUYS! CAN'T WE RESOLVE THIS PEACEFULLY?
WHAT'S WITH YOU?! GET OUT OF MY WAY, MAN!
FIGHTING DOESN'T RESOLVE ANYTHING!
SHUT UP!
WHUMP!
THUNK
STAY OUT OF THIS, JACKASS!

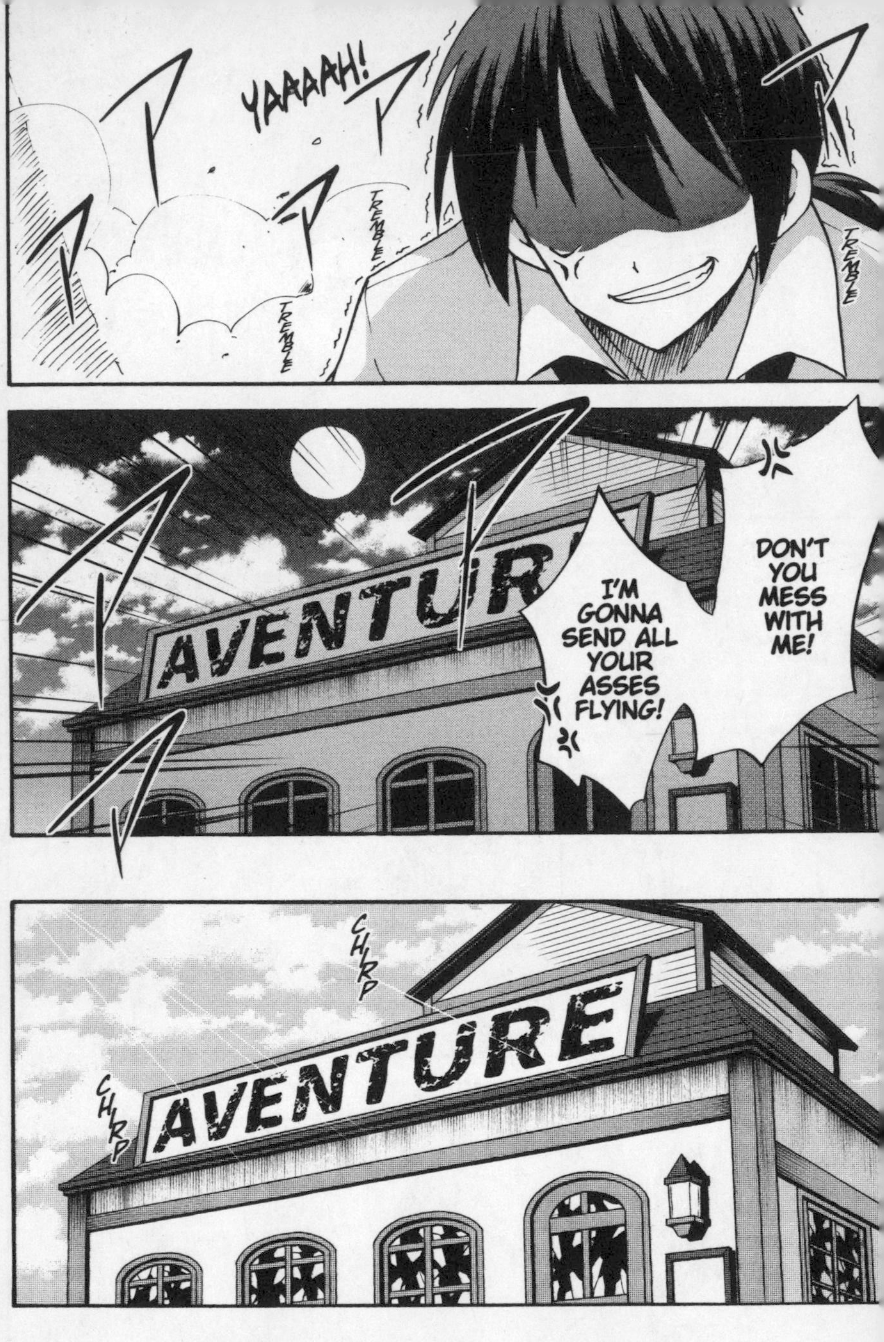
TREMBLE
YAAAAH!
TREMBLE
TREMBLE
DON'T YOU MESS WITH ME!
I'M GONNA SEND ALL YOUR ASSES FLYING!
AVENTURE
CHIRP
AVENTURE
CHIRP

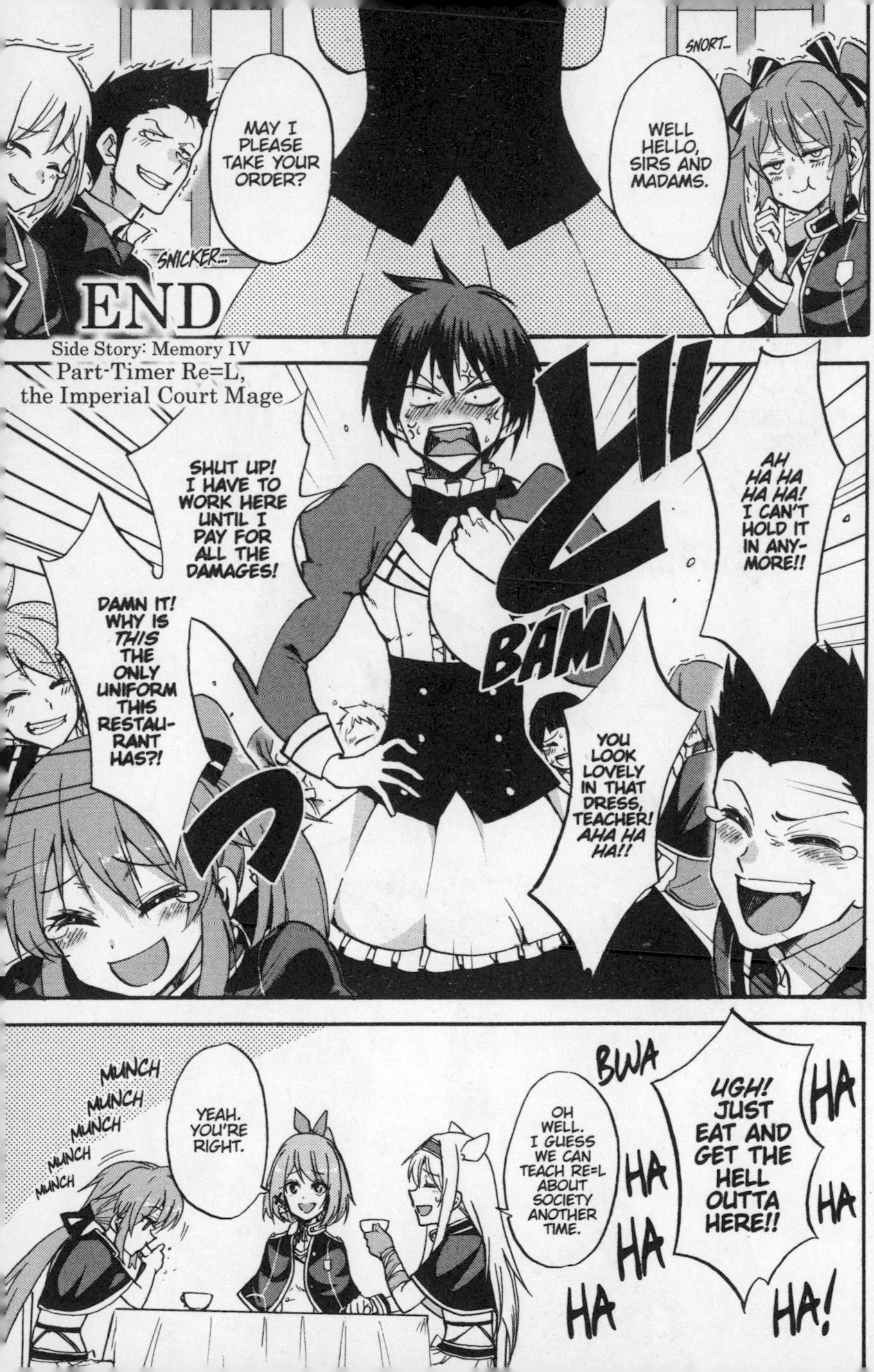
SNORT...
WELL HELLO, SIRS AND MADAMS.
MAY I PLEASE TAKE YOUR ORDER?
SNICKER...
END
Side Story: Memory IV
Part-Timer Re=L, the Imperial Court Mage
AH HA HA HA HA! I CAN'T HOLD IT IN ANY-MORE!!
SHUT UP! I HAVE TO WORK HERE UNTIL I PAY FOR ALL THE DAMAGES!
BAM
YOU LOOK LOVELY IN THAT DRESS, TEACHER! AHA HA HA!!
DAMN IT! WHY IS THIS THE ONLY UNIFORM THIS RESTAU-RANT HAS?!
HA HA HA!
UGH! JUST EAT AND GET THE HELL OUTTA HERE!!
BWA HA HA HA HA
OH WELL. I GUESS WE CAN TEACH RE=L ABOUT SOCIETY ANOTHER TIME.
YEAH. YOU'RE RIGHT.
MUNCH MUNCH MUNCH MUNCH MUNCH

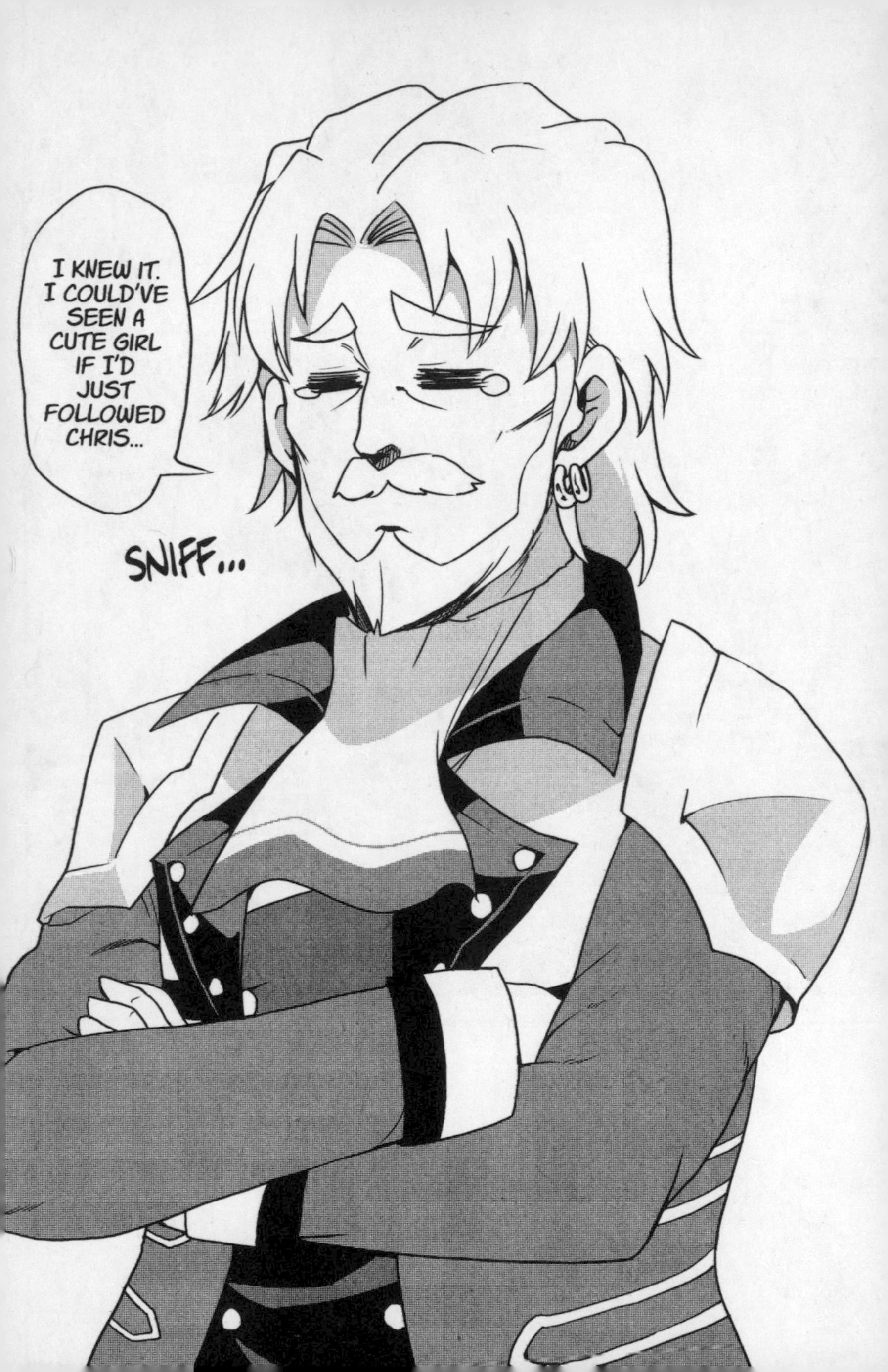
I KNEW IT. I COULD'VE SEEN A CUTE GIRL IF I'D JUST FOLLOWED CHRIS...
SNIFF...

Thank you for purchasing volume 11 of *Akashic Records of Bastard Magic Instructor*. This is Aosa Tsunemi.

I'm finally starting to run out of source material to adapt. It feels like it was just yesterday that the previous volume came out. It's all just been a dizzying blur. The story's starting to get to some really juicy parts, so I hope you continue to stay along for the ride.

Well, until next volume!

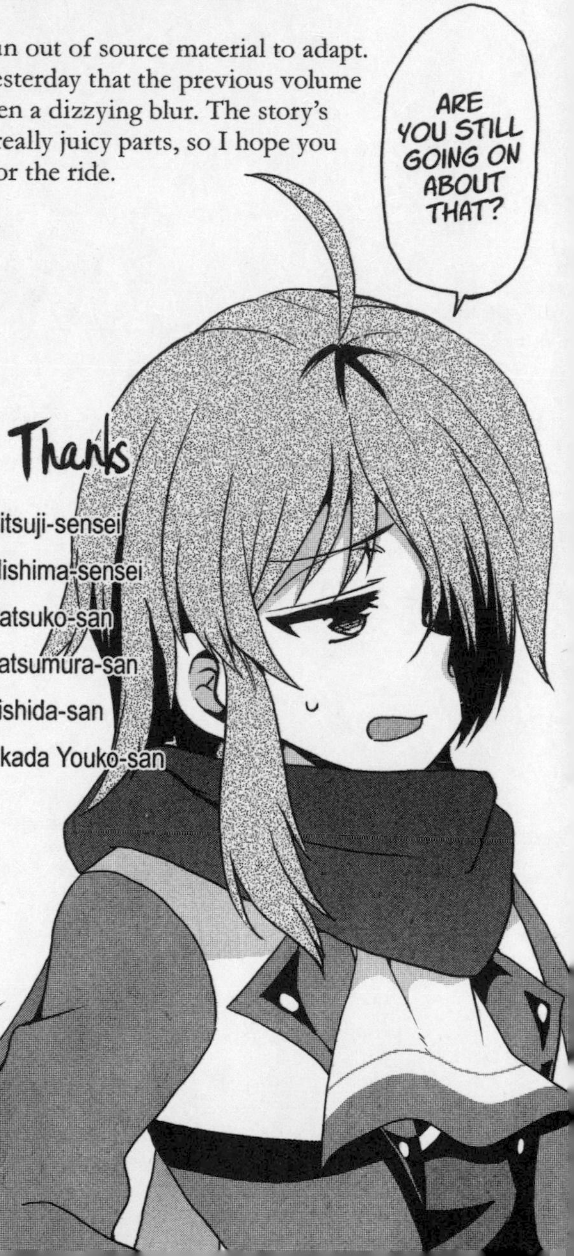
ARE YOU STILL GOING ON ABOUT THAT?

Staff

Asahi Ruyoru

Piko

Yoshimaru

Thanks

Hitsuji-sensei

Mishima-sensei

Hatsuko-san

Katsumura-san

Kishida-san

Okada Youko-san

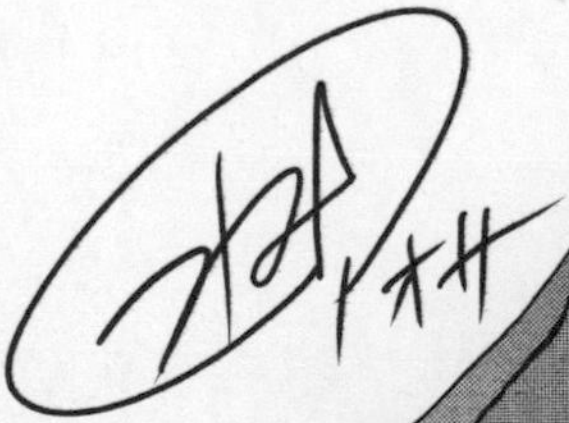

AKASHIC RECORDS OF BASTARD
MAGIC INSTRUCTOR

Story by Taro Hitsuji
Art by Aosa Tsunemi
Character design by Kurone Mishima

SEVEN SEAS ENTERTAINMENT PRESENTS

Akashic Records of Bastard Magic Instructor

VOLUME 11

story by TARO HITSUJI art by AOSA TSUNEMI original character designs by KURONE MISHIMA

TRANSLATION
Ryan Peterson

ADAPTATION
Bambi Eloriaga-Amago

LETTERING
Brandon Bovia

COVER DESIGN
Kris Aubin

PROOFREADER
Dawn Davis
Janet Houck

EDITOR
J.P. Sullivan

PREPRESS TECHNICIAN
Rhiannon Rasmussen-Silverstein

PRODUCTION MANAGER
Lissa Pattillo

MANAGING EDITOR
Julie Davis

ASSOCIATE PUBLISHER
Adam Arnold

PUBLISHER
Jason DeAngelis

ROKUDENASHI MAJUTSU KOSHI TO AKASHIC RECORD VOL. 11

Seven Seas press and purchase enquiries can be sent to Marketing Manager Lianne Sentar at press@gomanga.com. Information regarding the distribution and purchase of digital editions is available from Digital Manager CK Russell at digital@gomanga.com.

ISBN: 978-1-64505-799-4

Printed in Canada

First Printing: March 2021

10 9 8 7 6 5 4 3 2 1

FOLLOW US ONLINE: ***www.sevenseasentertainment.com***

READING DIRECTIONS

This book reads from ***right to left***, Japanese style. If this is your first time reading manga, you start reading from the top right panel on each page and take it from there. If you get lost, just follow the numbered diagram here. It may seem backwards at first, but you'll get the hang of it! Have fun!!

1
2
3
4
5
6
7
8
9

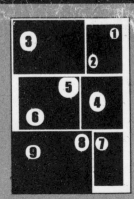